Landmark Copyright Cases in China

Landmark Copyright Cases in China

An In-Depth Analysis

Luo Dongchuan

Translated by
He Jiong

Published by:
Kluwer Law International B.V.
PO Box 316
2400 AH Alphen aan den Rijn
The Netherlands
E-mail: international-sales@wolterskluwer.com
Website: lrus.wolterskluwer.com

Sold and distributed in North, Central and South America by:
Wolters Kluwer Legal & Regulatory U.S.
7201 McKinney Circle
Frederick, MD 21704
United States of America
Email: customer.service@wolterskluwer.com

Sold and distributed in all other countries by:
Air Business Subscriptions
Rockwood House
Haywards Heath
West Sussex
RH16 3DH
United Kingdom
Email: international-customerservice@wolterskluwer.com

The title of Landmark Copyright Cases in China: An In-Depth Analysis by Luo Dongchuan is published and sold by Kluwer Law International, by permission of The Commercial Press, Ltd., 36 Wangfujing Street, Beijing, China, the owner of all rights to publish and sell same.

Printed on acid-free paper.

ISBN 978-90-411-9104-5

e-Book: ISBN 978-90-411-9126-7
web-PDF: ISBN 978-90-411-9127-4

© 2019 The Commercial Press

All rights reserved. No part of this publication may be reproduced, stored in a retrieval system, or transmitted in any form or by any means, electronic, mechanical, photocopying, recording, or otherwise, without written permission from the publisher.

Permission to use this content must be obtained from the copyright owner. More information can be found at: lrus.wolterskluwer.com/policies/permissions-reprints-and-licensing

Printed in the United Kingdom.

About the Chief Editor

Luo Dongchuan, Ph.D. (Peking University), is a senior judge (Grade 1) of China. He was a member of the Judicial Committee of the Supreme People's Court; President of the Fourth Civil Tribunal of the Supreme People's Court; supervisor for post-doctors at the China Institute of Applied Jurisprudence; professor at the National Judge College; professor at the IP Academy, Renmin University; research fellow at the International IP Research Center, Peking University; vice-president of the IP Law Association of China; standing council member of the Civil and Commercial Law Association of China; vice-director of IP Division of the Supreme People's Court; vice-director of the Research Department of the Supreme People's Court; director of the China Institute of Applied Jurisprudence; and vice-director of the Department of Politics of the Supreme People's Court.

Luo's published works include *Guidelines for Hearing IP Cases*, *Application of the Interpretations for Patent Law*, *Collection of IP Judicial Decisions*, *Studies of Remarkable Patent Cases*, *Studies of Chinese Patent Cases*, etc. He has also published numerous academic articles in IP field.

About the Translator

Dr. He Jiong acquired his Bachelor's in Law from East China University of Political Science and Law, China, and LL.M. and Ph.D. from the University of Aberdeen, UK. At present, Jiong is a lecturer at the Intellectual Property School, East China University of Political Science and Law.

Jiong is the Director of the Research Centre for Online Legal Service of ECUPL. He is also a Council Member of the China Law Association on Science & Technology. From 2013 to 2014, Jiong was a guest researcher at the Max Planck Institute for Intellectual Property and Competition Law (Germany) sponsored by the Max Planck Society and the Pujiang Program of Shanghai, China. In 2015, Jiong was appointed by the World Intellectual Property Organization as a lecturer of the WIPO Summer School on IP. In 2018, Jiong was appointed to teach IP law at the National University of Public Service of Hungary, sponsored by the EU Erasmus Program.

Jiong's research interests lie in the fields of international IP law, especially legal protection of software, and IP issues concerning "Belt and Road" Initiative of China. He has published over thirty articles in both Chinese and English language.

Table of Contents

About the Chief Editor — v

About the Translator — vii

Preface — xiii

The Commentary Committee — xv

Acknowledgment — xvii

Chapter 1
Introduction to the Chinese Copyright System — 1
§1.01　Emergence and Development of the Chinese Copyright System — 1
　　　[A]　Copyright System in the Late Qing Dynasty (Late 19th Century to 1911) — 2
　　　[B]　Copyright System in the "Republic of China" Period (1911–1949) — 2
　　　[C]　Copyright System in the People's Republic of China (1949 to Date) — 3
　　　　　　[1]　Copyright System Before the "Economic Reform and Opening-Up" Policy — 3
　　　　　　[2]　The Establishment and Development of Contemporary Copyright System — 4
　　　　　　　　　[a]　1990 Copyright Law — 4
　　　　　　　　　[b]　First Revision of Copyright Law in 2001 — 5
　　　　　　　　　[c]　Second Revision of Copyright Law in 2010 — 6
　　　　　　　　　[d]　Third Revision of Copyright Law in 2012 — 6
　　　　　　[3]　Basic Structure of the Contemporary Copyright System in China — 8
§1.02　Characteristics of the Chinese Copyright System — 9

Table of Contents

	[A]	A Dual-Track System	9
		[1] Administrative Enforcement of Law	9
		[2] Judicial Protection	10
	[B]	Necessity of Administrative Protection	11
	[C]	Dominant Role of Judicial Protection	12
§1.03		Mechanisms of Copyright Protection	14
	[A]	Enforcement by Administrative Enforcement	14
		[1] Law Enforcement System of Copyright Administration Department	14
		[2] Customs Enforcement System	15
	[B]	Enforcement by Judicial Adjudication	16
		[1] Development Overview	16
		[2] Four-Level Courts and Second-Instance System	17
		[3] The Method of Judicial Protection	18
		[a] Copyright Civil Litigation	18
		[b] Copyright Administrative Litigation	19
		[c] Copyright Criminal Procedure	19
		[d] "Three-in-One" Model	20
§1.04		Remedies for Copyright Infringement	20
	[A]	Administrative Enforcement Procedure	20
		[1] Scope of Penalties	21
		[2] Case Jurisdiction	21
		[3] Complaint Procedure	21
		[4] Active Investigation	22
		[5] Administrative Penalties	22
		[6] Channels of Relief	23
	[B]	Procedures of Judicial Relief	23
		[1] Civil Procedure	23
		[a] Standing to Sue	23
		[b] Jurisdiction	24
		[c] Limitation of Action	24
		[d] Preservation	25
		[e] Trial	26
		[f] Open Trial	27
		[g] Civil Liability	28
		[2] Criminal Procedure	29
		[a] Investigation	29
		[b] Public Prosecution	29
		[c] Private Prosecution	30
		[d] Jurisdiction	30
		[e] Trial	31
		[f] Criminal Liability	32
		[3] Administrative Procedure	32
		[a] Filing an Action	33

		[b]	Jurisdiction	33
		[c]	Trial	33
		[d]	Method of Judgment	34
§1.05	Challenge for the Copyright System in Facing New Technologies			34
	[A]	Impact of "Tri-Network Convergence" on the Conventional Structure of Interests		35
	[B]	Disputes Relating to Cloud Computing		35
	[C]	Internet TV and the Principle of "Technological Neutrality"		36
	[D]	Infringement by the Network Trading Platform		37
	[E]	Application of the Rule of "Notice-Takedown"		38
	[F]	New Method for Compensation Calculation of Damages		39
	[G]	Interplay of Copyright with Other IPs		39
		[1]	Interplay of Copyright with Patent Right: "Competition and Cooperation"	39
		[2]	Interplay of Copyright with Trademark Right: "Conflict"	40
		[3]	Anti-Unfair Competition and Copyright Law: "Supplement"	41

CHAPTER 2
Determination of the Nature of a Work — 45
Case 1. The Nature of Work of Applied Art — 45
Case 2. Originality in Architectural Works and the Relevant Remedy of "Stop Infringement" — 51
Case 3. The Nature of Opening Ceremony of the Olympic Games and Its Copyright Protection — 61
Case 4. The Nature of Fictional Character and Its Copyright Protection — 68
Case 5. The Nature of Music Video and Its Copyright Protection — 76
Case 6. The Nature of a Single Character from a Typeface Library and Its Copyright Protection — 86
Case 7. The Nature of Dispensatory and Its Possible Copyright Protection — 100
Case 8. The Nature of Technical Standard and Its Copyright Protection — 116

CHAPTER 3
Determination of Copyright Infringement — 127
Case 9. Originality of Works Inspired by Nonfictions and Copyright Infringement — 127
Case 10. Infringement of the Right of Adaptation — 132
Case 11. Protection of the Right of Authorship of Expressions of Folklore — 138
Case 12. Scope of Protection of Architectural Works — 144
Case 13. Infringement Relating to Internet TV — 151
Case 14. Liability of Service Providers of E-commerce Platform — 162
Case 15. Contributory Infringement by the Act of Inducement — 167

Table of Contents

Case 16.	Infringement of the Right of Communication by Apple's App Store	175
Case 17.	Internet Service Providers' Infringement of the Right of Communication Relating to Cloud Video Technology	180
Case 18.	The Nature of Real-Time Online Rebroadcast and Copyright Infringement	191
Case 19.	The Nature of Partial Communicating and the Nature of Full Reproducing Without Communicating	198
Case 20.	Infringement Relating to Making Available of Web Snapshot	208
Case 21.	Infringement of the Right of Revision of Computer Software Works	216
Case 22.	Infringement of Layout Designs of Integrated Circuits	227

CHAPTER 4
Other Issues concerning Copyright-Related Disputes   249
Case 23. The Principle of "Technological Neutrality" and Its Scope   249
Case 24. Availability of Preliminary Injunction in the Cases of Infringement
          of Moral Rights   253
Case 25. Enforceability of a Contract of Transferring Copyright of an
          Unfinished Work   259

Postscript   267

Preface

Since 2011, I have been teaching Chinese copyright law for international students in English language. In my course, I would translate some case excerpts to explain the rules and how the Chinese courts will apply them. Perhaps the most common question from my students is where to access the full English translation of Chinese cases. I also considered whether I should compile and translate such a casebook.

The idea itself is fascinating because I also believe in "the life of the law has not been logic; it has been experience." However, I did not get started for the following three reasons. First, regarding the legal system, China is generally a Germanic-style civil law system in which the rule of stare decisis does not apply, so previous cases are not binding on or persuasive for a Chinese court. Second, regarding the Chinese copyright law, since the legislation, particularly the 1990 and 2001 versions of the *Copyright Law*, were largely motivated by international pressure rather than domestic demands, they seem to be lacking philosophical integrity and are constantly in flux. The first copyright law of the People's Republic of China was legislated in 1990, as a part of the Sino-U.S. trade negotiation and for the membership of the *Berne Convention*, of which some provisions were directly "imported" from the *Berne Convention*. Since then, it has been amended twice. The first amendment was made in 2001 for the WTO membership, which was strongly influenced by the *TRIPS Agreement*. The second was made in 2010, right after China was complained by the United States in the WTO. The third reason is for the cases themselves. Because of the late start, the notion of copyright was new and unfamiliar not only to ordinary Chinese people but also to Chinese judges. As a result, most early copyright cases are of limited value to our current practice. Particularly for Internet-related cases, due to the wide range of *locus delicti*, even a court from less-developed areas has jurisdiction to hear the most sophisticated technology-oriented cases. Such forum shopping led to controversial judicial judgments for similar cases. The more cases we read, the more we might be confused.

However, recently, each year sees new improvements in judicial protection of copyright. First, even cases are not binding; the Supreme People's Court has still been selecting and publishing typical cases in its annual reports as references to all the Chinese courts. In those judicial opinions, the judges thoroughly explain the applied

Preface

interpretations of laws, which are not only good references for judges but also valuable study materials for lawyers and law students. Second, with the implementation of the *National Intellectual Property Strategy* of China, the legislative motivations of IP laws now concerns more domestic demands instead of external pressures. Currently, the third amendment of the *Copyright Law* is in process. The draft of the amendment reflects new issues which are mainly in relation to the domestic balance of interests. Thus, I am optimistic that the Chinese copyright law is becoming more stable and self-consistent. Third, the Chinese IP judges are also becoming more experienced and professional. Until now, three IP courts and serval IP tribunals have been established across the country, so that the disadvantages of forum shopping have been minimized. Therefore, it is time for introducing the world a casebook of the Chinese copyright law.

I am so lucky and honored to participate in the project of the English translation of the *Landmark Copyright Cases in China* edited by Chief Judge Luo Dongchuan, which is a unique and inventive selection of twenty-five landmark copyright cases decided by the Chinese courts. Those cases are carefully and inventively selected from the annual reports of typical cases by the Supreme People's Court, addressing various and new subjects in Chinese copyright law. It must be highlighted that each case in this book consists of not only the facts and rulings but also the comments from the judge of that particular case, who can provide us with the best reasoning for the decision. This is the most distinctive and valuable part compared with other casebooks of Chinese IP law.

Translating this casebook has been a long and laborious task. I would particularly like to thank Professor WANG Qian of ECUPL and Mr. QIU Anman, the former Deputy Director General of the National Copyright Administration of China, for their priceless comments. Last but not least, my family for their support and encouragement.

He Jiong
ECUPL
July 2018

The Commentary Committee

Chief Editor

LUO Dongchuan, Member of the Judicial Committee; Chief Judge and President, Fourth Civil Tribunal, the Supreme People's Court of China; First Degree Senior Judge; Professor

Editorial Committee

DING Wenyan

Commentators *(order by surname name in Chinese)*

DING Wenyan, DING Wenlian, FENG Gang, LI Dan, RUI Songyan, ZHANG Lingling, ZHANG Xiaojin, LUO Dongchuan, ZHOU Duo, JIANG Ying, XU Zhuobin, XU Cui, CUI Ning, QIANG Ganghua, TONG Haichao

Acknowledgment

CBI Financial Aid for Publication

CHAPTER 1
Introduction to the Chinese Copyright System

§1.01 **EMERGENCE AND DEVELOPMENT OF THE CHINESE COPYRIGHT SYSTEM**

The emergence of copyright has a close relationship with the emergence and development of printing technology. Since both papermaking technology and printing technology originated in ancient China, the history of publishing industry may be traced back to the Shang Dynasty, which is approximately 3,000 years ago. In pre-Qin era, the ancient Chinese scholars have already given birth to the ideas of protecting authorship and other moral rights in writing books (creating), copying books (reproducing) and selling books (communicating).[1] In the 11th century, the newly emerged printing technology largely reduced the cost of reproduction and communication of works. Since engraving and printing industries became popular, it was necessary to provide legal protection to the printing industries on their economic interests. As a result, a "concession" system was developed in the Nan Song Dynasty to protect the economic interests of certain publishers. However, since ancient Chinese rulers employed the strict "mind control" policy to prohibit the spread of any innovative ideas, the reproduction of books was strictly controlled. Therefore, the modern theory of copyright has not been introduced in China until the end of the Qing Dynasty, when China started to learn the modern legal system from the Western countries. Under the pressure from both the domestic Bourgeois reformists and Western countries, the Qing regime legislated the *Copyright Law of Qing* in 1910, which was the first copyright law in Chinese history. Afterward, in the eras of Beiyang government and Nanjing National Government, the development of copyright was postponed or even went in reverse.

---

1. 吴汉东 [Wu Handong],《关于中国著作权法观念的历史思考》["A Historical Perspective of Chinese Copyright Law"], http://wenku.baidu.com/view/2c667ae9551810a6f5248669.html?re=view.

The modern Chinese copyright system has been established since the birth of People's Republic of China, practically since the 1980s when China launched the "Economic Reform and Opening-Up" policy. In general, there are three stages of the history of modern Chinese copyright system.

[A]   Copyright System in the Late Qing Dynasty (Late 19th Century to 1911)

In 1903, the Qing Government was forced to conclude the *Sino-American Treaty of Commerce and Navigation* with the United States (U.S.). The notion of copyright was first introduced to China by this treaty. And the relevant article in this treaty emphasized that the restrictive obligation was "exclusively applied on Chinese citizens." In 1908, *chargés* and commercial counselor of Qing Government based in Berlin attended the Diplomatic Conference for Revising the *Berne Convention for the Protection of Literary and Artistic Works* as nonvoting delegates. In 1910, urged by the U.S., the Qing Government appointed Shen Jiaben to be in charge of the legislating procedure. With the aid of Japanese experts, *Copyright Law of Qing* was legislated as the landmark of the birth of modern copyright law in China. This Law took reference from the 1899 Copyright Law of Japan. Some fundamental copyright principles from both the common law system and civil law system have been taken into this Law in a harmonized manner.[2] It was the first time that Chinese copyright system was established by the form of statutory law and the structure of private law. There are five sections in the *Law*, which are general rules, term of protection, deposit rules, limitations of rights and appendix. In this fifty-five-article *Copyright Law*, the definition of copyright, the scope of protected works, the rights of the authors, the formality requirements of copyright grant, term of protection, limitations of right, remedies of infringement, etc. were regulated comprehensively. Since the theories of modern copyright were introduced into China for the first time, *Copyright Law of Qing* was a landmark in the history of copyright legislations in China. Despite that the Qing Dynasty soon collapsed after the Xinhai Revolution and this *Copyright Law of Qing* was "suspended" and never enforced, the spirits and ideas of the *Copyright Law of Qing* leave significant impact to the later Chinese copyright laws.

[B]   Copyright System in the "Republic of China" Period (1911-1949)

After the Xinhai Revolution of 1911, the Republic of China was established in January 1912. It changed hands three times, first by the Sun Yat-sen's Provisional Government (January 1912-1914), then by the Beiyang Government (1913-1928), and eventually by the Chiang Kai-shek's Nanjing National Government (1928-1949). In 1912, an official gazette by the Ministry of Interior of the Provisional Government provided that "the Law (*Copyright Law of Qing*) is temporarily suspended." In 1915, the Beiyang

---

2. 刘春田 [Liu Chuntian], 知识产权法 ["Intellectual Property Law"], 中国人民大学出版社 [China Renmin University Press] (2003), p. 48.

regime legislated the *Copyright Law of Beiyang Government*, who indiscriminately imitated the *Copyright Law of Qing*. In 1928, the Nanjing National regime legislated the Copyright Law, which was revised upon the *Copyright Law of Qing* that certain rights concerning politics of authors were deprived, according to Article 22 of the *Law*. In 1930, the Nanjing National regime promulgated the *Law of Publishing*, which further restricted the freedom of speech and clarified the news censorship system.

[C] Copyright System in the People's Republic of China (1949 to Date)

Since the People's Republic of China was founded, the Chinese government has made significant progress in copyright protection. During the decade of Culture Revolution (1966–1976), the whole legal system of China was destroyed, including the newly born copyright system. Therefore, the modern Chinese copyright system was actually formed after the Economic Reform and Opening-Up (1978). As the result of the last three decades' effort, a balanced copyright legal system to meet both the demands of the international treaty obligations and needs for domestic developments. A copyright protection system with Chinese characteristics which consist of both administrative and judicial protection has been established. Within such copyright legal system, the *Copyright Law of the People's Republic of China* which was first legislated in 1990 is the fundamental and most important law. This *Law* plays the leading role in regulating both copyright-related activities and legal relationships.

[1] Copyright System Before the "Economic Reform and Opening-Up" Policy

Since the People's Republic of China was founded in 1949, all prior laws and regulations enacted by the former Republic of China regime were abolished. From 1949 to 1976, a Temporary Regulation for Protecting Copyright of Published Work was drafted but never promulgated. There was no specific law or regulation of copyright, except few principles from the *Constitutional Law* and relevant laws. For instance, according to the *1954 Constitutional Law*, outstanding social science works and literary and artistic works shall be encouraged and rewarded. During the First National Conference on Publishing Industry in September 1950, a *Decision on Improving and Developing Publishing Industry* was made to provide principles of copyright protection. It provided that "publishing industry shall respect the copyright and the right of publishing. Any act of copying, plagiarising or tampering is prohibited." In a long period of time, this *Decision* was served as the legal basis for copyright dispute. Until 1966 when the Cultural Revolution started, several regulations were made to provide indirect protection for copyright. During the Cultural Revolution, the whole legal system of China was destroyed. So was the newly born copyright system.

[2] The Establishment and Development of Contemporary Copyright System

After the Third Plenary Session of the Eleventh Central Committee of the Chinese Communist Party, from 1977 to 1984, the State Administration of Publishing and the Ministry of Culture promulgated a series of administrative regulations to protect copyright. Among all the regulations, the *Tentative Regulations for Books and Journals* promulgated by the Ministry of Culture in June 1983 was the first specific law to protect copyright in the New China. The twenty-four article *Tentative Regulations* clarified the purpose of copyright, subject matters, term of protection, transfer and inheritance of rights, limitations, remedies for infringement, etc. In January 1985, the *Implementing Rules of the Tentative Regulations for Books and Journals* was promulgated. The *Tentative Regulations* and *Implementing Rules* built up the infrastructure for the contemporary copyright system in China. The other landmark administrative legislation is the *Tentative Rules for Book Remuneration*, which was promulgated in September 1984 and put into tentative use in December the same year. It provided the rules for the right of publishing, the right of translation, the right of adaptation, the ownership of rights and term of protection. In April 1986, the *General Principles of Civil Law of China* was promulgated. According to Article 94, "citizens and legal persons shall enjoy copyright and shall be entitled to sign their names as authors, issue and publish their works and obtain remuneration in accordance with the law." Article 118 provided that "if the rights of authorship (copyright), patent rights, rights to exclusive use of trademarks, rights of discovery, rights of invention or rights for scientific and technological research achievements of citizens or legal persons are infringed upon by such means as plagiarism, alteration or imitation, they shall have the right to demand that the infringement be stopped, its ill effects be eliminated and the damages be compensated for." The *General Principles of Civil Law* is the first civil code to regulate copyright as an important part of civil rights in the New China. It provided the positive grounds for commercializing the domain over knowledge and became an essential piece of puzzle for a completed copyright system.[3] In September 1986, the *Tentative Rules for Audio and Video Publications was* promulgated, which provides legal grounds for protecting the legitimate interests of authors, performers and audio and video publications producers.

[a] 1990 Copyright Law

The Third Plenary Session of the Eleventh Central Committee of the Chinese Communist Party provided the best opportunity for China to develop its socialist literature, art and science. In China, it was urgent to make copyright law to protect intellectual creations for the promotion of national culture and science. Internationally, the *1979 Sino-American Implementation Protocols for Cooperation in the Field of High Energy*

---

3. 刘春田 [Liu Chuntian], 知识产权法 ["Intellectual Property Law"], 中国人民大学出版社 [China Renmin University Press] (2003), p. 49.

Physics mentioned the bilateral cooperation on copyright for the first time. To meet the demands, China started to launch the legislative effort to draft the first copyright law. The most controversial issue was to find the balance between the international copyright treaties' basic requirements and China's actual needs. According to a Sino-American intellectual property (hereinafter, "IP") negotiation document signed in 1989, China promised to enact its copyright law as soon as possible. In September 1990, the *Copyright Law of China* was adopted at the Fifteenth Session of the Standing Committee of the Seventh National People's Congress and effective as of on June 1, 1991. It consists of six sections and fifty-six articles in total, which protects authors', other right owners' and communicators' legitimate interests by providing the articles concerning the purpose of the legislation, definitions and rights of copyright, licensing, liabilities for infringement. This version of the *Copyright Law* takes care of both the Chinese demands and international copyright principles. It keeps three balances of interests, which are the balance among individuals, employers and the State, the balance between authors and communicators, and the balance between authors and public interests. In regard to the economic rights of copyright, the protection is practical and consistent with the international standard. In regard to the moral rights of copyright, the protection level is even higher than the international standard, which indicates the Chinese characteristics.[4] This version of the *Copyright Law* also provides proper protection to foreign authors for their legitimate interests.[5] The *1990 Copyright Law* is a landmark that modern copyright system has been established in China. Later on October 15 and October 30, 1992, China became a Member State of the *Berne Convention* and the *Universal Copyright Convention*. On September 25, 1992, the State Council promulgated the *Provisions on the Implementation of the International Copyright Treaties* and enacted on September 30, 1992. In 1997, crime of copyright infringement was introduced into the Criminal Law of China. Thus, the modern copyright system has been established.

[b]   *First Revision of Copyright Law in 2001*

Since the *1990 Copyright Law* was promulgated before China launched its Socialist Market Economy, the law was made in the planned economy style. With the development of economic system, the culture and science were making huge progress. As a result, the notions of IP including copyright were respected more by the Chinese people. Thus, the *1990 Copyright Law* seemed out of date and could not catch up with the development of China. In order to solve the problem, the National Copyright Administration recommended revising the *1990 Copyright Law*. Meanwhile, in order to enter WTO, it was also necessary for China to modify its *1990 Copyright Law* to satisfy the requirements of *TRIPS Agreement*. On October 27, 2001, the *National People's Congress's Standing Committee's Decision on Revising the Copyright Law* was promulgated to revise thirty-six articles of the *1990 Copyright Law*. The rules concerning the

---

4. 吴汉东 [Wu Handong],《知识产权基本问题研究》 ["The Fundamental Issues of Intellectual Property"], 中国人民大学出版社 [China Renmin University Press] (2009), p. 10.
5. *Ibid.*

rights to be protected, the protection of acrobatic works and architectural works, the limitations and exemptions of rights, collective licensing system, enforcement measures, statutory damages, administrative punishment for infringement concerning public interests and free use of works by broadcasting and TV stations were modified. The revised version contains sixty articles in total, while the former version was fifty-six articles in total.

[c] Second Revision of Copyright Law in 2010

Since 2001, new challenges have arisen with the globalization and new technologies to the *2001 Copyright Law*. In 2008, China launched to implement the *National Intellectual Property Strategy Outline*. In order to promote the industrialization of copyright and the systematization and harmonization of IP, it is necessary to further revise the *2001 Copyright Law*. In 2009, the WTO experts made the arbitral decision of the IP disputes between U.S. and China that Article 4 of the *2001 Copyright Law* violated the *Berne Convention* and the *TRIPS Agreement*. Thus, on February 26, 2010, the Thirteenth Session of the Standing Committee of the Eleventh National People's Congress promulgated the *National People's Congress's Standing Committee's Decision on Revising the Copyright Law* to revise the *2001 Copyright Law*. This was a minor revision. The regulation concerning illegal publishing in Article 4 was deleted. In addition, the new regulation concerning the copyright pledge was introduced into the *Copyright Law* for the first time by Article 26. Thus, there are six sections and sixty-one articles in total in the *2010 Copyright Law*.

From 1990 to 2010, the two revisions of the *Copyright Law* were made due to both domestic motivation and international pressure. Compared with the domestic demands of economic reform and cultural development, the international pressure from the U.S. and the obligation of WTO membership were of more significance. Since the two revisions were partial and lack of self-motivation, some practical copyright issues occurred during the social and economic reform remain unsolved.

[d] Third Revision of Copyright Law in 2012

With the rapid development of digital and internet technologies, the 21st century is the era of globalization of economy and culture. In this era, China launched the national strategy to further develop its socialist culture. Hence, the conflict between the growing demands for better copyright protection and the current protection provided by the dated *Copyright Law* became more severe. In order to improve the situation, the National Copyright Administration launched the third revision of the Copyright Law on July 13, 2011.

Different from the last two revisions, the third revision must be comprehensive, systematic and self-motivated. It is made for the implementation of national IP strategy and the demands of globalization and information network technologies. This third revision must follow the following three principles: the principle of independence, the principle of balance and the principle of international standard. The principle of independence requires the new copyright law to be based on China's actual conditions and to reflect the Chinese characteristics. It also requires the new copyright law to solve the problems happened in China by taking the Chinese reality into consideration. The principle of balance requires the new copyright law to build up the sophisticated balance among creators of works, communicators of works and public interests. The principle of international standard requires the new copyright law to reflect the trend of international copyright protection and promote the national image of China in the international community.[6] This new revision is expected to be legislated in a short period of time with adequate quality, so that the problems in copyright practice may be solved as many as possible. Since July 2011, huge efforts have been made by the experts appointed by the National Copyright Administration. Now the *Third Draft of Copyright Law Revision* has been completed.

Compared with the *2010 Copyright* Law, the *Third Draft* has made the following modifications: First, in regard to the main structure, the *Third Draft* has been expanded from six sections and sixty-one articles into eight sections and ninety articles. Second, in order to pay higher respect to intellectual creations, the content of rights has been expanded, including the rights enjoyed by both authors and owners of related rights. For instance, rental right is granted to the performers for the first time in China. In addition, performers of audiovisual performances may enjoy the right to make contractual arrangement for the ownership of their copyright. Those modifications are consistent with the international copyright treaties. Third, the *Third Draft* has made huge modifications to create effective, reasonable and standard licensing mechanisms and trading modes. Fourth, the level of protection has been raised. For instance, new administrative measures, higher standard for statuary damages and new notion of punitive damages have been introduced into the new revision.[7] In December 2012, the National Copyright Administration submitted the *Manuscript of the Draft of the Copyright Law*. During June 6–July 5, 2014, the Legislative Affairs Office of the State Council then requested a public consultation for further comments of this *Manuscript*. The consultation paper will be examined by the State Council and submitted to the Standing Committee of the National People's Congress.

With the three revisions of the Copyright Law and expansion of copyright subject matters, the State Council also simultaneously enacted five administrative regulations, including the *Regulations on the Protection of Computer Software* and the *Regulations for the Implementation of the Copyright Law*. The *Copyright Law*, the *Provisions on the Implementation of the International Copyright Treaties* and the above five administrative regulations are known as the "one law and six regulations." Meanwhile, the Supreme People's Court published copyright-related interpretations and judicial policies, including the *Interpretation of the Supreme People's Court Concerning the Application of Laws in the Trial of Civil Disputes over Copyright*. Hence, the copyright

---

6. National Copyright Administration,《关于〈中华人民共和国著作权法〉（修改草案）的简要说明》 ["Brief Explanation of the Draft of Copyright Law of China"], http://www.law-lib.com.
7. 王自强 [Wang Ziqiang], 著作权法第三次修订工作回顾 ["Review of the Working Progress of the Third Revision of the Copyright Law"],《中国新闻出版报》[China News Publishing] (2003).

framework of China has been made of the *Copyright Law*, relevant international treaties, administrative regulations, judicial interpretations and policies, departmental rules, local decrees, and local government rules and normative documents. Within this copyright framework, "one law and six regulations" are considered as the fundamental infrastructure.[8]

[3] Basic Structure of the Contemporary Copyright System in China

The basic laws are: the *Copyright Law* (promulgated on September 7, 1990, first revised on October 27, 2001, and second revised on February 26, 2010, effective as of April 1, 2010); the *General Principles of the Civil Law* (promulgated on April 12, 1986 and effective as of January 1, 1987);the *Tort Liability Law* (promulgated on December 26, 2009 and effective as of July 1, 2010); the *Contract Law* (promulgated on March 15, 1999 and effective as of October 1, 1999); and the *Criminal Law* (promulgated on July 1, 1979, fifth revised on March 14, 1997 at the Fifteenth Session of the Standing Committee of the Eighth National People's Congress, and effective as of October 1, 1997).

The administrative regulations are: the *Provisions on the Implementation of the International Copyright Treaties* (promulgated on September 25, 1992 and effective as of September 30, 1992); the *Regulations on the Protection of Computer Software* (promulgated on December 20, 2001 and effective as of January 1, 2002); the *Regulations for the Implementation of the Copyright Law* (promulgated on August 2, 2002 and effective as of September 15, 2002); the *Regulations of Copyright Collective Management* (promulgated on December 28, 2004 and effective as of March 1, 2005); the *Regulation on Protection of the Right to Network Dissemination of Information* (promulgated on May 18, 2006 and effective as of July 1, 2006); and the *Interim Measures for Payment of Remuneration by Radio and Television Stations for Broadcasting Sound Recordings* (promulgated on November 10, 2009 and effective as of January 1, 2010).

The judicial interpretations are: the *Interpretation of the Supreme People's Court concerning Several Issues on Application of Law in Hearing Correctly the Civil Copyright* (promulgated on October 12, 2002 and effective as of October 15, 2002); the *Provisions of the Supreme People's Court concerning Several Issues on Application of Law in Hearing Correctly Civil Dispute Cases of Infringement of Information Network Dissemination Right* (promulgated on November 26, 2012 and effective as of January 1, 2013); the *Interpretation of the Supreme People's Court and the Supreme People's Procuratorate on Several Issues of Concrete Application of Laws in Handling Criminal Cases of Infringing Intellectual Property* (promulgated on December 8, 2004 and effective as of December 22, 2004); and the *Interpretation II of the Supreme People's Court and the Supreme People's Procuratorate on Several Issues of Concrete Application of Laws in*

---

8. 阎晓宏 [Yan Xiaohong], 中国版权保护的现状与发展态势 ["The Status Quo of Copyright Protection in China and Its Future"], 《中国法律》 [China Law] (2007), 2.

Handling Criminal Cases of Infringing Intellectual Property (promulgated on April 4, 2007 and effective as of April 5, 2007).

The judicial policies are: the speeches of the leaders of the *Supreme People's Court in the Annual National Intellectual Property Trials Conferences (2007–2010)*; the *Opinions of the Supreme People's Court on Several Issues Regarding the Implementation of the National Intellectual Property Strategy* (promulgated on March 23, 2009); the *Opinions of the Supreme People's Court on Several Issues concerning Intellectual Property Trials Serving the Overall Objective under the Current Economic Situation* (promulgated on April 21, 2009); and the *Opinions of the Supreme People's Court on Issues concerning Maximizing the Role of Intellectual Property Right Trials in Boosting the Great Development and Great Prosperity of Socialist Culture and Promoting the Independent and Coordinated Development of Economy* (promulgated on December 16, 2011).

The International treaties are: the *Berne Convention* (came into force in China on October 15, 1992); the *Universal Copyright Convention* (came into force in China on October 30, 1992); the *Phonograms Convention* (came into force in China on April 30, 1993); and the *TRIPS Agreement* (came into force in China on December 11, 2001).

§1.02 CHARACTERISTICS OF THE CHINESE COPYRIGHT SYSTEM

The Chinese copyright system is a relatively complete copyright system based on international experience and is gradually established, developed and improved with the national conditions and international rules. It is an institutional choice from the nature of Chinese society and the stage of social development. The Chinese copyright system, a dual system of judicial protection and administrative enforcement, the judicial finality and complementary advantages, differs from the western copyright systems.

[A]   A Dual-Track System

The dual-track system of copyright protection refers to the protection system in which administrative enforcement and judicial protection perform their duties and cooperate with each other to safeguard the legal order of copyright and protect parties' rights and interests.

[1]   *Administrative Enforcement of Law*

The administrative protection of copyright includes administrative management and especially administrative enforcement of law. It refers to the legal protection in which the copyright administration authorities, in accordance with legal procedures, use powers in law to deal with various copyright infringements, safeguard the order of the copyright market and effectively protect the legitimate rights of copyright subject. The protection mainly includes administrative punishment, administrative investigation, administrative mediation and administrative adjudication.

Article 48 of the *2001 Copyright Law* provides that he who commits any of the eight types of infringements that damage public interests, the copyright administration department may order him to cease the act of infringement, may confiscate his illegal gains, confiscate and destroy the reproductions of infringement and impose a fine on him. It provides legal basis for the copyright administrative department to exercise administrative penalties. Article 2 of the *Measures for Copyright Administrative Penalty Implementation* further clarifies that the National Copyright Administration and the local copyright administrative departments are the subjects of copyright infringement administrative penalty.

According to Article 37 of the *Regulations for the Implementation of the Copyright Law*, the copyright administrative department of the State Council or the copyright administrative department of the local government is responsible for investigating, punishing the infringements which are listed in Article 48 of the *Copyright Law* and damage the public interests. It shows that the copyright administrative authority has the power of administrative investigation and control for copyright infringement that damages the public interests.

According to Article 55 of the *Copyright Law*, copyright infringement disputes can be settled through mediation. Article 23 of the *Regulations on the Protection of Computer Software* also provides that software copyright infringement disputes may be mediated. Although the above provisions do not explicitly authorize the right to mediate disputes to the copyright administration authority, for the eleven violations of Article 47 of the *Copyright Law* and the six violations of Article 23 of *Regulations on the Protection of Computer Software*, the copyright administrative department presided over mediation of a large number of disputes, according to the parties' autonomy.

The copyright administrative authority's jurisdiction over copyright infringements does not be stipulated clearly in copyright laws and regulations. Nevertheless, in practice, when the copyright administrative department imposes administrative penalties or conducts administrative investigations on copyright infringements, it is usually necessary to identify the infringing act first by exercising administrative discretion. Therefore, administrative adjudication is an important part of copyright administrative enforcement of law as well.

In 2012, according to statistics, copyright enforcement departments across the country investigated 2,249 copyright cases, of which 1,524 were administratively closed, 858 criminal cases were transferred to the judicial authorities for investigation.[9] In 2013, the number of investigated cases reached 3,567.[10]

[2] Judicial Protection

Judicial protection refers to the method that IP rights owners or public prosecution departments protect copyright through civil, administrative or criminal lawsuits in law.

---

9. 国家知识产权局 [State Intellectual Property Office], "2012年中国知识产权保护状况" [China's intellectual property protection in 2012], http://www.sipo.gov.cn, last visit time: August 23, 2014.
10. *Ibid.*

Judicial protection, indispensable for IP protection as IP a private right, the "final adjudication" principle for IP protection established in the *TRIPS Agreement*, the most basic, powerful and ultimate legal remedy for copyright protection in China, plays a major role in copyright infringement and piracy disputes. Judicial protection of IP rights has played a leading role in China, after the implementation of the *Outline of the National IP Strategy* in 2008. Currently, judicial protection of copyright includes copyright civil litigations (including infringement and contract disputes), criminal litigations and administrative litigations for disputes concerning penalties by copyright administrative departments.

Of the *2001 Copyright Law*, Articles 47–55 provide civil remedies for copyright and civil sanctions, and Articles 48 and 56 provide administrative penalties for copyright infringements and administrative litigation, remedies of refuses to accept punishment. In addition, Articles 217–218 of the *Penal Code* provide for criminal liability for crimes of copyright infringements.

[B] Necessity of Administrative Protection

The modern IP protection system of China was established in the 20th century, when China's national conditions decided the dual copyright protection model. As IP was new and unfamiliar at that time, most judges were lack of skill and experience in hearing IP cases. Meanwhile, administrative enforcement of law has been dominant in China in tradition. The administrative enforcement departments have more mature methods of enforcement, so that they could effectively punish infringements of IP rights.

Administrative enforcement of law has the following advantages over judicial protection: (a) Much easier to accept cases. For copyright infringement, usually it is difficult for copyright owner to collect the evidence or identify the infringer. The copyright administrative departments can play a more active role. Even without complete evidence or information, administrative department will still accept the case, as long as the complainant provides clues in relation to the infringement. After the case is filed, the administrative department investigates the infringement by exercising its enforcement power. (b) Much lower cost for the right owners. Generally, all complainants need to submit to the copyright administrative department are an application for investigation, a certificate of ownership, an infringed work or product and other acquired evidence. Besides, when necessary, the copyright administrative department may request the complainant to attend the relevant hearings. Since there are no more obligations beyond the above, it can effectively save costs such as attorneys' fees and investigation fees and does need any property guarantee; it is less expensive for copyright owners to protect their rights by administrative enforcement. (c) Much lighter burden of proof. The complainants only need to submit the infringed works or products, or submit the relevant information of the infringement. Once the complaint is accepted, the copyright administrative department will conduct investigations based on their authority and collect relevant evidence of infringement. Moreover, the collected evidence during the enforcement process and the punishment decision issued by the administrative enforcement department can be used directly as the evidence of infringement in civil litigations. It improves the efficiency of evidence collection and reduces the cost of proof. (d) Much more efficient procedures. Comparatively, the judicial protection focuses more on pursuing justice, while the administration focuses more on efficiency. Usually, the first priority for copyright owners is to stop the infringement as soon as possible, so that they may occupy the market and gain commercial opportunities, rather than to obtain economic compensation. Therefore, some owners prefer administrative enforcement procedures to protect rights.

Since copyright is different from other private rights in nature, it is necessary to provide administrative protection on it. Copyright, which was derived from the privilege of ancient feudal society, is the result of state power. The *TRIPS Agreement* clearly states that despite IP is recognized as a private right, the goal of IP protection is not only to protect right owners but also for "Recognizing the underlying public policy objectives of national systems for the protection of IP, including developmental and technological objectives." Therefore, the protection of copyright does not only protect owners' rights and interests but also the communication of intellectual achievements for China and even for the international society. The purpose of copyright law is not only to protect moral and economic rights of authors but also to keep the balance of interests among authors, communicators and users. Since judicial protection is passive, administrative protection is necessary for achieving the public policy goals.

Therefore, Article 46 of the *1990 Copyright Law* provides that: For any of the seven types of copyright infringements such as plagiarism of other people's works, the copyright administrative department shall impose penalties such as confiscation of illegal gains, fines, etc., which grant them the power of administrative enforcement of copyright infringement. Although Article 48 of the *2001 Copyright Law* amended this provision, it still retains the administrative enforcement powers of the copyright administrative authorities, but it only imposes restrictions on the administrative enforcement powers in the case that the public interests are damaged.

[C] Dominant Role of Judicial Protection

Since copyright administrative enforcement is effective and relatively simplified, it plays an irreplaceable role in copyright protection. However, there are also some deficiencies: (a) Institutional voids. First of all, there is no systematic rule or regulation concerning the standards for the determination of infringement, the determination of the amount and the penalty procedures. Second, there is no systematic method of penalties, such as suspending production, suspending or revoking business licenses, etc. Third, there is no systematic cohesion mechanism between administrative enforcement and judicial remedy, which results in the conflicts between law enforcement standards and judicial standards. (b) Lack of standardized law enforcement. There are numerous administrative departments that are authorized to protect copyright. Besides the copyright administrative department authorize by the *Copyright Law*, there are also cultural, public security, industry and commerce, and customs departments that are authorized in accordance with different administrative regulations. Those departments have unclear responsibilities, varying standards, unclear procedures and competing interests with each other. Somehow, the above defects deviate from the goal that administrative enforcement protects the public interests of copyright.

By contrast, judicial protection of copyright is final, normative and more comprehensive: (a) The comprehensiveness. Compared with the administrative departments, the courts are able to provide a more comprehensive protection and relief for IP rights via civil, administrative and criminal litigations. Judicial litigations not only comprehensively protect the moral rights and economic rights of the works but also supervise the copyright administrative department, and provide criminal sanctions for IP crimes. (b) The finality. Judicial protection is the ultimate remedy of copyright protection and has the final effect of right protection. The effective judgment of the court conforms to the principle of "justice first, then efficiency" and is final which makes the legal effect of the judicial judgments more authoritative than the administrative decisions. Therefore, it is the ultimate solution to settle disputes and safeguard justice. (c) The function of normative guidance. Regarding the new copyright disputes, when there is still no consensus on how to solve the issue, the judicial judgments of such new and difficult cases will have the important function of normative guidance, so that both right owners and the public can predict the similar behaviors according to the judicial judgments of similar disputes in the future. Nowadays, with the rapid development of new technology and new copyright disputes, it is of great importance to have judicial protection that can clarify the legal standards. (d) The compensation for damages. In civil litigations, the court can order the infringer to compensate economic losses, reasonable expenses for safeguarding rights, and even to impose punitive damages in law, which makes significance to fully compensate for the right owners' loss of infringement, and to encourage authors to keep creating good works.

Since copyright is a private right, judicial protection is inevitable. IP rights are the tools for market competition, thus they have the nature of private rights. The nature determines that IP rights should be mainly protected by judicial protection, instead of the active participation and intervention of public power. Thus, the main task for the state is to establish a fair and efficient judicial system for IP.

In conclusion, both administrative enforcement and judicial protection have their own advantages for the protection of IP rights. However, judicial protection is essential for the IP rights due to the nature of private rights and plays a leading role in the protection. The *Outline of the National Intellectual Property Strategy in 2008* requires China "to improve the law enforcement and management system of IP rights," to build the dual-track system of judicial protection and administrative law enforcement, and that judicial protection plays a leading role in IP protection. In order to achieve the above goals, China has adopted a series of measures since 2008: First, China has established specific IP courts and IP tribunals, which hear civil, administrative and criminal cases of IP rights (including copyright), in order to achieve the professionalization of IP trials. Second, China has optimized the rule of jurisdiction, so that more local courts shall have jurisdiction over copyright disputes, facilitating litigants to participate in litigation. Summary procedures are applied in accordance with the law to simplify the procedure and shorten time to meet the need for judicial protection of copyright. Third, the rule of preliminary protection has been introduced into judicial protection to minimize copyright owners' dependence on administrative protection. Fourth, China has improved the rule of compensation, including punitive damages, to increase the compensation. The above measures have greatly enhanced the capability of judicial protection, encouraging more copyright owners to protect copyright by judicial approach. According to statistics, cases of copyright disputes handled by courts across the country have increased significantly from 2008 to 2013. On August 31, 2014, the 10th meeting of the 12th NPC Standing Committee promulgated the *NPC Standing Committee's Decision on the Establishment of Intellectual Property Courts in Beijing, Shanghai and Guangzhou*. It is great significance to optimize the IP protection system, harmonize the relationship between judicial protection and administrative law enforcement, strengthen the leading role of judicial protection of IP rights and unify the judicial IP protection standards.

§1.03 MECHANISMS OF COPYRIGHT PROTECTION

As mentioned above, the dual-track of administrative enforcement and judicial protection is the characteristic of the Chinese copyright protection. Accordingly, the Chinese copyright protection system consists of two parts, which are the administrative system and the judicial system.

[A] Enforcement by Administrative Enforcement

[1] Law Enforcement System of Copyright Administration Department

According to Article 7 of the *Copyright Law*, the copyright administrative department under the State Council shall be responsible for the nationwide administration of copyright. The copyright administrative department of the government of each province, autonomous region or municipality directly under the Central Government shall be responsible for the administration of copyright within its own jurisdiction. Therefore, copyright administration and administrative law enforcement are mainly handled by the State Copyright Administration and local copyright administrative departments.

According to the *Copyright Law* and the *Regulations for the Implementation of the Copyright Law*, the national Copyright Administration, being an administrative department for copyright matters under the State Council, is responsible for the nationwide administration of copyright (including software copyright) by mainly carrying out the following functions: (a) It shall implement copyright laws, regulations and entrustment by the National People's Congress and its Standing Committee to draft copyright laws. Besides, it shall be entrusted by the State Council to draft and formulate administrative regulations related to copyright administration. (b) It shall investigate and redress cases of infringement of copyright that are of nationwide influence, infringements where a foreign party is involved, and infringements that should be redressed by the National Copyright Administration, as the Administration might think. (c) It shall approve the formation of and to supervise the operation of collective administration of copyright, copyright agent business dealing with cross-border transactions and arbitration scheme for disputes in relation to copyright contracts. (d) It shall undertake administration as far as external copyright relation is concerned. (e) It shall administer copyright of which the State is the owner and which be enjoyed by the State according to the *Copyright Law*. (f) It shall provide guidance for local copyright departments with their performance of administrative functions, and supervise them. (g) It shall carry out other duties assigned by the State Council in relation to copyright administration.

The copyright administrative departments of the government of each province, autonomous region and municipality directly under the Central Government, some cities specifically designated in the state plan, and some special regions or cities, shall be responsible for the administration and administrative law enforcement of copyright within their own jurisdiction according to the law. They are authorized to: (a) redress the infringements against copyright and copyright-related rights; (b) preside over the mediation of copyright disputes; (c) make registration of licensing contracts for overseas publishing of books, audio-visual recordings, electronic publications, computer software, etc., as well as the pledge of copyright; (d) deal with voluntary registration of works; (e) issue certificates for foreign-related copyright.

[2]   Customs Enforcement System

According to Article 44 of the *Customs Law*, the customs shall protect IP rights including copyrights that are related to import and export goods. Article 91 provides that whoever imports or exports goods, which constitute infringement of IP, the infringing goods shall be confiscated by customs and a fine shall be imposed thereof; where the case constitutes a crime, the person or persons concerned shall be investigated for criminal liability. Customs is authorized to impose confiscation and fines on the import and export of goods that infringe IP rights according to the above provisions. In December 2003, in order to fulfill the requirements of the *TRIPS Agreement*, the State Council issued the *Regulations on Customs Protection of Intellectual Property Rights* which provides detailed rules of customs for IP administrative enforcement.

According to the *Regulations on Customs Protection of Intellectual Property Rights*, customs protect copyright and copyright-related rights that are related to import and export goods by the Chinese laws and administrative regulations. Its responsibilities include: (a) dealing with declaration and recording of IP rights for import and export goods; (b) accepting the application for impoundment of goods imported and exported that suspected of infringing upon rights; (c) detaining import or export goods that are suspected of infringing upon rights upon IP rights in law; (d) confiscating or destroying the goods confirmed as having infringed upon IP rights after investigation; (e) pursuing the criminal liability of person or persons concerned according to the law, where the import or export of goods that infringe upon IP rights constitutes a criminal offense.

In China, custom protection of copyright has formed its legal system initially, although starting late. The protection is even more than the obligations of the *TRIPS Agreement* in some way. In terms of the scope of protection, China protects the IP rights of both imported and exported goods, while *TRIPS Agreement* only covers imported goods. Regarding the protecting object, *TRIPS Agreement* only explicitly requires protecting counterfeit and pirated goods, but the Chinese custom also covers other copyright infringements. Besides, the time limit is also stricter. However, there are also some deficiencies in the Chinese copyright customs protection. For example, the substantive and procedural laws are mixed together, which results in the inappropriate procedure, especially the procedures for transferring copyright crimes are only in principle but not in details.

In addition, administrative departments for industry and commerce, journalism, publishing, radio, film and television, culture, public security, science and technology, education and technical supervision at all levels shall also perform their respective functions that assist copyright administrative departments to manage copyright and undertake some functions of copyright administrative law enforcement.

[B] Enforcement by Judicial Adjudication

In accordance with the constitution law, the courts are authorized to exercise judicial power, while the procuratorates are authorized to exercise procuratorial power on behalf of the state. In general, the judicial protection of copyright refers to protecting copyright by civil litigations. According to Article 2 of the *Law on the Organization the People's Courts*, the adjudicatory authority of China is exercised by local courts at various levels, military courts and other special courts, and the Supreme People's Court. The local courts at various levels are divided into: basic people's courts, intermediate people's courts and higher people's courts. The Supreme People's Court shall be the highest judicial departments of the state and supervise the administration of justice by the local people's courts at various levels and by the special people's courts. There are criminal, civil, economic, administrative and IP tribunals in the courts. The institutional system of China's copyright judicial trials consists of the IP judicial departments set up by basic, intermediate, higher people's courts and the Supreme People's Court.

[1] Development Overview

It has been over thirty years since China started to launch the judicial protection of copyright in the 1980s. A complete judicial system and mechanism has been formed. The *General Principles of Civil Law* was promulgated and implemented in April 1986. For the first time, copyright was enumerated as an important part of civil rights. Article 94 and Article 118 explicitly provide for the protection of citizens' copyright, providing a legal basis for the courts to accept copyright disputes.

However, in the beginning, due to the weak awareness of copyright of the public and the lack of experience of the courts, copyright disputes were judged by civil tribunals but not specific IP tribunals. In August 1993, Beijing No. 1 Intermediate People's Court took the lead to establish the first IP tribunal in China, successively followed by higher people's courts, intermediate people's courts and even some basic courts where IP cases emerged intensively. Since then, IP judges have gained experience from the practice, especially that there are a good number of professional judges in Shanghai, Beijing and other well-developed areas. By 2012, 420 IP tribunals have been set up in courts across the country; 2,759 judges are engaged in IP trials, 97.5% of which are undergraduates or above, and 41.1% are postgraduates. On August 31, 2014, the 10th Meeting of the 12th NPC Standing Committee voted and passed the *NPC Standing Committee's Decision on the Establishment of Intellectual Property Courts in Beijing, Shanghai and Guangzhou*. Accordingly, the specific IP courts shall be established in Beijing, Shanghai and Guangzhou. It will make most of the leading role of judicial protection of IP under the dual-track protection model, achieve the unification of standards of the judgments and promote the standards of administrative enforcement and judicial adjudication. The judicial protection of copyright is going to embark on a new stage.

[2]   Four-Level Courts and Second-Instance System

In accordance with Article 12 of the *Law on the Organization the People's Courts*, the courts shall adopt the system whereby the second instance is the final instance. Thus, the judicial protection system for copyright in China implements a "Four-level Courts and Second-instance System," that is, a trial system in which a copyright case is terminated after the first-instance and second-instance procedures of the four-level courts. Four-level courts refer to basic people's courts, intermediate people's courts, higher people's courts and the Supreme People's Court. The basic people's courts may establish a number of people's tribunals. However, they are not trial departments, but agencies from basic people's courts and hear cases in the name of the basic people's courts. According to Articles 198 and 199 of the *Civil Procedure Law*, if there is any mistake in a judgment or adjudication that has already taken effect, it may be re-tried through trial supervision procedures. In October 2002, the Supreme People's Court issued the *Interpretation of the Supreme People's Court on Issues Concerning the Application of Law in the Trial of Cases of Civil Disputes over Copyright* to establish a copyright trial system that suits the national conditions of China. According to Article 1, the courts accept the civil cases of dispute over copyright as mentioned below: (a) The cases of dispute over the possession, infringement and contract of copyright or copyright-related rights and interests; (b) The cases of plead for stopping the infringement upon copyright or copyright-related rights and interests before the institution of an action or for attachment of property or evidences before the institution of an action; (c) Other cases of dispute over copyright or copyright-related rights and interests. Article 2 provides that a civil case of dispute over copyright usually shall be subject to the jurisdiction of the intermediate people's court, while the higher people's court becomes the second-instance court. Meanwhile, some of the basic people's courts shall be the first-instance court for trying civil cases of dispute over copyright, while the intermediate people's court becomes the second-instance court. The number of IP tribunals in China is determined by the Supreme People's based on the types and the number of IP cases. By 2013, 160 basic people's courts have had jurisdiction over copyright cases. Three specific IP courts shall be established in Beijing, Shanghai and Guangzhou according to the *Decision of the Standing Committee on Establishing IP Right Courts in Beijing, Shanghai and Guangzhou*. In Beijing, Shanghai and Guangzhou, the IP Courts will be the courts of appeal for the first-instance cases by the basic people's courts in Beijing, Shanghai and Guangzhou respectively. In the cases where IP Courts in Beijing, Shanghai and Guangzhou are the first-instance, the higher people's courts of that city will be the courts of appeal.

[3] The Method of Judicial Protection

[a] Copyright Civil Litigation

The *TRIPS Agreement* states that IP rights are private rights. Since the ultimate remedy of IP rights is judicial civil litigation by which IP owners to safeguard their legal rights and obtain financial compensation, civil litigation plays the fundamental role in judicial protection. In other words, civil copyright litigation is the most important method to regulate the interests among copyright owners, users of works, and communicators. Article 118 of the *General Principles of Civil Law* provides that if the copyright, patent right, right to exclusive use of trademarks, right of discovery, right of invention or right for scientific and technological research achievements of citizens or legal persons are infringed upon by such means as plagiarism, alteration or imitation, they shall have the right to demand that the infringement be stopped, its ill effects be eliminated and the damages be compensated for. Articles 46 and 48–54 of the *Copyright Law* are the basic legal basis for copyright civil litigation, which stipulated the civil compensation standards, property preservation, behavior preservation, evidence preservation and contracts for copyright. According to the *Provisions on Causes of Action in Civil Cases of the Supreme People's Court*, civil disputes accepted by the courts include three major types of forty-two types of disputes, namely copyright contract disputes, copyright ownership and infringement disputes, and the recognition of noninfringement of copyright disputes, covering all areas of copyright civil litigation.

The legal system regulating the civil copyright litigation consists of the substantive law and the procedural law. The substantive legal system includes the *General Principles of Civil Law*, the *Tort Liability Law*, the *Contract Law*, the *Copyright Law*, the *Regulations for the Implementation of the Copyright Law*, the *Regulations on the Protection of Computer Software*, the *Regulations on the Protection of the Right of Communication of Information on Networks*, the *Interpretation of the Supreme People's Court on Issues Concerning the Application of Law in the Trial of Cases of Civil Disputes over Copyright*, etc., while the procedural legal system is mainly composed of the *Civil Procedure Law* and its judicial interpretations. The legal system concerning foreign-related copyright contains the *TRIPS Agreement* and the *Berne Convention*, etc.

[b] Copyright Administrative Litigation

Copyright administrative litigation is a litigation activity and system that the courts conduct judicial review of the legitimacy and reasonableness of law enforcement such as confirmation and management of copyright, handling of copyright disputes, etc., carried out by the copyright management departments at all levels. Thus, copyright administrative litigation is the most important method to regulate the copyright-related interests among the State, copyright owners, users of works, and communicators. Article 55 of the *Copyright Law* states that any party that objects to an administrative penalty may bring a lawsuit to the courts within three months as of the date when it received the written decision on the penalty. If a party neither brings a lawsuit nor implements the decision within the above time, the copyright administration department concerned may apply to the court for enforcement. Who intending to initiate legal litigations directly with a court shall be required to do so within three months of its being notified of the particular administrative action that it wishes to contest. The legal basis for copyright administrative litigation includes above provisions. So, any party who objects to an administrative penalty may bring a lawsuit to the court in accordance with Article 47 of the *Copyright Law* and Article 38 of the *Regulations for the Implementation of the Copyright Law*.

In China, the legal system regulating domestic copyright administrative litigation also consists of the substantive law and the procedural law. The substantive legal system includes the *Copyright Law*, the *Regulations on the Protection of Computer Software*, the *Regulations on the Administration of Audio and Video Products*, and the *Measures for Copyright Pledge Contract*, the *Measures for the Implementation of Administrative Penalties for Publications*, etc. The procedural legal system is mainly composed of the *Administrative Procedure Law* and its judicial interpretations.

[c] Copyright Criminal Procedure

The criminal procedure of copyright is the method of judicial remedies to the criminal law and the criminal procedure law for severe IP infringements which constitute a criminal offense. In some foreign countries, the criminal protection of copyright was launched in the 1970s. By contrast, in China, the criminal liability for copyright infringements was not provided in the *1990 Copyright Law*. It results that no matter how serious the infringements were, the infringers would never bear any criminal responsibility, which causes criticisms from the international community. On July 5, 1994, the 8th Meeting of the Standing Committee of the National People's Congress promulgated the *Decision on the Punishment of the Crimes of Copyright Infringement*, which is the first specialized law for the criminal copyright protection. It is to respond to the pressures of the international community, especially the *Sino-US Memorandum on the Protection of IP* for the growing necessities concerning piracy of books, sound and video recordings, computer software and other works and products. The *1997 Criminal Law* provided the crimes of IP infringement in the eighth section of the third chapter. Articles 217 and 218, incorporating the *Decision on the Punishment of the*

Crimes of Copyright Infringement, provided crimes of copyright infringement and the sale of infringing copies, which has been the fundamental basis of copyright criminal law protection.

[d] "Three-in-One" Model

As mentioned earlier, the dual-track system of administrative enforcement and judicial protection was implemented at the beginning of the establishment of the Chinese IP system. In order to unify the litigation standards under the dual-track system, in 1996, Pudong District People's Court of Shanghai started to explore a "three-in-one" model for civil, administrative and criminal IP litigations. Normally, civil, administrative and criminal IP cases are heard respectively by the civil, administrative and criminal tribunals. Under this "three-in-one" model, all IP cases shall be heard by a specific IP tribunal, so that the litigation standards of IP cases can be unified. After Pudong, in 2006, Guangdong Higher People's Court started to apply this "three-in-one" model in Tianhe District People's Court of Guangzhou, Nanshan District People's Court of Shenzhen and Nanhai District People's Court of Foshan. Since then, Jiangsu, Zhejiang, Chongqing and Hubei provinces also started to apply the "three-in-one" model, and gradually established the "three-in-one" model, providing a three-dimensional protection of administrative, civil and criminal protection of IP. By 2013, seven higher courts, seventy-nine intermediate courts and seventy-one basic courts across China had carried out the "three-in-one" IP litigations.

With the growing judicial institutional mechanisms, judicial copyright protection has been much more important to play the leading role in copyright protection. From 2011 to 2013, the number of first-instance and second-instance of copyright cases was increasing significantly year by year. According to the *Judicial Protection Status of IP in China (2010–2013)* and the *Geographical Distribution of IP Cases (2011–2013)*, in 2011, there were 24,719 copyright cases heard in China, which was an increase of 61.54% 2010. In 2012, there were 53,848 copyright cases heard, which was an increase of 53.04% over 2011. In 2013, there were 51,351 copyright cases heard, which was slightly less than that of 2012. Among all the IP litigations, copyright disputes accounted for the largest proportion, exceeding 70% for two consecutive years of 2011 and 2012.

§1.04 REMEDIES FOR COPYRIGHT INFRINGEMENT

[A] Administrative Enforcement Procedure

The *Measures for the Implementation of Copyright Administrative Punishment* issued by the National Copyright Administration explicitly stipulates both the administrative punishments by copyright administrative departments and the administrative law enforcement procedures.

[1] Scope of Penalties

The illegal acts of the copyright administrative department that has the power to enforce administrative penalties include the following: First, the infringements which damage the public interest, stipulated in the *Copyright Law*; Second, the infringements which damage the public interest, stipulated in the *Regulation on the Protection of Computer Software*; Third, the infringements stipulated in the *Regulations on the Protection of the Right of Communication of Information on Networks*; Fourth, the acts subjects to administrative penalty as provided by the *Regulations on Collective Management of Copyright*; Fifthly, other illegal acts that should be given administrative penalties as stipulated in copyright laws, regulations and rules.

[2] Case Jurisdiction

The infringing act of copyright is generally investigated by administrative departments of the place where the infringement act takes on, the place where the infringement results take place, the place where the infringing product is stored, or the place where distrained according to law. However, for the infringement of the right of communication of information on networks, it shall be investigated by the administrative departments of the infringer's domicile, the place where such equipment as the network server, where computer terminal involved in the alleged infringement located and the place where the infringement is recorded and registered. The National Copyright Administration and the local copyright administrative departments are responsible for investigating, with different jurisdiction of the illegal acts. The National Copyright Administration may, in accordance with the authority, investigate and redress illegal acts that have significant influence, as well as other illegal acts that should be investigated by it. The local copyright administrative departments are responsible for investigating illegal acts in their own jurisdiction respectively.

[3] Complaint Procedure

If the copyright owner believes that his rights have been infringed, he may file a complaint with the copyright administrative departments. The complainant shall submit an application, a certificate of rights, the infringed works or products, and other evidence if he is going to file a case for investigation. The right owner may entrust the agent to apply for investigation with the letter of attorney. In addition to accepting complaints, the administrative department of copyright may also decide to file a case for investigation or to investigate according to the materials transferred by the relevant department, or to file a case according to the complaint or report of the infringer, interested party or other insiders.

[4] Active Investigation

Whether it is a complaint case or a case decided to be investigated by the departments, investigators of the copyright administrative department shall promptly conduct an investigation and require the party bearing the burden of proof to submit evidence within the time limit specified by the copyright administrative departments. The evidences may include: the copyright-related manuscripts, originals, legitimate publications, copyright registration certificates, copyright contract registration certificates, certificates issued by the certification authorities, contracts for licensing or assignment, and infringing copies and invoices collected by the parties or attorneys. When obtaining evidence, the investigator may collect the relevant evidence by: Inspecting and copying documents, books and other written materials; Sampling evidence of the infringing products; And registering and preserving the suspected infringing products, the equipment that stores suspected infringing products, the website of the alleged infringing website, the alleged infringing website server and the materials, tools and equipment mainly used for illegal activities.

[5] Administrative Penalties

For acts of copyright infringement, the copyright administrative department may impose the following administrative penalties while ordering the infringer to stop the infringement: Warnings, fines, confiscation of illegal income, confiscation of infringing products, confiscation of equipment for installation of infringing products, confiscation of materials used primarily for the production of infringing articles, tools, equipment, etc., and other administrative penalties stipulated by laws, regulations and rules.

Regarding the amount of fines, Article 36 of the *Regulations for the Implementation of the Copyright Law* explicitly stipulates: Where the total amount of the illegal business is RMB 50,000 or more, the copyright administrative department may impose a fine of more than one time but no more than five times the total amount of the illegal business; Where there is no amount of the illegal business or the total amount is less than RMB 50,000, the copyright administrative department may, based on the circumstance of the case, impose a fine of not more than RMB 250,000. Article 24 of the *Regulations on the Protection of Computer Software* makes a special provision about the amount of fines to infringing computer software: Who commits the acts as reproducing the software of the copyright owner wholly or partly, or distributing, renting, or communicating of information on networks the software of the copyright owners to the public shall be concurrently imposed a fine of RMB 100 per copy or not exceeding five times the value of the copies. The infringer who commits the act as knowingly circumvent or sabotage the technological measures adopted by the copyright owner for protecting his software copyright, or knowingly remove or alter any digital rights management information for software right management, or transferring or licensing another person to exploit the software copyright of the copyright owners shall be concurrently imposed a fine of no more than RMB 200,000. In addition, the copyright administrative department may also confiscate materials, tools and equipment for making infringing products in the following cases: The amount of illegal income is over RMB 2,500; the total amount of illegal business is over RMB 15,000; the operation of the infringed products over 250 copies; the recommitment of copyright infringement and other serious infringements.

[6] Channels of Relief

If the party disagrees with the administrative punishment of the State Copyright Administration, he may apply to the State Copyright Administration for administrative review. If the party disagrees with the administrative punishment of the local copyright administrative department, he may apply to the government at the corresponding level or its superior copyright administrative department for administrative review. Any party who objects to an administrative penalty may bring a lawsuit to the court within three months as of the date when it received the written decision on the penalty. If a party neither brings a lawsuit nor implements the decision within the team, the copyright administration department may apply to the court for enforcement.

[B] Procedures of Judicial Relief

[1] Civil Procedure

Civil IP litigation plays a major role in protecting IP rights and promoting independent innovation. Copyright cases account for a large proportion of civil IP cases. In 2013, the local courts across China had accepted 88,583 first-instance civil IP cases. Among them, 51,351 (57.97%) were copyright cases.[11] The judicial procedures involved in civil copyright litigations mainly include the following aspects:

[a] Standing to Sue

According to Article 119 of the *Civil Procedure Law*, Filing of a lawsuit shall satisfy the following conditions: (1) the plaintiff must be a citizen, legal person or any other organization that has a direct interest in the case; (2) there must be a definite defendant; (3) there must be specific claim or claims, facts, and cause or causes for the suit; and (4) the suit must be within the scope of acceptance for civil actions by the courts and under the jurisdiction of the court where the suit is entertained. When a lawsuit is brought, a statement of complaint shall be submitted to the court, and copies of the statement shall be provided according to the number of defendants.

---

11. 《2013年中国法院知识产权司法保护状况》白皮书 [the White Paper of Judicial Protection of Intellectual Property in Chinese courts in 2013].

[b] Jurisdiction

The copyright cases are professional, especially in Internet-related copyright cases, which often involve the most novel Internet technology, with the technical and legal issues intertwined. Such cases are challenging to the courts. In 2002, in order to ensure the quality and efficiency of the litigations and to provide guidance to all the courts, the Supreme People's Court issued the *Interpretation of the Supreme People's Court on Issues Concerning the Application of Law in the Trial of Cases of Civil Disputes over Copyright* which makes a relatively centralized jurisdiction on civil copyright cases. According to Article 2 of the *Interpretation*, in principle, civil copyright cases shall be under the jurisdiction of the intermediate people's courts. According to this rule of level jurisdiction, the first-instance of civil copyright case is under the jurisdiction of an intermediate people's court, and the second instance is heard by a higher people's court. However, since unbalanced regional development in China, there are much more copyright disputes in the developed coastal areas and provincial capital cities, each High People's Court may, based on its actual situation, designate several basic People's Courts to hear civil copyright cases for the first instance.

Article 4 of the *Interpretation of the Supreme People's Court on Issues Concerning the Application of Law in the Trial of Cases of Civil Disputes over Copyright* provides:

> The civil action instituted on the ground of copyright infringement shall be subject to the jurisdiction of the court where the infringing acts take place, where the reproductions are stored, detained or confiscated, or where the defendant dwells. The place where the infringing reproductions are stored refers to the place where large quantities of infringing reproductions are stored or concealed for business purposes. The place of detention or confiscation is the place where the infringing reproductions were lawfully sealed up or detained by the administrative departments of customs, copyright, administrations for industry.

Furthermore, for the Internet-related copyright disputes, the *Interpretation of the Supreme People's Court on Several Issues Concerning the Application of Law to Trial of Civil Dispute Cases of Infringement of the Right of Communication of Information on Networks* was promulgated by the Supreme People's Court to facilitate civil copyright litigations. According to this *Interpretation*, in Internet-related copyright cases, the place where the infringing act occurs includes the locations of the network servers, computer terminals, or other equipment by which the act of infringement carried out. If both the place where the infringing act occurs and the defendant's domicile are unable to be determined or outside the territory of China, the place of the computer terminals or other equipment by which the plaintiff discovers the infringement may be considered as the place where the infringement occurs.

[c] Limitation of Action

In accordance with the *General Principles of the Civil Law*, the period of limitation of actions on a request to the court for the protection of civil rights is two years. And the period of limitation of actions shall be calculated from the time it was known, or should have been known, that a right was infringed upon. The statute of limitations for copyright also applies to civil copyright disputes. In addition, if more than twenty years have passed, however, since the date of the infringement of the right, the court shall offer no protection. However, since some acts of copyright infringement are continued, Article 28 of the *Interpretation of the Supreme People's Court on Issues Concerning the Application of Law in the Trial of Cases of Civil Disputes over Copyright* provides: Where the right owner institutes an action after two years, and if the infringing act still continues when the action is instituted, and is within the protection period of the copyright, the court shall rule that the defendant shall stop the infringing act, and the amount of compensations for damages shall be calculated two years from the date when the copyright owner instituted the lawsuit with the court.

[d] *Preservation*

Compared with general torts, copyright infringement is easier to implement, costs less and its damage is easier to expand. In order to prevent infringements that are being or are about to be implemented, to preserve key evidence of infringement, to avoid further damage or irreparable damage, Article 50 of the *TRIPS Agreement* provides for "provisional measures," which is that the judicial authorities shall have the power to order prompt and effective provisional measures to prevent the infringing goods from entering the channels of commerce and to preserve relevant evidence of the alleged infringement. In the light of the *TRIPS Agreement*, the *Copyright Law* stipulates three types of provisional measures, including cessation of the relevant act before the lawsuit (the preliminary injunction), pretrial evidence preservation and prior measures of attachment on property. Article 50 of the *Copyright Law* provides the rule concerning preliminary injunction and prior measures of attachment on property: where a copyright owner or owner of a copyright-related right who has evidence to establish that another person is committing or will commit an act of infringing his right, which could cause irreparable injury to his legitimate rights and interests if the act is not stopped immediately, he may apply to the court for ordering cessation of the related act and for taking the measures for property preservation before instituting legal proceedings. Article 51 of the *Copyright Law* provides the rule of the preservation of evidence before the lawsuit: For the purpose of preventing an infringing act and under the circumstance where the evidence could be lost or is difficult to obtain afterward, the copyright owner or the owner of a copyright-related right may apply to the court for evidence preservation before initiating legal proceedings.

On the basis of the successful experience of provisional measures in IP case, the *2012 Civil Procedure Law* provides for three types of preservation measures: evidence preservation, property preservation and behavior preservation before and during litigation. Article 81 stipulates that: Where there is a possibility that evidence may be extinguished, lost or too difficult to obtain afterward, any litigation participants may apply to the court for the preservation of the evidence. The court may also take preservation measures on its own initiative; Where any evidence may be extinguished or may be hard to obtain at a later time, if the circumstances are urgent, an interested party may, before instituting an action or applying for arbitration, apply for evidence preservation to a court at the place where the evidence is located or at the place of domicile of the respondent or a court having jurisdiction over the case. Article 100 stipulates that: For cases in which the action of a party to the lawsuit or any other reason causes difficulty in enforcement of a judgment or causes other harm to the litigants, a court may, pursuant to an application by a counterparty litigant, rule on preservation of its property or order the counterparty to undertake certain acts or prohibit the counterparty to undertake certain acts; Where the litigants do not make an application, a court may rule that preservation measures be adopted where necessary. Article 101 further stipulates that: In the event of urgent circumstances where the legitimate rights and interests of an interested party will be subject to irreparable damages if the interested party does not forthwith apply for preservation, the interested party may, prior to filing of lawsuit or application for arbitration, apply to the court at the location of the properties to be preserved or the respondent's domicile or a court which has jurisdiction for the case for adoption of preservation measures.

[e] Trial

As mentioned above, China implements the "Four-level Courts and Second-instance System," that is, a copyright case is terminated after the first-instance and second-instance procedures of the four-level courts. Any party, who refused to accept the judgment or ruling of the first instance of the local court, may appeal to the court at a higher-level court within the statutory time limit. The judgment and ruling made by the second instance court are the final judgment and ruling. Thus, if the parties do not file an appeal within the statutory time limit, the judgment or ruling made by the first instance will have legal effect. The judgment and ruling of the Supreme Court have legal effect directly. If any parties consider to have a mistake in the judgment or ruling that have already come into effect, they may apply to the higher-level court for re-trial. Where the president of a court at any level discovers an error in a written judgment, ruling or mediation of this court which has come into legal effect and deemed that there is a need for re-trial, the matter shall be submitted to the Judicial Committee for discussion and decision. Where the Supreme People's Court discovers an error in a written judgment, ruling or mediation of a local court at any level which has come into legal effect or where a higher-level court discovers an error in a written judgment, ruling or mediation of a lower-level court which has come into legal effect, it shall have the right to arraign or order the lower-level court to re-try the case. If the procuratorate files a case for protest, the court shall retry the case.

The first instance procedure is including the following stages: Filing and acceptance of lawsuits, pretrial preparation, hearing, deliberation and pronouncing judgment or ruling. A hearing generally includes: announcement of court in session, court investigation, court debate and closing statement. The litigants shall be responsible for providing evidence for their assertions. In short, the "burden of proof is borne by claimant." Where unable to gather evidence on his own due to objective reason, the litigant may apply to the court for the investigation. In the case of evidence deemed by the court to be necessary for the trial of the case, the court shall investigate and gather the evidence. According to the principles of "party autonomy" and "lawfulness," the court may carry out mediation. However, if a mediation agreement cannot be reached, the court shall render judgments without delay.

For trial of general procedures, it shall be completed within six months from the acceptance. Where there is a need for extension of time under special circumstances, the approval of the president of the court is required and an extension of time of six months may be granted; where there is a need for further extension of time, the approval of the higher-level court is required.

In the second instance, the court shall examine the relevant facts and applicable laws for the appeal. Except for specific circumstances stipulated by the *Civil Procedure Law*, the general procedures for first instance shall apply to the second instance. The second-instance court shall take the following actions in accordance with the following circumstances: Where the facts ascertained in the original judgment or ruling are clear, and the application of laws is correct, the appeal shall be dismissed by a judgment or ruling, and the original judgment or ruling shall be affirmed; Where the facts ascertained in the original judgment or ruling are wrong or the application of laws is wrong, the original judgment shall be amended, revoked or modified by a judgment or ruling; Where the basic facts ascertained in the original judgment are unclear, the second-instance court shall rule to revoke the original judgment, and the case shall be remanded to the original court for re-trial, or the original judgment shall be amended upon ascertainment of facts; Where a litigant is omitted in the original judgment or the judgment in default is passed illegally which violates statutory procedures seriously, the second-instance court shall rule to revoke the original judgment, and the case shall be remanded to the original court for re-trial. Where the court which originally heard the case has made a judgment on a remanded case, and the litigants file an appeal, the second-instance court shall not remand the case for re-trial again.

For trial of second-instance procedures against a judgment, it shall be completed within three months from the acceptance of the second instance. Where there is a need for extension of time under special circumstances, the approval of the president of the court is required. For trial of second-instance procedures against a ruling, it shall be completed within thirty days from the acceptance of the second instance.

In the cases subject to re-trial by a court pursuant to the procedure for trial supervision, where the judgment or ruling made by the first-instance court has come into legal effect, the case shall be tried pursuant to the procedure for trial of first instance, the litigants may file an appeal for the judgment or ruling; Where the judgment or ruling made by the second-instance court has come into legal effect, the case shall be tried pursuant to the procedure for trial of second instance, the judgment or ruling is a judgment or ruling which has come into legal effect.

[f]   Open Trial

In principle, civil cases shall be tried by way of open hearing, except where: State secret or personal privacy is involved or otherwise stipulated by the law; for a divorce case or a case which involves commercial secrets, where a litigant applies for closed hearing, the lawsuit may be tried in closed hearing.

Evidence should be presented in court and cross-examined by the parties, but evidence concerning state secret, trade secret and personal privacy should be kept confidential and not presented at open hearings.

[g]   Civil Liability

Article 47 of the *Copyright Law* stipulates that he who commits acts of infringement shall bear the civil liability for such remedies as ceasing the infringing act, eliminating the effects of the act, making a public apology or paying damages, depending on the circumstances.

Regarding ceasing the infringing act: If the infringement is still continuing during the judgment, the court may order the infringer to cease the act of infringement. Regardless of the subjective wrong of the infringer, once his act constitutes an infringement, the infringement should be ceased immediately.

Regarding eliminating the effects of the act: When the infringer's infringement results in damage to the reputation of the author or his work, the court may order the infringer to clarify the fact within a certain scope to eliminate the damage on the infringed or his work in the public. Generally, the infringer shall be ordered to eliminate the effects in the scope of the damage.

Regarding making a public apology: The author's copyright includes moral rights. When the moral rights are damaged, the economic compensation alone cannot make up for the damage. In this case, the court may order the infringer to confess the mistakes and make an apology.

Regarding paying damages: Damages are usually applied to the infringement of the economic rights of copyright. The court may order the infringer who does economic damages to compensate for the economic losses. Article 49 of the *Copyright Law* provides that the infringer shall, when having infringed upon the copyright or the rights related to copyright, make a compensation on the basis of the copyright owner's actual losses; where the actual losses are difficult to be calculated, the compensation may be made on the basis of the infringer's illegal gains. Where the copyright owner's actual losses or the infringer's illegal gains cannot be determined, the court shall, on the basis of the seriousness of the act of infringement, adjudicate a compensation of up to RMB 500,000. This provision indicates that there are three steps of calculating the amount of compensation: The first step is to calculate according to the actual losses of the copyright owner. The second step is to calculate according to the illegal gains of the infringer if the actual losses cannot be ascertained. The third step is to apply the statutory compensation where the copyright owner's actual losses or the infringer's illegal gains cannot be determined, and the court shall adjudicate a compensation of up to RMB 500,000. The statutory compensation will be determined based on the following facts including the types of infringed works, the reasonable license fees, the nature of the infringement and the consequences. Moreover, the amount of compensation shall also include the reasonable expenses paid by the copyright owner for stopping the infringement, including the reasonable expenses of investigating by the copyright owner or his agent. The attorney's fees may also be included as reasonable expenses in accordance with the relevant laws and regulations.

[2] Criminal Procedure

Since copyright is private in nature, generally infringers only bear civil liability. However, certain serious copyright infringement will not only damage legitimate rights and interests of copyright owners but also undermine market order and prejudice the public interests. To punish the illegal acts of serious copyright infringement, Articles 217 and 218 of the *Criminal Law* provide two crimes relating to copyright infringement. According to the *Criminal Procedure Law*, the judicial procedures of criminal copyright cases is mainly including the following steps of investigation, prosecution, trial, execution etc.

[a] Investigation

The investigation of criminal copyright cases is carried out by public security department. The investigation first goes through three steps, including accepting cases, preliminary examination and case filing. Accepting cases refers that investigative departments accept the report, complaint, information and self-incrimination. Preliminary examination refers to the phase to examine the materials and determine whether they are adequate for case filing. Case filing is determination by the investigating departments of whether the case should be treated as a criminal case for investigation in compliance with the law. After the case is filed, the investigating departments may, according to the case, take interrogation of the suspect, interview the witness, conduct an inquest or examination, search, seize and impound material evidence and documentary evidence, identify, take wanted orders etc.

After the investigating department has concluded its investigation of a case, it shall make a written opinion recommending prosecution, which shall be transferred, together with the case file and evidence, to the procuratorate at the same level for examination and decision. Meanwhile, the investigating department shall inform the criminal suspect and the defense attorney of the transfer.

[b] Public Prosecution

Criminal procedures can be classified as public prosecution procedures and private prosecution procedures. Public prosecution refers to the procuratorate's prosecution of criminal suspects' acts to the court, which requires the court to determine the facts of the crime and punish the criminal through the trial procedure. The public prosecution procedure includes five steps: filing, investigation, prosecution, trial and execution. A procuratorate may remand the case to a public security department for supplementary investigation or conduct the investigation by itself. Supplementary investigation may be conducted twice at most. Where, after supplementary investigation has been conducted twice for a case, the procuratorate still deems that evidence is insufficient and the case does not meet the conditions for prosecution, the procuratorate may decide not to initiate a prosecution. Where a procuratorate deems that the facts of a criminal suspect's crime are clear, that evidence is sufficient, and that the criminal suspect shall be subject to criminal liability, it shall make the decision to initiate a prosecution; and, according to the provisions of jurisdiction, initiate a public prosecution in a court and transfer the case file and evidence to the court. Where a criminal suspect has no criminal facts or the circumstances of responsibility, a procuratorate shall make a decision not to initiate a prosecution. With respect to a case that is minor and the offender need not be given criminal punishment or need be exempted from it according to the *Criminal Law*, the procuratorate may decide not to initiate a prosecution.

[c] *Private Prosecution*

Private prosecution case is a criminal case that the victim or his legal agent or close relatives shall directly bring a lawsuit to the court, which shall directly accept the case, in order to investigate the criminal responsibility of the accused. Cases of private prosecution include the following: Cases to be handled only upon complaint; Cases, for which the victims have evidence to prove that those are minor criminal cases, whereas, the procuratorates do not institute prosecution; Cases for which the victims have evidence to prove that the defendants should be investigated for criminal liability according to law because their acts have infringed upon the victims' moral or economic rights, whereas, the public security departments or the procuratorates do not investigate the criminal liability of the accused. It shall be mentioned that if the infringement is so serious that prejudices the social order and national interests, then private prosecution will be no longer applicable.

Regarding the cases of private prosecution, the court may conduct mediation; and the private prosecutor may voluntarily reach a settlement with the defendant or withdraw the private prosecution before a judgment is announced.

[d] *Jurisdiction*

Regarding the jurisdiction by levels of courts: a basic-level court shall have jurisdiction as a Court of First Instance over ordinary criminal cases; however, when necessary, a court at higher level may try criminal cases over which a court at lower level have jurisdiction as a Court of First Instance; a court at higher level may instruct a court at lower level to transfer the case to another court for trial.

Regarding the territorial jurisdiction: The *Criminal Procedure Law* provides that a criminal case shall be under the jurisdiction of the court in the place where the crime was committed. Where it is more appropriate for the case to be tried by the court in the place where the defendant resides, then that court may have jurisdiction over the case. However, in judicial practice, a large number of crimes of Internet-related copyright infringement are cross-regional crimes. Thus, the principle is no longer sufficient for those Internet-related crimes. To solve the problem, Article 2 of the *Interpretation of the Supreme People's Court on the Application of the Criminal Procedure Law*, which came into effect on January 1, 2013, specifically stipulates that the places of crime of Internet-related copyright infringement include the place where the crime occurred and the place where the crime results occurred. The places of crime are including the location of the network server used to carry out the criminal act; the location of the network access; the location of the website creator or operator; the location of the infringed computer system or its operator; the location of computer system used by the suspect or the victim; and the location of the loss of the victim's property. On May 4, 2014, the *Opinions of the Supreme People's Court, the Supreme People's Procuratorate and the Ministry of Public Security on Several Issues Concerning the Application of Criminal Procedure in the Application of Criminal Cases in Internet-Based Crimes* were promulgated. Article 2 further clarifies that the places of crime are including the location of the network server used to carry out the criminal act; the location of the network access; the location of the website creator or operator; the location of the infringed computer system or its operator; the location of computer system used by the suspect or the victim; the location of the loss of the victim's property; in the Internet-related cases with multiple links, if the suspect provides any assistance for the crime, the public security department of the place where the crime is committed or the place of the suspect's residence may file a case for investigation. The above-mentioned judicial interpretation is aimed at the characteristics of cybercrime, clarifies the specific circumstances of the cybercrime case and is conducive to cracking down on crimes of Internet-related copyright infringement.

[e] Trial

Similar to civil litigation, criminal litigation is also subject to the second-instance system. Thus criminal trial procedures are, including, first-instance procedures, second-instance procedures and re-trial procedures. A hearing of a criminal case generally includes: announcement of court in session, court investigation, court debate and closing statement of the defendant.

After deciding to hold a court session to hear a case, the court shall determine the members of the panel, and serve a copy of the indictment of the procuratorate upon the defendant and the defense attorney thereof no later than ten days before the court session is opened. Before a court session is opened, the judges may call together the public prosecutor, parties concerned, defense attorney, and agents *ad litem* to gather information and hear opinions on trial-related issues, such as challenges, list of witnesses to testify in court, and exclusion of illegally obtained evidence. In principle, a first-instance court shall hear cases openly. However, if a case involves any state secret or personal privacy, it shall not be heard in open court; and if a case involves any trade secret, it may not be heard in open court, by the request of the concerned party.

In the public prosecution case, the burden of proof for the defendant's guilt is borne by the procuratorate, which is different from the rule of civil litigation. However, in the case of private prosecution, it is borne by the private prosecutor.

[f]   Criminal Liability

The criminal liability for copyright infringement refers to the legal liability that the infringer should bear in violation of the provisions of Article 217 or 218 of the *Criminal Law* for his infringement of copyright. According to Article 217 of the *Criminal Law*, the criminal liability for the crime of copyright infringement includes: If the amount of illegal gains is relatively large, or if there are other serious circumstances, he shall be sentenced to fixed-term imprisonment of not more than three years or criminal detention and shall also, or shall only, be fined; If the amount of illegal gains is huge or if there are other especially serious circumstances, he shall be sentenced to fixed-term imprisonment of not less than three years but not more than seven years and shall also be fined. According to Article 218 of the *Criminal Law*, the criminal liability for the crime of selling infringing copies include: if the amount of illegal gains is huge, he shall be sentenced to fixed-term imprisonment of not more than three years or criminal detention and shall also, or shall only, be fined. If the unit commits the crime of copyright infringement or the crime of selling the infringing copy, the unit shall be fined. And the persons who are directly in charge and the other persons who are directly responsible for the crime shall be punished in accordance with the above provisions.

[3]   Administrative Procedure

Administrative litigation of IP has significant judicial function. First of all, it can give full play to the judicial review function of the court to safeguard the legitimate rights and interests of private party in administration. On the other hand, it can support the administrative department to carry out administration according to law to improve administrative protection of IP rights.

Administrative litigation may be classified from different perspectives. Generally, administrative copyright cases can be classified as: administrative cases of act, administrative cases of non-act and administrative cases of compensation. From the perspective of the nature of the specific administrative act being sued, administrative IP cases can be classified as: administrative cases of grant and confirmation of IP rights, administrative cases of ruling, and administrative cases of penalty. It must be emphasized that in the administrative cases of grant and confirmation of IP rights are only applicable to issues of patent and trademark, but not copyright in China. Since copyright is automatically granted to the copyright owners in China in the light of the *Copyright Law* and the *Berne Convention*, there is no administrative case of grant and confirmation of copyright in China. Despite that there is a copyright registration system in China in accordance with the *Trial Measures for Voluntary Registration of Works*, the copyright registration is totally voluntary and does not affect the ownership of copyright. The copyright registration certificate may be used as a preliminary proof of resolving copyright disputes, so that the copyright owner may protect their copyright more efficiently.

[a] Filing an Action

According to the *Administrative Procedure Law* and the *Interpretation of the Supreme People's Court on the Application of Administrative Procedure Law*, the concerned parties shall meet certain conditions to bring an administrative copyright lawsuit: The plaintiff must be qualified; there must a specific defendant; there must be specific claims and corresponding factual basis; the alleged specific administrative acts must fall within the scope of cases acceptable to the courts; the court must have jurisdiction and the case must be in line with the limitation of actions.

[b] Jurisdiction

Regarding the jurisdiction by levels of courts: A basic-level court shall have jurisdiction as a Court of First Instance over ordinary administrative cases; however, when necessary, a court at a higher level may try administrative cases over which a court at lower level have jurisdiction as a Court of First Instance; A court at higher level which has the jurisdiction may transfer the case to a court at lower level.

Regarding the territorial jurisdiction: An administrative case shall be subject to the jurisdiction of the court in the place where the administrative department that initially undertook the specific administrative act. An administrative case which has been reconsidered may also be subject to the jurisdiction of the court in the place where the reconsideration department is located.

[c] Trial

Administrative litigation is also subject to the second-instance system, thus administrative trial procedures are including first-instance procedures, second-instance procedures, and re-trial procedures. In principle, a first-instance court shall hear cases openly. However, if a case involves any state secret, personal privacy or other conditions in law, it shall not be heard in open court. The burden of proof is borne by the defendant. The alleged copyright administrative department shall provide evidence and regulatory documents on which the act has been based. During the legal proceedings, the defendant and its agent *ad item* are not allowed to collect evidence from the plaintiff, a third party or witnesses on its own initiative.

Regarding the scope of examination of administrative copyright cases: Article 5 of the *Administrative Procedure Law* stipulates that the hearing court shall examine the legality of the specific administrative act in the administrative case. Accordingly, the court can only examine the specific administrative act of the copyright administrative department, but not the abstract administrative act. Moreover, when hearing an administrative case, a court shall check the legality of the relevant administrative act but not the rationality of the act. This indicates the court's respects for the administrative judgment and administrative discretion made by the administrative department by its expertise.

Article 97 of the *Interpretation of the Supreme People's Court on the Application of the Administrative Procedure Law* stipulates that the court may refer to not only the *Administrative Procedure Law* and the *Interpretation of the Supreme People's Court on the Application of the Administrative Procedure Law*, but also the relevant provisions of civil procedure.

[d]   Method of Judgment

Where the evidence for taking a specific administrative act is conclusive, the application of laws and regulations is correct, and the legal procedure is complied with, the court shall reject the claims of the plaintiff. Where a specific administrative act has been taken under any of inadequacy of essential evidence, erroneous application of the law or regulations, violation of legal procedure, exceeding authority, abuse of powers or obvious unfairness, the court shall make a ruling to cancel or cancel partially the administrative act, or may rule the defendant to make a new administrative act. Where the court finds that the defendant has failed to perform its statutory duty, a fixed time shall be set by judgment for its performance of the duty. Where the administrative penalty is obviously unfair, the court may decide to change.

§1.05   CHALLENGE FOR THE COPYRIGHT SYSTEM IN FACING NEW TECHNOLOGIES

As a tradition, the judicial protection of copyright tend to protect authors' creative enthusiasm and encourage authors to create more and better works in the fields of literature, art and science, and to maintain the balance of interests between the copyright owners and the public. However, in modern society, copyright is closely connected with technological innovation and industrial development. On the one hand, the new Internet-related copyright disputes emerge with the rapid development of information technology. Whenever there is new information technology, a relevant new copyright dispute will arise simultaneously. On the other hand, the commercialization of Internet-related copyright has continuously created new business models, which leads the Internet-related cultural industry to become a new growth point in the national economy. With the ambiguity caused by the lag of copyright legislation, the copyright litigations play a significant role of "daring to try and foretasting" and "legislation from judicial feedback." Meanwhile, interplay of Copyright with Other IP in the process of commercialization of works makes the issue of judicial copyright protection even more complicated. There is no doubt that the judicial protection of copyright is no longer for the protection of the creation, but to adjust the sophisticated balance of interests among the copyright owners, Internet service providers and the public, and to coordinate copyright with other IP rights. Indeed, it is a new challenge for the copyright system.

[A] Impact of "Tri-Network Convergence" on the Conventional Structure of Interests

On June 25, 2014, the U.S. Supreme Court ruled in a 6–3 decision that the service provided by Aereo, Inc., allowing subscribers to view live and time-shifted streams of over-the-air television on Internet-connected devices, violated copyright laws, and infringed the copyright of the American Broadcasting Company, the Columbia Broadcasting System, the National Broadcasting Company and the Fox Broadcasting Company etc. In fact, the dispute is a war between conventional radio and television companies and the new network television service providers.

In China, the similar issue also arises, particularly in the process of promoting the national policy of "Tri-Network Convergence" (the convergence of telecommunication networks, radio and television networks and the Internet). With the advancement of the "Tri-Network Convergence," there are new ways of communicate in various types of works such as text, music and video. The business fields and customer ranges of the three major operating entities of the telecommunication network, radio and television network, and the Internet tend to be the same. Because of the overlapping of the market, the subject of operation which originally belongs to the different interests' pattern has conflict of rights and interest to aggravate, which brings about new problems in the Internet-related field. For example, IPTV is able to play TV program in an interactive way by its function "review service," which makes IPTV different from conventional TV. At first, IPTV records and stores the live TV programs. When users choose the "review service," they may access to the TV programs stored in the IPTV. Does this service constitute an infringement of the right of communication of information on networks? Given that the copyright laws do not explicitly provide an answer, the question should be answered by the courts in their judgments.

In regard to such challenge by the "Tri-Network Convergence," the Chinese courts have made some progress in defining the rights boundary and settling disputes. For example, an effective judgment holds that if the broadcasting organization right is extended to the Internet, the scope of the right of communication of information on networks will be decreased, which will cause the unbalanced interests between the copyright owners and the related-right owners. Therefore, the scope of the right of broadcast shall not be extended to the Internet. Regarding the act of communication of IPTV, the broadcasting organization may claim on the basis of the right to fix its TV program on a video recording, depending on whether there is prior recording by the IPTV operator. Besides, the broadcasting organization may also try to protect its right and interests by the *Anti-Unfair Competition Law*.

[B] Disputes Relating to Cloud Computing

As the commercialization of the notion of cloud computing, new network technologies such as cloud video and cloud storage are constantly emerging, which has resulted in new types of Internet-related copyright disputes. Regarding the conventional link service, the Chinese courts generally apply the approach of "server standard" or the approach of "user perception standard." According to the "server standard," whether the involved information has been uploaded or stored in the server is the key factor to determine the infringement. The one who actually uploads or stores the information is the one who exercises the right of communication of information on networks. According to the "user perception standard," even the network service provider does not upload or store the information in the server, as long as its external appearance of the technical service makes ordinary network users feel that the information is provided by the network service provider, it can also be determined as the one who exercises the right of communication of information on networks.

In the cloud video service, video works are stored on the cloud server and controlled by the operator of the cloud server, but users perceive that the cloud video website and the cooperative website are providing content services simultaneously. Therefore, the conventional approaches of "server standard" and "user perception standard" seem no longer applicable in the copyright cases of cloud video. In the case that the cloud video website is authorized to communicate the work on its website and it is obligated to provide cloud service to a third party, does it constitute an infringement if the cooperative website uses the cloud service? In 2012, the *Jidong Network* case held that: The act of the Cloud video website to provide cloud video services to cooperative website shall be identified as the act of uploading the work to its own server, but not an act of re-authorizing to the cooperative website. Meanwhile, since the act of the cooperative website to play the uploaded work via the cloud technology shall be identified as an exploitation of the cloud service, it does not constitute any copyright infringement. Since this case correctly presented the legislative spirit of the copyright law concerning the technical characteristics and commercial operation of cloud computing, it was nominated as one of the "Top Fifty Typical IP Cases of 2012" by the Supreme People's Court. Such correct and timely judgment has positive significance in encouraging the development of cloud computing and promoting the prosperity of Internet-related culture and provides effective judicial protection for Internet-related technological innovation as well.

[C] Internet TV and the Principle of "Technological Neutrality"

The Internet TV, also known as "TV box," is a host computer for connecting the TV terminal and the Internet, so that the TV can play the videos from the Internet. Generally, a "TV box" only provides web searching and link services, but does not download or store any cinematographic work in itself. Since the emergence of such "TV box," there have been several disputes of the infringement of the right of communication of information on networks. In such cases, the plaintiffs often claim that the defendant shall cease the infringement by stopping manufacturing and selling "TV box" which is linking to the involved cinematographic works. On the other hand, the defendants usually argue that they cannot examine the ownership of works on the IPTV platform as that they are just hardware manufacturers, which should not bear the liability.

The emergence of IPTV brings challenges to the principle of "technological neutrality." However, even if the new Internet technology is neutral, does it necessarily mean that the relevant business model is neutral as well? The technology of the "TV box" should be treated separately from the business model of "TV box." If the main purpose of the business model is to obtain commercial benefits from the copyright infringement, then the principle of "technological neutrality" shall be no longer applicable.

As a good reference to China, the *Grokster* case of U.S. rules that: Anyone who distributes a device with the object of promoting its use to infringe copyright, as shown by clear expression or other affirmative steps taken to foster infringement, is liable for the resulting acts of infringement by third parties, regardless of whether the device has legitimate use.

In China, the courts have actively formed an approach to resolve the disputes on the basis of different situations: Where there is a cooperation agreement between the "TV box" provider and the Internet TV platform provider, it is determined that the Internet TV platform provider is liable for infringement, while the "TV box" provider is not liable. Where the "TV box" provider searches and links to works without authorization, the determination of the liability shall be made based on whether the "TV box" has "substantial noninfringement purposes." If the "TV box" is neutral, the developer, manufacturer and the seller can apply a technical measure to avoid copyright infringement, then according to the principle of "technological neutrality," the defendant will no longer be liable to stop manufacturing and selling the product. Such a conclusion is to protect the innovative development of Internet technology.

[D] Infringement by the Network Trading Platform

In conventional trading markets, market operators lease stalls or counters to actual operators to engage in wholesale and retail operations within the business scope approved by the administrative departments. Thus, they shall assume corresponding market management responsibilities. However, on the Internet, the service providers of the network trading platform, as known as e-commerce platform service providers, are confronted with numerous online sellers and a huge number of goods of various types. The online sellers on the e-commerce platform can be classified as enterprise sellers, individual sellers, and the operator of the e-commerce platform itself as a seller. For enterprise sellers, the e-commerce platform service providers should examine their business licenses and other relevant licenses. By contrast, for individual sellers, the e-commerce platform service providers usually examine their personal ID information.

The judicial rules of the determination of copyright infringement of e-commerce platform service providers are of great importance not only for the protection of copyright, but also for the development of e-commerce. Taking into consideration the balance of interests of both copyright owners and the development of e-commerce, the Chinese courts have developed an approach to determine the infringement by the e-commerce platform service providers: First, in principle, e-commerce platform service providers do not have an obligation to examine the commodities in advance.

Since there may be hundreds of thousands of commodities on the platform, it will be impractical to examine the commodities one by one and identify the copyright status. Second, in principle, e-commerce platform service providers shall not bear infringement liability for compensation of economic losses. In judicial practice, when the seller has been determined copyright infringement, the courts usually rule that the actual seller shall be liable for the compensation for the economic losses, while the e-commerce platform service provider shall just be liable for ceasing the infringement. Third, when the e-commerce platform service provider notices that its seller may sell infringing goods, it shall fulfill the duty of care and actively stop the sale. Otherwise, the e-commerce platform service provider shall still bear the liability.

With the rapid development of e-commerce, new e-commerce models are emerging. For example, online group buying is a new form of e-commerce which provides goods and services at significantly reduced prices on the condition that a minimum number of buyers would make the purchase. In online group-buying transactions, the online group-buying service providers and the sellers are more collaborative. Whether to buy largely depends on the reputation of the online group-buying service providers. Therefore, the higher degree of participation of online group-buying service providers, the more duty of examination the online group-buying service providers shall take.

[E]   Application of the Rule of "Notice-Takedown"

Due to the massive and rapid information transmission on the Internet, the rule of "Notice-Takedown" is provided by the *Tort Liability Law* and the *Regulations on the Protection of the Right of Communication of Information on Networks* in order to reasonably reduce the infringement liability of Internet service providers. Besides, the Supreme People's Court timely promulgated the *Provisions of the Application of Law in Hearing Civil Dispute Cases Involving Infringement of the Right of Communication of Information on Networks* to keep the balance of interests among copyright owners, network service providers and the public in regard to the new technologies. For example, Article 13 stipulates: Where a network service provider fails to take necessary measures to promptly delete, block, break links after receiving the notice of the copyright owners in writing, faxed, electronic mail or other forms, the courts shall deem that the network service provider has clearly known the act of infringement upon the right of communication of information on networks. The terms "notice in writing, faxed, electronic mail or other forms" and "deleting, blocking, breaking links" in this article clarify and refine the rule of "Notice-Takedown." Meanwhile, the Supreme People's Court has issued relevant judicial opinions by summing up the trial experience. In the *Annual Report on IP Cases of the Supreme People's Court (2012)*, the Supreme People's Court pointed out that when the copyright owner has repeatedly sent adequate notices and the network service provider has had certain understanding of the alleged infringement, the network service provider should not ignore the notices merely because the notices do not meet the corresponding conditions, but should actively contact and negotiate with the copyright owner to determine how to take reasonable measures. Those who are negligent of duties shall bear corresponding liability for the expansion of losses caused by the direct infringement. The rule of the "Notice-Takedown" has established guidance for the Chinese courts to apply.

[F] New Method for Compensation Calculation of Damages

Article 49 of the *Copyright Law* stipulates a three-step approach of calculating the amount of compensation: The first step is to calculate according to the actual losses of the copyright owner. The second step is to calculate according to the illegal gains of the infringer if the actual losses cannot be ascertained. The third step is to apply the statutory compensation where the copyright owner's actual losses or the infringer's illegal gains cannot be determined, and the court shall adjudicate a compensation of up to RMB 500,000. In practice, due to the intangible nature of copyright and the difficulty in obtaining evidence, actual losses and illegal gains are often difficult to be accurately calculated. However, in some cases, the actual losses and illegal gains are obviously over RMB 500,000 in fact. Thus, the compensation for infringement damages is expected to be calculated in an innovative way, in which the actual losses or illegal gains shall be determined over the statutory compensation. On the basis of evidence, the court may take into consideration the market price and license fee and the average price in the same industry etc.

In recent years, the Chinese courts of various levels have explored a new method for compensation calculation of damages in judicial practice for "large amount of compensation" exceeding RMB 500,000. For example, in the case that the defendant company uses pirate software for commercial purpose, the court determined the economic losses of the plaintiff on the basis of the number of illegal users in the defendant company and the market price of each legitimate copy of the involved software. In another case that the defendant continuously distributed the infringing copies, the court determined the compensation on the basis of average daily distribution of the infringing copies.

[G] Interplay of Copyright with Other IPs

The commercialization of copyright leads to the overlap of protection fields among the copyright law, patent law, trademark law and anti-unfair competition law. The Chinese IP protection system is formed by the collaboration of different IP laws.

[1] Interplay of Copyright with Patent Right: "Competition and Cooperation"

For the IP of computer software, there are three available protection modes: copyright protection, patent protection and trade-secret protection. Since the encryption measures of software may be deciphered, the trade-secret protection mode is not common. To protect software by copyright is a common practice all around the world, since copyright protection is automatic and lasts for a long period. However, copyright only protects the expression of source code, object code, etc., but cannot be extended to the ideas as the design, process and operation method, which seems insufficient. Thus, besides copyright, U.S. and some European countries started to protect software by patent. The patent protection mode can effectively protect core intellectual creation of software, such as inventive methods. However, given the short period of software life cycle, and long period of examination of patent application, it is difficult for patent protection to timely protect the market value of software. Thus, it can be concluded that both the copyright protection mode and the patent protection mode have their own advantages and disadvantages. Only when the two protection modes work together can the software be better protected. In China, both the *Copyright Law* and the *Patent Law* stipulate to protect computer software. In accordance with the *Copyright Law*, China has specially legislated the *Regulations on the Protection of Computer Software*. Article 8 of the *Regulations* stipulates that software copyright owners enjoy the rights of publication, authorship, revision, reproduction, distribution, rental, communication of information on networks and translation. The *2010 Guidelines for Patent Examination* provides: "The invention relating to computer programs refers to solutions for solving the problems of the invention which are wholly or partly based on the process of computer programs and control or process external or internal objects of a computer by the computer executing the programs according to the above mentioned process." According to the above provision, after the examination, patent right may be granted to the software owner.

With the rapid development of electronic devices, particularly mobile tablet devices, the graphical user interface (GUI) of electronic devices has become the focus of market competition. For example, the U.S. case *Apple Inc. v. Samsung Electronics Co., Ltd.* in 2012 was regarding the GUI of smartphones and tablet computers. Regarding the protection of GUI, Western countries including the U.S., Japan, European Union (EU) members, etc. have already amended the domestic patent laws. China has also made progress. In the *2013 Guidelines for Patent Examination*, which was amended on September 16, 2013, the protection of GUI is explicitly added into the Chinese patent system.

The above laws and regulations provide the court with the right basis for protecting computer software from both copyright and patent rights.

[2]   Interplay of Copyright with Trademark Right: "Conflict"

A trademark is a symbol of characters, graphics, letters, numbers, three-dimensional signs, color combinations, sounds, etc. as well as combination of the above elements, which identifies commodity or services of a particular source from those of others. Generally, the protection of trademark is focused on the distinctiveness, while the protection of copyright is focused on the originality.

However, once some designs of trademarks contain high originality, they may also be recognized as works of copyright. Thus, this situation may cause an overlap of copyright and trademark rights. For example, when the plaintiff enjoys both trademark right and copyright upon a pattern, if the defendant uses the pattern on his goods without permission, then he may infringe both the trademark right and the copyright of the plaintiff. The plaintiff may choose to sue on the basis of one of the rights according to the principle of "selection of IP rights." However, if there is a same pattern, but the owner of the relevant trademark right and the owner of the relevant copyright are not the same, then there will be conflicts between the copyright and trademark rights. Under the situation that a trademark is also a work, the copyright owner enjoys the copyright when the creation is completed, but the trademark right can only be granted by the trademark administrative department afterward. In another word, the pattern must be created before the trademark registration. Therefore, regarding the pattern, the copyright is the prior right of the trademark. The *Trademark Law* explicitly provides that a trademark to be registered shall not conflict with any prior legitimate rights obtained by others, or harm existing prior rights of others, and the prior rights owner may file an opposition to the trademark administrative department within three months from the date of publication. If the opposition is justified, no registration shall be approved. The above provision shows the principle of "protecting prior rights" in the conflict between trademark right and copyright, which means trademark right cannot be granted if there is a prior copyright. However, Article 45 of the *Trademark Law* stipulates that any owner of prior rights may, within five years from the date of registration, request that the "Trademark Review and Adjudication Board" make a ruling to invalidate the trademark's registration. Where the registration was obtained with malicious intent, the owner of a well-known trademark shall not be bound by the five-year limitation. This five-year limitation has positive significance in maintaining social and economic stability, protecting consumers' rights and interests and promoting the right owners to exercise their rights timely. It provides a legal basis for the courts to deal with the conflicts between trademark rights and copyright in different situations.

[3] Anti-Unfair Competition and Copyright Law: "Supplement"

The *Copyright law* is a special law to the *Anti-Unfair Competition Law*. When the *Copyright Law* has relevant provisions, they shall be applied first, which can reduce the instability caused by the application of the general provisions of the *Anti-Unfair Competition Law*. When the *Copyright Law* does not have relevant provisions, then the *Anti-Unfair Competition Law* should be applied to protect the order of the market economy. For example, in the case that the third-party software has changed the application function of the main software without authorization, if such an act infringes the copyright of the owner of the main software, then the copyright law should be applied to regulate it; If such an act does not infringe the copyright, then the *Anti-Unfair Competition Law* should be applied to protect the legitimate rights and interests of the owner of the main software. At present, the Internet-related competition is getting wild. Some network operators deliberately take advantage of other competitors, such as setting up search keywords to get "free-riding." Some network operators maliciously undermine the competitive advantages of others, such as mutual interference between similar network software and mutual resistance between network security software.

When dealing with such new Internet-related unfair-competition cases, the courts mainly apply Article 2 of the *Anti-Unfair Competition Law*, which is a provision of general principle of the *Law* that: "A business operator shall, in his market transactions, follow the principles of voluntariness, equality, fairness, honesty and credibility and observe the generally recognized business ethics. Unfair competition refers to a business operator's acts violating the provisions of this Law, infringing upon the lawful rights and interests of another business operator and disturbing the socio-economic order. A business operator refers to a legal person or any other economic organization or individual engaged in commodities marketing or profit-making services."

However, the provision of general principle is relatively abstract, which requires the courts to further develop a specific and concrete standard of adjudication in practice. Thus, in the judgment of the case *Qihu v. Tencent*,[12] the Supreme People's Court pointed out that: "The free competition and free innovation are based on the premise that the legitimate rights and interests of others shall not be prejudiced."

The development of the Internet needs an orderly market environment and well-defined competition rules. Whether it is a lawful free competition and innovation of the spirit of the Internet should be determined by whether it is favorable for establishing an equal and fair competition order and for the general interest of consumers and the public, but not by the technology itself. Otherwise, anyone can use technology as an excuse to interfere with other's technology. No one can apply the "jungle law" in the name of innovation. Innovation can stimulate competition, and competition can promote innovation in return. Although technology is neutral, it can still become a tool for unfair competition. Innovation should become an instrument of fair and free competition, but not an excuse to interfere with the legitimate business model of others. The above statement clarifies the boundaries of technological innovation, free competition and unfair competition, which is an important guidance for the application of the general principle of the *Anti-Unfair Competition Law*, particularly for Internet-related cases.

With the rapid development of the Internet, new problems are constantly emerging with new technologies. In order to cope with the impact of the Internet, currently China is greatly revising the *Copyright Law* that the draft of the revision has been published. In recent years, the Supreme People's Court has issued judicial interpretations including the *Provisions of the Supreme People's Court on Several Issues concerning the Application of Law in Hearing Civil Dispute Cases Involving Infringement of the Right of Communication of Information on Networks* etc., in response to the new issues in the trial of copyright, clarifying the standards for the application of law and unifying the standards of judgments. The Supreme People's Court has also carried out the research to clarify new issues and provide new approach to deal with. In doing

---

12. (2013) Min San Zhong Zi No. 5.

so, the Supreme People's Court has established specific judicial policies for IP. Besides, the Supreme People's Court has been publishing the annual *Top Ten Cases of Judicial Protection of IP Rights in the Chinese Courts*, *Top Ten Innovative Cases of Judicial Protection of IP Rights in the Chinese Courts* and *Top Fifty Typical Cases of IP Protection in the Chinese Courts.* Those case reports play the guiding role in all the Chinese courts. In facing the challenges, the Chinese courts will continue to actively promote the development of the copyright protection and make contribution to the national strategy of innovation.

LUO Dongchuan, DING Wenyan and TONG Haichao

CHAPTER 2
Determination of the Nature of a Work

Case 1.   The Nature of Work of Applied Art

Inter-IKEA Systems B.V. v. Taizhou Zhongtian Plastic Co., Ltd.
Case of Copyright Infringement Dispute
Case Index: *Inter-IKEA Systems B.V. v. Taizhou Zhongtian Plastic Co., Ltd.*; Shanghai No. 2 Intermediate People's Court, Hu Er Zhong Min Wu (Zhi) Chu Zi [2008] No. 187, August 22, 2009

Facts:

The Plaintiff, Inter-IKEA Systems Co., Ltd. (hereinafter, "IKEA") alleged that the Plaintiff, established in 1943, was world's largest furniture retailer and had over 190 stores in thirty-one countries and regions. The Mammut children's furniture was designed by designer Morten Kjelstrup and fashion designer Allan Östgaard under the supervision of and on behalf of the Plaintiff. In 1994, the Mammut children's chair was awarded "Furniture of the Year" in Sweden. The Mammut products had been reported in some books and commodity catalogs for several years. The Plaintiff noticed that the Defendant copied the designs of Mammut products in which the Plaintiff was the copyright owner, without the Plaintiff's authorization. Meanwhile, the Defendant produced and marketed the infringing children's stools and chairs with the models ZTY-522, ZTY-525, ZTY-525A and ZTY-525B, and exhibited the infringing commodities on its website. Such infringement still occurred until now. Since 2004, the Plaintiff had continuously demanded the Defendant to stop the infringement via lawyer's letters. However the Defendant ignored the demands completely and even applied for design patent for the infringing designs, while such patents were examined to be invalid by the authority. Hence, the Plaintiff requested the court to order that the Defendant: (1) shall cease the copyright infringement concerning the Mammut products immediately; (2) shall immediately recall all the infringing products in the market, destroy all the infringing products in stock and molds for the production thereof, and destroy all packages and advertisements concerning the infringing products; (3) shall immediately remove the images of infringing products exhibited at www.ztpc.cc; (4) shall compensate the Plaintiff RMB 500,000 for economic losses, including the reasonable expenses. (5) shall eliminate the negative impact by publishing a statement concerning the infringement on *Xinmin Evening News* and *Qianjiang Evening News*.

The Defendant, Taizhou Zhongtian Plastic Co., Ltd. (hereinafter, "Zhongtian") argued that: (1) the Plaintiff was not eligible to be a party to this case; (2) the Plaintiff did not provide evidence to prove it owned the copyright in Mammut products. Even if the Plaintiff had relevant rights, Mammut products were not qualified as works of applied art, but practical industrial goods since they did not have the characteristics such as innovative and artistic that a work of applied art should do; (3) before the design of the Plaintiff's products was completed, furniture which are generally identical with its products had already appeared in cartoons; (4) the products produced by the Defendant were independently designed by the Defendant's designer and thus did not infringe other's copyright.

After the trial, the court made the following findings that: by comparison, among the fifteen models of products exhibited at www.ztpc.cc that were alleged to be infringing products, children's stools (ZTY-525S, ZTY-525M and ZTY-525L) were basically identical with Mammut children's stools of the Plaintiff in the general shape. The children's stools (ZTY-534, ZTY-533, ZTY-537, ZTY-536, ZTY-541, ZTY-322, ZTY-325, ZTY-326 and ZTY-542) were slightly different in the shape of stool surface from Mammut children's stools but were basically identical with Mammut children's stools in the shape of legs, and therefore were similar in the general structure to the Plaintiff's Mammut children's chairs. By comparison, among children's chairs and stools of the Defendant which were bought by the Plaintiff under notarization were basically identical with Mammut children's chairs and stools in the general shape.

Ruling and Reasoning:

Shanghai No. 2 Intermediate People's Court held that: The key issue was whether the Mammut children's stools and chairs were recognized as works of applied art under the *Copyright Law of China*. A work of applied art referred to a result of intellectual creation with utility, artistry and other elements of a work. This meant a work of applied art must be of utility, artistry, originality and replicability. According to the Chinese copyright laws, works of applied art are protected as works of fine art. A work of fine art refers to a two- or three-dimensional shape of work consisting of lines, colors or other medium with aesthetic value, including painting, calligraphy and sculpture. Therefore, the artistic level of a work of applied art must meet the minimum standard for that of a work of fine art. The concerned Mammut children's chair (*see* Figure 1) consisted of three parts, including chair back, cushion and legs. The chair back was made up of three rectangular battens and a piece of trapezoidal solid wood which took up approximately half of the space of the whole chair back. The chair cushion had the basic structure of ordinary chair. The chair legs were four upright cones that were narrow on the top and broad at the bottom. The concerned Mammut children's stools consisted of two parts, including chair cushion and legs. The stool surface was a round solid surface with equal top and bottom sides that are similar to other ordinary stools. The stool legs were four spindle rods. This court held: The key design of the concerned Mammut children's chair and stool was relatively simple and did not reach meet the artistic level for a work of fine art. As a result, they were not qualified as works of applied art within the category of works of fine art, thus not protected under the Chinese copyright laws. Therefore, the alleged act of the Defendant did not constitute copyright infringement of the Plaintiff's. The court ruled that: the claims of the Plaintiff, IKEA were dismissed.

Figure 1   Mammut Children's Chair

Commentary:

1. Protection of works of applied art is different from that of ordinary works

In regard to the copyright protection of applied art and works of applied art, there have been numerous judicial cases in China, while academics also have been continuously discussing this topic. However, there is still no consensus yet. This article is focusing on the copyright protection of works of applied art. As a work of applied art, it must be qualified as a work, which meets the statutory requirements of originality and been able to be reproduced. In addition, it must be literary, artistic or scientific intellectual creation. However, due to their characteristic of utility, works of applied art cannot be protected as ordinary works. According to the current *Copyright Law of China*, there is no explicit provision concerning work of applied art as a copyrightable subject matter. Correspondingly, the definition and explanation of the work of fine art provided by the *Regulation for the Implementation of the Copyright Law of China* can hardly be extended to cover the work of applied art. The *Provisions on the Implementation of the International Copyright Treaties* promulgated by the State Council in 1992 mentions the copyright protection on works of applied art. Article 1 clarifies that such protection only covers foreign works. Article 6 further stipulates that the term of protection for foreign work of applied art is twenty-five years after the making; such provision is not applicable on works of fine arts (including the designs of cartoon figures) that are made for industrial products.

　　In summary of the current Chinese laws and regulations, first of all, works of applied art can be copyrightable subject matter, but only foreign works. Second, the term of protection for work of applied art is only twenty-five years, while the term of protection for ordinary works is fifty years. However, if a work of fine art is used on industrial product, this will not decrease its copyright protection from fifty to twenty-five years. Such phenomenon can be explained that: in order to meet the minimum standard of international treaties, special provisions are legislated in domestic law to provide special protection on foreign works. Such protection is ultra-national treatment. Even if they meet the requirements of works, domestic works of applied art still cannot enjoy the same protection as their foreign counterparts can. Some scholars argued that based on the above *Provisions* and the revision of *Copyright Law of China* in 2001, it may be concluded that the Chinese copyright laws also protect works of applied art.[1] This argument is questionable. If copyright law intends to vest protection on certain category of works, it should express such intention directly. Due to the utility of works of applied art, it is an exception to vest copyright protection on them, while not vesting protection is a more ordinary approach. Even according to the *Bern Convention*, the term of protection for works of applied art is only twenty-five years, which is different from ordinary works. The key reason for such difference is that a work of applied art is a mixture of artistry and utility, while copyright generally only protects artistic works. During the making of works of applied art, the creators consider not only the artistic elements but also the functional elements for daily use, which may be common in all useful items of the same kind. For such a mixture of artistry and utility, what copyright intends to protect is the artistic part, or the result of intellectual endeavor concerning the artistic molding, appearance design, coloristic decoration, etc. What copyright intends not to protect is the functional aspect. Of course, the decision whether a work is classified as a work of applied art or a work of fine art should be made case by case. However if a work is classified as work of applied art, the Chinese copyright laws must be applied strictly that copyright protection is exclusively vested in foreign works of applied art. For Chinese works of applied art, the protection will be available only if the Chinese copyright laws are revised to clarify the protection explicitly.

2. Separability of utility and artistry

Since the protection for utility is not the task of copyright law, even if works of applied art are copyrightable, the protection exclusively covers the artistic part, but not the functional part. When a work of applied art is protected by copyright, the functional part must be eliminated, otherwise the function of copyright will be misplaced. In another word, due to its utility, even a foreign work meet the standards for an ordinary work, the term of protection will be decreased to twenty-five years, and its functional part will be excluded for copyright protection at the same time. Nowadays both in academic and judicial practice, it has become a consensus that copyright law only protects the artistic part of a work of applied art, but not the functional part. In addition, the artistic part needs to meet the standard of originality of a copyrightable work to get the protection. From the perspective of comparative law, U.S. copyright law only protects the useful items in which the artistic characteristics may be separated

---

1. *See* Guan Yuying, The Approach of Legal Protection on Works of Applied Art, *Intellectual Property* (《知识产权》), 7 (2012), p. 57.

Chapter 2: Determination of the Nature of a Work

from the functional elements. Under the Japanese law, the Japanese courts held that the copyright protection on works of applied art may jeopardize the legal basis of industrial design system; therefore generally copyright protection must not extended to the designs of useful items, unless the law expresses explicitly that the massive-produced useful products with certain aesthetic function and technological characteristic may be protected as works of fine art.[2] According to this book's opinion, first of all, a work of applied art needs to meet all the requirements for ordinary works, including originality and being able to be reproduced. Then it may be recognized as a copyrightable work of applied art and gets a copyright protection, which is weaker than that of ordinary works. In case the item does not meet the requirement for copyrightable works, but still has certain level of aesthetic value as well as novelty, it may apply for an industrial design patent, for which the term of protection is even shorter.

3. Level of originality

Originality is the fundamental characteristic of works. Originality requires the author to create the work by his/her own, and such work must represent the author's distinctive personality and idea. The standard of originality for works of fine art requires the distinctive creativity and concept in aesthetic field. For the subject matter which contains both aesthetic and functional value, whether it can be protected as a work of fine art is depending on the distinctive characteristic and creativity generated by the intellectual endeavor of the author inside the aesthetic field. The intellectual endeavor outside the aesthetic field is not relevant to the originality. Therefore, the key factor of the final judgment is whether a work of allied art can be qualified as an original work of fine art after its functional part is eliminated. The artistic standard for works of applied art must not be lower than that for works of fine art. However, because the utility is usually thoroughly mixed with artistry, it is of great difficulty to separate the utility from artistry due to the limit of subjective vision. According to the current judicial practice, for those works of applied art which their artistic part can be physically separated from the functional part, the artistic standard for the artistic part is the same as that for works of fine art. This means that a minimum degree of aesthetic value will meet the artistic standard to be qualified as an original work. For those works of applied art which their artistic part can hardly be physically separated, but can be conceptually separated from the functional part, because the artistic part, the abstract medium of shape and color, and the functional part are mixed together, thus the artistic standard for the artistic part can be slightly higher than that for works of fine art. This means that the subject matter must be at an adequate level of originality and distinctive characteristic to satisfy the artistic standard to be qualified as an original work.[3] In this case, the artistic part and functional part of the Mammut children's chairs and stools can hardly be physically separated, but can be conceptually separated from each other, while the creativity of the products is presented by their shape, therefore the artistic

---

2. *See* Zhou Yunchuan, Copyright Protection on Works of Applied Art, *Chinese Patent and Trademark*) (《中国专利与商标》), 4 (2013), p. 67.
3. Hu Mi, The Artistry of Works of Applied Art Should Meet a Sufficient Standard, *People's Court Daily* (《人民法院报》) (2010), p. 6.

standard should be higher. Artistry itself is an abstract and subjective concept, while the appearance of the concerned chairs and stools in this case did not present significant difference and distinctive characteristic when being compared with other chairs and stools. As a result, the court ruled that because the concerned chairs and stools did not meet the minimum standard for works, they were not within the scope of copyrightable works of applied art. Despite that the products of the Defendant and Plaintiff are similar, the Defendant did not infringe any copyright.

It should be mentioned that the concepts of applied art and works of applied art appears to be similar to each other, but in fact they are basically different. Works of applied art is a part of applied art. Since they meet the standard for works of fine art, works of applied art are vested an automatic twenty-five-year copyright protection. The applied art that does not meet the standard for works of fine art may only seek for a ten-year patent protection. In this case, the concerned products of the Plaintiff did not meet the standard for works, thus the court ruled that there was no copyright infringement. However the Plaintiff may still apply for industrial design patent. Otherwise, any copycat will not infringe any intellectual property right. Imitation is also a fundamental approach for the progress of literature, arts, natural science, social science and engineering. This means that the successors are eligible to make use of the same ideas, process method of predecessors to design and produce the similar products.

—**Comments by DING Wenlian and XU Zhuobin**

Chapter 2: Determination of the Nature of a Work

Case 2.   Originality in Architectural Works and the Relevant Remedy of "Stop Infringement"

Porsche AG v. Beijing Techart Automobile Sales Service Co., Ltd.
Case of Copyright Infringement Dispute
Case index: *Porsche AG v. Beijing Techart Automobile Sales Service Co., Ltd.*; Beijing No. 2 Intermediate People's Court, Er Zhong Min Chu Zi [2007] No. 01764, December 19, 2007; Beijing High People's Court, Gao Min Zhong Zi [2008] No. 325, December 19, 2008.

Facts:

On July 22, 1999, Dr. Ing. h.c.F. Porsche Aktiengesellschaft (hereinafter, "Porsche AG") signed a contract with a Dutch design company named Cepezed. In accordance with the contract, the Porsche AG was entitled to revise the specific design of Cepezed, who was the winner of the Stuttgart-Zuffenhausen Design Competition held by Porsche AG in 1997. Later, the Porsche AG revised this design, and then such design became the basic model for all trading firms of the Porsche AG. By doing so, the Porsche AG's trading firms all over the world would appear with the unified architectural characteristics. Cepezed was entitled to the copyright of the designs, outlines and miniatures as such, which were created by it in the competition and in the process of later revised design. The Porsche AG and Cepezed shared the copyright of the later revised design and the works of architecture. Cepezed freely transferred all rights to use, namely all economic rights and interests, from the copyright in the works created in the competition and later revised design to the Porsche AG. The assignment should be valid all over the world. The rights were exclusive. Without written permission by the Porsche AG in advance, Cepezed was no longer entitled to use.

On December 9, 10 and 17, 2003, the *China Automotive News*, the *Economic Information Daily*, the *Beijing Youth Daily* and the *China Business Times* successively reported the completion of the Beijing Porsche Center Building. According to the reports, the Beijing Porsche Center Building was invested by the Beijing Bardelli Automobile Import and Export Group Co., LTD and would start business in the Beijing Economic and Technological Development Area. The Center was the first Porsche 3S shop in mainland China, providing services of car retail, customer service and original parts supply

The Porsche AG acquired the copyright registration certificate (No. 2006-L-06050) on November 20, 2006, which specified that the Porsche AG as transferee was entitled to have the copyright in the Porsche Center Building which was a work created and first published in Beijing in October 2003 by Cepezed. During the trial of the case, the Porsche AG acknowledged that the Porsche Center Building was the Beijing Porsche Center located in the Beijing Economic and Technological Development Area. According to the photograph in the copyright certificate, the characteristics of the external appearance of the building were:

(1) The facade of the building presented a circular arc, which was divided into upper and lower parts. The upper half was awash with rectangular building materials, while the lower half was the exterior wall of glass.
(2) The entrance and its upper parts of the building located in the center of the facade of the building were made of glass. The top of the entrance parts indented into the interior of the building and extended to the top. The entrance and its upper parts of the building divided the facade of the building into left and right wings. The billboard of "PORSCHE" was on the left top, while the billboard of "Bardelli (in Chinese language)" was on the right top.
(3) The rear and right side of the building was a rectangular work area whose external wall was comprised of lateral stripped dark color.
(4) The color of the exhibition hall of the building was in silver grey and the work area was in dark grey.

The characteristics of the internal appearance of the building were:

(1) The arc-shaped glass wall in the lower part of the exhibition hall and the part of glass ceiling presented a T-shape appearance at the entrance of the exhibition hall. This provided a road sign from the entrance to the main retail area.
(2) The top parts of the internal wall of the exhibition hall were made of aluminum and other metals. They were organized in rectangular-shaped and integrally within grey hue. The metal cylinder of grey hue in the exhibition hall was bright pillar, which was standing out clearly against the internal wall and arc-shaped glass.
(3) The floor in the retail area was in dark grey, so that the cars could be more obvious.
(4) The main reception counter in the center of the exhibition hall was in white curved. The center of the hoarding behind the counter was white and the two symmetrical sides were black. The logo of "PORSCHE" and the "shield" trademark were on the white hoarding.
(5) Above the main reception counter was a wide metal-look outer trim on the floor of the second floor, with air conditioning vents below it.
(6) The second floor was located on the back side of the exhibition hall. The metal staircase was set up to provide a large space, so that the exhibition hall would be giant and transparent.

During the trial, Beijing Bardelli Automotive Import & Export Group Co., Ltd. issued a statement to the court stating that the construction of the Beijing Porsche Center Building strictly complied with the building and decoration standards set in the Porsche's internal construction manual. It confirmed that the copyright of the Beijing Porsche Center Building was owned by the Porsche AG.

On November 29, 2006, Chang'an Public Notary Office downloaded the relevant web page at the website "http://imp.porsche.com." The page showed all the Porsche Centers in China including Shanghai, Beijing, Chengdu, Guangzhou, Hangzhou,

Chapter 2: Determination of the Nature of a Work

Qingdao, Shenyang, Wuhan, Dalian, Xiamen, Hong Kong, Macau, Chongqing and Wenzhou. The appearances of the Porsche Center Buildings in Chengdu, Shenyang, Xiamen, Shanghai and Beijing were similar to each other. In addition, the Porsche AG also submitted the notarized pictures of the Porsche Centers in Australia, Germany, France and UK, showing that the characteristics and styles were also similar. Beijing Techart Automobile Sales & Service Co., Ltd. (hereinafter, "Techart") did not approve the evidence by submitting pictures of Porsche Centers in Japan and Germany that were notarized by Beijing Notary Office. Based on those pictures, Techart argued that the features and styles of Porsche Centers around the world were not consistently similar.

Techart was established on June 21, 2005. Its business scope included retail of the imported Techart automobiles, automobile parts, service for Class 1 automobiles, information consultation (except intermediary), import and export of goods. The registered capital was RMB 10 million. On July 28, 2005, Techart signed a contract titled the "Agreement on Techart Automotive Design Co., Ltd.'s Importers and Foreign Bases" with the Techart Co. of Germany. The contract stipulated that Techart Co. of Germany authorized Techart to sell, modify and market its products in mainland China, Hong Kong and Macau. Techart had the exclusive dealership and marketing rights and was authorized to use Techart trademarks and brands. On November 21, 2005, the National Automobile Industry Administration issued the list of automobile dealers, which indicated that Techart was the general dealer of Techart automobiles, and its business scope included retail of the imported Techart automobiles. Media including Sohu.com, PacificCar.com, AutoMarket.com and magazines including *Casual Fashion* and *Fashion Car* reported the stories that Techart did the business of modifying the Porsche automobiles.

On June 15, 2005, Techart signed a contract titled the "Agreement on the Design of the Beijing Techart Center" with Zhongfangjianke Company. According to the contract, Techart would provide the required design information, and Zhongfangjianke would complete the design of the Beijing Techart Center Building. The consulting fee was RMB 70,000. On October 7, 2005, Techart signed a contract titled the "Contract for Construction of Beijing" with Mingdianshijia Company. The contract stipulated that Mingdianshijia was contracted to do the interior decoration project of the exhibition hall of the Beijing Techart Center Building. The project price was RMB 900,000.

On February 14, 2006, Mingdianshijia displayed the pictures titled "Techart Porsche Showroom" in the category of "Latest Project Cases" on its website http://www.mdsj.com.cn, in which the "PORSCHE" and "Shield" logos were visible behind the reception desk and in the exhibition hall. Such scenario was notarized by the Chang'an Notary Office.

On March 15, 2006, after being certified by the Chang'an Notary Office, the agent of the Beijing IntellecPro Intellectual Property Agency Co., Ltd. obtained a volume of *Special Design of Steel Structure Design Project* from CHEN Dongwei of the Architectural Design Office of China Zhongfang Group. In this book, the introduction of the "Porsche 4S Auto Shop" with the picture embodying "PORSCHE" and "Shield" logos could be found, and the owner's name of the "Porsche 4S Auto Shop" was Techart.

Porsche AG argued that Techart's unauthorized copying of the architectural works constituted the infringement of copyright, thus filed the lawsuit. The Plaintiff Porsche AG claimed that the Defendant should cease the infringement by modifying the architectural characteristics of the infringing building, compensate the economic loss and issue a public statement to eliminate the negative influence.

According to the court's investigation, the exterior appearance of the Techart Center Building located in the Beijing Golden Harbor Motor Park was basically similar to the feature Nos. 1, 2 and 3 of the Porsche Center Building. The differential features were: there was a 1-meter-high platform below the entire building; the building was surrounded by railings and the lower side below the arc of the building was not a glass wall so that the area was more spacious for car parking; the left side of the building was the work area, which was opposite to the layout of the Beijing Porsche Center Building; the upper part of the building has the billboard "Techart (in Chinese language)" and the upper right side "TECHART;" the exhibition hall was in grayish black, and the work area was in silver grey. The interior of the exhibition hall of the Techart Center Building was basically similar to the features Nos. 1–6 of the Porsche Center Building. The main difference from the interior of the Beijing Porsche Center exhibition hall was that: the different location of the staircase; the two rows of workshops on the second floor; perforated aluminum panels at the ceiling of the exhibition hall; aluminum-plastic panels at the interior walls; bright metal paint on the bright columns; and the lighting area in the center of the exhibition hall; the customer rest area mainly under the second floor; the pretest workshop separated from the exhibition hall; and the "TECHART" logo behind the main reception desk.

During the first instance trial, Techart modified the Techart Center Building. Materials in white were used both inside and outside the building. However the Porsche AG considered that the modified building still constituted an infringing copy of the work of architecture, and argued that the modifications of the appearance of buildings were common. Thus, the Plaintiff Porsche AG submitted the evidence concerning modifications of buildings that was downloaded from the relevant website.

Ruling and Reasoning:

In the first instance, Beijing No. 2 Intermediate People's Court held that: The key issues of this case were whether the Beijing Porsche Center Building could be recognized as a copyrighted work under the Chinese copyright law, whether the Plaintiff Porsche AG was the owner of the exclusive right to use the economic rights of the work relating to the Porsche Center, and whether the Techart Center Building was an infringing copy relating to the Plaintiff's rights and thus should bear legal responsibilities.

The first issue was whether the Beijing Porsche Center Building could be recognized as a copyrighted work under the Chinese copyright law, and whether the Plaintiff Porsche AG was the owner of the exclusive right to use the economic rights of the work relating to the Porsche Center.

According to the Chinese copyright law, a work of architecture refers to the work with aesthetic effect which is expressed in the form of buildings or structures. As the subject matter of copyright protection, the appearance of the building must be original design elements with aesthetic value and originality. Based on the facts of this case, the Beijing Porsche Center Building applied circular arc design. The upper half was aligned with rectangle construction materials and the lower half was glass wall. The building was divided into left and right wings by the entrance. The entrance and the upper part were made of glass. The rectangular work area made of transverse ribbon dark material was connected to the exhibition hall. The exhibition hall was silver-gray and the work area was dark gray. The above characteristics indicated that the Beijing Porsche Center Building had a unique appearance and architectural modeling, and it fitted the definition of work of architecture protected by the Chinese copyright law with aesthetic value and originality. The Defendant Techart asserted that the circular arc design and glass curtain wall were ordinary design patterns. Besides, the glass curtain wall and the glass in the upper part of the building were common functional designs of car showrooms. Since the material of buildings decided the appearance of the work area, the Plaintiff's building was lack of originality. In the lack of sufficient evidence by the Defendant, the court decided not to adopt the Defendant's argument.

Based on the existing evidences, it should be concluded that: According to the agreement with Cepezed, the Plaintiff Porsche AG obtained the exclusive right to use the economic rights of the unified architectural image design and the work of architecture. The Beijing Porsche Center Building involved in this case was built according to the relevant unified architectural style and characteristics of the Porsche AG. Moreover, the Plaintiff Porsche AG had obtained the copyright registration certificate for the work of architecture in China. Thus, the Plaintiff was entitled to claim for the exclusive right to use the economic rights of the work of architecture. The Defendant Techart claimed that since the agreement with Cepezed was made before the completion of the Beijing Porsche Center Building, the Plaintiff was not entitled to claim based on the later work of architecture. However, the later completed work was constructed according to the Porsche's unified architectural characteristics and design style of the agreement between the Plaintiff and Cepezed. Thus, the Plaintiff was entitled to the exclusive right to use the work of architecture embodying the above characteristics and design style. Accordingly, the arguments by the Defendant were groundless. The court would not support.

The second issue was whether the Techart Center Building was an infringing copy relating to the Plaintiff's rights and thus should bear legal responsibilities.

By comparison, the basic features of the Defendant's Techart Center Building and the Beijing Porsche Center Building of the Plaintiff Porsche AG were identical. Despite that there existed slight differences between two buildings in some parts, including the location of the platform, railing, exhibition hall and work area, the partial arc appearance and the integral color. The Techart Center Building was still similar to the Plaintiff's work of architecture. Thus, the Techart Center Building was an infringing copy of the original work of architecture. Despite that the Techart Center Building was designed and decorated by the third parties, including Zhongfang Jianke and Mingdian Shijia; however, as the owner and the actual user of the architecture, the Defendant Techart should bear the relevant legal responsibility. The Defendant claimed that the copyright of the infringing building belonged to Zhongfang Jianke and Mingdian Shijia, thus the Defendant shall not bear the responsibility. Since this argument was groundless, the court decided not to accept it. As the work of the architecture under the Chinese copyright law was the architecture appearance and modeling in the form of construction, interior decoration features of the construction were not covered. The Plaintiff claimed that the Defendant's Techart Center Building infringed the relevant copyright of the Plaintiff because the architectural interior characteristics were protected by the copyright law. Since this claim was groundless, the court should not uphold.

In summary, the construction and use of the Techart Center Building by the Defendant constituted the infringement of the Plaintiff's exclusive right relating to the Beijing Porsche Center. The claims by the Plaintiff Porsche AG that the Defendant should cease the infringement and make the compensation were reasonable. Thus, the court would support the above arguments. In regard to the actual approach of ceasing the infringement, the court made the approach based on both the Plaintiff's request of reconstructing the infringing building and the specific facts of the case. The Beijing Porsche Center Building was composed of the features including "the facade of the building presented a circular arc, which was divided into upper and lower parts. The upper half was awash with rectangular building materials, while the lower half was exterior wall of glass. The entrance and its upper parts of the building located in the center of the facade of the building were made of glass. The top of the entrance parts indented into the interior of the building and extended to the top. The entrance and its upper parts of the building divided the facade of the building into left and right wings." Hence, the Defendant should reconstruct the Techart Center Building to avoid the same or similar appearance of the characteristics mentioned above. In regard to the amount of compensation of the economic loss, the court would take into account the factors including the mode and scope of the infringement and the degree of subjective fault, as well as the cost of the design. Since the Plaintiff Porsche Ag was only entitled to the economic right relating to the Beijing Porsche Center, there was no evidence that the infringement caused any damage to the Plaintiff's reputation. Therefore, the Plaintiff's claim of eliminating negative effects was groundless and should not be upheld by the court.

In accordance with Article 10.1 (5), Article 10.2, Article 47 (1) and Article 48 of the *Copyright Law of China*, the ruling was made as follow:

(1) The Defendant, Beijing Techart Automobile Sales Service Co., Ltd., should reconstruct the infringing Techart Center Building within six months from the effective date of ruling. The reconstructed building should not contain the same or similar architectural characteristics of the Beijing Porsche Center Building. The court would review the effect of the reconstruction.
(2) The Defendant, Beijing Techart Automobile Sales Service Co., Ltd., should compensate the Plaintiff, Porsche AG, for the economic loss of RMB 150,000 and reasonable expenses of RMB 17,079 within ten days from the effective date of ruling.
(3) Other claims made by the Plaintiff, Porsche AG, were dismissed.

Chapter 2: Determination of the Nature of a Work

The Defendant Techart refused to accept the first-instance judgment and made an appeal to the Beijing Higher People's Court, requesting the court to abrogate the judgment and dismiss the claims by the Porsche AG. The court of second instance dismissed the appeal and sustained the judgment of the first instance.

Commentary:

The case, a new type of case concerning copyright protection of works of architecture, was awarded by the Supreme People's Court as one of the ten cases of Chinese judicial protection of intellectual property rights in 2008. How to determine the scope of protection of works of architecture and how to determine the originality of works of architecture are issues that need to be studied and explored in judicial practice. This case concludes that the architectural work has a unique appearance and shape, is full of beauty, has originality and belongs to the works of architecture by comprehensively analyzing the characteristics of the Plaintiff's buildings involved. The Court also supported the Plaintiff's request, ordering Defendant to renovate the building in question so that it is no longer the same as or similar to the main features of the Plaintiff's architectural appearance, in the judgment according to the specific conditions of the parties' construction, which creates effectively explorative meaning for the application of the civil liability of stopping the infringement in copyright infringement cases involving construction works.

1. Questions on the originality of works of architecture

The Berne Convention for the Protection of Literary and Artistic Works, to which China has acceded, expressly includes works of architecture in copyright protection. In the interpretation of the Convention, the World Intellectual Property Organization pointed out that works of architecture refer to works expressed in three-dimensional shapes, including The architectural model also including the building itself. After China's "Copyright Law" was revised in October 2001, Article 3, paragraph 4 of the article clearly states that works of architecture and fine artworks are the objects of copyright protection. At the same time, paragraph 7 of this article stipulates engineering design drawings and product design drawings. Graphic works and model works such as maps, sketches and other works are protected by copyright law. Article 9 Item 9 of the "Implementation Regulations of the Copyright Law" makes it clear that works of architecture refer to aesthetic works expressed in the form of buildings or structures. Based on this, it can be seen that buildings, architectural design drawings, architectural models, etc., can all be protected by China's copyright law.

However, not all buildings can be protected by the copyright law. Only the elements of "work" that conform to the provisions of the copyright law of our country can be protected by law as works of architecture. In accordance with the relevant provisions of China's copyright law, works refer to intellectual creations in the fields of literature and arts that have originality and can be reproduced in some tangible form. As a building, its reproducibility is self-evident, so how to judge its originality has become a controversial issue. In this case, the Court comprehensively analyzed the features of the construction of the "Porsche 3S Center" built by the Plaintiff claiming rights, and determined that the building has a unique appearance and shape, is full of beauty, has originality and belongs to the works of architecture protected by China's copyright law.

As a work with a large amount of practical functions and value, a building first has features that functionally satisfy the actual needs of people in production and life, and its design style is often limited by construction purposes, urban planning and surrounding construction environments. Its originality should be judged by the prevailing views of China's copyright law on the low originality requirements of other works. The design of related buildings should first of all be independently created, and its appearance and shape should have original design components and be of aesthetic design. If only the ubiquitous "matchbox" shaped buildings are not protected as works of architecture. In other words, if the building is completely composed of functional elements such as ordinary entrances, windows, roofs, etc., this standard feature should not be protected by the copyright law, but the special selection, arrangement and combination of such standard elements should be subject to Protection is reflected in relevant U.S. jurisprudence. In this case, the Court found that the involvement of the Porsche Center building in Beijing was rounded from the front, the upper half was made up of rectangular building materials and the lower part was the glass exterior wall; the entrance to the building and the top of the building divided the front of the building into two parts. The entrance part of the building and its top was composed of glass and other major features. It has a unique appearance and shape, full of beauty and originality, belonging to the works of architecture protected by China's copyright law. The circular arc design and glass curtain wall proposed by the Court to the Defendant TechArt belonged to the common design pattern. The glass curtain wall and the glass above the building belonged to the functional design commonly used in lighting in the auto showroom. Therefore, the construction works involved were not the idea of originality was not adopted.

As it is known, copyright only protects the expression of the work but does not protect the ideological content of the work. For the copyright protection of works of architecture, combined with the characteristics of works of architecture, should be limited to the appearance and shape of the building, does not include the interior features and structural characteristics of the building. The internal features of the building that the Plaintiff Porsche proposed to the building also belong to the object protected by the works of architecture, and the Court did not support it. Moreover, the Court also clearly identified the inevitable design of the 4S shop workspace and the horizontal banding due to the construction materials used. It is also not a category of works of architecture protected by copyright law.

In addition, during the trial of the first instance of this case, the Defendant had conducted the infringement of the building involved in the case.

The reconstruction changed the overall color of the building from dark gray to white, and it was therefore proposed that the reconstructed building was not the same as the Plaintiff's claimed work. The Court held that although the Defendant changed the color of the building, it did not change the main design features of the building and therefore it still belonged to the infringing building. Obviously, the color of a building is usually not a major part of the protection of a building work. The copyright law mainly protects its appearance, and specific features such as color can generally be excluded from the scope of protection of copyright law.

2. Determination of the specific methods of stopping infringement of works of architecture

According to the relevant provisions of China's copyright law, infringement of copyrights generally shall bear the civil legal responsibility of stopping infringements, making apologies, eliminating influences, and compensating for losses. For the specific remedies for infringement of the copyright of works of architecture, the law does not make special provisions. How to deal with infringement works and how to stop the infringement is another issue that is controversial in this case. One view is that works of architecture are special types of works, their practicability and functional characteristics are more than artistic features, and usually the cost of architectural design is only 3%-4% of the total cost of construction projects. Even if it constitutes infringement, the infringer shall not be ordered to reconstruct or demolish the building. Instead, the owner of the work of architecture should be compensated of the license for the use of the work and other economic compensation; another view is that the owner of the works has the right to demand infringement. People stop infringement, but taking into account factors such as the waste of the enormous social wealth caused by the demolition or destruction of buildings, consideration may be given to asking infringers to renovate infringing buildings.

Judging from the treatment of infringement buildings by Courts in various countries of the world, there are also the aforementioned two viewpoints. For example, the Swiss Copyright Law stipulates that the remedies used to remove or destroy illegal copies used in general copyright infringement disputes do not apply to existing ones. Buildings; section 83 of Article 83 of the Austrian Copyright Law also stipulates that copyright holders shall neither require the removal or reconstruction of illegal buildings nor require the transfer of illegal buildings to themselves. However, Courts in the U.S. often issue temporary injunctions against infringing construction works that are still in the process of construction. German Courts generally prevent the infringement from continuing, that is, prohibiting infringers from further construction. But in the case of *Tri-L Construction, Inc. v. Jackson*, the building involved was a house, and part of the buyers of the house had already sold their current homes. If construction of the buildings involved is prohibited, the life of this part of the subscribers will be greatly affected. Therefore, the U.S. court refused to issue a construction prohibition order against the Defendant.

In this case, the Court finally found that the protection of works of architecture should not be simply decided to stop the infringement, because it involves not only the waste of social wealth but also may be related to social public interests, municipal planning and many other issues. For this reason, the Court, after careful consideration, determined that the Defendant should be reconstructed for the infringing buildings, and that the reconstructed buildings should not have the same or similar composite architectural features as those involved in the Porsche Center building in Beijing. It can be seen that the protection of works of architecture should emphasize the protection of specific features of such works, especially in determining the specific ways of stopping the infringement. The handling of this case has positive exploration significance for how to apply the civil liability for stopping infringement in the infringement cases involving construction works and effectively stop the infringement.

How to balance the interests between the copyright holders of works of architecture and owners of infringement buildings in the disputes of infringement of copyright in works of architecture is a matter for further study. At present, the Courts of many countries have increased the application of legal liability for damages, such as requiring the infringer to pay the right holder all the infringement profits or require the infringer to pay for the architectural design fees. Increasing the application of legal liability for compensation for damages, although carrying nature of punishment to the infringer, does not satisfy the rights holder's request to stop the infringement. For example, the Plaintiff Porsche insists that he has the right to claim the Defendant as the right holder. Stop infringement. Therefore, on the premise that the Court comprehensively examined the possibility of reconstructing a building, the Court used the method of requiring the Defendant to renovate the infringing building to stop the involved infringement.

3. Determination of the amount of compensation for damages

How to determine the amount of damages and how to show the protection of intellectual property rights is a common problem encountered in all kinds of intellectual property rights infringement cases. In this case, Porsche Company only proposed the amount of damages for infringement according to the relevant provisions of Article 48 of the Chinese Copyright Law on the amount of compensation and has not failed to provide proof of this. When determining the amount of compensation, the Court must first find out the Plaintiff's loss due to infringement or the Defendant's gains from infringement. In the event that both cannot be ascertained, the Court will apply the principle of fixed compensation. Even if a fixed amount of compensation is applied, it does not mean that the parties do not need to provide evidence. On the contrary, the parties should provide proof of the relevant factors in determining the amount of compensation, such as the related architectural design costs incurred in the construction works involved in the case, the costs of transferring the works of architecture of the Dutch company Sempcider to Porsche, and the construction works involved in the construction of Porsche in the world. The percentage of intangible assets in the marketing of the center and the design expenses of the Defendant's construction costs. Considering these factors comprehensively will help the Court to make a judgment and determine a reasonable amount of compensation.

—Comments by ZHANG Xiaojin

Chapter 2: Determination of the Nature of a Work

Case 3. The Nature of Opening Ceremony of the Olympic Games and Its Copyright Protection

CCTV International Network Co., Ltd. v. Shanghai Quantudou Culture Communication Co., Ltd.
Cases of the right of communication of information on networks dispute
Case Index: *CCTV International Network Co., Ltd. v. Shanghai Quantudou Culture Communication Co., Ltd.*; Minhang District People's Court of Shanghai [2013] No. 241, Min Min San (Zhi) Chu Zi, October 22, 2013; Shanghai No. 1 Intermediate People's Court [2013] No. 227, Hu Yi Zhong Min Wu (Zhi) Zhong Zi, February 14, 2014

Facts:

On July 28, 2012 (July 27, 2012 in London), the opening ceremony of the 30th Olympic Games (hereinafter, "London Olympic Games") was held in London, UK. The opening ceremony mainly involved performance, entry of athletes from all countries, releasing of peace doves, speeches of the Olympic Committee officials, flag-raising ceremony, outfield torch relay, oaths of the representatives of athletes and referees, infield torch relay and handover, lighting of the main torch and fireworks.

On August 8, 2012, Christophe De Kepper, the general manager of the International Olympic Committee (hereinafter, "IOC") and Howard Stupp, the director of the Legal Department of IOC issued a "To Whom It May Concern" document, declaring that the IOC is the exclusive owner of the rights of broadcast and exhibition of the London Olympic Games.

According to this document, on March 25, 2009, IOC and China Central Television signed the "Agreement on the Rights of Broadcast and Exhibition of the London Olympic Games in China." According to the Agreement, IOC authorized China Central Television to exclusively exercise the Internet dissemination right and Internet interactive communication rights of the London Olympic Games, including but not limited to, the right of communication of information on networks and the right to interactively broadcast and exhibit on the Internet and mobile network. The region of authorization is China (including Macau, but not including Hong Kong and Taiwan) and the term of authorization is from March 25, 2009 to December 31, 2012. Besides, China Central Television is entitled to the right to take necessary actions against any unauthorized broadcast and exhibition of the London Olympic Games by third parties. Such necessary actions are including signing and issuing warning notices, complaining to the Chinese law enforcement authorities, and filing lawsuits to the Chinese courts.

The above document was notarized by a Swiss notary office and was also certified by the Chinese Embassy in Switzerland. The Changan Notary Office of Beijing issued a notarial deed for the document that is in conformity with the original copy, and the certificate number is "(2012) No. 19555 Jing Chang An Nei Jing."

On April 20, 2009, China Central Television issued a letter of authorization to CCTV International Network Co., Ltd. (hereinafter, "CCTV International"). According to this letter of authorization, China Central Television has authorized the Plaintiff CCTV International to exclusively exercise the rights of communication, broadcast, and making available to the public on networks (including but not limited to the Internet) of all the TV programs (including but not limited to the current and new variety shows, such as Spring Festival Gala, etc., talk shows, documentaries) that have been shot, produced or broadcasted by China Central Television, who is entitled to the copyright and the related rights. CCTV International is authorized as the exclusive agent for international trade of the above rights. In addition, as the exclusive licensee of the above rights, CCTV International is entitled to exercise and claim for the above rights in its own name; to license or prohibit others from exercising or partially exercising the above rights; to adopt various legal measures on its own name or entrust an attorney to sue against any infringement. All of the mentioned authorizations took effect on April 28, 2006 and will expire on the date when China Central Television makes a written statement to cancel the authorization.

The Defendant Shanghai Quantudou Culture Communication Co., Ltd. (hereinafter, "Tudou") is the operator of www.Tudou.com, which provides information storage service for the registered users. On the website of www.Tudou.com, Tudou sets up channels for original video, TV dramas, movies, sports, etc. The registered users can choose the relevant channels to upload videos. In order to minimize the legal risk of copyright infringement, Tudou has a full-time specific video-reviewing department to examine the videos uploaded by its users. All the contents of uploaded videos will be examined manually. Besides, there is an automatic filtering system to filter the keywords and sensitive words before the information is published. This three-step examination system runs continuously.

On August 1, 2012, the Plaintiff applied for evidence preservation at the Jingan Notary Office of Shanghai. With the notary, Yu Jing, the attorney of CCTV International, operated an Internet-connected computer to do as follows: (1) open the IE browser and enter www.Tudou.com; (2) view the related information of Tudou, such as "License for Audio-visual Programs Transmitted over Information Network," "License for Network Culture Operation," "License for Broadcasting and Television Program Production and Operation," etc., showing that the website is owned by the Defendant, which has relevant qualifications of the communication of information on networks; (3) input the keywords "Full Version of the Opening Ceremony of 2012 London Olympic Games" in the search bar of the homepage of www.Tudou.com, and click to play the video "Opening Ceremony of 2012 London Olympic Games" uploaded by the Tudou user "qixing0311" three days ago, and has been played for 97,494 times. (With the logo of CCTV and Olympic Rings, the program involved performance, entry of athletes, torch relays, and lighting ceremony, etc. The video commentary clearly broadcasted the Opening Ceremony of the London Olympic Games.) During the play, the screen was recorded by the screen recording software "Camtasia recorder" and some pages were taken screenshots. Cui Yaxia, a notary at the Jingan Notary Office of Shanghai, and Xu Jing, a member of staff, supervised the above-mentioned operation and issued the certificate "(2012) No. 2989 Hu Jing Zheng Jing Zi" on August 10, 2012. The notarization fee is RMB 1,200.

The Plaintiff claimed that: The Defendant shall compensate the economic losses of RMB 1,000,000. Right after being sued, the Defendant deleted the involved video on www.Tudou.com, and argued that the opening ceremony of the Olympic Games was not a copyrighted work.

Ruling and Reasoning:

In the first instance, Minhang District People's Court of Shanghai held that:

> According to the copyright, the term "works" means intellectual creations with originality in the literary, artistic or scientific domain, insofar as they can be reproduced in a tangible form. The "Opening Ceremony of 2012 London Olympic Games" involved in the case was composed of performance, torch relays, and lighting ceremony. Through the creative work of the key staff, the theme of the Olympic Games and the spirit of the Olympic Games were embodied. Since it has certain originality, it can be identified as a work in accordance with the copyright law. The "Opening Ceremony of 2012 London Olympic Games" is an essential part of the London Olympic Games. According to the organization rules of the Olympic Games and related agreements, IOC is the right owner of the London Olympic Games. According to Article 2 of the *Copyright Law*, any work of a foreigner or stateless person which is eligible to enjoy copyright under an agreement concluded between the country to which the foreigner belongs or in which he has habitual residence and China, or under an international treaty to which both countries are party, shall be protected by the *Copyright Law*. IOC is an international, nonprofit organization established in Switzerland. Since both China and Switzerland are members of the *Berne Convention for the Protection of Literary and Artistic Works*, IOC enjoys the copyright of the "Opening Ceremony of 2012 London Olympic Games" in China. According to the *Copyright Law*, IOC is entitled to the right of communication of information on networks of the "Opening Ceremony of 2012 London Olympic Games." According to the "To Whom It May Concern" document by IOC, IOC authorized China Central Television to exclusively enjoy the Internet dissemination right and Internet interactive communication rights of the "Opening Ceremony of 2012 London Olympic Games." The mentioned "Internet dissemination right and Internet interactive communication rights" shall be determined as the right of communication of information on networks under the Chinese copyright law. Meanwhile, according to the letter of authorization issued by China Central Television, China Central Television has exclusively authorized CCTV International the rights of communication, broadcast, and making available to the public on networks (including but not limited to the Internet) of all the TV programs. Therefore, it can be concluded that the Plaintiff CCTV International is entitled to the right of communication of information on networks of the involved work "Opening Ceremony of 2012 London Olympic Games." Within the term and region of the authorization, in the absence of fair use, any unauthorized act of communication of information on networks of the involved work will constitute the infringement of the right of communication of information on networks of the Plaintiff.

When providing Internet services, if the Internet service provider (hereinafter, "ISP") aids or abets network users to infringe the right of communication of information on networks, it shall bear the corresponding liabilities. The Olympic Games has great popularity and influence throughout the world. Its opening ceremony has always been an essential part of the Olympic Games and attaches much attention. If TV stations, ISPs and other agencies want to communicate the opening ceremony, they need to sign agreements or obtain authorizations with IOC. In this case, right after the opening ceremony of the London Olympic Games, the involved work was available on www.Tudou.com operated by the Defendant Tudou. The uploader was an ordinary registered user who did not obtain any authorization from the copyright owner. As the operator of a specialized video-sharing website of video, entertainment, sports and other services, Tudou should have known that the uploader was not the copyright owner; however, Tudou did not take any necessary measures including deleting, blocking, or disconnecting the link in time, willfully allowing the infringement. As an ISP of network storage service, although Tudou did not directly upload the involved work, it willfully facilitated others to commit the infringements. Since there is a subjective wrong, Todou's act constitutes contributory infringement and shall bear the corresponding liabilities. Whereas the Plaintiff CCTV International failed to prove the actual losses by the infringement or the illegal income of the Defendant Tudou, the Court determined the compensation by comprehensively considering the factors including the type of involved work, popularity, times of communication and degree of the subjective wrong, and the nature of the infringement. The Court ruled that: The Defendant Tudou shall compensate the Plaintiff for economic losses of RMB 80,000 and reasonable expenses of RMB 7,000.

In the second instance, Shanghai No. 1 Intermediate People's Court held that:

> Works refer to intellectual creations with originality in the literary, artistic or scientific domain, insofar as they can be reproduced in a tangible form. The "Opening Ceremony of Olympic Games" contains a unified theme and expresses in a constant manner. When expressing the theme, it combines modern science and technology with the spirit of Olympic Games, portraying characters and creating atmosphere. These ingenious ideas and unique aesthetic expressions give the audience abundant visual enjoyment. On the other hand, those expressions are not the only expressions based on the specific patterns or merely mechanical or skillful labor. In fact, from the arrangement and design of the content, the selection of spotlights and background music, and guidance of the participants' performance activities, one can find that the "Opening Ceremony of Olympic Games" consists of unique arrangements and individualized choices of the participating creators, which reflects the creators' higher degree of creativity. Besides, the "Opening Ceremony of Olympic Games" can be completely reproduced and communicated based on a medium of fixation. Therefore, it can be identified as work that should be protected by the copyright law.

According to Article 7 of the *Olympic Charter*, "the Olympic Games are the exclusive property of the IOC which owns all rights and data relating thereto, in particular, and without limitation, all rights relating to their organization, exploitation, broadcasting, recording, representation, reproduction, access and dissemination in any form and by any means or mechanism whatsoever, whether now existing or developed in the future." The "Opening Ceremony of Olympic Games" is an essential part of the 2012 London Olympic Games. IOC has a rational basis for enjoying its copyright, not only the Internet dissemination right and Internet interactive communication rights mentioned by the "To Whom It May Concern" document. According to the *Berne Convention for the Protection of Literary and Artistic Works* and the *Copyright Law*, the copyright enjoyed by IOC is protected by the *Copyright Law* in China. According to Article 10 of the *Copyright Law*, the right of communication of information on networks

Chapter 2: Determination of the Nature of a Work

is the right to communicate to the public a work, by wire or wireless means in such a way that members of the public may access these works from a place and at a time individually chosen by them. Since the "Internet dissemination right and Internet interactive communication rights" mentioned in the "To Whom It May Concern" document are in line with the connotation and characteristic of the right of communication of information on networks, it can be determined as the right of communication of information on networks under the Chinese copyright law.

In accordance with the huge influence and popularity of the involved work, and the general practice of the authorization of the similar opening ceremony of the Olympic Games, as an operator of a specialized video-sharing website of video, entertainment, sports, etc., the Defendant should have the corresponding professional capability, and should have fulfilled the reasonable duty of care. Otherwise, the Defendant shall bear the liabilities for the infringement. Therefore, the appeal is dismissed, and the original judgment is affirmed.

Commentary:

The key issue of this case is the nature of the involved opening ceremony of the Olympic Games and the ownership of the copyright. In this case, the Plaintiff distinguished the opening ceremony of the Olympic Games with the TV program of the opening ceremony of the Olympic Games, clearly asserting that its claims were based on the opening ceremony of the Olympic Games itself, not the TV program. Is the opening ceremony of the Olympic Games a copyrighted work? If it is a work, what type of work is it? In recent years, there are not only the copyright disputes concerning the opening ceremony of the Olympic Games but also the disputes concerning the opening ceremony of the World Cup. Therefore, it is of great practical significance to clarify this issue.

1. Whether opening ceremony of the Olympic Games can be identified as a work

According to Article 2 of the *Regulations for the Implementation of the Copyright Law*, "works are original intellectual creations in the literary, artistic and scientific domain, insofar as they are capable of being reproduced in a certain tangible form." Therefore, the constituent elements of works are "originality" and "can be fixed and reproduced in some form." There are many similarities in different opening ceremonies of the Olympic Games, such as the flag-raising ceremony, entry of athletes and lighting ceremony of the Olympic Flame. However, the Olympic Games held in different cities have different performance and expressions, and they have obvious differences. Therefore, regarding the originality, the opening ceremony of each Olympic Games is closely connected with the national culture and the Olympic spirit. For example, the opening ceremony of the Athens Olympic Games shows that Greece is the birthplace of the Olympic Games, the opening ceremony of the Beijing Olympic Games shows the 5,000 years history and culture of China, and the opening ceremony of the London Olympic Games shows the history and culture of England such as Shakespeare, the Industrial Revolution, and the Queen. The opening ceremony is actually a large-scale stage show with various types of performances. Its program planning, arrangement, screening and combination are all reflected the individual choice of the host. Its expression reflects the high originality of the creators, and the manpower and material resources devoted in maybe even higher than most films. At the same time, live performances at the opening ceremony of the Olympic Games can be completely fixed through filming and can be reproduced in tangible form. Therefore, the live performance of the opening ceremony of the Olympic Games should be protected as a work in the sense of *Copyright Law*.

2. What type of work is the opening ceremony of the Olympic Games?

In this case, the Plaintiff stated that the opening ceremony of London Olympic Games was "a work created by a process analogous to cinematography" according to the *Copyright Law*. The "works created by a process analogous to cinematography" means works which are recorded on some material, consisting of a series of images, with or without accompanying sound, and which can be projected with the aid of suitable devices or communicated by other means. This kind of work enjoys the same protection as the cinematographic works. They should essentially refer to works such as TV shows to distinguish them from video recordings. However, since the Plaintiff had already clearly distinguished the TV programs of the opening ceremony of the Olympic Games from the opening ceremony of the Olympic Games itself, and explicitly stated that the rights they claim were based upon the opening ceremony of the Olympic Games itself, then it is necessary to think how to classify the opening ceremony of the Olympic Games. The opening ceremony of the London Olympic Games includes songs, dances, acrobatics, etc., as well as lighting ceremony of the Olympic Flame, entry of athletes, fireworks, etc. These works and non-works are arranged, screened and connected under the theme of the Olympic Games. Works derived from compilation of some preexistent works or parts, data which do not constitute the works or other materials of the preexistent works, reflect the compiler's originality of selection and arrangement of the content. Therefore, the opening ceremony of the Olympic Games can be classified as a works of compilation under the *Copyright Law*.

3. Concerning the programs that have been produced

In this case, the Plaintiff was protecting the right of the opening ceremony of the London Olympic Games, which could be based on the opening ceremony itself, or on the TV program of opening ceremony that produced by the Plaintiff. Even if the TV program is identified as a video recording, it does not impede it enjoys the right of communication of information on networks. However, if the opening ceremony of the Olympic Games itself can be identified as a work of compilation, the Defendant may constitute infringement for communicating all the TV programs of the opening program, not only produced by China Central Television, but also by all other television stations. In another word, if it is only based on the TV program of opening ceremony of the Olympic Games produced by China Central Television, the Plaintiff can only claim the right of communication of information on networks of this particular TV program produced by China Central Television.

Chapter 2: Determination of the Nature of a Work

Some scholars argue that although the opening ceremony of the Olympic Games was completed by a camera team alone, the goal is to restore the grandest scene of the opening ceremony. The object and perspective of the filming is entirely based on the circumstance of the live performance, and the space for creation and personal expression is limited. That is to say, even if you change a camera team of the same level, the actual effect of the camera's object, angle, etc. should be basically the same. Therefore, the opening ceremony of the Olympic Games does not satisfy the requirement of originality and cannot be protected as a work. It can only be used as a sound and video recording to enjoy related rights. In my opinion, in this case, whether the TV program of opening ceremony of the Olympic Games produced by China Central Television is a video recording or a TV program (a work created by a process analogous to cinematography) still has room for discussion. Although the TV program was based on live performances of the opening ceremony of the Olympic Games, the purpose was also to broadcast the real circumstance of the opening ceremony to the audience. However, not only a fiction can be a work, a documentary can also be a work. For the production of live performances, different camera teams have different perspectives, screen switching methods and commentary words. If the audience watches opening ceremony of the Olympic Games produced by different TV stations, it can be said that the visual experience is very different. Different producers have different expressions of the same facts (completed TV program), reflecting the originality of the producers. Why cannot they become works? In my opinion, the opening ceremony of the London Olympic Games produced by China Central Television itself can be identified as work. In terms of the type of work, it is a work created by a process analogous to cinematography, which was based on facts of the opening ceremony of the London Olympic Games. Because the opening ceremony itself was a work of compilation, then the TV program was also a derivative work. The producer, China Central Television, was the copyright owner of the opening ceremony TV program.

—**Comments by XU Zhuobin**

Case 4. The Nature of Fictional Character and Its Copyright Protection

Shanghai Character License Administrative Co., Ltd. v. Hubei A-best Supermarket Co., Ltd.
Case of Copyright Infringement Dispute
Case Index: *Shanghai Character License Administrative Co., Ltd. v. Hubei A-best Supermarket Co., Ltd.;* Wuhan Intermediate People's Court of Hubei Province, Wu Zhi Chu Zi [2011] No. 378, August 11, 2011; Hubei Higher People's Court of, E Min San Zhong Zi [2012] No. 23, March 16, 2012

Facts:

Shanghai Character License Administrative Co., Ltd. (hereinafter Huachuang) sued that: Huachuang is the exclusive licensee in China of the right of reproduction, the right of distribution, the right of showing, the merchandising right of characters and the right of sublicensing of the above-mentioned rights of the cinematographic work *ULTRAMAN TIGA* (fifty-two episodes) owned by the Tsuburaya Company of Japan. In this work, Tsuburaya Company created the character Ultraman Tiga, who is a mighty hero fighting for peace of the universe. Some manufacturers produced and marketed toys of Ultraman Tiga without Huachuang's authorization. Despite that A-best Supermarket Co., Ltd. (hereinafter, "A-best") should have known that Huachuang is entitled of the copyright of this work, A-best still marketed the infringing toys. Since A-best had subjective wrong, it shall be liable for its copyright infringement. Thus, Huachuang claimed that: (1) A-best shall immediately cease infringement by stopping marketing any toy relating to the character Ultraman Tiga. (2) A-best shall immediately destroy all the infringing samples, semi-finished products, finished products and relevant packages. (3) A-best shall compensate Huachuang RMB 300,000 for direct economic losses. (4) A-best shall make a public apology to Huachuang. (5) A-best shall be liable for the expenses of the litigation.

A-best asserted that: (1) as a work of fine art, the image of the character Ultraman Tiga should be owned by the copyright owner of the work of fine art; (2) there are significant differences between the image on the package of the toy marketed by A-best and the image of Ultraman Tiga; (3) since the products involved in this case were purchased from a legitimate source, A-best had already fulfilled its duty of care and should not be liable for the infringement. Therefore, A-best required the court to dismiss the claims by Huachuang.

Ruling and Reasoning:

Wuhan Intermediate People's Court of Hubei Province found that: On April 7, 1996, Tsuburaya Company created the cinematographic work of *ULTRAMAN TIGA* (fifty-two episodes) and published it in Japan on September 7, 1996. A character Ultraman Tiga was created in this cinematographic work, whose main characteristics are: helmet-shaped head, oval-shaped eyes, ridged brow, rectangular ears, no eyebrow or hair. Shanghai Audio and Video Publishing House was authorized to import the cinematographic work to China and published and distributed a DVD-ROM version, with the

Chapter 2: Determination of the Nature of a Work

copyright import information (No. 102 of 2005) in the DVD. On November 20, 2006, Tsuburaya Company applied for copyright registration at the Copyright Protection Center of China as the producer of the work. On February 13, 2009, Tsuburaya Company and Huachuang reached a copyright license agreement, stating that Huachuang is the exclusive licensee in China of the right of reproduction, the right of distribution, the right of rental, the merchandising right of characters and the right of sublicensing of the above-mentioned rights of the cinematographic work *ULTRAMAN TIGA* from February 1, 2009 to January 31, 2012. The agreement was approved by the Shanghai Municipal Copyright Administration (Record No. SH-2009-034) on April 13, 2009.

On July 8, 2010, Huachuang found that A-best sold the infringing toys at its Qingnian Road Store in Wuhan Supermarket at Wuhan, which infringed the copyright of the character Ultraman Tiga, thus applied for evidence preservation at the Wuhan Chuxin Notary Office of Hubei Province. After examining and comparing the images in the package of the toy "superhero" with the image of the character Ultraman Tiga, the Court found that the main characteristics of the two images were similar.

Wuhan Intermediate People's Court of Hubei Province held that: Since the work involved in this case was the image of the character Ultraman Tiga, the key issue of this case is whether the image of the character Ultraman Tiga is a work under the *Copyright Law* and whether Huachuang is entitled of the copyright of the work. Since the image of the fictional character Ultraman Tiga was created by the designers, which contains specific characteristics, it meets the requirement of originality. Besides, it can be fixed and reproduced. Therefore, it can be identified as a work of fine art, which is created in lines, patterns, colors or other expression methods under the *Copyright Law*. However, since the image of the fictional character Ultraman Tiga could be separated from the cinematographic work of *ULTRAMAN TIGA*, the image should be identified as an independent work. Thus, the ownership of the copyright of the image of the character Ultraman Tiga needs to be identified. In this case, Huachuang did not provide any evidence relating to either the identification of the designer of the image of the character Ultraman Tiga or the ownership of the work of fine art. Based on the above grounds, the Court ruled that: The claims by Huachuang are rejected.

Huachuang appealed to revoke the first-instance judgment, insisting that all the claims by it should be supported.

In the second instance, the Higher People's Court of Hubei Province found that the facts determined by the first instance were correct. Besides, the second instance court further found that: On April 13, 2009, the Shanghai Municipal Copyright Administration approved the copyright license agreement between Tsuburaya Company and Huachuang (Record No. SH-2009-034). According to this copyright agreement approval certificate, Tsuburaya Company granted Huachuang the exclusive license regarding the right of reproduction, the right of distribution, the right of rental, the right of exhibition etc. of sixteen cinematographic works (Chinese version) of the *Ultraman* series from February 13, 2009 to January 31, 2012. Compared with the certificate of authorization issued by Tsuburaya Company on February 13, 2009, the copyright agreement approval certificate does not mention either the merchandising right of sixteen cinematographic works or the right of reproduction, the right of distribution and the merchandising right of characters from the sixteen cinematographic works. The character Ultraman Tiga is the leading character in the works of *Ultraman Tiga*. The main characteristics of the character Ultraman Tiga are: helmet-shaped head, oval-shaped eyes, ridged brow, rectangular ears, no eyebrow or hair, red and blue stripes tight coat with a blue sign on the chest. In the episodes of the cinematographic works, when alien monsters invade the Earth, Ultraman Tiga will instantly change his shape from an ordinary citizen into the great hero to fight bravely against the monsters. In the second instance, Huachuang stated that the image of "Ultraman" was created in the 1960s by Eiji Tsuburaya of Tsuburaya Company and "Ultraman Tiga" was a re-creation of "Ultraman" based on the original "Ultraman" in the 1990s by Kazuo Tsuburaya of Tsuburaya Company. The screenshots of the series of *ULTRAMAN TIGA* showed that the work was "Created by Kazuo Tsuburaya" and "Produced by the Tsuburaya Company."

The Higher People's Court of Hubei Province held that: The character image of Ultraman Tiga is identified as a separate work that was independent from the cinematographic works, whose author had the independent copyright. It cannot be simply or directly assumed that the copyright owner of the cinematographic works is the owner of the character image. The use of reproducing the character image of Ultraman Tiga in the toy was an exploitation of the copyright of the character image which can be used separately from the cinematographic works, but not the exploitation of the copyright of the cinematographic works themselves. Despite that Huachuang had obtained the rights of the cinematographic works, it was not entitled to enjoy the rights of the character images from the cinematographic works. The character image of Ultraman can only be protected as a work of fine art, whose owner is the author. Therefore, Huachuang needs to prove that it is entitled to enjoy the copyright of the work of fine art of Ultraman Tiga, but not to make the claims based on the cinematographic works of *Ultraman Tiga*. In the absence of relevant evidence, Huachuang shall bear the legal consequences of the inability of proof. Based on the above grounds, the Court ruled that the appeal was dismissed and the first-instance judgment was affirmed.

Commentary:

Ultraman Tiga is the leading character of the series *Ultraman Tiga*. When the alien monster attacks humans, the fictional character Ultraman Tiga will bravely fight against the monster to maintain the peace of the universe. Regarding the definition of fictional characters, some scholars hold that fictional characters refer to characters, animals and robots that appear in animation, TV programs, movies, etc.[4] and the vocal figures may also be fictional characters. The images of fictional characters refer to the artistic images with characteristics that are formed by original works. Such an image consists of unreal artistic elements including names, appearances, iconic moves, pet

---

4. Wu Handong (Editor), *Research on the Copyright System of Western Countries*, China University of Political Science and Law Press, 2009, p. 54.

Chapter 2: Determination of the Nature of a Work

phrase etc.[5] The images of fictional characters may be human or animals and can be further classified as literary characters, audio-visual characters and cartoon characters. The character image of Ultraman Tiga in this case is an audio-visual character from a cinematographic work.

1. Can a fictional character be individually identified as a work under the *Copyright Law*?

The World Intellectual Property Organization classifies character images into two types, which are the images of "real person" and the images of "fictional character."[6] In the U.S., for real person, the images are protected by the "right of publicity" that is "the right for people to exploit their own identity for commercial use;"[7] while for fictional character, the images are protected by the "rights in characters" to protect "people, animals and robots from movies, TV programs, animations, etc., and the vocal figures."[8]

Fictional characters are the artistic images created in from the works of animations, movies and TV programs. Generally speaking, "characters from novels, drama, and movies are usually played by people. Despite the make-ups and unique appearances, they cannot be identified as works."[9] Based on this ground, some scholars argued that the character Ultraman Tiga itself could not be an independent work but a part of the cinematographic work of *Ultraman Tiga*, because the character could not exist independently from the cinematographic work of *Ultraman Tiga*. Whether a fictional character can be individually identified as a work should be determined by the *Regulations for the Implementation of the Copyright Law*. Article 2 of the *Regulations* stipulates: "The term works as referred to in the *Copyright Law* means intellectual creations with originality in the literary, artistic or scientific domain, insofar as they can be reproduced in a tangible form." Therefore, the works protected by the *Copyright Law* must meet the following three requirements: First, the works must be intellectual achievements in the literary, artistic or scientific domain; second, they must be original; third, they must be able to be reproduced in a tangible form. Some scholars hold that "originality is the key element in determining the rights relating to images."[10] For example, the *Nichols* standard formed by the *Nichols v. Universal Picture Corp* case of U.S., also known as the "distinctively delineated" standard, requires the character must be distinctive enough to get the protection, and the more sophisticated the character is, the more it may be protected. Moreover, in the determination of

---

5. Wu Handong, Commercialization of Image and Image of Commercialization, *Science of Law*, 10 (2004).
6. *See* WIPO, Character Merchandising, WC/INF/10847998/1PLD, p. 9.
7. Li Mingde, The Right of Publicity under US Law, *Global Law Review*, Winter (2003).
8. Lin Ya'na & Song Jing, The Legal Model of Protecting Fictional Characters in US, *Journal of Guangxi Politics and Law Management Cadre College*, 5 (2003).
9. Chen Jinchuan, *Copyright Judgment: Principle Interpretation and Practice Guidance* (2014 Edition), Law Press, 2014, p. 8.
10. Ding Zhaozeng, Research on Commercial Use of the Right of Publicity: A Comment of the *Ultraman Tiga* Case, *Journal of Fujian Normal University (Philosophy and Social Sciences Edition)*, 6 (2011).

infringement, the infringed character should be originally conceived and fully described.[11]

In this case, the key factor in determining whether the fictional character Ultraman Tiga is a work is originality. The originality of a work consists of two aspects, which are "independently originated" and "a minimum degree of creativity."[12] First of all, Ultraman Tiga is a re-creation based on the Ultraman of the 1960s, and thus can be considered as "independently originated." The first image of Ultraman was created by Eiji Tsuburaya in the 1960s. Ultraman Tiga is a re-creation by Kazuo Tsuburaya in the 1990s based on the Ultraman of the 1960s. Compared with Ultraman, Ultraman Tiga is distinctive from the shape of helmet, the color of coat and the pattern on the chest, which reflect the independent concept of the author rather than imitation, making Ultraman Tiga a new fictional character that is different from Ultraman. Second, the fictional character Ultraman Tiga is of creativity. Although Ultraman Tiga is a role played by a real person and has a human body shape, it is not a character figure created by simple make-up, but a robot-like image created in a creative way, whose main characteristics are: helmet-shaped head, oval-shaped eyes, ridged brow, rectangular ears, no eyebrow or hair, red and blue stripes tight coat with a blue sign on the chest. Those characteristics are generated from the personal choice, arrangement and design, reflecting the unique personality of the author. Some scholars argued that: "The originality does not include the requirement of aesthetic value. As long as the expression is originated by the author independently and can reflect a certain degree of personal choice, arrangement, design, and combination, it can be determined as a work."[13] According to this standard, since Ultraman Tiga is conceived and created independently by the author, it should be protected by the *Copyright Law*. In the commodity economy, fictional characters can be commercialized independently from the relevant cinematographic works, so that the owner of the fictional characters can exploit economic benefits from the work. Therefore, fictional characters are works that are independent of the relevant cinematographic works.

2. What type of work are fictional characters?

According to the facts of this case, Tsuburaya Company licensed the rights of reproduction, distribution, rental and merchandising right of the cinematographic works of *ULTRAMAN TIGA* series and their images in China to Huachuang. Thus, it can be concluded that the rights licensed by Tsuburaya Company to Huachuang could be divided into two items: the first was the reproduction rights, distribution rights, and rental rights of the cinematographic works of *ULTRAMAN TIGA*; the second was the merchandising right of the image of the fictional character Ultraman Tiga. The identification of the type of work of the fictional character of Ultraman Tiga is a prerequisite for determining the type of right and the scope of protection.

---

11. Lin Ya'na & Song Jing, T The Legal Model of Protecting Fictional Characters in US, *Journal of Guangxi Politics and Law Management Cadre College*, 5 (2003).
12. Chen Jinchuan, *Copyright Judgment: Principle Interpretation and Practice Guidance* (2014 Edition), Law Press, 2014, p. 1.
13. Li Chen, *Keywords of Intellectual Property Law*, Law Press, 2006, p. 27.

One opinion is that the fictional character Ultraman Tiga should belong to the works of character image. Accordingly, the owners of such works of character image enjoy merchandising right. According to a character merchandising report published by WIPO in 1993, character merchandising can be defined as the adaptation or secondary exploitation, by the creator of a fictional character or by a real person or by one or several authorized third parties, of the essential personality features (such as name, image and appearance) of a character relating to various goods and services with a view to creating in prospective customers a desire to acquire those goods and to use those services because of the customers' affinity with that character.[14] Some scholars argue that the fictional character should be protected independently, "Namely, to establish an independent merchandising right, formally establish the legal status of merchandising rights in legislation, and no longer allow the merchandising right to become the shadow of civil rights such as the rights of personality, copyrights and trademark rights."[15] However, since there is no such merchandising right of fictional characters in the current Chinese legal system, thus the right to commercialize the image of the fictional character Ultraman Tiga cannot be protected.

The other opinion is that the fictional character Ultraman Tiga should belong to the works of fine art. Some scholars argue that "in some Western countries, fictional characters belong to a special subject matter of copyright, but not an independent type of works. The images of fictional characters are recognized as a work of art and the characters from a literary work are recognized as a part of the literary work, so that the characters may be protected by copyright." [16] According to Article 4 (8) of the *Regulations for the Implementation of the Copyright Law*, "Works of fine art are 2D or 3D works created in lines, colors or other medium which, when being viewed, impart esthetic effect, such as paintings, works of calligraphy, sculptures and works of architecture." In this case, the image of Ultraman Tiga is robot looking with a helmet-shaped head, inimitable face and red and blue stripes tight coat with a blue sign on the chest. In essence, it is an aesthetic artwork composed of lines, colors and patterns. Based on this ground, the fictional character Ultraman Tiga can be identified as a work of fine art protected by the *Copyright Law* in China.

It should be emphasized that the scope of protection of the works of fine art is smaller than the scope of protection of the rights of the image of characters. Children love the character image of Ultraman Tiga not only for its unique aesthetic exterior appearance but also for the heroic and peace-keeping personality of the character. Thus, the infringing goods exploited not only the external appearance of Ultraman Tiga, but also the internal personality of Ultraman Tiga that was deeply loved by the fans. Therefore, according to the theory of protecting the merchandising rights of fictional characters, both the external appearance and internal personality jointly make Ultraman Tiga a comprehensive fictional character image work. However, according to

---

14. Li Fumin, Legal Protection of Fictional Characters in Works, *Social scientist*, 5 (2012).
15. Liu Yajun & Cao Junjing, The Legal Protection of Fictional Characters Commoditization Rights and the Enlightenment of American Practice, *Contemporary Law*, 7 (2008).
16. Wu Handong, Commercialization of Image and Image of Commercialization, *Science of Law*, 10 (2004).

the "idea expression dichotomy" of copyright, as a work of fine art, the copyright protection of the image of the fictional character Ultraman Tiga covers only the artistic expression of the external appearance, but not the internal personality that belongs to the idea of the work.

3. How to identify the copyright owner of a fictional character?

In the Chinese judicial practice, there is no consensus in relation to the ownership of the copyright of fictional characters. Taking the fictional character Ultraman or Ultraman Tiga as an example, one opinion is that since Ultraman is a fictional character from the literary work and cinematographic work, the copyright owner of it shall be the same copyright owner of the relevant literary work and cinematographic work. [17] The other opinion is that the copyright owner of the image of the character Ultraman Tiga shall be the copyright owner of the work of fine art of Ultraman Tiga. Therefore, in this case, Huachuang must prove that it is entitled to the copyright of the work of fine art of Ultraman Tiga, rather than the copyright of cinematographic work.[18]

According to Article 15 of the *Copyright Law*, "The copyright of cinematographic works shall be enjoyed by the producer of the work, but the screenwriter, director, cameraman and lyricist shall enjoy the right of authorship in the work and shall be entitled to remuneration according to the contract signed with the producer. The authors of screenplay, musical works and other works that are included in a cinematographic, television or video-graphic work which can be exploited separately shall be entitled to exercise their copyright independently." As mentioned above, the fictional character Ultraman Tiga is similar to the screenplay and musical work from cinematographic works, which can be exploited separately from the relevant cinematographic works. In this case, since the infringing product was a copy of the image of Ultraman Tiga, such an act was a separate exploitation of the work of fine art of Ultraman Tiga, rather than the overall exploitation of the cinematographic work of *ULTRAMAN TIGA*.

According to the *Copyright Law*, the copyright owners of works of fine arts are the authors of the works, while the copyright owners of cinematographic works are the producers of the works. In this case, the work of fine art of Ultraman Tiga created by Kazuo Tsuburaya was used in the cinematographic work of ULTRAMAN TIGA created by the Tsuburaya Company. Huachuang failed to provide any evidence to prove whether Kazuo Tsuburaya had made any agreement with the Tsuburaya Company in relation to the copyright of the work of fine art of Ultraman Tiga. Even if the author of the fine artwork of Ultraman Tiga authorized the Tsuburaya Company to use the fine artwork in the cinematographic work of *ULTRAMAN TIGA*, it still could not be determined that Kazuo Tsuburaya had assigned his copyright of Ultraman Tiga, including the rights of reproduction, distribution, and rental, to Tsuburaya Company and authorized Tsuburaya Company to file lawsuits.

In conclusion, the copyright owner of the fictional character Ultraman Tiga should be Kazuo Tsuburaya, who is the author of the work or fine art of Ultraman Tiga.

---

17. Sun Meilan & Kong Dingying, Reflections on the *Ultraman* Case, *Science of Law*, 7 (1999).
18. Hubei Higher People's Court (2012) E Min San Zhong Zi No. 23.

Despite that Huachuang obtained the authorization from the copyright owner of the cinematographic work of *ULTRAMAN TIGA*, in the absence of evidence in relation to the copyright authorization of the work or fine art by Kazuo Tsuburaya, it cannot be asserted that Huachuang is entitled to the separate exploitation of the work of fine art of Ultraman Tiga from the cinematographic work of *ULTRAMAN TIGA*.

—**Comments by TONG Haichao**

Case 5. The Nature of Music Video and Its Copyright Protection

Beijing Huaxiajinma Culture Communication Co., Ltd. v. Wuhan Ledixiong Music & Entertainment Co., Ltd.
Case of Right of Showing Infringement Dispute
Case Index: *Beijing Huaxiajinma Culture Communication Co., Ltd. v. Wuhan Ledixiong Music & Entertainment Co., Ltd.* Wuhan Intermediate People's Court of Hubei Province, Wu Zhi Chu Zi [2009] No. 38, September 3, 2009; Hubei Higher People's Court, E Min San Zhong Zi [2009] No. 84, December 22, 2009.

Facts:

The Plaintiff, Beijing Huaxiajinma Culture Communication Co., Ltd. (hereinafter, "Huaxiajinma"), alleged that: The Defendant, Wuhan Ledixiong Music & Entertainment Co., Ltd. (hereinafter, "Ledixiong"), illegally copied seven music videos including *Hurt*, *When a Wolf Loves a Sheep*, *Angry Lover*, *Never Regret for Loving You*, *Your Name Warms Me Up*, *Will You Miss Me When I Am Missing You* and *Once You Change Your Mind* to the video-on-demand system in the Holiday Karaoke Club operated by the Defendant and showed to the public for commercial purpose, which infringed the right of reproduction and the right of showing. The Plaintiff claimed that: The Defendant shall cease the infringement immediately and compensate the Plaintiff RMB 401,114 in total including RMB 380,000 for the economic losses and RMB 21,114 for the reasonable expenses. The Defendant argued that: (1) Except the work of *When a Wolf Loves a Sheep*, since six of the seven music videos involved in this case were not made by virtue of an analogous method of film production, they cannot be defined as cinematographic works or works created by virtue of an analogous method of film production, and are not works protected by copyright. (2) Since the right of showing itself covers the step of reproducing for the showing, the Defendant did not infringe the right of reproduction. (3) Even if the Defendant's act constitutes infringement, since there is no actual damage to the Plaintiff, the Plaintiff obviously claimed an excessive amount of compensation, thus such claims shall be dismissed.

In the first instance, Wuhan Intermediate People's Court found that: On October 10, 2005, Huaxiajinma signed the first contract with Beijing Chuanqixing Culture Communication Co., Ltd. to commission it to make the music video of *When a Wolf Loves a Sheep*, performed by Tang Chao. The music video was made on 16 mm film, which cost RMB 110,000 in total. According to the contract, Huaxiajinma owns the copyright of this work. In addition, Chuanqixing agreed not to remake, alter, play, and show the work to public and not to use or authorize any third party to use the costume, character image, voice-over and other audio-video design. On February 15, 2006, Huaxiajinma signed the second contract with an outsider, Beijing Jingying, to commission it to make the music video of *Never Regret for Loving You*, performed by Tang Chao. The music video was made on 16 mm film, which cost RMB 80,000 in total. According to the contract, Huaxiajinma owns the copyright of this work. Beijing Jingying agreed not to remake, alter, play, and show the work to public and not to use or authorize any third party to use the costume, character image, voice-over and other audio-video design. On March 3, 2006, Huaxiajinma signed the third contract with another outsider, Lin Xia, to commission it to make four music videos including *Hurt, Your Name Warms Me Up, Will You Miss Me When I Am Missing You* and *Once You Change Your Mind*. The music video was made in Adobe Flash format. According to the contract, *Your Name Warms Me Up* had been accomplished and the cost had been paid; the rest three music videos including *Hurt, Will You Miss Me When I Am Missing You* and *Once You Change Your Mind* would cost RMB 2,700 each and RMB 8,100 in total. Huaxiajinma owns the copyright of the four music videos. Lin Xia agreed not to alter the work, not to authorize any third party to publish or distribute, or upload to the Internet for commercial view or download. In summary, in accordance with the contracts, Huaxiajinma has made payments to all the photographers, producers and performers of seven music videos, and all of them declared that Huaxiajinma is the copyright owner of the seven music videos. In addition, on April 13, 2009, Tang Chaojun (whose stage name is Tang Chao) stated to confirm that he is the author and performer of the relevant seven music works; the seven music videos including *Hurt (Flash version), When a Wolf Loves a Sheep (disc version), Angry Lover (Flash version), Never Regret for Loving You, Your Name Warms Me Up (Flash version), Will You Miss Me When I Am Missing You (Flash version)* and *Once You Change Your Mind (Flash version)* performed by him were produced by Huaxiajinma and Huaxiajinma is the copyright owner of the seven music videos.

According to the civil judgment of Hai-Min-Chu-Zi [2006] No. 25641 by Beijing Haidian District People's Court, it is ascertained that Tang Chao is the state name of Tang Chaojun. The above-mentioned seven music works are included in the album of *When a Wolf Loves a Sheep by Tang Chao*, published and distributed by Guangdong Feile Film and Television Products Co., Ltd. (hereinafter, "Feile").

In the first instance, the Court organized both parties to check the album by submitted by Huaxiajinma. Both parties confirmed: (1) The music video of *When a Wolf Loves a Sheep* lasts 4 m 55 s on a 16 mm film. (2) The music video of *Never Regret for Loving You* lasts 4 m 2 s in Adobe Flash format, with live folk dance of Northeast China and street dance in it. (3) The music video of *Angry Lover* lasts 5 m 12 s. (4) The music video of *Your Name Warms Me Up* lasts 3 m 56 s. (5) The music video of *Once You Change Your Mind* lasts 3 m 47 s. (6) The music video of *Hurt* lasts 4 m 2 s. (7) The music video of *Will You Miss Me When I Am Missing You* lasts 4 m. The last five music videos are all in Adobe Flash format. In the video content, all of the seven music videos are marked the name of Huaxiajinma as the producer and the logo of Feile as the publisher and distributor. In addition, in the music video of *Angry Lover*, there is also another mark of "Edited by Lingdu." On September 1, 2008, Huaxiajinma applied to Wuhan Qintai Notary Office for evidence preservation. On September 10, 2008, the delegated notary accompanied Huaxiajinma's lawyer Zhou Jiaqi to Holiday Karaoke Club, located at No. 61 Jianghan Road, Wuhan, for evidence preservation, then issued the notarial certificate that Zhou jiaqi, as an ordinary consumer, operated the video-on-demand system in Room 303 of this Club to play the following music videos: *House,*

Hurt, Word Feel China, That Feeling, Love Thieves, When a Wolf Loves a Sheep, Angry Lover, Hometown Heilongjiang, Mom I miss you, The Power of Smile, Love and Hurt, Love and Hurt (audition version), Once You Change Your Mind, Never Regret for Loving You, You Are My Good Friend, I fall in Love with You, You are the Prettiest Girl I Love, and *Will You Miss Me When I Am Missing You*. The music video of *When a Wolf Loves a Sheep* was No. 5 on the Top Song List in the system. After operating the system, the music videos were played on the screen, while Zhou Jiaqi used a video recorder to videotape the whole process. Then Zhou Jiaqi paid the Club RMB 190 for the karaoke service and RMB 74 for food and beverage. On May 19, 2009, the Court of First Instance organized both parties to do a field visit to the Holiday Karaoke Club operated by the Defendant. Both parties confirmed that the music videos are stored in the computer server and can be selected and played via the video-on-demand ordering system. After ordering, the digitized music videos will be transmitted to the screen in the room via a local network. The process during the field visit is consistent with the process recorded by the notarial certificate; however, none of the music video involved in this case was accessible during the field visit. Meanwhile, both parties confirmed that Holiday Karaoke Club's business area is 1427.5 m^2, with sixty-seven private rooms, and the business hours is between 8:00 am to 2:00 am the next day.

During the trial, the Court organized both parties to make comparison between notarized videos and the seven music videos of the Plaintiff. It was found that the characters, images, subtitles, animation plots are the same with the mark of Huaxiajinma and the logo of Feile, except *When a Wolf Loves a Sheep* in which there is a mark of "Made by Qinyin."

The expenses of Huaxiajinma consists of RMB 50 for business investigation fee, RMB 800 for notary fee, RMB 190 for karaoke service at Holiday Karaoke Club, RMB 74 for food at Holiday Karaoke Club, and RMB 20,000 for the attorney fees.

Ruling and Reasoning:

In the first instance, Wuhan Intermediate People's Court held that: The Plaintiff Huaxiajinma is the copyright owner of the seven music videos including *When a Wolf Loves a Sheep* etc. The Defendant Ledixiong infringed the right of showing of the Plaintiff by showing to the public the seven music videos without any authorization. Thus, the Defendant shall be liable for the civil liability of cease the infringement and compensation for economic losses. Since it has been confirmed by both parties that the infringement had been actually stopped, the Defendant Ledixiong shall no longer be liable for cease the infringement. According to Article 3, Article 10, Article 15, Article 47 and Article 48 of the *2001 Copyright Law*, and Article 128 of the *2007 Civil Procedure Law*, the Court ruled that: (1) Ledixiong shall compensate RMB 15,000 for economic losses; (2) Ledixiong shall compensate Huaxiajinma RMB 11,040 for reasonable expenses; (3) other claims by Huaxiajinma are dismissed. Regarding the litigation expense of the first instance, Huaxiajinma shall pay RMB 1,463.4, and Ledixiong shall pay RMB 5,853.6.

Chapter 2: Determination of the Nature of a Work

Both the Plaintiff and the Defendant filed an appeal. The second instance court ruled that all the petitions were dismissed and the original judgment was affirmed.

Commentary:

This dispute is relating to the infringement of the right of showing of music videos created by virtue of an analogous method of film production. The Defendant infringed the right of showing by playing the music videos without authorization. I would like to analyze the case from the following four perspectives: the type of work involved, the Plaintiff's legal capacity to sue, the right infringed by the Defendant, and the calculation of damages.

1. The type of work involved in the case

Regarding which type of work music video shall be classified as and what rights the copyright owner shall be granted, there are still controversial arguments. The *Copyright Law* distinguishes the "cinematographic works and works created by a process analogous to cinematography" with the "sound and video recordings." According to Article 4 of the *Regulations for the Implementation of the Copyright Law*, cinematographic works and works created by a process analogous to cinematography refer to works which are recorded on certain material, consisting of a series of images, with or without accompanying sound, and which can be projected with the aid of suitable devices or communicated by other means. According to Article 5 of the *Regulations*, sound recordings refer to aural fixations of sounds of performances or other sounds; video recordings refer to fixations of a connected series of related images or pictures, with or without accompanying sounds, other than cinematographic works and works created by a process analogous to cinematography.

Regarding the type-of-work issue, the first opinion is that: In this case, except the music video of *When a Wolf Loves a Sheep* that can be identified as a work created by a process analogous to cinematography, the other six music videos can only be identified as sound and video recordings. According to Article 41 of the *Copyright Law*, the owners of sound and video recordings are only able to authorize another person to exercise the rights of reproduction, distribution, rental, communication of information on networks and receive remuneration. Therefore, the Plaintiff is not entitled to make claims for the infringement of the right of showing that can be only enjoyed by the owner of cinematographic works and works created by a process analogous to cinematography.

The other opinion is that: All of the seven music videos in this case can be identified as a work created by a process analogous to cinematography. Therefore, the Plaintiff is entitled to make claims for the infringement of the right of showing in accordance with Article 10 of the *Copyright Law*.

The key factor for determining whether the music videos are identified as works created by a process analogous to cinematography or sound and video recordings is originality. The word "originality" has two meanings, which are "originated from" and "creativity." So, from the perspective of copyright, what is the real meaning of "originality?"

In UK, which is the birthplace of modern copyright law, and other common law system countries including U.S., Canada, Australia, New Zealand, even if no intellectual creation is embodied in the labor achievement, as long as the labor achievement includes the author's "independent hard work" and has practical value, it can satisfy the "originality" requirement of the copyright law. Such a standard of "originality" is also known as the "sweat of the brow" doctrine. According to the "sweat of the brow" doctrine, compilation of facts, such as telephone directory, is "original" enough to get copyright protection, regardless of whether the editor's intellectual creativity is reflected in the selection and arrangement.[19] However, this may lead to a monopoly on the facts themselves. In the example of telephone directory, as soon as the first company obtains the copyright of the first telephone directory by "sweat of the brow," no one can ever publish a similar telephone directory without infringing the copyright, but can only collect and arrange the telephone numbers again independently. In the example of map, a UK court even declared on the basis of the "sweat of the brow" doctrine that: "For a book about a road, one must calculate mileage on his own. For a newly discovered island map, one must complete all measurements himself as he has never seen previous maps. Usually, without his own independent labor, he has no right to use a word from previously published information."[20] Obviously, the "sweat of the brow" doctrine has, to a certain extent, prevented the unfair free riding of labor results, but it will inevitably hinder others from using the facts and data in the results of previous labor. Such a consequence is against the fundamental purpose of copyright law for encouraging the next generations to "stand on the shoulders of their predecessors" to create new works. Therefore, there are few countries that still stick to the "sweat of the brow" doctrine. It is clear that U.S. and Canada have already demolished this doctrine.[21]

According to the *Regulations for the Implementation of the Copyright Law*, only labor products with "originality" can be identified as works to be protected by the *Copyright Law*, but there is no provision to clarify the degree of "creativity" in "originality." Therefore, the Chinese courts eventually reach a consensus that if the music video is simply a composition of sounds and images, or a mere recording of live concerts, it can only be identified as a sound and video recording but not a work, since it does not achieve the "creativity" of "originality." Meanwhile, even the video recorder is adjusted manually during the shooting process, if the adjustment is just for the quality of the sound and image, the music video can only be identified as a sound and video recording. In addition, if a music video is just the result of post-processing and simple editing, it can only be identified as a sound and video recording.

On the other hand, if a music video has been produced to present the vivid combination of the performers and the background elements, representing the creative work of the scriptwriter, director, photographer, and editor, etc., it will meet the requirements of "creativity," then can be identified as a work created in analogous

---

19. *See* WANG Qian, *Intellectual Property Law Course*, China Renmin University Press, 2011, p. 29.
20. *Ibid.*, p. 30.
21. *Ibid.*

method of film production. For example, if a music video can tell a complete story, it can be identified as an original work.

In this case, except *When a Wolf Loves a Sheep*, the other six music videos are made in Adobe Flash format. A Flash artwork is an animation with sound and subtitle created by computer software. Those six music videos in Flash format are recorded on certain material, consisting of a series of images, with or without accompanying sound, and which can be projected with the aid of suitable devices or communicated by other means. The content of the work is the design of characters, scenes, plots, etc. of a musical theme and lyrics meaning, expressing the creator's idea, which embodies the creative work of writing, directing, filming, editing and compositing. It represents certain degree of originality and is not a mere reproduction of sounds or images. Hence, the six music videos can be identified as the works created in analogous method of film production.

Another opinion is that the six music videos cannot be identified as works created in analogous method of film production, because they were not made on films. As it is known, the process of movie producing is changing continuously with the development of technology. Nowadays, movies can be made by computer software, fixed in media such as film, videotape, flash memory, laser disk and hard disk and can be played not only in a theater but also in a personal computer. According to the *Regulations for the Implementation of the Copyright Law*, cinematographic works and works created by a process analogous to cinematography shall be "recorded on certain material" to meet the requirement of fixation. Such an expression of "recorded on certain material" does not exclude the method of production by using the Adobe Flash software and the method of fixation by storing them on CDs. Thus, this opinion is not well established.

2. The Plaintiff's legal capacity to sue

In this case, the Plaintiff is the producer of seven music videos. According to Article 15 of the *Copyright Law*, the Plaintiff enjoys the copyright of the seven works and has the legal capacity to sue.[22] The reason why the issue of legal capacity to sue should be discussed and further clarified is that there were a large number of similar cases held by the courts in Hubei Province for infringement of the rights of reproduction, performance, and authorship, in which the plaintiffs are authors of songs and lyrics and the defendants are karaoke operators.

So the question is: Besides the producers, do authors of songs and lyrics have the legal capacity to sue karaoke operators for the unauthorized exploitation of the music videos?

Regarding this question, there are controversial judgments in China. First of all, if the music video involved in this case is identified as a sound and video recording, all

---

22. Article 15 of the *Copyright Law* stipulates that: "The copyright in a cinematographic work and any work created by an analogous method of film production shall be enjoyed by the producer of the work, but the scriptwriter, director, cameraman, lyricist, composer, and other authors thereof shall enjoy the right of authorship in the work, and have the right to receive remuneration pursuant to the contract concluded with the producer."

the Chinese courts agree that the author of the song and lyric has the legal capacity to sue the karaoke operators for the unauthorized exploitation of his music work. This is because the music video is a product formed on the basis of original musical work, while there is no new work or copyright to be formed. Thus, as the copyright owners of music work, authors of songs and lyrics are entitled to sue without any doubt.

However, if the music video involved in this case is identified as a work created in analogous method of film production, do authors of songs and lyrics still have the legal capacity to sue karaoke operators?

There are two controversial opinions in the judicial practice. According to the first opinion, the author of music work is not entitled to sue if the work created in analogous method of film production is infringed. Because according to Article 15 of the *Copyright Law*, when music lyrics are combined with the efforts by screenwriters, directors, and photography to jointly form a work created in analogous method of film production, the copyright, including the rights of reproduction, performance, etc., are enjoyed by the producer. The author of music work only has the right of authorship of his music work and the right to receive remuneration pursuant to the contract concluded with the producer, and cannot claim the reproduction right of the work created in analogous method of film production.[23]

According to the second opinion, the author of music work is entitled to sue for the following two reasons: First, in January 2007, Justice Cao Jianming, vice-president of the Supreme People's Court, stated in a speech at the national forum on intellectual property trials: "Music and lyric are more important than images in music videos. This is the main difference between music videos and other general cinematographic works. Also, usually producers will not buyout songwriter's rights. Hence, for the works of music videos, songwriters can still claim rights to users for commercial use directly." In this speech, Justice Cao classified music videos into two categories, which are the works created in analogous method of film production and the sound and video recordings. Even in the case of works created in analogous method of film production, authors of music works can still directly use the infringers. Second, the China Music Copyright Association is a copyright collective management organization that manages copyrights for composers and lyricists. According to Announcement No. 1 issued by the National Copyright Administration in 2006, the China Music Copyright Association is entitled to collect karaoke copyright royalties in China. If authors of music works are not allowed to sue infringers, they will not be able to locate the unauthorized music video producers, which is not adequate for protecting authors of music works.

However, regarding the second opinion, there are still two questions that need to be answered. First, given that no matter the music video is identified as a work created in analogous method of film production or a sound and video recording, the author of music work is always entitled to sue, then why bother distinguishing music videos into works created in analogous method of film production and sound and video recordings? Second, if an author of music work successfully sues the unauthorized karaoke operator for the exploitation of the music video, is it possible for the producer of the

---

23. *See* (2010) Yue Gao Fa Min San Zhong No. 67.

same music video to sue the same karaoke operator on the basis of a "bigger" copyright of the work created in analogous method of film production? If the court ruled again that the karaoke operator shall be liable for the same infringement, it is obviously against the principle of *"Non bis in idem,"* and unfair for karaoke operators.

3. The right infringed by the Defendant

In this case, the Plaintiff claimed that the Defendant had infringed the right of reproduction and the right of showing. According to Article 10 of the *Copyright Law*, the right of reproduction, that is, the right to produce one or more copies of a work by printing, photocopying, lithographing, making a sound recording or video recording, duplicating a recording, or duplicating a photographic work or by any other means; the right of showing, that is, the right to show to the public a work, of fine art, photography, cinematography and any work created by analogous methods of film production through film projectors, overhead projectors or any other technical devices. What the Defendant did in this case was: (1) storing the music videos in its computer server of video-on-demand system; (2) when consumers select one of the music videos via video-on-demand system, showing the music video on the monitor.

In the judicial practice, there is no major dispute on whether the Defendant infringed the Plaintiff's right of showing, except that someone argues that the Defendant infringed the Plaintiff's the right of communication of information on networks. In regard to the identification of using music videos by video-on-demand system that similar to a jukebox, it has been suggested that the courts shall identify it as an act of showing, instead of an act of communication of information on networks in the local network, to avoid any confusion for future judicial practice.

In regard to the infringement of the right of reproduction, there are three major opinions: The first opinion is that the Defendant's act of storing music videos on its server was apparently an act of reproduction of the original work, but such an act was for the purpose of showing the work. The necessary technical preparations were made for showing, but not copying. The protection of the right of showing covered the protection of the right of reproduction. Therefore, the Defendant only infringed the right of showing but not the right of reproduction.

The second opinion is that: as a karaoke operator, the Defendants did not produce the video-on-demand system. The acts of copying the music video into the system and selling the system were performed out by the video-on-demand system manufacturer for commercial purpose. Meanwhile, the maintenance of the music videos was also by the video-on-demand system manufacturer. Since the karaoke operator did not perform any act of copyright, the video-on-demand system manufacturer should be the infringer and take the responsibilities.

In some cases relating to music videos, the plaintiffs may also sue the karaoke operators that their right of authorship is infringed, since the karaoke operators involved in this case do not show the authors' name in the music videos. Regarding the infringement of the right of authorship, since karaoke operators do not participate in the production process of music videos and also impractical to monitor tens of thousands of music videos in the system, it is incorrect to determine that karaoke operators infringe the right of authorship.

The third opinion is that: whether the karaoke operator infringes the right of reproduction and the right of authorship should be determined from the perspective of the burden of proof. To be more specific, if the karaoke operator fails to prove that the works and recordings in its system were copied by others, then it shall be regarded as the one who performed the act of copying the works and recordings; if the karaoke operator successfully proves that the works and recordings in its system were copied by others, then it can be determined that the karaoke operator did not perform the act of copying the works and recordings. This approach is also applicable in the cases of infringement of the right of authorship.

Currently, the third opinion is the most common opinion that is agreed by the author himself. The advantage of this approach is that it encourages the karaoke operators to provide the information of the video-on-demand system manufacturer, which can effectively prevent the copyright infringements at the source, and crack down those who actually perform the infringement.

4. The calculation of damages

In this case, the Plaintiff failed to submit the amount of the actual losses of profits from producing, distributing and licensing the music videos involved in this case that caused by the infringement. Neither did the Plaintiff submit any amount of illegal income of the Defendant from the infringement. Therefore, the Court calculated the statutory damages in accordance with Article 48 of the *Copyright Law*[24] and Article 25 of the *Interpretation of the Supreme People's Court on Several Issues Concerning the Application of Law in the Trial of Civil Disputes over Copyright*.[25] The court referred to the following factors in determining the amount of compensation: (1) Type of work: The works in this case are similar to those created in analogous method of film production, and *When a Wolf Loves a Sheep* was quite popular in the karaoke market. (2) Nature of the infringing act: Since the Defendant knew that the Plaintiff was the copyright owner of the music videos, but still unauthorized showed the works to the public, it can be determined that the Defendant had subjective wrong. (3) Consequences of the

---

24. Article 48 of the *Copyright Law* stipulates: "Where a copyright or a copyright-related right is infringed, the infringer shall compensate for the actually injury suffered by the right owner; where the actual injury is difficult to compute, the damages shall be paid on the basis of the illegal income of the infringer. The amount of damages shall also include the appropriate fees paid by the right owner to stop the infringing act. Where the right owner's actual injury or infringer's illegal income cannot be determined, the People's Court shall judge the damages not exceeding RMB 500,000 depending on the circumstances of the infringing act."
25. Article 25 of the *Interpretation of the Supreme People's Court on Several Issues Concerning the Application of Law in the Trial of Civil Disputes over Copyright* stipulates: "Where it is difficult to determine the actual injury suffered by the right owner or illegal income of an infringer, the People's Court shall apply, at the request of the interested party or within the capacity, the provision of Article 48, para. 2 of the *Copyright Law*, to the determination of the amount of damages. The People's Court, in determining the amount of damages, shall take account of the circumstances, such as the type of the work, reasonable royalty, nature of the infringing act or consequences of the infringement, and make a comprehensive determination."

Chapter 2: Determination of the Nature of a Work

infringement: The seven music videos involved in the case were played in the Holiday Karaoke Club operated by the Defendant, with a business area of 1427.5 m^2 and sixty-seven private rooms. The opening hours were from 8:00 to 2:00 the next day. (4) Reasonable expenses for investigating and stopping the infringement.

Therefore, the Court finally determined that the Defendant should pay for compensation in accordance with the standard of RMB 2,000 for each piece of work. Since *When a Wolf Loves a Sheep* was more popular, the court determined that the compensation standard for this work was RMB 3,000. So the total compensation for the Plaintiff's economic losses was RMB 15,000, while the reasonable expense was RMB 11,040.

In this case, the Plaintiff Huaxiajinma also claimed that the amount of compensation should be calculated in accordance with the standard of the China Audiovisual Copyright Collective Management Association, which is calculated based on the number of private rooms. The Court held that the standard of the China Audiovisual Copyright Collective Management Association was designed for collective management but not for a single song, thus such standard was not applicable.

During the hearing of this case, the Court received a letter from the China Audiovisual Copyright Collective Management Association, trying to persuade the Court to determine a less compensation. According to the opinion of the China Audiovisual Copyright Collective Management Association, some individual right owners, such as Huaxiajinma of this case, are reluctant to join in the copyright collective management organization, but decide to obtain benefits through commercial litigations. As a result, a large number of karaoke operators have been sued even after they had paid fees to the copyright collective management organization. Thus, those karaoke operators are no longer willing to continue paying fees. The China Audiovisual Copyright Collective Management Association believes that the Court should comprehensively consider the negative impact caused by such litigations, and that the karaoke operators that have already paid the royalties will be liable for less compensation to maintain the orders between the copyright collective management organizations and karaoke operators. That will promote the construction and development of copyright collective management system in China. This opinion seems reasonable: if all copyright owners join in the collective management organization, it will undoubtedly promote the development and growth of the organization. However, this opinion clearly violates the principle of "equality before the law." The copyright owners cannot be promoted to join the organization by lowering the compensation. The essence of the intellectual property system is to protect the interests of right owners. When the right owners try to defend their rights, judges should be more likely to be biased toward the right owners. The development of copyright collective management organizations should depend on factors such as the improvement of management systems and management skills for the copyright owners' interests, rather than requesting the courts to classify the amount of compensation.

—**Comments by XU Cui**

Case 6. The Nature of a Single Character from a Typeface Library and Its Copyright Protection

Beijing Founder Electronics. Co., Ltd. v. Guangzhou P&G Co., Ltd. and Beijing Carrefour Co.
Case of Copyright Infringement Dispute
Case Index: Beijing Founder Electronics. Co., Ltd. v. Guangzhou P&G Co., Ltd. and Beijing Carrefour Co.; Haidian District People's Court of Beijing, (2008) Hai Min Chu Zi No. 27047, December 2010 Judgment; Beijing No. 1 Intermediate People's Court, (2011) Yi Zhong Min Zhong Zi No. 5969, Judgment of July 5, 2011

Facts:

In this case, the Plaintiff, Beijing Founder Electronics Co., Ltd. (hereinafter, "Founder") designed and developed "Qianti," which is a specific typeface library of Chinese characters. Guangzhou P&G Co., Ltd. (hereinafter, "P&G") commissioned NICE, which was a design company, to design its product logo. Then NICE legitimately purchased Founder's Qianti typeface library and used the Chinese character "Piaorou" from the typeface to design the commodity logo of a shampoo produced by P&G. Founder asserted that although the design company purchased the Qianti typeface library, each character from the typeface constitutes an independent work of fine art. Since the user's agreement between Founder and users explicitly restricted the users' commercial use of the characters, P&G should have obtained a separate license from Founder, if it wants to use one of the characters in the logo of the commodity.

It is found that the users' license agreement is attached in the CD-ROM of the Founder's Qianti typeface, but the users do not need to click "yes" when installing the typeface library. The content of the agreement reads that: "This product cannot be copied, rented, or transmitted on the Internet, in whole or in part, without the written permission by Founder; It is forbidden to use all or part of the typeface library for republishing purposes (including but not limited to releases by TV, movie, picture, webpage, commercial printed matter, etc.); It is forbidden to embed any character of the typeface into portable documents (including but not limited to PDF or other formats); This product cannot be used in any network or multi-users environment unless all the users of the network have acquired the authorization." If the user requires exceeding the limits, he needs to contact Founder for the corresponding authorization.

Founder claimed that: After a large amount of creative work, Founder completed the typefaces of Founder Qianti typeface series. In the creation process, Founder's technical staff put a large amount of creative work into Qianti typeface. Each of these characters is created based on unique strokes, structures and sequences. It belongs to works of fine art which is protected by copyright law, and Founder enjoys the copyright for this typeface and every single character in it. P&G's unauthorized use of the character "Piaorou" in the packaging, logos, trademarks and advertisements of the products infringes the copyright of the Founder's. Carrefour sells products of infringing typefaces and should also be liable for the infringement. Accordingly, P&G shall cease the infringement and compensate the economic loss of RMB 500,000 and a reasonable expense of RMB 119,082; Carrefour shall stop selling the above infringing products; the two Defendants shall make public apology and eliminate the negative impact.

P&G argued that: Chinese characters belong to the public domain and are not the subject matter of copyright protection. They cannot be owned by anyone. The typeface in this case is a deductive work, which is based on the existing Chinese character typefaces with some certain design styles and features. Only the original elements created by Founder can enjoy copyright protection. However, there is little difference between the Qianti typeface and the typefaces from the public domain, thus the Qianti typeface is not qualified as a work under the copyright law. The mechanical process that is accomplished by technical means cannot create new and original works. Text is the main carrier of information transmission, and it is a tool with practical value. Its primary function is to convey feelings and emotions. Art appreciation is just a secondary function. The protection of typeface should be kept to an appropriate limit so as not to affect the primary function of texts that has been there for thousands of years. In addition, the design company purchased the typeface software of Founder and used it to design the product logo for P&G. Since P&G paid for the design, its behavior shall not be determined as copyright infringement. In summary, the claim of Founder shall be dismissed.

Carrefour argued that the products of P&G, which are sold by Carrefour, are all purchased through legitimate sources. Since the duty of care has been fulfilled, Carrefour does not infringe the copyright.

Ruling and Reasoning:

Haidian District People's Court of Beijing held that: The typeface and corresponding software of the typeface library developed by Founder are a collection of textual representations with certain originality. Founder has invested in intellectual creation, making the collection of aesthetic typefaces a certain degree of originality, in line with the characteristics of the works of fine art according to the *Copyright Law*, and shall be protected. The reproduction of the whole typeface library shall be determined as copyright infringement. However, typeface libraries are also industrial products which are the results of the implementation of preset rules. Only the unique style and digitized expression of the whole typeface library shall be protected by copyright. Therefore, the protection only covers the overall use of typeface library and the digital reproduction, where the single character cannot satisfy the requirement of the work of fine art. From the perspective of social effect, if it is determined as an infringement just because one character from a typeface library is similar to one character from another typeface library, then Chinese language can no longer maintain its function of communication. Such a conclusion is against the original purpose of copyright law. Therefore, there is insufficient legal basis for each character from a typeface library to enjoy the copyright of the work of fine art. According to Article 4 of the *Regulations on the Implementation of the Copyright Law*, the Court decided to dismiss all the claims by Founder.

Founder Appealed to Beijing No. 1 Intermediate People's Court

Beijing No. 1 Intermediate People's Court held that: Founder needs to prove all the following facts: (1) The character "Piaorou" in the case constitutes a work; (2) Founder is the copyright owner of the character "Piaorou"; (3) The act committed by P&G should be determined as copying the character "Piaorou"; (4) The act committed by P&G is unauthorized, neither by express or implied license. If any of the above facts are not proved successfully, then the claims by Founder shall not be supported.

After examining the elements of the case, the Court found that the behavior of P&G had been actually approved by Founder, which is the fourth fact. Therefore, regardless of the other three facts, P&G does not constitute copyright infringement.

The Court's determination was based on the key fact that the character "Piaorou" was designed by NICE, who is the owner of the Founder's "genuine" typefaces products. As the owner of the legitimate copy, NICE is entitled to use the specific characters from the Qianti typeface to make advertisement and allow its customers P&G to present the follow-up copy of its design results. Therefore, the alleged behavior carried out by P&G shall be deemed to be authorized by Founder. Correspondingly, the alleged behavior carried out by Carrefour was also deemed to be authorized by Founder.

The Court explained that NICE was implied licensed by Founder to carry out the above behavior. When someone legitimately purchases a copy of a carrier of intellectual property, he shall have the right to use it in a reasonably expectable manner, and such use shall be regarded as having been implied licensed by the right owner. In this case of typeface library, based on its essential function of communication, to display any the specific character on the computer screen shall be considered as a reasonable and expectable use and shall be determined as having been implied licensed by the copyright owner. In the case of typeface libraries of Chinese characters, if the copyright owner does not provide "clear, reasonable and effective" restrictions, the purchaser's subsequent use of displaying the characters on the screen belongs to the reasonable and expectable use. It shall be regarded as having been implied licensed by the right owner.

As to what kind of restrictions are reasonable restrictions, the court held that the division of products into personal (or home) and corporate versions according to the nature of the buyer to distinguish between commercial use and non-commercial use should generally be considered as reasonable restrictions. Whether or not other restrictions are reasonable depends on the circumstances. However, in principle, the characteristic of the instrumentality of Chinese characters should be considered, and the use of Chinese characters and the extensiveness of the scope of use should be taken into consideration. It must not cause unreasonable effects on the use behavior and interests of purchasers or the public through restrictions.

In this case, the Court held that both the use of the specific character of the typeface to design advertisement and the follow-up reproduction and distribution of

Chapter 2: Determination of the Nature of a Work

the advertisement were reasonable and expectable, and thus should be regarded as having been implied licensed by Founder. Despite that the users' agreement provided by Founder expresses to retain copyrights except "screen display" and "printout"; the agreement is compulsory to be ticked during installation. Since there is no evidence to prove that NICE agreed to sign the license agreement when installing the typeface product, it could not be determined that NICE accepted the restriction. In addition, since Founder did not classify the products of Qianti typeface into personal (or home) edition or enterprise edition, this sales model was sufficient to enable buyers for commercial purpose to reasonably believe that Founder did not restrict commercial use. Whereas buyers for commercial purpose will definitely include design companies such as NICE. For such buyers, the main purpose of their purchase is to use the specific characters to design and provide their design results to customers. This is their main business mode to obtain commercial benefits. If such use is forbidden, it will be difficult for such buyers to do business. Without any substantial value, this purchase will not achieve the reasonable expectations of the buyer. In view of this, the Court reasonably determined that the above restriction clause which excluded the buyer's main rights was not a reasonable contract clause.

In summary, NICE has the right to use the results of the "Piaorou" design of the specific characters in the Qianti typeface to provide P&G with follow-up reproduction and distribution. The alleged behavior by P&G and Carrefour should be regarded as a behavior that has been authorized by Founder, and the above behavior does not need to obtain another permission of Founder.

Therefore, in accordance with Article 153of the *Civil Procedure Law of China*, Beijing No. 1 Intermediate People's Court rejected the appeal and uphold the original judgment.

Commentary:

1. Whether a single character from a typeface library constitutes a work

Regarding whether a specific character in a character library constitutes a work, the existing views are generally divided into two categories, namely, that a single character constitutes or does not constitute a work. However, through the trial of the case, the author believes that the answer to this question under the existing copyright law framework in China should be based on the "specific form of the typeface library," but it cannot be generalized. No answer to this question is arbitrary and lacks factual basis without knowing exactly how the specific typeface is formed.

1.1 The situation in which a single character cannot constitute a work

If each character in the typeface is not written by the writer one by one, it is first written by the writer as part of the example character, and then the typeface maker, the strokes, the radicals, the positional relationship and the writing style of the example character are analyzed. Determine the standard, and under the guidance of this standard, design all the characters in the typeface, then the characters in such typefaces do not belong to the original intellectual achievements, not the object of copyright protection and cannot constitute works.

The reason why the author holds this view is that each character in this typeface is made up of "modularized points, tenders, and enamels, and other stroke parts, as if they were assembled from the same standard components."[26] For this type of typeface product, its creative work is reflected in the extraction and formulation of standards, rather than the final formation of specific characters. In the final formation of specific characters, the finisher can only be implemented in accordance with the standard. Even if it is done by different people, the resulting character will not be different in the form of expression. Because the specific characters in such typefaces can no longer reflect the differences and individualization of the intellectual achievements of different authors required by originality, the process of completion of specific characters based on specific criteria is not the original work of copyright requirements, and it is finally formed. The specific character does not belong to the category protected by copyright law.

1.2 The situation in which a single character constitutes a work

If the characters in the typefaces have the same style, but each of them is designed and modified by the designer, the characters in such typefaces belong to original intellectual achievements and are objects protected by copyright law. If such objects have "significant characteristics" in the expression of the characters and "significantly different from the existing ones," they can be deemed to have achieved a basic degree of originality and can be determined to constitute a work.

The characters in such typefaces constitute the object of copyright law protection, because for designers, even if they write the design according to the same style, it is impossible for each specific character they obtain to be completely consistent, even in different characters. Containing the same components, the design of the component will not be the same; therefore, whether it is written using traditional writing tools (such as Founder's static buds completely written by Xu Jinglei using the signature pen one by one).[27] It is also designed using tool software. The design of each specific character embodies the individuality and diversity of the designer's intellectual activities. Therefore, it is the result of the designer's original work. On this basis, because the copyright law clearly stipulates that calligraphy works belong to the category of fine artworks, each specific character in such a typeface is a work of fine art that protects objects in copyright law.

On this basis, the reason why the characters in the typeface only have "significant features" in the shape of the characters and are obviously different from the existing

---

26. *See* Wu Hongmei & Wu Fang, *Fundamentals of Font Design*, Guangxi Fine Arts Publishing House, 2009, p. 12. Quoted from Wang Kun, *On the Legal Issues of the Art Group, Intellectual Property Rights*, 5 (2011).
27. *See* "Interview Xu Jinglei Tan Jinglei," http://jaintizi.com/news/4.html, last accessed on Oct. 10, 2011.

"character shape" is that they basically reach a level of originality, taking into account the following factors:

- First, this requirement is in line with the legislator's legislative intent. The Interpretation of the Copyright Law of the People's Republic of China written by the legislature clearly states that "calligraphy generally refers to the art of writing Chinese characters with a brush." As it is known, compared to the pen writing instruments, Chinese characters written with a brush are more concerned with the use of pen and ink, the intensity of writing, and shading, which all lead to higher artistry and higher creative space. Despite the fact that current brushwork is not the main writing tool for Chinese characters in the current copyright law, the legislature still restricts calligraphy works mainly to brush calligraphy. This approach can reasonably be understood as a higher creative level for calligraphy works.
- Second, this requirement meets the essential requirements of the originality of the work. Originality requires that works be independently created by the author. The so-called independent creation means that before the creation of the work, it did not "reach into" and the work of the work constitutes a "substantial approximation." For calligraphy works with Chinese characters as their constituent elements, the inherent communicative functions of Chinese characters use such artists, and the number of people who use them and their length of time are unmatched by other works. The existence of this situation must make this possible. The creators of the works are more likely to "contact" other people's works than other types of works, and this can be realized with the general knowledge of the public. A judge can certainly recognize this as a member of the public. One point does not require the parties to provide another evidence. At the same time, because Chinese characters have been used for a long time and in large quantities, there is not much space for their creation. Therefore, in the case of existing large-scale Chinese characters, there are only "significant features" in the appearance of the characters. It is obviously different from the existing typefaces that it does not constitute a "substantial approximation" with the existing typefaces.

Again, this practice is in line with the principle of balance of interests. Although the copyright is a private right, the interests of the copyright owner cannot be absolutely protected. As a tool for people's daily communication, Chinese characters are bound to affect the public's use of Chinese characters if they do not set reasonable originality requirements. For example, if the originality of the characters in the typeface is too low, then a large number of characters in the typeface can be identified as constituting the work, which will result in the user not only needing to purchase the genuine typeface software for the multi-database, but when you use it again, you should still obtain permission from the copyright owner again. This situation obviously will greatly affect the use of Chinese characters. Obstructing people's normal exchanges is contrary to the legislative purpose of the copyright law to promote cultural development.

1.3 Character "Piaorou" of Qianti typeface library does not constitute a work

Adapting the above analysis to this case can be seen that judging whether the "Piaorou" involved in the case constitutes a work, it should first consider whether it belongs to the object protected by copyright law, that is, whether the Qianti typeface library belongs to a typeface library designed according to a certain standard. Judgment on this issue should be based on solid facts. Only when the 6,763 characters in the Qianti typeface library are verified and compared with each other, it is possible to determine whether each character is designed individually. And then to conclude whether it belongs to copyright law to protect the object. Although this practice can make a precise judgment as to whether it belongs to the object of copyright protection, it is undeniable that the identification of this fact takes a lot of time. From the standpoint of litigation economy, the court's task is to resolve disputes most efficiently under the existing legal framework. It is obviously not wise to verify such complicated facts in cases where disputes can be effectively resolved from other angles. Therefore, although the court has conducted a systematic understanding of the formation process of Qianti typefaces, and from the above understanding process, it can be basically confirmed that the Qianti typeface library is not assembled according to a certain standard, but the court does not have any. The formation process was investigated one by one, so the court ultimately held a rigorous attitude and did not determine whether it constituted the object of copyright protection.

However, the author believes that even if the Qianti typeface database can constitute the object of copyright law protection, it has not yet reached the basic originality level that should be achieved in the library. The author has pointed out in the previous article that only the glyphs of specific characters in a typeface can have a "significant feature" and "significantly different from the existing glyphs" before they can be identified as achieving the basic height of originality required by the work. However, it can be seen from the character "Piaorou" that it is only a conventional art typeface, which is not significantly different from the existing ones. It obviously does not reach the basic height of originality and does not constitute a work.

After the verdict of the second instance verdict was pronounced, there was a view that since the verdict was taken as the reason for implied permission; the implication was that the court had defaulted the character "Piaorou" to constitute the work. This understanding was indeed a misunderstanding of the verdict. The judgment did not mean this. The judgment in this case has clearly stated that as long as it does not meet any of the infringement requirements in the determination of infringement, it cannot be concluded that it constitutes infringement. When it is determined that the Defendant's use is an act of implied permission, the act obviously does not meet the infringement requirement of "unauthorized." Therefore, regardless of whether the right object claimed by the Plaintiff constitutes a work, it cannot constitute Infringement.

Chapter 2: Determination of the Nature of a Work

1.4 Considerations in the judgment that have not been identified from the perspective of the work

In the trial of this case, the author has been paying close attention to the opinions and viewpoints of the industry and academic circles on this case, and also clearly saw the urgent expectations of the outside world on this issue. However, the ultimate reason why the court failed to resolve the dispute in the case from the point of view of the work is mainly to hope that the verdict can not only solve the dispute in this case but also prevent the upcoming such disputes to the maximum extent and to take into account the principle of litigation economics. From the analysis above, it is obvious that if disputes are resolved from the perspective of the object of copyright protection, this means that in this case and in subsequent cases, it is necessary to first identify the formation process of all the characters in the typeface, which will inevitably lead to each case. The tedious inspection work must be carried out in China and it is not conducive to the litigation economy. On this basis, even if it can be determined that the characters in a particular typeface belong to the object protected by copyright law, it is inevitably necessary to consider whether or not it reaches a basic height of originality. However, original judgments are extremely individual cases. In this case, the court found that the character "Piaorou" in the case did not reach the original height, and did not mean that the characters in other typefaces did not reach the original height. This means that in the case of other such cases that may arise in the future, one must conduct original judgments one by one, which means that the judgment in this case will have lower guiding value for the subsequent cases. In this case, in the case where the court can use the implicit permission of this approach, which is more instructive for the subsequent case, the issue of the court's failure to design a design work is also a result of the court's trade-off.

2. Identification of implied permission behavior of purchasers of genuine typeface products

2.1 The principle of determining the intellectual property implied license

In the existing cases of intellectual property rights, there is very little recognition of implied licenses, and perhaps because of this, the use of the principle of implied license in this case has caused such a big debate. In the judgment of this case, it was pointed out that if the right holder's sales act would enable the purchaser to objectively believe that the infringer did not prohibit the purchaser from using the intellectual property subject of its ownership in a specific way, thus reasonably expecting the exercise of this right, the above used method shall be deemed to have been implicitly permitted by the owner of the intellectual property rights, and the purchaser will not be required to obtain additional licenses.

The author believes that the implied license in this case fully complies with the basic principles of modern civil law (i.e., the principle of affirmation and fairness of meaning). The determination of implied license, in essence, is the identification of the right holder's meaning. In modern civil law, the determination of the parties' true intentions is based on the principle of the intentional expression of the person's actions: from the point of view of the general public, an objective analysis of the behavior is performed to infer its true meaning, rather than absolute meaning in his heart.[28] The specific case of intellectual property rights depends on the meaning of the general public's inference from the right holder's sales behavior, rather than the right of the right holder. If the right holder's sales conduct will make the buyer objectively believe that the right holder does not prohibit the purchaser from using the intellectual property object it carries on in a specific way (i.e., the judgment of the effect of the right holder on the expression of the effect, rather than the meaning of the inner effect judgment), so as to produce a reasonable expectation of the exercise of this right, the above-mentioned expected behavior is the content of the meaning expressed by the right holder's expression.

The above points of view are consistent with the basic principle of fairness in civil law, while complying with the principle of meaning and recognition. In practice, any purchaser pays for the purchase of a product, usually because the consideration is exchanged for the use value of the product that he reasonably expects when purchasing. The reasonable expectation that the purchaser produces is also a reasonable explanation based on the expression of the meaning of the sales behavior.

If an extra price is needed to pay for the expected behavior, the original purchase will be meaningless. Such results will jeopardize the interests of the buyer, which is unfair and against the market order.

2.2 General recognition principle of implied license for Chinese character typeface products

Taking into account the characteristics of the Chinese character typeface products, the author believes that the following behaviors are reasonably expected to be used by buyers of typeface typefaces and should be regarded as the implicit permission of the copyright owner:

(1) The behavior of calling specific characters in the typeface on the computer screen.
(2) The purchaser makes a reasonable "subsequent use" of the specific characters displayed on the screen, unless the copyright owner has made clear, reasonable and effective restrictions.

Subsequent use of behavior includes both noncommercial and commercial use. The commercial use behavior includes both the purchaser's use of specific characters in the typeface within its internal scope (such as the editing of documents on the computer in the business process, the behavior of advertisement design for the customer, etc.), and also includes buyers use their results of subsequent reuse (such as

---

28. Participating in Liang Huixing, *The General Theory of Civil Law*, Law Press, 2007, p. 172.

publicly displaying edited documents, allowing advertising design results to allow advertisers to make subsequent reuse, etc.).

The reason why the author holds this view is based on the following considerations:

- First of all, Chinese character typeface products are mainly functional tools and supplemented by aesthetic functions.

  Chinese character typeface products are products designed according to national standards. Designs based on national standards are usually only industrial products suitable for mass production, and may not be pure artwork. Therefore, Chinese character typeface products must have practical functions as a Chinese character tool. Of course, this does not deny that Chinese character typeface products may also have aesthetic functions. The reason why the purchaser chooses between different typeface products is precisely the difference in the beauty of different typeface products. However, it should be noted that even for a Chinese character typeface product with distinctive features and high artistry, the purchaser's first consideration when buying is the instrumentality rather than its aesthetic function. If the purchaser simply wants to enjoy visual aesthetics, he or she will choose to purchase a calligraphy work in the usual sense, instead of a Chinese character typeface product. It can be seen that Chinese character typeface products are mainly functional tools and supplemented by aesthetic functions.
- Second, because the typeface product is mainly based on practical functions, the main purpose of any purchaser to purchase the product is to use it. Therefore, the normal and reasonable use of Chinese characters belongs to the reasonably expected usage behavior of the purchaser of the typeface. Obviously, the above methods of use are all normal and reasonable ways for the public to use Chinese characters. Therefore, all of them are reasonably expected to be used by buyers.

Again, the purchaser's above-mentioned use behavior is a reasonably expected use behavior and does not mean that the right holder cannot explicitly limit the purchaser's subsequent use behavior. If the owner of the typeface product has a "clear and reasonable" restriction on this, and the purchaser has accepted this restriction, it shall be deemed that the subsequent use behavior does not belong to the reasonably expected use behavior of the purchaser.

As to which restriction is "clear and reasonable," it should be determined according to the specific circumstances. In principle, the characteristics of the instrumentality of Chinese characters should be considered, and the use of Chinese characters and the extensiveness of the scope of use should be taken into consideration. Unreasonable impact on the use behavior and interests of buyers or the public. At the same time, this restriction should also be made clear to the purchaser before the product is purchased, so that the purchaser can decide whether to continue his purchase if he knows the content of the restriction.

For example, if the right holder divides the product into the personal version and the enterprise version to distinguish between commercial use and noncommercial use behavior, it is generally difficult to determine the use behavior if the user of the personal version purchases the commercial use behavior. It is a reasonably expected use behavior. This is because this restriction is more "clear and reasonable." On the other hand, the buyer is aware of the restriction at the time of purchase and decides to continue purchasing in this case. It should be bound by this restriction. However, if the right holder does not impose any restrictions on the sale, but in the installation process after the sale of the product, the user must be forced to agree to the restrictions in the license agreement, and the restrictions on the commercial use of the user is prohibited, In this case, because the restriction clause does not inform the user in advance, and the clause is difficult to be identified as a reasonable restriction clause, it will be difficult for the user to restrict it.

2.3 Determination of the implied license of Founder Qianti typeface product in this case

Specifically, in this case, the character "Piaorou" used by P&G was commissioned by NICE to use the genuine Founder typeface product design. Therefore, whether P&G copied and distributed the word "Piaorou" could be recognized as a result of Founder. The key to the use of company licenses lies in whether or not NICE's commercial use of the words in the company's words has been implicitly licensed by Founder. Considering the following factors, NICE's behavior should be regarded as an implied license of Founder.

First of all, the product involved in the Qianti typeface does not distinguish between the enterprise version and the personal version. This practice makes the product "commercial use" a use behavior that the purchaser reasonably expects. Whereas commercial buyers will of course include design companies like NICE, for such buyers, the main purpose of their purchase is to use the specific words in the product to design and provide their design results to customers for subsequent use. If it is forbidden to implement the above-mentioned behaviors, or if its customers are required to obtain the permission of Founder in the subsequent use of their design results, it is difficult for such buyers to conduct business operations as a tool, and the products will not with actual value, this purchase will not achieve the reasonably expected benefits of the purchaser. In this regard, rights holders are clearly aware.

Second, the restriction clauses in the user license agreement of the Qianti typeface product concerned cannot restrict the use behavior of the purchaser. Some people think that there is a clear licensing agreement in the Founder CD-ROM and a clear authorization for the usage and scope of the typeface library. It explicitly prohibits commercial use such as re-issuance. Therefore, there is no implied license. [29] In this regard, the author believes that although the user license agreement for the Sci-Tech typeface product only permits users to "screen display" and "print out" specific words

---

29. *See* "Font Industry Faces 'Model Crisis,'" http://www.eb.com.cn/1634427/20110722/246203.html, last accessed on Nov. 28, 2011.

in the typeface, they have made reservations about other commercial use behaviors. However, as far as the facts involved are concerned, the restriction clause cannot play the above restriction. The main reason is not merely whether the above restrictions are "reasonable" yet to be explored. What's more important is that it does not disclose the above-mentioned restrictions to buyers at the time of purchase. This means that the purchaser is not aware of the above restrictions. At this time, it is obviously unfair to limit the reasonable expectations of the purchaser at the time of purchase if the purchaser's "post-awareness" restriction clause is used. In addition, even if it is not considered whether this fact is explicitly stated in advance, because the user license agreement of the product involved in the Qianzi typeface is not required to be installed at the time of installation, NICE cannot agree to be bound by the restriction clause.

In summary, NICE has the right to use the results of the "Piaorou" design of the specific word "Liupu" in the product in question to provide P&G with subsequent reproduction and distribution. In this case, P&G Co., Ltd. copied and distributed the alleged infringement. The behavior of the product should also be regarded as an act authorized by Founder and no separate approval from Founder is required.

2.4 Considerations for the use of implicit permission theory in judgments

As mentioned in the previous article, if disputes are resolved from the point of view of a recognized work, this may result in uneconomical litigation and restrict the resolution of this case to individual cases. However, if you use the existing implicit license, the situation is obviously different. In accordance with this principle, the use of genuine product purchasers can be considered to belong to the scope of implied licenses in most cases, which means that a considerable proportion of allegations of infringement against genuine typeface product buyers can be excluded. It is possible to avoid a large number of disputes in the future.

3. Other considerations in the trial of this case

The author hereby wishes to stress that the handling of this case is based on a large number of investigations and studies, and after careful consideration, in addition to the factors already described in the previous article; the following factors have also played a certain role in the conclusion of this case.

First of all, it is an international mainstream practice to protect the words in the typeface from copyright law.

According to the author's investigation, although the respective perspectives adopted are different, the existing major countries or regions do not basically provide copyright protection for the words in the typeface. This research result has also been confirmed by Beijing Founder. In the process of hearing the case, despite repeated requests, the materials submitted by Beijing Founder failed to prove that there existed legislative and judicial cases in which the copyright protection of the words in the typeface was carried out in various countries. Of course, I also do not think that the practices adopted by other countries will necessarily suit China, but it cannot be denied that when an approach is adopted by most major countries or regions, it can also explain the rationality of this approach to a certain extent. In addition, the author has always believed that the protection of intellectual property rights is to a large extent a tool of protection in developed countries. As a developing country, China's protection level of intellectual property should not be higher than the general international level, especially for those with the weakest regional characteristics of copyright protection. Even more so, it will do more harm than good. In the case of typeface products, if copyright protection is provided for words in Chinese typefaces products, it is bound to protect Western typefaces, and the number of Western typeface products is several times or even several times that of Chinese typefaces products. This protection result obviously will have a greater impact on the general public.

Second, there is no inevitable link between the protection of the copyright protection provided by the word in the typeface and the development of the typeface industry.

Typefaces companies have always advocated that the protection of the words in the typeface will not directly affect the development of the typeface industry in China. However, the author does not agree with this. On the one hand, because the typeface database company does not provide sufficient data support for this, on the other hand, because if this view is established, it can be reasonably inferred that for countries that do not provide single-word copyright protection. It will be difficult to have a well-developed typeface industry. However, according to relevant statistics, the U.S. typeface company Mona Corporation's annual revenue exceeds USD 100 million. [30] However, U.S. copyright law explicitly excludes the words in typefaces products from the protection object of copyright; Japan and South Korea also do not protect single words. Cases, but the developments of their typeface companies are far stronger than our country. From this it can be seen that the profitability of the typeface store company is not directly related to whether or not to provide the protection of the word in the typeface. In fact, the typeface company itself also admits that the status quo in China's typeface industry is mainly caused by piracy, rather than the free use of end users. Taking "static buds" as an example, genuine software only sold more than 2,000 sets, but there are hundreds of thousands of pirated copies on the market. The status quo of the industry is that the market share of genuine typefaces is still less than 0.01%. And if all typeface design companies can get 5% of the typeface market, the company can operate normally.[31] However, it is clear that by limiting the use of words by end users, piracy cannot be solved.

Third, protecting the words in the typeface provides copyright protection will greatly affect the public's use of the text.

If the end-user is provided copyright protection using the words in the typeface, the inevitable consequence is that any user must first consider whether the typeface is a work when using computer typefaces and whether the typeface should be authorized by the copyright owner. Due to the popularity and practicality of computers, computer

---

30. See "The Font Factory Struggles for Piracy," http://news.hexun.com/2011-04-20/128905003. html, last accessed on Nov. 28, 2011.
31. See "Piracy, National Character Industry Urgently Needed Protection," http://tech.ifeng.com/internet/detail_2011_03/31/5488903_0.shtml, last accessed on Nov. 28, 2011.

typeface products have become an essential word processing tool for people. Therefore, the above results will affect all aspects of the use of words by the public, including both the commercial use of the company and the use behavior of individual users. Undoubtedly, it will seriously affect the communication function of Chinese characters.

Although the typeface company stated that the public can use the typeface products that have entered the public domain, but in the current copyright law system, even for judges, it is not easy for them to point out which typeface has been in the public domain. Therefore, it is reasonable that ordinary people are not able to distinguish. Therefore, it is required to judge whether a certain typeface has entered the public domain before using any typeface, and it is objectively completely inoperable, and the result can only make the user at a loss.

Finally, providing no copyright protection for the words in the typeface does not mean that there is no legal protection for the typeface products. The interests of the typeface library can be remedied through the protection of other laws.

Although it is more appropriate to consider not providing copyright protection to the words in the typeface in consideration of the public interest, it goes without saying that the development of each typeface product has taken a lot of manpower and financial resources of the typeface library company, according to the current national standard typeface development standards. The number of words in each typeface is at least 6,673 Chinese characters and no more than 21,000 Chinese characters at most. Typefaces companies of course have the right to obtain corresponding benefits based on their input. As for how to better protect the interests of the typeface companies, the author believes that the biggest problem affecting the development of the typeface library industry is the prevalence of piracy, and the most effective method of protection against piracy problems is to provide overall protection for the typeface library products. This protection method is precisely the practice adopted by some countries. Therefore, under the existing legal framework of our country, it is more appropriate for the regulation of such infringements to be the good faith clause of Article 2 of the Anti-Unfair Competition Law to determine that piracy violates the principle of good faith and constitutes unfair competition.

—**Comments by RUI Songyan**

Case 7. The Nature of Dispensatory and Its Possible Copyright Protection

Shaanxi Jinfang Pharmaceutical Co., Ltd. v. Jinan Sanyouli Biotechnology Co., Ltd. Case of Patent Right and Copyright Infringement as well as Unfair Competition Dispute
Case Index: *Shaanxi Jinfang Pharmaceutical Co., Ltd. v. Jinan Sanyouli Biotechnology Co., Ltd.*; Jinan Intermediate People's Court of Shandong, Ji Zhi Chu Zi [2001] No. 31; Shandong Higher People's Court Lu Min San Zhong Zi [2001] No. 3, January 30, 2002

Facts:

The Plaintiff, Xi'an Hi-tech Shaanxi Jinfang Pharmaceutical Co., Ltd. (hereinafter, "Jinfang Pharmaceutical") alleged that: Zhao Cunmei, the deputy general manager and chief engineer of the Plaintiff, has the patented invention of ZL94113652.3 Shuangcuotai effervescent tablets and its preparation method. Since August 15, 2000, this patent right has been assigned to the Plaintiff by Zhao Cunmei. The Defendant, Jinan Sanyouli Biotechnology Co., Ltd. (hereinafter, "Sanyouli Company") produced and sold XinTing Shuangcuotai Vaginal effervescent tablets that covered the Plaintiff's claims of patent right without the Plaintiff's authorization, therefore constituted the infringement of patent right. The Plaintiff has the copyright of his own directions for use of Shuangcuotai effervescent tablet. However, the Defendant plagiarizes the above directions for use to apply to the product of the same category without the Plaintiff's authorization, therefore constituted the infringement of the Plaintiff's copyright. The trade name, Shuangcuotai, was a unique name of a well-known commodity several to the Plaintiff, however, the Defendant used this name to produce and sell the product of the same category without authorization, and assaulted the Plaintiff's market by dumping at bottom price, which constituted unfair competition and caused huge economic losses to the Plaintiff. Hence, the Plaintiff requested the court to order that: The Defendant shall cease the patent right and copyright infringement as well as the act of unfair competition. Also, the Defendant shall make an apology and compensate for a loss of RMB 1.8 million. The Defendant, Sanyouli Company argued that: the Plaintiff, not being the patentee of the patent in this case, was not eligible to be a party to this case; Shuangcuotai was a name which had been used in prior product, prior patent and trademark that registered before, so the Plaintiff's claim that his product was well-known departed from actual realities. The Defendant did not sell commodities at a price lower than cost, not alone aim to push competitors aside. Therefore, the Defendant requested to dismiss the claims of patent infringement and unfair competition of the Plaintiff. The product description of the Plaintiff consisted of two parts. The first part was content related to the medicine attribute, including the name, main ingredients, pharmacodynamics, indication symptom, and usage and dosage while the second part was pictures and characters above the description. The above-mentioned second part had nothing in common with the Defendant's description, while the first part was the content which all statutory medicine descriptions shall be annotated and reflected medicine attribute objectively and faithfully. This part was completed by the Defendant independently through the reference to the pharmacopeia and its content reflected medicine attribute. This part of the Plaintiff's description was almost the same with the record of pharmacopeia and prior description by others, and it did not include intellectual creation with originality of the Plaintiff, so it did not have ingredient of a work under copyright and did not belong to a work under the protection of copyright.

In the first instance, Jinan Intermediate People's Court, after the trial, made the following findings that: On December 9, 1994, Zhao Cunmei applied for grant for a patent for invention of Shuangcuotai effervescent tablets and its preparation method to National Patent Office, and obtained the authorization on April 9, 1998. The patent number was ZL94113652.3, and the inventor and patentee is Zhao Cunmei. On August 15, 2000, Zhao Cunmei made a statutory declaration that: the patented invention of ZL94113652.3 belongs to service invention, and its intellectual property pertains to the Plaintiff. On May 9, 2001, the notary office in Baoji city, Shaanxi notarized the above declaration through Bao Zheng Zi [2001] No. 944 certification. On July 4, 2001, the copy of ZL94113652.3 patent register from State Intellectual Property Office indicated that: the current patentee of the patent is Zhao Cunmei. Both the product descriptions submitted by the Plaintiff and the Defendant can be divided into two parts. The first part being at the top of the description shows their trade name, trademark, and registration number, and the second part was at the bottom of the description, all of which were the content related to medicine attribute, including the product's name, main ingredients, pharmacodynamics, indication symptom, and usage and dosage. On February 26, 1993, Jinzhou Pharmaceutical Factory No. 5 applied to register trademark "Shuangcuotai" to the State Administration for Commodity Inspection, and obtained ratification on May 21, 1994. Its Wei Yao Zhun Zi [90] No. X-108 medicine name was "Shuangcuotai Plug." On August 30, 1993, Yan Shan Factory, the branch of Jinzhou Pharmaceutical Factory No. 2, applied for grant for a patent for invention of Shuangcuotai Paste and its preparation method to National Patent Office, and obtained the authorization on October 11, 1997 and the patent number was ZL93115777.3.

Jinan Intermediate People's Court held that: according to patent laws, for the infringement of the patent right without the authorization of patentee, the patentee or the party interested shall file a lawsuit to people's court. Hence, the proper Plaintiff of patent infringement lawsuit is patentee or party interested. Although Zhao Cunmei has made a declaration to assign the patent right to the Plaintiff, which was notarized, the parties did not register and announce the assignment of patent right in National Patent Office. Therefore, the Plaintiff did not have sufficient evidence to bring a lawsuit of patent infringement. According to Regulation for the Implementation of the Copyright Law of China, the work under copyright refers to literary, artistic or scientific intellectual creation which has originality and is able to be reproduced, that is, the work under the protection of copyright shall be original and reproductive. Combining the requirements of the pharmaceutical administration regulations of China on directions to use a medicine, and comparing directions for use of medicine of the same category, Shuangcuotai effervescent tablets' direction for use of the Plaintiff, Jinfang Pharmaceutical is not original, so it does not belong to a work under the protection of copyright. According to Anti-Unfair Competition Law, operators shall not use the unique name of a well-known commodity, causing confusion with other operators' well-known commodities, and mislead buyers that it is that well-known commodity;

operators shall not sell commodities at a price lower than their cost with the express purpose of pushing competitors aside. Otherwise, it shall constitute unfair competition. Before the Plaintiff, Jinfang Pharmaceutical used the trade name "Shuangcuotai," others had already used it in prior product, prior patent, and prior trademark, hence, the Plaintiff's claim that "Shuangcuotai" was a unique name for its well-known commodity did not come into being. The Plaintiff alleged that the Defendant made unfair competition through dumping commodities at a low price; however, he did not provide relative evidence to substantiate that his claim was established. In summary, the Plaintiff, Jinfang Pharmaceutical's claims of infringement of patent right and copyright as well as unfair competition are lack of either sufficient evidence or valid reason. The court ruled that: the claims of the Plaintiff, Xi'an Hi-tech Shaanxi Jinfang Pharmaceutical Co., Ltd. were dismissed. Jinfang Pharmaceutical Company filed an appeal during legal time limit. He requested to recall a judgment of the original jurisdiction and supported his claims in the first instance.

Ruling and Reasoning:

In the second instance, Shandong Higher People's Court, after the trial, made the following findings that: On December 9, 1994, Zhao Cunmei applied for grant for a patent for invention of Shuangcuotai effervescent tablets and its preparation method to National Patent Office, and obtained the authorization on April 9, 1998. The patent number was ZL94113652.3, and the inventor and patentee is Zhao Cunmei. The statement abstract in this patent's description is that: this invention involves a new antimicrobial and antiphlogistic medicine "Shuangcuotai" effervescent tablets and its preparation method. Each effervescent tablet contains metronidazole, clotrimazole, chlorhexidine acetate, and the ingredients of an effervescent agent. This ingredient of effervescent agent contains sodium carbonate, citric acid, boric acid and starch, and it also contains tween. The tablet of this invention is prepared by separating the above-mentioned raw ingredient into alkaline composition A and acidic composition B and making them into granules respectively, and then tableting them after mixing two granules. The patent claim of this patent is consisted of three parts. The first part is the title of invention and its recipe, the second part is main features of this invention, and the third part is the preparation of this invention. On July 10, 2001, in the statement relating to the ownership of patent that Zhao Cunmei submitted to the original court, she made a declaration the exclusive assignee of this patented invention was Xi'an Hi-tech Shaanxi Jinfang Pharmaceutical Co., Ltd. On November 19, 2001, the copy of ZL94113652.3 patent register from State Intellectual Property Office indicated that: the current patentee on this patent is Xi'an Hi-tech Shaanxi Jinfang Pharmaceutical Co., Ltd., and the registration date for the transferring the patent is October 18, 200.

In addition, Shandong Higher People's Court also made the following findings that: At the top of description of the appellate, Jinfang Pharmaceutical Company, there is a phase "only once per day, broad spectrum, instant, and high efficiency." The pharmacological effect is that: this medicine is developed from ingredients recipe as well as three drugs including metronidazole inhibiting and killing anaerobes, trichomonas, and amoeba, clotrimazole which inhibits and kills fungus, chlorhexidine acetate which inhibits and kills aerobes. Antimicrobial experiments and clinical studies have confirmed that the various components of this medicine in the efficacy maintain every drug's effect of inhibiting and killing the biological activity of bacteria, fungus and trichomonas, and they also have synergistic therapeutic effects, especially effective for mixed infection. Matters need attention: (1) during the treatment period, the patient should take a bath frequently, and frequently change his clothing and other Articles of daily use, shoes, and socks in order to improve the curative effect; (2) generally, sex partner should receive treatment at the same time; (3) very few patients have a feeling of vaginal burning but do not affect curative effect; (4) during the use, very few patients have pain, which is because the vagina, particularly the vulva, has heavy infection and the mucous membranes have been damaged. It is recommended to adhere to medication or suspension of use. At the bottom of description of the appellee, Sanyouli Company, there is a phrase "broad spectrum, instant, high efficiency, and convenient." The effect is that: this medicine is developed from Chinese medicine and ingredients recipe and three drugs including metronidazole of amoeba inhibiting and killing anaerobes and trichomonas, clotrimazole which inhibits and kills fungus, chlorhexidine acetate which inhibits and kills aerobes. Antimicrobial experiments and clinical studies have confirmed that the various components of this medicine in the efficacy maintain every drug's effect of inhibiting and killing the biological activity of bacteria, fungus and trichomonas, and they also have synergistic therapeutic effects, especially effective for mixed infection. Matters need attention: (1) during the treatment period, the patient should change and wash his underwear frequently; (2) generally, sex partner should receive treatment at the same time; (3) very few patients have a feeling of vaginal burning but do not affect curative effect; (4) during the use, very few patients have pain, which is because the vagina, particularly the vulva, has heavy infection and the mucous membranes have been damaged. It is recommended to adhere to medication or suspension of use; (5) the patient suffering from elderly vaginal dryness should not use it; (6) pregnant women use it with caution. The pharmacological part of "Shuangcuotai Plug" from Jinzhou Pharmaceutical Factory No. 5 is that: this medicine is developed from three drugs including metronidazole inhibiting and killing anaerobes, trichomonas, and amoeba, chlorhexidine acetate which inhibits and kills aerobes as well as clotrimazole which inhibits and kills mold. In vitro and clinical studies have confirmed that the various components of this medicine in the efficacy maintain every drug's effect of inhibiting and killing the biological activity of bacteria, fungus and trichomonas, and they also have synergistic therapeutic effects, especially effective for mixed infection. Also, in the second instance, the appellate provided sales invoice for the appellee's products in several places, such as Shenyang, Qinhuangdao and Shenzhen, and their prices range from RMB 3.5 to RMB 18. The other findings made by Shandong Higher People's Court were consistent with that of the original jurisdiction.

Shandong Higher People's Court held that: regarding whether the appellee constituted an infringement of the appellant's patent right, the appellate lacked the right proof when he filed an appeal, so it was appropriate for the court to dismiss his claims in the first instance. Since the appellate had no standing of subject of procedure to this infringement of patent, whether the appellate constituted an infringement of the patent of the appellee shall no longer be tried. As to whether the appellant constituted an unfair competition against the appellant, Jinzhou Pharmaceutical Factory No. 5 and Yan Shan Factory, the branch of Jinzhou Pharmaceutical Factory No. 2 had used the trade name "Shuangcuotai" in products, paten right and trademark before the appellate used it. Therefore, the claims of the appellate that "Shuangcuotai" was a unique name for his well-known products were not formed. The invoice, given when the appellee sold his products, provided by the appellate was not sufficient to prove that the appellee dumped at a low price and caused damage on the appellate, so the claims of the appellate that the products of the appellee dumped at a low price and caused unfair competition were not supported. As to the claims of the appellate that the appellee did not get the registration number for producing medicine and selling nondrugs as medicines, which was beyond the trial of this case, it shall be investigated and dealt with by the relevant medical administrative department.

As to whether the appellee constituted an infringement of the copyright of the dispensatory for use of the appellate, comparing the dispensatory for use of the appellate and that of the appellate, it shall be found that both were basically the same in terms of pharmacological effects, indications, adverse reactions, and precautions, so it shall be confirmed that the product description of the appellee copied the dispensatory for use of the appellate. However, according to Article 3 of *Copyright Law of the People's Republic of China* and Article 2 of *Regulations for the Implementation of the Copyright Law of the People's Republic of China*, a work protected by copyright shall be literary, artistic or scientific intellectual creation which has originality and is able to be reproduced. That is to say, a work can only be protected by copyright if it is original and replicable. From the dispensatory for use of the appellate, its format strictly observed the stipulations of the pharmaceutical administration regulations of China on the format of dispensatory for use. Its pharmacological effects and precautions were all objective descriptions of medicine attributes, and it lacked originality in text combination, while the advertising language "broad spectrum, instant, and high efficiency" failed to highlight the characteristics that were obviously different from other pharmaceutical advertisements. Meanwhile, the dispensatory for use of the appellate was not original after comparing it with the direction for use of "Shuangcuotai" of Jinzhou Pharmaceutical Factory No. 5. Hence, the claims of the appellate that his dispensatory for use enjoyed copyright lacked sufficient evidence, and the court did not support his above claims.

In summary, the claims of the appellate that the appellee constituted an infringement of his patent right and copyright as well as constituted the unfair competition lacked sufficient evidence, so his claims did not support. In the first instance, the court's adoption of facts was clear, the laws applied were correct, and the judgment result is appropriate. Therefore, the claims were dismissed and the original judgment was affirmed.

Commentary:

This case is a dispute involving three types of infringements: patent infringement, unfair competition, and copyright infringement, which is very complicated. This article is focusing on the copyright of dispensatory for use. One of the key issues if that whether the Defendant constituted an infringement of the copy of dispensatory for use of the Plaintiff, and the premise to solve this problem is to figure out that whether dispensatory for use is under the protection of copyright.

1. Different opinions on whether medicine description shall be protected by copyright in China's juridical practice

In recent years, with the modernization and nationalization of the biopharmaceutical industry, the competition in the pharmaceutical market has become more intense, and the awareness of drug manufacturers to protect their intellectual property right has been strengthened. Besides the traditional protection strategies for patents, trademarks, trade secrets and technical secrets, copyright has increasingly become a strategy for drug companies to seek competition in this industry. Disputes over copyright of medicine description have become a new issue in China's jurisdiction of intellectual property. Due to different interpretations of copyright originality standards and the attribute of drug descriptions, different courts gave completely different answers.

In this case, both courts of different levels in Shandong did not support Jinfang Pharmaceutical Company's claims that his medicine description enjoyed copyright; in the dispute that Xiangbei Wellman Pharmaceutical Co., Ltd sued Suzhou Erye Pharmaceutical Co., Ltd. for the latter infringing the copyright of dispensatory for use, both courts of different levels in Changsha city held that Suzhou Erye Pharmaceutical Co., Ltd. constituted an infringement of the copyright of medicine description of Xiangbei Wellman Pharmaceutical Co., Ltd.; in the dispute that Xiangbei Wellman Pharmaceutical Co., Ltd. sued Hongxing Pharmaceutical Co., Ltd. in Foshan City, Guangdong for the latter infringing the copyright, the court held that the medicine description was inappropriate to be identified as a work under the protection of copyright, so there is no act of constituting an infringement of copyright. Therefore, the claims of Xiangbei Wellman Pharmaceutical Co., Ltd. were dismissed. The three cases represent two different views on the copyright of medicine description in current juridical practice in China, that is: negative theory and positive theory.

The negative theory held that: the medicine description, a description of the drug's objective attribute, was written by strictly observing the requirements of the pharmaceutical administration regulations of China on the format of dispensatory for use. The medicine description has no originality in expression, so it shall not constitute a work making sense to copyright. The reason is as follows: whether a work has originality or not is a premise to decide whether it shall be a work making sense to copyright and under the protection of the copyright. Since the medicine description has no originality, it need not be protected by copyright. According to Article 3[32] of *Drug Instruction and Label Management Regulations* of State Food and Drug Administration, the content of medicine description shall be ultimately examined and approved by the State Food and Drug Administration before it shall be used, so the medicine description is not completed by the registrant for drug declaration or the producer of research and development alone. According to Article 9[33] of *Drug Instruction and Label Management Regulations,* The State Food and Drug Administration has strict stipulations and restrictions on the content, format, and writing requirements of medicine descriptions, and the power to decide whether they need to revise or how to revise the content is in the State Food and Drug Administration, so the drafter of medicine description almost has no chance and power to create. Therefore, it is very difficult to have originality in the medicine description itself, so it does not fall under the protection of copyright.

The positive theory held that: the medicine description itself does not belong to administrative documents and the medicine description which contains the experimental process of the medicine and experimental data that belongs to unique intellectual creation shall be under the protection of copyright.

2. Reasons for different views

The differences in the understanding of whether medicine description is under the protection of copyright stem from the following reasons: first, the uncertainty of the stipulation on the standard of a work in copyright; second the uniqueness that the medicine description itself is different from ordinary works.

2.1 Uncertainty of the originality standards of Chinese copyright

The key to judge whether a work constitutes a work making sense to copyright and under the protection of copyright is to figure out whether it has the originality required by copyright, that is, the substantive standard of a work.

The uncertainty of the substantive standard of a work, namely, the originality of a work, is the causa sine qua non to lead to different view on the adoption of works' standard in juridical practice. Although originality is viewed as a substantive standard for constituting a work making sense to copyright in the interpretation of countries of Anglo-American Law and civil law system, international covenant, and World Intellectual Property Organization, there is considerable controversy over the meaning of originality both in theory and legislation and juridical practice because countries have different specific circumstances, different philosophical and historical foundation for legislation. Taking "Commercial Copyright Theory" as philosophical foundation for legislation, countries of Anglo-American Law hold that the essence of copyright system

---

32. In *Drug Instruction and Label Management Regulations,* Art. 3 clarifies that the instruction and label shall be examined and approved by State Food and Drug Administration.
33. In *Drug Instruction and Label Management Regulations,* Art. 9 clarifies that: Drug descriptions should contain important scientific data, conclusions, and information on the safety and efficacy of drugs to guide the patient to use it safely and rationally. The specific format, content, and writing requirements of medicine description are formulated and published by the State Food and Drug Administration.

is to protect the asset value of a work, and "works worth replicating are also worth protecting." Legislation focuses on promoting the creation and dissemination of new works by stimulating people's investment in the creation of works, expecting little on works' originality, and it stipulates originality as that the works shall be "investments of work, skill or capital."[34] Just as the British judge Peterson pointed out that: the copyright, not requiring that the expression shall be novel, only requires that the work is not plagiarism of the other work and is created by the author independently.[35] Federal Supreme Court of the U.S. also established "independent completion" as the standard for judging the originality of works through the case of *Bleistein v. Donald Lithographing Co.*[36] in 1903. The copyright of civil law countries takes personality values as philosophical foundation for its legislation, makes the protection of the author's interest as the center and starting point and uses "Author right" to definite copyright.[37] The aim of legislation of copyright is, though protecting copyright, to encourage people to employ their creation to engage in intellectual activity with creation. For instance, Article 2 of *Copyright Law* of Germany clarifies that a work shall be the intellectual creation with originality of individual, which emphasizes the factor of "intellectual creation with originality" of a work, and a work shall constitute a work making sense to copyright and be under the protection of copyright only when its creation reach some level. With the development of international communication and cooperation, countries of Anglo-American Law gradually raise their requirements on originality, while civil law countries lower their requirements on that by take relatively flexible approaches step by step. The interpretation of originality of World Intellectual Property Organization is more consistent with that of Anglo-American Law, and it points out that: works protected by copyright must be original works. The thoughts reflected in the works are not required as new ones, but their literary and artistic expressions must be created by the authors for the first time. They are not plagiarized at all or basically not from another works, and they shall originate from the author's labor.[38]

According to Article 3 of the *Copyright Law* and Article 2 of the *Regulations for the Implementation of the Copyright Law,* a work under copyright shall take originality as substantive standard, which is consistent with the stipulation of countries of both Anglo-American Law and civil law system and the interpretation of World Intellectual Property Organization. However, China's laws and related judicial interpretation do not stipulate and explain the interpretation of originality and lack essential stipulation on originality. Hence, in the juridical practice, the judgment of originality relies on the

---

34. *See* Zhao Rui, Rethinking and Cognizing the Standard of Works' Originality, *Intellectual Property* (《知识产权》), (2011), 9.
35. *See* William R. Cornish, *The Copyright Law of United Kingdom*, in International Copyright Law, Barbara Ringer & Hamish Standison (eds), 1989, p. 67.
36. *See* US239 SCt298, 4FLEd460. Cited in WU Hangdong, *Research on Basic Issues of Intellectual Property*, China Renmin University Press, 2009, 35.
37. *See* Zhao Rui, Rethinking and Cognizing the Standard of Works' Originality, Intellectual Property (《知识产权》) (2011), 9.
38. World Intellectual Property Organization: *Intellectual Property Talk*, p. 217, cited in WU Hangdong, *Research on Basic Issues of Intellectual Property*, China Renmin University Press, 2009, 37.

interpretation and discretion of the court (in fact, it relies on the judge undertaking the case), which inevitably leads to a lack of uniformity of the judgment standard to originality. In this case, the court directly confirmed that Jinfang Pharmaceutical's description lacked originality in text combination and did not belong to a work in the sense of copyright on the grounds that its format strictly observed the stipulations of the pharmaceutical administration regulations of China on the format of dispensatory for use; yet in the case where Xiangbei Wellman Pharmaceutical Co., Ltd sued Suzhou Erye Pharmaceutical Co., Ltd., the court obviously did not deny the originality of the medicine description on the grounds that the medicine description strictly observed the stipulations of the pharmaceutical administration regulations of China on the format of dispensatory for use. This indicates different standards to judge originality.

2.2 Legal Provision on medicine description

2.2.1 Stipulation on the format and content of medicine description

According to Article 9 of the *Drug Instruction and Label Management Regulations*, medicine descriptions are important scientific data, conclusions and information on the safety and efficacy of drugs and are used with medicine package and label at the same time to guide the patient to use it safely and rationally. It is a necessary and important component of medicine certification documents ratified by the State Food and Drug Administration and plays a crucial role in ensuring the safety when people are taking medicine and the right of knowing the facts of a case of pharmaceutical products. Hence, all countries have stipulated the content and format of medicine description.

Famous for its perfection and preciseness, the pharmaceutical management laws and regulations of the U.S. also established a complete system for the management of medicine description and label. American Food and Drug Administration (hereinafter, "FDA") manages the descriptions and labels of prescription medicine and nonprescription medicine in different ways. Instead of requiring nonprescription medicine to include medicine description, it only requires that the label of nonprescription medicine shall have enough direction for use, while it emphasizes that each type of content on prescription medicine descriptions shall explain information that is accurate, specific, professional, comprehensive and detailed.[39] In order to improve the format of prescription medicine descriptions and highlight the most important information in the description and improving its clarity and readability, FDA issued *Regulations on the Format and Content Management of Prescription Drugs and Biological Products* on January 18, 2006. While managing prescription medicine and nonprescription medicine in different ways, FDA classified the medicines into original drugs and generic drugs, and stipulated that the Labeling of generic drug shall be the same as Labeling of the referenced original drug, and the content and format must be the same as those of

---

39. *See* Hua Congxiao & Gao Chenyan, *Comparison of Management Status of Chinese and American Drug Description*, National Drug Evaluation Center Data, http://ishare.iask.sina.com.cn/f/182 42413.html?from, Last access time: Mar. 15, 2012.

the referenced original drug and updated accordingly.[40] Labeling, however, includes label, medicine description and any other characters, printing, and pictures of the drug's container, accompanying Articles, and envelop. The EU does not require that the description of a generic drug shall be consistent with that of the referenced drug, but it has strict and specific requirements for the format of description. A description model for patients, issued by the EU in 2005, was divided into six parts including what the drug is, the situation before taking this drug, how it can be used, possible untoward effect, how it can be kept in storage, and other information, and emphasized to use the language that readers can understand.[41]

In *Pharmaceutical Administration Law* of China, Article 54 clarifies that: the pharmaceutical packaging must be printed or affixed with the label and attached with description according to stipulation. The label or description shall be annotated with the drug's common name, ingredient, specification, manufacturing enterprise, registration number, batch number of the product, date of manufacture, duration of validity, indication or major function, usage, dosage, contraindication, untoward effect, and matters need attention. *Drug Instruction and Label Management Regulations* stipulates specific requirements on the format and content of the medicine description: it is required that manufacturing enterprise of drugs shall clearly and comprehensively indicate the relevant project contents in medicine description. It is emphasized that the description shall provide accurate, clear, detailed and comprehensive drug information. *Rules for Normalization Description of Chemical Drugs and Biological Products for Therapeutic Use* stipulates the specific format and content of description, including name of the drug, registration number, main ingredient, usage and dosage, contraindication and caution, slow release and controlled-release, date of manufacture, batch number of the drug, etc. and gives interpretation to every part.

It is because of restrict stipulations and requirements from laws and regulations of countries and drug supervision department on the content of medicine description, the content of medicine description is mainly objective introduction on the drug's attribute. Meanwhile, pharmaceutical administration regulations of China stipulate the format of dispensatory for use, which further restricted the expression of medicine description. Therefore, despite the author in writing medicine description may still have a certain expression of the space, whether a description written under a specific format and content requirements is the expression of the drafter's personal thoughts and reflects the originality in expression is worthwhile to be studied.

2.2.2 The stipulation of the procedure of medicine description

General works are produced by the completion of the author's creation, but the formation of medicine description is different. Since medicine description is related to public health, all countries stipulate that medicine description shall be released to the public after getting approved by drug supervision department. In the U.S., Drug Review

---

40. "A Comparative Analysis of the Registration Management System of Generic Medicines in China, the United States and Europe," http://gllow8.com/a/danganguanli/20111023/2262.htm, Last access time: Mar. 23, 2012.
41. *Ibid.*

and Research Center under FDA is responsible for the review of medicine description and label. Generally, the corporation will draft the description and provide FDA research data supporting content of the medicine description at first, and the FDA has a check on the description and forms a final draft by further discussion with the corporation. The description ratified by FDA and the approval letter will be put together on the FDA's website.[42] In China, according to relevant laws and stipulations, the content of medicine description need to be filed by the registered applicant, and technical review organ examines and approves on the basis of declaration material and relevant review opinions. Only when technical review finishes and the conclusion is that the application for listing is approved, it is possible to completely start review work of important technical documents like quality standards and description of the medicine proposed by registered applicant.[43] Therefore, the process for drafting, reviewing and revising the medicine description is a process of reconciliation between the technical review agency and the applicant for registration on the relevant content after repeated communication. This process not only involves registered applicant and drafter of medicine (sometimes, both are the same subject) but also technical review experts and agency for examining and approving.

The process of the formation of medicine description indicates that the date of its completion is not the date on which the drafters completed the essay writing, but the date when it gets the approval from the drug supervision department and its completion does not depend on the drafter's day of completion, but on the drug supervision department. This also determines the particularity of the medicine description in terms of its production procedure and use: that is, the medicine description is made for the purpose of selecting drugs and guiding the safe and rational use of drugs. Since its creation, it can only be used with the subject medicine, and it loses its own meaning when it is separated from its subject. Therefore, it has no independent use value and value. Works in copyright often express certain ideas and can be used independently to bring certain spiritual joy to human beings. They have certain powers and functions, and have independent value and use value. This particularity of production and use has led to people's controversy over whether the medicine description belongs to administrative document, and it is also one of the reasons why different opinions on whether medicine description is a work.

3. Relevant regulations and case studies in the U.S. and Taiwan area of China

In order promoting the development of generic drug and balancing the interests between the manufacturer of original drug and manufacturer generic drug, the U.S. issued *Drug Price Competition and Patent Term Restoration Act* in 1984. Both this Act

---

42. *See* Hua Congxiao & Gao Chenyan, *Comparison of Management Status of Chinese and American Drug Description*, National Drug Evaluation Center Data, http://ishare.iask.sina.com.cn/f/182 42413.html?from, Last access time: Mar. 15, 2012.
43. *See* Zhou Siyuan, *Research on Work Procedures of Reviewing and Revising Quality Standard, Description and Package Label of the Medicine*, http://www.chinabaike.com/z/yiqi/2011/032 6/619873.html, Last access time: Mar. 10, 2012.

and relevant federal regulations require that the labeling of generic drug shall be the same with that of the original drug. Its legislative logic is that: the safety and efficacy has been confirmed in clinical trials and use of very long years, and the requirement that every generic drug completely repeated clinical trials is not only a waste of resource but also a breach of ethics, so generic drug manufacturers do not need to repeat the clinical trials of safety and efficacy that have been done by original drug manufacturers. The data of safety and efficacy required to submit for the application of generic drugs is replaced by the bioequivalence or similar data of the original drug relative to that generic drugs. The reason that generics drug can simplify the process of listing is on the basis of its consistency of the ingredients, dosage forms, efficacy and dose of the original drug, and all the drug information which shall be recorded in the description of generic drug is neither the production of the trial report of bioequivalence nor subject availability trial report, and data before clinical trials still is dependent on trial result of the drug of reference.[44] Therefore, due to the considerations of science and drug safety, *Drug Price Competition and Patent Term Restoration Act* requires that the labeling of generic drug shall be the same with that of the original labeling. Hence, in the case of *Smith Kline Beecham Consumer Healthcare, L.P. v. Watson Pharmaceuticals, Inc.*,[45] American court held that: the copyright dispute of labeling is only a means or method of competition in drug market; the FDA requires manuals and tapes of generic drugs to be consistent with that of the original drug which is in accordance with the law; the consumer manuals and tapes of the original drugs are protected by the copyright, however, in the conflict of *Food and Drug and Cosmetic Act* and copyright, the former shall be applied first. The judgment of the case did not directly make adoption of the copyright of medicine description, but it determined that use manual and tape of original drug are under the protection of copyright and excluded the illegality of the manual and tapes of generic drugs, consistent with the original drugs, produced in accordance with the *Food and Drug and Cosmetic Act*. Also, it established the principle that in the conflict of *Food and Drug and Cosmetic Act* and copyright, the former shall be applied first, and balanced the interest between the original drug and generic drug. In addition, it promoted the availability of generic drugs as soon as possible, and it also provided an example for solving the problem of the relationship between generic drug's description and reference drug's description.

In Taiwan area of China, the management of medicine description, with reference to the relevant principles of *Drug Price Competition and Patent Term Restoration Act*, does not require data that shall attach with the listing of generic drugs to provide the safety and efficacy data of clinical trial. In guidelines for examination and registration of drugs, Article 20 clarifies that: generic drug's description shall check and ratify in accordance with the first medicine description checked, and unmonitored drug shall be translated follow the original description. On the basis of this situation, courts

---

44. *See* Gong Zhaolong: *The Development Trend of Generic Drug and the Comparison Between Requirements of Chinese and American Generic Drug Registration and Declaration*, http://www.doc88.com/p-49735454403.html, Last access time: Apr. 3, 2012.
45. *See Smith Kline Beecham Consumer Healthcare, L.P. v. Watson Pharmaceuticals, Inc.*, 211 F.3d.

in Taiwan area of China, when dealing with the dispute of the copyright of medicine description, have formed three adjudication opinions: (1) In the second instance judgment of Taiwan Taipei District Court, Zhi Zi [1993] No. 81 case, the court, directly on the basis of the reliance of client to the drugs regulations and according to Article 39 of drug law and Article 20 of guidelines for examination and registration of drugs in Taiwan area, held that the alleged infringement of medicine description was produced in accordance with the translation for the original medicine description, so it was difficult to regard it as an unlawful infringement of copyright of others. (2) In the civil judgment of Taiwan Taichung High Court, Zhi Shang Zi [1995] No. 9, the court held that the originality of medicine description did not comply with the requirements of the originality of a work under copyright and had academic value, and was unable to use independently and was with extremely low mental effect; the alleged medicine description was produced on the reliance of the regulation while guidelines for examination and registration belong to statutory order, so the people shall be restricted by it. The alleged infringer produced medicine description and also had obligation to observe it too. The appellate also had the obligation to bear and restricted by the guidelines, while the appellee used it rationally, which did not constitute an infringement of copyright. (3) In the judgment of Taiwan High Court, Zhi Shang Zi [1994] No. 17, the court held that the content of medicine description was mainly about the record of some respects related to the drug that consumer used such as, pharmacological effect, pharmacodynamics, drug interaction, indication, usage and dosage, matters need attention, and side-effect, which always need repeated and giant scientific experiments, and research to draw this conclusion. From these repeated and giant trial records, one can concentrate, analyze, choose and regroup scientifically meaningful data, and explain and describe it through characters to compile it into lucid expression that can easily understand. This process needed the drafter's professional training, judgment and deduction, which had much creativity. It did not only belong to the drug's operation, concept, principle, and findings, but presented as the objective form of medicine description; since its content belonged to academic discourse in science, therefore, medicine description shall belong to a work under copyright. However, generic drugs accepted administrative examination and approval for applying listing and reproduced or translated original drug's description, which are a rational use of legitimate purpose.

In summary, although there are different opinions on the identification of whether medicine description is a work in Taiwan area, the reason of the problem that the infringement of copyright of medicine description has been known. Generic drug description is produced in accordance with drug law and guidelines for examination and registration of drugs in Taiwan area; although it is the same with reference drug's description, it does not constitute an infringement of copyright on the basis of the client's reliance on regulations and rational use of reference drug's description. This is consistent with the opinion of American judgment.

4. Several problems involved in the resolution of dispute

4.1 The standard of judgment of a work's originality and analysis of the legal nature of medicine description

As mentioned above, medicine description, on the basis the stipulation of pharmaceutical administration regulations of China on the format of medicine description is a relevant introduction on medicine attribute, usage, dosage, side-effect and contraindication. The key to judging whether a medicine description shall be under the protection of copyright is to judge whether it has originality. It is the different opinions on originality's standard that lead to different opinions on such problems in China's juridical practice. Therefore, according to China's specific condition of copyright protection and the consideration of the reality and development trend of national legislation and jurisdiction of countries of Anglo-American Law and civil law system, the legislative body or judiciary organ determines the judgment of originality standard of a work under copyright is a sure resolution to the judgment of whether something like medicine description or patent description is a work.

4.1.1 The judgment of the originality of medicine description

Intellectual property law has always been the choice of public policy. Selective policy arrangements for intellectual property are made according to the needs of the country at different stages of development, which is a common practice[46] in Western countries and an experience for everyone to learn. In the current situation about the lack of original standard of a work, namely, nature of identification of a work, the essence of the copyright dispute of medicine description and the fundamental purpose of the pharmaceutical industry to serve the public health shall be considered, and adjust Chinese pharmaceutical industry to make full use of the period of strategic opportunity for generic drugs production created by the current expiration of patent medicine. Not only attention is paid to the introduction of technology and independent innovation in pharmaceutical industry but also protecting copy and innovative practical needs in copy. From the original intention of copyright legislation, the standard "modest originality level"[47] shall be used to identify whether medicine description is a work. The standard "modest originality level" is neither different from the standard "intellectual creation" in civil law country nor the standard "independent completion" in countries of Anglo-American Law. This standard not only insists that originality is a natural standard for constituting a work but also differentiate the originality that required by copyright from novelty and creativity required by patent. As long as a work is completed by the author independently rather than plagiarizing or imitating others' work and showing some personalized features, its originality shall be recognized. This

---

46. Wu Handong, *No "Too High" or "Too Low" Problem in Overall Level of Intellectual Property Protection*, http://www.hinews.cn/news/system/2008/11/05/010349601_01.shtml, Last access time: Dec. 6, 2011.
47. Beijing No. 1 Intermediate People's Court Intellectual Property Trial Court, Summary of Classification Cases of Intellectual Property Trial, *Intellectual Property Press* (2008), 9.

standard neither excluded some factual works like map and sketch map because of high standard nor included in the scope of protection of some simple collections of facts. Moreover, this standard has been indicated in some judicial adjudication. For instance, Beijing No. 1 Intermediate People's Court, Yi Zhong Min Chu Zi [2002] No. 4378 dispute of Huang Cheng Old Mama sued Huang Rong Old Mama for constituting an infringement of copyright, the court expressed such opinions.

According to this standard, medicine description, in the content, follows the format stipulated in pharmaceutical administration regulations of China, and introduces drug attribute, usage, dosage, side-effect, and contraindication. The vocabulary and language used by medicine description are basically scientific research language which is precise and standard such as physics, chemistry and pharmacy that are commonly used as well as unit of measurement commonly used by international community. It does not need and never use original vocabulary and language, so the expression has a very large limitation. Hence, generally, medicine description is not expression of thoughts of some natural person or group; it is difficult to reflect modest originality, so it shall not be a work in a sense to copyright and protected by copyright. It cannot be denied that the experimental data and conclusions, expressed in the medicine description, themselves are results of drug research and development personnel and involves creative works of the personnel; however, the character expression of experimental data and conclusions(i.e., the content of description) as well as experimental data and conclusions themselves are different definitions and coverage. The literal expressions are protected by copyright. The data and results generated from experiments are protected by patent. The notion of originality of copyright shall not be misunderstood as the notion of novelty of patent.

4.1.2 Whether medicine description is an official document

In *Methods of Handling the Official Documents of State Administrative Organizations*, issued by the State Council in 2000, Article 2 clarifies that: administrative official document is a document with legal effect and standard format formed in the administrative management process of the administrative authority. Accordingly, administrative official document has the following features: it is written by the staff of administrative authority. It is formed in the process of administrative management. It has legal effect and standard format. It severs for public administration. Only when the above conditions are met, it is an official document. Since the liability subject of medicine description is pharmaceutical R&D and production enterprise rather than administrative authority or its staff, and drug supervision department is a subject that checks and manages medicine description rather than the lability subject of writing and revising; the fundamental purpose of writing *medicine description* is to instruct doctors and patients to use drugs and meet the needs of public health instead of severing for administrative management. On the contrary, the administrative supervision of drug supervision department also severs the ultimate purpose of public health. Therefore, it is not suitable to identify medicine description as an administrative official document.

It should be noted that Hunan High People's Court made civil judgment of Xiang Gao Fa Min Zai Zhong Zi [2013] No. 73 in July 1, 2013, which revised the judgment of Changsha, Hunan Intermediate People's Court, Chang Zhong Min San Zhong Zi [2010] No. 0437 in August 3, 2010, and confirmed that medicine description is not a work protected copyright. Since then, courts throughout our country have formed a consensus that medicine description is out of protection of China's copyright in legally effective judgment.

4.2 Improving management regulations on consistency between generic drugs and reference drugs

The essence of copyright infringement of medicine description is that drug manufacturer seeks to use the chronicity of copyright protection making up the limitation of patent protection so as to prolong patent protection duration and strengthen enterprise competitiveness. At the present stage of China's pharmaceutical industry that the overall quality is not high, the innovative ability is low, most varieties have not yet formed specialization and scale production, and generic drug dominates, China's IP protection on medical biological field shall not only adjust the trend and requirements of international development as well as actively fulfill international liability, but also maximize the protection of national interests and insist technology introduction and independent innovation. Meanwhile, it shall protect imitation and the principle that make innovation in imitation, especially to make full use of the historical opportunities that drug patent's expiration of transnational companies appears a peak and to enlarge the market of generic drugs. This needs laws and regulations to provide enough protection on the listing of generic drugs, and the stipulation on generic drug's description is certainly included. With reference to American *Drug Price Competition and Patent Term Restoration Act* as well as drug law and guidelines for examination and registration of drugs in Taiwan area of China, improving mechanism of examining and approving as well as managing, and examining and approving generic drug's description according to reference drug's description which is already checked as well as defining both of them in laws and regulations, all of which provide reliable reference of laws and regulations for writing generic drug's description on the basis of reference description, and are of profound significance for solving the problem of copyright dispute in judicial judgment fundamentally, and providing reliable law protection on the development of generic drugs, and meeting the needs of common interests.

—**Comments by DING Wenyan**

Case 8. The Nature of Technical Standard and Its Copyright Protection

The Forschungsinstitut Hohenstein Prof. Dr. Jurgen Mecheels GmbH & Co. KG v. Intertek Testing Services Shanghai, Ltd.
Case of Copyright Infringement Dispute
Case Index: *The Forschungsinstitut Hohenstein Prof. Dr. Jurgen Mecheels GmbH & Co. KG v. Intertek Testing Services Shanghai, Ltd.;* Shanghai No. 1 Intermediate People's Court, Hu Yi Zhong Min Wu (Zhi) Chu Zi [2007] No. 198, October 15, 2010; Shanghai High People's Court, Hu Gao Min San (Zhi) Zhong Zi [2010] No. 90, September 2, 2011

Facts:

The Plaintiff Forschungsinstitut Hohenstein Prof. Dr. Jurgen Mecheels GmbH & Co. KG alleged that Oeko-Tex Association (hereinafter, "QEKO-TEX") was the internationally famous organization which was established in accordance with the Swiss law specializing in the research on the certification and inspection of the ecological textiles. "Oeko-Tex Standard 100" was the technical requirement which was published by the OEKO-TEX and initiator on the basis of the research achievements of many years aiming to test the ecological textiles established by 1992. After that, OEKO-TEX annually updated and modified the standard according to the latest research achievement, which formed the different versions of the standard (such as 2001, 2002–2006). OEKO-TEX decided and signed "Copyright transfer agreement" to transfer the copyright and all the related rights (including the right to sue any infringement) within the jurisdiction of the People's Republic of China (except Hong Kong, Macao and Taiwan area) to the Plaintiff on December 12, 2005. Then the Plaintiff applied to the China Copyright Registration Center for the copyright registration of the "Oeko-Tex Standard 100" and obtained copyright license on March 27, 2007. The Defendant Intertek Testing Services Shanghai, Ltd. was a product testing, inspection and certification company established in Shanghai. In 2005, OEKO-TEX found the Defendant launched authenticating service of Intertek ecological products and distributed certification manual and leaflets on different occasions. OEKO-TEX found that the core content of these publicity materials (such as formats, test items and limited editions) replicates the content of the "Oeko-Tex Standard 100" (especially the 2002 version). During the trial, the Plaintiff further advocated that the Defendant plagiarized "LIMIT VALUES AND FASTNESS" and notes in Annex 5 of the Oeko-Tex Standard 100 (2002). OEKO-TEX hired the lawyer and sent the Defendant a notice to require him stop plagiarism on February 2005. The Defendant replied the notice and did not deny the relevant facts. The Plaintiff sued to the Court and requested the Court to order that: (1) the Defendant stopped copying and publishing the publicity material; (2) the Defendant had the responsibility to apologize on the notice published on "Textile Guide" and eliminate influences; (3) The Defendant compensated the Plaintiff for the loss of RMB 500,000 due to the infringement.

The Defendant objected to the Plaintiff's first claim because there was no plagiarism neither publication. There was also an objection to the claim for compensation and apology. The Plaintiff did not clearly state who the copyright owner of Oeko-Tex standard 100 was. The Plaintiff did not clarify the subject of the resolution made by OEKO-TEX on December 12, 2005, nor did it prove the legitimacy of the subject. The Plaintiff filed an application on the basis of the resolution but did not provide relevant evidence. The publicity materials charged with the infringement were used for the internal publicity, so there was no public offering. The forms of the Defendant's publicity material were words and tables, then what was the Infringing typography claimed by the Plaintiff? "Oeko-Tex standard 100" had seven versions; the Plaintiff did not define what content in which version was infringed by the Defendant. The infringement acts accused by OEKO-TEX's lawyer actually referred to replication and imitation, no mention of plagiarism. The Defendant categorically denied infringement act in the reply to the Plaintiff. The Plaintiff did not provide factual evidence regarding the Defendant's copying behavior. There is no factual or legal basis for the amount of compensation claimed by the Plaintiff.

After the first trial, The Shanghai Municipal First Intermediate People's Court made the following findings that: "Oeko-Tex standard 100" is a technical requirement standard for eco-textile testing. It was produced by OEKO-TEX in German, English and French using its own printing system and was released in Zurich, Switzerland. Since the first announced in 1992, the organization successively published different updated and modified versions (including the version of 1992, 2000, 2001, 2002, 2003, 2004 and 2005). OEKO-TEX decided to transfer the copyright and all the related rights (including the right to sue any infringement) within the jurisdiction of the People's Republic of China to the Plaintiff on December 12, 2005 so that the Plaintiff had the right to file a lawsuit against the Defendant. On the same day, OEKO-TEX signed "Copyright transfer agreement" with the Plaintiff to agree on the specific content and district sphere of the transferred rights. Thereafter, the Plaintiff applied to the China Copyright Registration Center for the copyright registration of the "Oeko-Tex Standard 100" and obtained copyright license on March 27, 2007. The Annex 5 of the "Oeko-Tex standard 100" (2002) was "LIMIT VALUES AND FASTNESS."

The Defendant was established in Shanghai in 1994. It is a company engaged in product certification and management system certification, providing quality technical services such as product standards and testing for enterprises. On June 2004, the Defendant commissioned outsider to print "Intertek Eco-Certification" brochure (1,000 in Chinese and 1,000 in English). The Annex 1 of the brochure was "TESTING PARAMETERS AND LIMIT VALUES."

On February 2005, OEKO-TEX hired the lawyer and sent the Defendant a notice to require him stop plagiarism. The Defendant replied the notice and denied the alleged infringement.

In the "LIMIT VALUES AND FASTNESS" table which was claimed the copyright by the Plaintiff, the testing productions were divided into four types: Baby, In Direct Contact with Skin, with No Direct Contact with Skin and Decoration Material. Meanwhile, the table specified the testing parameters and maximum values of the four types of products. The table structure was five columns and fifty-seven rows. The first column on the left was the name of testing parameters, the second, third, fourth and fifth columns, respectively, represented the limit values of the four products. The first row on the top was the name of product classification and the other fifty-six rows listed fourteen types and thirty-four items testing parameters and the limit values of each item in each type. Twelve notes were attached on the table.

The Chinese-English "TESTING PARAMETERS AND LIMIT VALUES" table printed by the outsider commissioned by Defendant divided the testing products into: product for babies, product for adults and product for decoration. Meanwhile, the table specified the testing parameters and maximum values of the three types of products. The table structure was four columns and forty-nine rows. The first column on the left was the name of testing parameters; the second, third, fourth columns, respectively, represented the limit values of the three products. The first row on the top was the name of product classification and the other forty-eight rows successively listed thirteen types and thirty-nine items testing parameters and the limit values of each item in each type. Thirteen notes were attached.

The similarities between the above two forms were as follows: there were ten type testing parameters having same names and the same order in the table. There were twenty-three items that had the same name and limited value. In the notes, the notes 1, 11, 12 in Plaintiff's table were totally same as the note 9, 12, 13 of the Defendant's. The note 10 in Plaintiff's table is similar to the note in Defendant's.

On November 22, 2002, Administration of Quality Supervision Inspection and Quarantine (AQSIQ) published the national standard of "Technical specifications of ecological textiles." The preface of the standard states that: the product classification and requirement of the standard adopted OEKO-TEX 100-2002 "Ecological textiles – General and special technical requirements" to classify the ecological textiles and regulate the limited values and test method of every index, as well as add the specific indicator of the baby product saliva color fastness and the definition of the ecological textiles. The ecological textiles classification and requirement in this standard was entirely the same as the content in the "LIMIT VALUES AND FASTNESS." There was a little difference in the formal of tabulation (adding the measurement unit as a sole column).

The laws of the US, the EU, Japan and Thailand made prohibition regulations to part of the textile testing parameter of the standards formulated by the Plaintiff and the Defendant.

Ruling and Reasoning:

In the first instance, Shanghai No. 1 Intermediate People's Court held that: According to the Article 3 in "Copyright Law of the people's republic of China," the works protected by law should be created in some forms, that is, the work should be the expression with originality. Thus, the work protected by the copyright law must meet the requirements of originality and the protection only reach the expression, not contain the idea, technique, process and mathematical concept. By extension, the work without originality or with the unique expression is not protected by the copyright law. Since the scope of protection for works of low originality is narrow, the determination of infringement is also more strict. In this case, "Oeko-Tex standard 100" (2002) was a normative document published by OEKO-TEX, which aimed to describe various conditions of gaining authorization to use the mark of "Oeko-Tex standard 100." The document belonged to the work in copyright law and was definitely protected. The Annex 5 "Limit value and fastness" and annotation of "Oeko-Tex standard 100" (2002) in this case expressed the standards of classification, prohibited items and maximum when detected the textiles. However, only when put in the full text of "Oeko-Tex standard 100" (2002), the content of the document could be clearly understood. Thus, the Annex 5 and annotation was only a component of the "Oeko-Tex standard 100" (2002) rather than an independent work. Certainly, the component of a work was also protected by the copyright law as long as meet the requirement of originality and the plaintiff had the right to stop plagiarism. But the form of the annex was a general table and the content was chemical element and numerical value, the expression was unique and the annotation was simple normal expression. So, the annex and annotation could not be regarded as original and protected by copyright law. Accordingly, the court held that plaintiff's claim had no legal basis and dismissed all the claims.

The plaintiff refused to accept and appealed to the court. The two parties negotiated a settlement through mediation of Shanghai Higher People's Court.

Commentary:

All claims of the plaintiff in the first instance were refused. Although two parties negotiated a settlement under the auspices of the court in the second trial and cleared the relevant content of the test item, limitation table and banned chemicals in the brochures and other documents. It should be noted if the defendants need to learn from Chinese standards and other countries' standards and the defendants were not allowed to use Annex 1 (test item and limitation table) and Annex 2 (banned chemicals) of the "Intertek authenticating of ecological products" brochure. However, as for the Annex 5 and annotation of the "Oeko-Tex standard 100" (2002), it is worth exploring whether it has copyright. By extension, whether the various technical standards frequently used in the enterprise management are protected by copyright and how to guarantee the interest of the relevant subjects should be identified by the law and justice.

1. Whether the technical standard can be the objective of the copyright.

"Standard" is a kind of normative document commonly and repeatedly used which made by consensus and approved by notarial offices aiming to get the best order within certain range.[48] "Standard" is a uniform rule of the repetitive things and concepts. As common criteria and basis, it is on the basis of the comprehensive achievements of the scientific technique and the practical experience and approved by the authorities and

---

48. *See* GB/T20000.1-2002 "Standardization Work Guide Part 1: General Vocabulary for Standardization and Related Activities." Quoted from the Baidu Encyclopedia "standard" word entry, http://baikebaidu.com/view/8079.htm? Fr = aladdin, last visit time: Oct. 16, 2015.

published by the certain form.⁴⁹ Technical standard is regulated by law as a kind of standard. According to the binding degree, standards can be divided into compulsory standards and recommendatory standards. According to the published subjects, the standards can be divided into national, trade, local and enterprise standards. There are different views on the problem that whether the standard can be the subject of the copyright law. Some scholars argue that compulsory standards and recommendatory standards both belong to "corporate works." The competent administrative authorities are the owner of the standards and enjoy the copyright (except the owner of the enterprise standard). ⁵⁰ Other scholars argue that the standard can be regarded as the work in copyright law, but it may not be protected by the copyright law. The national, trade and local standard are all legislative and administrative documents belonging to formal official documents which made and published by state organs and should not be protected by copyright law. The enterprise standard is set and only adopted by the enterprises themselves and not a kind of official document. It can be protected by the copyright law. Thus, compulsory standards and recommendatory standards should not be included in the protection range of the copyright law.⁵¹

The technical standard is generally called as a kind of intellectual property which mainly expressed in the form of words in the scientific field, undoubtedly, has originality and meets the requirement of works. According to the laws, technical standard is not explicitly excluded as the subject of the copyright. Thus, at least the copyright can exist on the "standard" and it is proper for standard to be the subject of copyright. However, on the basis of exception regulation of the copyright law, not all standards can be protected by the copyright law. According to the Article 5 of the *Copyright Law*, this law shall not be applicable to the laws and regulations, resolutions, decisions and orders of state organs, other documents of a legislative, administrative or judicial nature and their official translations. It has a key impact that whether the standard has the legislative, administrative and judicial nature to whether the standard can be protected by the copyright law. Thus, when judging if technical standard can be the subject of the copyright, the main step is to identify whether it has the legislative, administrative and judicial nature. The author thinks that the legislative, administrative and judicial nature that has been called mainly means that whether a document belongs to the laws, regulations, administrative rules, normative documents and judgments and ruling of the judicial organs. In essence, there are two main factors: one is exercising the public rights; another is having the power of enforcement. The whole system of the copyright law is to grant the oblige certain right to control the spreading of the works, including replication, distribution and internet communication and allow the obligee enjoy the exclusive right in prescribed period to gain financial payoff. As for the document of legislative, administrative and judicial nature, the author undoubtedly

---

49. *See* "Company for providing product quality standards, testing and other quality technical services, product certification and management system certification business," quoted from Baidu Encyclopedia "standard" entry, http:// baike.baidu.com/view/8079.htm?fr = Aladdin.
50. Ling Shengen, *Discussion on the Copyright of Technical Standards and Related Policies*, China Publishing, 2007, 7.
51. Zhou Yingjiang & Xie Guanbin, Analysis of the Copyright Issues of Technical Standards, *Intellectual Property*, 2 (2010).

gives certain original work, the reason why the laws rule that this kind of document cannot be protected by the copyright law is to avoid limiting the spreading of the document. The limitation of the copyright on these documents has legitimacy since the widespread of these documents is the need to ensure the public management and maintain public benefits. As described above, the standards can be divided into compulsory standards and recommendatory standards, and there is obvious difference on the legal effect between two standards. According to Article 7 of the "Standardization Law:" national and trade standards divide into compulsory standards and recommendatory standards. The standards to guarantee the human health and personal and property safety and the standards which are enforceable regulated by the laws and administrative regulations are the compulsory standards, others are recommendatory standards. The local standards formulated by standardization administration departments of provinces, autonomous regions and municipalities directly under the central government for the safety and sanitary requirements of industrial products shall be compulsory standards within their respective administrative areas. Article 14 stipulates that: compulsory standards must be complied with. The products, which fail to meet the mandatory standards, shall be prohibited from producing and selling. The State encourages enterprises to voluntarily adopt the recommendatory standards. Article 20 stipulates: whoever produces, sells or imports products that do not conform compulsory standards shall be dealt with according to law by the competent administrative authorities as prescribed by the laws and administrative rules and regulations. In the absence of this prescription, his products and unlawful proceeds shall be confiscated and shall be currently fined by the administrative authorities for industry and commerce. According to Article 23 of the *Regulation for the Implementation of the Standardization Law*: Any units and individuals that are engaged in scientific research, production and operation must strictly implement compulsory standards. The products which do not measure up to the compulsory standards may not be allowed to be produced, marketed or imported. Article 33 regulates the corresponding administrative penalties of the behaviors that produce, sell or import products that do not conform compulsory standards. According to the above laws and administrative regulations, the compulsory standards are compulsively implement by the public power. The consequence of the violation is as same as breaking the laws. In my opinion, some specific compulsory standards have the equal legal effect with the laws, regulations and departmental rules which compulsively implement this standard and certainly have legislative, administrative or judicial nature. Thus, they are in accordance with Article 5 of the *Copyright Law* and there is no copyright on them.

  As for recommendatory standards, there is a view that recommendatory standards are similarly drawn up, examined and approved and published by the state organs in accordance with the legal duties and procedures, just as the permissive regulation in the contract law, having the nature of laws and administrative regulations, thus they should not be protected by the copyright law. [52] Some scholars argue

---

52. *Ibid.*

that recommendatory standards belong to the technical specification adopted voluntarily and have no nature of laws. Since the creative labor should be paid during the process of setting recommendatory standards, and the standards have the character of the creative intellectual achievements. If conforming to other conditions of the works, it should be within the protection extent of the copyright law.[53] The author holds that recommendatory standards cannot be treated the same. Although recommendatory standards are one of the national and trade standards, they are not completely drawn up by the relevant administrative departments. Sometimes the administrative departments only introduce and the standard itself may be an enterprise standard. The enterprise standards do not change into the standards with coercive force or laws or administrative regulations simply due to the administrative departments treat as recommendatory standards. However, in my opinion, since the recommendatory standards are set up by the legislative or administrative departments to encourage enterprises to adopt the standards, it is not suitable for them to be protected by the copyright law. If there is copyright on the standard, the spread will be limited, causing a situation with disorganized aim mixing the encouragement and limitation. The enterprise standards are set and adopted by the enterprises themselves. In general, there is no reason to exclude them to the outside of the protection scope of the copyright law.

In this case, the source obligee of the involved standard was a foreign nongovernmental organization. Thus, the standard was actually an enterprise standard in terms of the domestic law. Although the administrative department regarded it as a recommendatory standard it also made it clear that referenced the enterprise standard. The substance content was same. Thus, the standard did not translate into the work introduced by the administrative department, it still was an enterprise standard and could be protected by the copyright law.

2. The technical proposal in the technical standard

The technical standard is the work in the form of words and table. As mentioned above, the enterprises own the copyright to the standards set by them. The basic rights of the copyright such as copyright, distribution right and information network propagating right are embodied in the protection of the technical standard, that is, others are not allowed to copy, publish and propagate the technical standard on the network without the permission. In real market society, there are some enterprises making money by setting standard and certified products. These enterprise standards are of certain authority and accepted by the society and production enterprises. Sometimes, the standards even own higher degree of authority and social recognition since the enterprise standards are stricter than the national compulsory standards. This operation mode objectively is beneficial to the unification of products or service standards and the promotion of the quality. It should be encouraged by laws, at least not be banned. Under this mode, the copyright protection of the enterprise standard is

---

53. *See* Intellectual Property Tribunal of the Supreme People's Court [1998] Zhi Ta Zi No. 6.

especially important. However, when apply and protect the technical standard, it should distinguish the boundary of the idea and expression. The distinction between the idea and expression is one of the basic copyright theories. Only the original expression of the idea can be protected by the copyright law. As for the technical standard, it involves considerable operation methods, produces, parameters and steps, belonging to the technical scheme or the part of it. In terms of the copyright law, it belongs to the idea scope, thus manufacturing products and providing services according to the technical standard whose copyright owned by others do not infringe others' copyright. If the obligee wants to seek legal protection on the technical scheme, he should apply for a patent and accept the enabling conditions.

In this case, although a lot of testing parameters' names and limited values of the defendant's brochure were the same as the plaintiff's technical standard, these content terms belonged to technical schemes which were within the idea scope. Obviously, they do not have copyright. Although the plaintiff repeatedly claimed that the expression of norms was original and the figures were from scientific experiment, so they should be protected by copyright. However, the research achievement actually was a technical scheme which should seek patent or business secret protection. If obtaining protection from copyright law, it obviously did not conform to the legislative purpose and the function of copyright law.

3. The uniqueness of expression

Work is the expression of idea. But if there is only sole or limited expression, the copyright protection on this expression may handicap the spread of idea and then damage the basic freedom of expression. Thus, based on the public interest, the dissemination of ideas should not be restricted and the work of unique expression should not be protected. It is the basic principle of copyright law. The issue whether the technical standard exists the uniqueness of expression should make a concrete analysis according to the specific case. In this case, the plaintiff claimed the copyright on the attached table of the technical standard. The first instance court held that the form adopted by the plaintiff was general form and the content exists the uniqueness of expression. The notes of the form belonged to simple habitual expression. Thus, the form and notes could not be protected by the copyright law. In my opinion, the form also conveys the content of the technical standard, the form of general forms did not obstruct the copyright protection. The form should be interpreted as a whole rather than denying content due to form. As for the content of the form, it shows the testing parameters and relevant values in tabular form to make readers more intuitively to read and more convenient to use. But the character of the tabular form is omitting adjectives, verbs and adverbials. The sentences with SOV structure in the technical standard text are in the form of correspondence of tables. From the point of expressing certain ideas, the tabular form indeed exits some limitation and the optional expression method is limited. As described above, the technical scheme of the technical standard is impossible to become the subject of the copyright law. The testing parameters and values in the table, even indeed from the research which plaintiff devote a lot of manpower and material resources, are not protected by the copyright law.

4. The policy consideration of infringement judgment

It should be noted that the underlying issue of the technical standard copyright infringement disputes is not the problems in copyright law such as the replication and distribution of the technical standard but the enterprise profit-making mode of the product certification on the basis of the technical standard, as well as the resulting market competition issue. The source author of the involved technical standard, in this case, OEKO-TEX, was an organization specializing in the research on authentication and testing of ecological textiles, while the defendant was a company providing quality technical services such as product standard and testing to engage in product certification and management system certification business. Both business areas had overlapping; there inevitably was competition on providing textile production enterprises testing and certification services. The reason why plaintiff brought lawsuit was that he thought that the scientific research achievement on textiles testing was freely used by others to compete in the testing and certification market. From the angle of the defendant's usage, the contents in the involved table and plaintiff's table were quite similar, especially some testing parameters and values were totally same. It should be said that the defendant indeed used the plaintiff's relevant scientific research. The above had illustrated that it was not going to work that protect the scientific research by the copyright law, since the scientific was technical scheme in nature rather than the subject of copyright law. The plaintiff's technical standard belonged to enterprise standard and the author certainly enjoyed the copyright on the whole. But it should be seen that related administrative department published it as recommendatory standard. As the enterprise standard published by foreign nongovernment agency, the involved technical standard could be regarded as recommendatory standard by the domestic government agency. It should be said that the standard was pretty authority and more likely to be highly recognized in the industry. It was also possible to make enterprises in the industry from the "path dependence" which depend on the standard. In any case, technical standard was with certain public nature, since the manufacturing enterprises would distribute the products to the market in the end, relating to the personal and property safety of common consumers. Even for the enterprise standard, when protected by the copyright law, the protection intensity should be different from the general literature and fine art. At the same time, as national recommendatory standard, the protection intensity of the enterprise standard should further weaken. There was a view holding that it should be treated as general work when judging whether to infringe the enterprise standard copyright. [54] In my opinion, since the enterprise standard, which as recommendatory standard, was recommended by the administrative department, its technical standard had a certain advantage in the market. If granting stronger copyright protection, its competitive superiority would further

---

54. Shen Qiang, Copyright Protection of Technical Standards of NGOs, *World Trade Organization Dynamics and Research*, 7 (2008).

become intensive. The reason why grant technical standard is a weak copyright protection was that the strong protection would make the technical standard copyright become the tool used by superior certification enterprise to beat competitors, causing the monopoly of the standard certification market, and then harming the public interest.

—**Comments by DING Wenlian and XU Zhuobin**

CHAPTER 3
Determination of Copyright Infringement

Case 9. Originality of Works Inspired by Nonfictions and Copyright Infringement

Qian Jiang v. Tang Hao and Beijing Youth Daily
Case of Copyright Infringement Dispute
Case Index: *Qian Jiang v. Tang Hao and Beijing Youth Daily*; Chaoyang District People's Court of Beijing, Chao Min Chu Zi [2013] No. 8853, August 13, 2013; Beijing No. 3 Intermediate People's Court, San Zhong Min Zhong Zi [2013] No. 00116, November 19, 2013.

Facts:

Qian Jiang is the author of the books *History of Ping Pong Diplomacy* and *Story behind Ping Pong Diplomacy*, and the article of *Glen Cowan and His Mother in Ping Pong Diplomacy*. He filed the lawsuit against the Defendant Tang Hao that: In his book *Inside the Ping Pong Diplomacy* by Tang Hao, Tang Hao copied the Plaintiff' works for approximately 72,000 words which counts one-third of the whole book, even the whole pages or paragraphs were copied. The Defendant Tang Hao asserted that "Ping Pong Diplomacy" was one of the major historical events that shocked the whole world in the 20th century and had become a public resource, and thus the topic could not be owned by someone. *Beijing Youth Daily* serialized Tan Hao's book *Inside the Ping Pong Diplomacy* in fifteen issues on its newspaper and communicated Tan Hao's book *Inside the Ping Pong Diplomacy* on the Internet via the websites www.ynet.com and www.qianlong.com. Qian Jiang asserted that Tang Hao and *Beijing Youth Daily* caused his economic and reputation losses and moral damages.

In the first instance, Chaoyang District People's Court of Beijing found that: The Eastern Publishing Co., Ltd. published and distributed the book *History of Ping Pong Diplomacy* in January 1987 and the book *Story behind Ping Pong Diplomacy* in November 1997, with the author's name Qian Jiang on the cover and copyright page of the two books. Qian Jiang also published the article of *Glen Cowan and His Mother in Ping Pong Diplomacy* in the journal of *5 Biographical Literature (2007)*. In April 2012, the Contemporary Chinese Publishing House published the book by Tang Hao. According to the copyright page, this book counts 180,000 words in total and the price is RMB 29. Comparing *Inside the Ping Pong Diplomacy* with *History of Ping Pong Diplomacy*, *Story behind Ping Pong Diplomacy* and *Glen Cowan and His Mother in Ping Pong Diplomacy*, it can be found that there are approximately 60,651 words in Tang Hao's book that are identical to the corresponding content of *History of Ping Pong Diplomacy*, 99 words are identical to *Glen Cowan and His Mother in Ping Pong Diplomacy*, and 2,409 words are identical to *Story behind Ping Pong Diplomacy*. Most of the contents are identical in a page-to-page or paragraph-to-paragraph manner.

In the first instance, the Court held that: In accordance to the signature in *History of Ping Pong Diplomacy*, *Story behind Ping Pong Diplomacy* and *Glen Cowan and His Mother in Ping Pong Diplomacy*, it could be concluded that, in the absence of evidence to the contrary, Qian Jiang is the author of above works and is entitled to the copyright. After comparing, it has been found that *Inside the Ping Pong Diplomacy* of Tang Hao is similar to the above three works of Qian Jiang. The similar part counts over 60,000 words in a page-to-page or paragraph-to-paragraph manner, which is approximately one-third of the whole book *Inside the Ping Pong Diplomacy*. Since the three works of Qian Jiang were published earlier than the book of Tang Hao, Tang Hao has the possibility to access to the works of Qian Jiang. In addition, Tang Hao admitted that he referred to relevant works of Qian Jiang, but failed to prove that he obtained the similar content from other lawful sources. Thus, the Court ruled that: Since Tang Hao plagiarized the relevant content of Qian Hao's works and infringed the copyright of Qian Jiang, Tang Hao should bear the liabilities of apologizing and compensating for the economic losses.

Ruling and Reasoning:

In the second instance, Beijing No. 3 Intermediate People's Court confirmed the finding made by the first instance.

Beijing No. 3 Intermediate People's Court held that: Qian Jiang is the author of *History of Ping Pong Diplomacy*, *Story behind Ping Pong Diplomacy* and *Glen Cowan and His Mother in Ping Pong Diplomacy* and entitled to the copyright. After comparing, it has been found that over 60,000 words of *Inside the Ping Pong Diplomacy* are identical to the content of the three works of Qian Jiang, which is one-third of the whole book. Tang Hao claimed that the similar part was from other sources; however, some relevant works submitted by Tang Hao as evidence for the second instance were published later than the works of Qian Jiang involved in this case. Some other relevant works submitted by Tang Hao as evidence for the second instance were published earlier than the works of Qian Jiang, but Tang Hao failed to prove that the similar part was actually from those works, instead of the works of Qian Jiang. Thus, the Court cannot support Tang Hao's argument that the similar part was from other sources. The themes of the works of Tang Hao and Qian Jiang are the major historical events "Ping-Pong diplomacy," which is an idea but not expression protected by copyright.

However it does not mean that the works of this topic cannot satisfy the requirement of originality to get copyright protection. In other words, works created on the basis of historical events are still copyrightable, but not public resources that anyone may use freely. The original content is exactly the subject matter of copyright. Thus, the Court did not support Tang Hao's argument that the contents of the works involved in the case were relating to historical event and anyone might use such public resources freely. In addition, it was reasonable for the first instance court to take into account the factors, including the degree of originality of Qian Jiang's work, the number of copied words and the degree of subjective wrong, to determine the damages in line with the relevant regulations of the remuneration rate. Therefore, the appeal was rejected and the original judgment was affirmed.

Commentary:

In the Chinese judicial practice, there are some disputes in relation of works inspired by nonfictional historical events. The two key issues are: First, whether such work is original and protected by the copyright. Second, how to determine the infringement?

1. The originality of works inspired by nonfictions

Originality is one of the prerequisites for copyright protection. Therefore, the key element for an intellectual creation inspired by nonfictions to be protected by copyright is whether it satisfies the requirement of originality.

When dealing with the same topic, different people may take different expressions to connect the ideas, characters and plots with words. Such expression embodies author's personality and judgment.[1] Originality can be determined from two aspects which are "originated independently" and "of minimal creativity." "Originated independently" requires the authors to create a new work independently without plagiarizing or copying others' work. "Of minimal creativity" means the works should be the achievement of intellectual activities and embody authors' personal ideas and judgments, and they do not need to be of high artistic value.[2] Some scholars argue that the works inspired by nonfictions are the descriptions of the historical events which are facts, thus they do not satisfy the requirement of originality. Therefore, when considering whether the works inspired by nonfictions are original, the focus is on whether there are authors' personal creative expressions in the descriptions.

Works relating to historical events can be classified into two categories. The first category is the objective description of historical event without any creative expression, or there is only one available expression to describe the historical event.[3] Since historical events all happen in real life before the creation of the relevant works, the works cannot be considered original if the author just merely pays physical labor to describe the facts. Such works mainly are the statistical data and investigation reports.

---

1. Chen Jinchuan, *Copyright Judgment: Principle Interpretation and Practice Guidance* (2014 Edition), Law Press, 2014, p. 2.
2. Wang Qian, *Intellectual Property Law Course*, Reming University Press, 2007, pp. 28–35.
3. This situation is covered by the "merger" doctrine.

However, in practice there is an situation when the authors claim that although the expression in the historical works are only about "five basic factors" ("when, where, who, what, how"), they have worked so hard to consult and explicit these factors, so they should be entitled to the rights of discovery and first disclosure even if the works are not original enough. This argument is similar to the "sweet of the brow" doctrine of U.S. copyright law that was dated. As is known to all, the purpose of copyright law is to promote the creation and dissemination of culture. Too much protection on discovery and first disclosure by copyright law or even by civil law will be against the legislative purpose of copyright law, as it may not be able to "stand on the shoulders of a giant." Thus, one should be more careful when making the decision to protect discovery and first disclosure either by copyright law or by civil law.

The second category is the works inspired by nonfictional historical events. In this situation, authors have their own creative expression when describing the historical events. These original words are the key element for a work to be protected by copyright. Copyright laws do not protect the abstract ideas and objective facts, but protect the expressions of those abstract ideas and objective facts, as long as the expressions are original. Usually, those protected works are not rigorous history survey report, but historical novel and artistic works. In another word, for artistic works, there is enough space for authors to describe the historical events in an original way, so that the works are the subject matters of copyright law.

2. The determination of infringement of works inspired by nonfictions

It is clear that original works inspired by nonfictions are the subject matters of copyright. The next issue will be how to determine the infringement. The determination shall be made based on the following aspects:

2.1. The scope of copyright protection

As mentioned above, mere historical facts are not the subject matters of copyright. Only the original expression of describing the historical event can be protected by copyright. From the perspective of copyright law, ideas, themes, facts and scenes do not fall into the scope of copyright, while whether the plots in the works can be protected are generally based on whether involved in plagiarism. For the literary works such as novels, it is important to protect the plots in the works. However, when the plot of the real historical event is certain, there may be a problem that if the purpose of a work is to reestablish the event, then the expressions of different authors are probably similar. The reason is the creative space of historical works is limited, so there is a need to distinguish different kinds of works and analyze whether the works are protected case by case.

2.2. The special circumstances of deep plagiarism

As mentioned above, the space of creativity of works inspired by nonfictions is thin, since the arrangement of plots should be consistent with the sequences of the historical events. But it is not ruled out that the plot arrangement is consistent with the facts as well as original. If the plots in the works are copied in this situation, the originality of the arrangement should be considered and the plot should be included in the scope of copyright. Yet there is no such case in the Chinese judicial practice, but the possibility of this situation shall not be ruled out.

2.3. The standard of determining infringement should be strict

Different scope of protection shall be applied to different types of works. Also, different standards of determination of infringement shall be applied based on different types of works. For fictitious works, since the authors have more creative spaces to freely arrange the "five basic factors" ("when, where, who, what, how"), the expressions of different authors are more likely to be different, and the possibility of creating same or similar content is low. Thus, a lower infringement standard is more suitable to be applied to this kind of works.

On the other hand, for works inspired by nonfictions, if the content is a real event in history and the purpose of author is to reestablish the event instead of adapting and deriving, then the author's creative space is limited. In this situation, it is usual and logical that different authors may describe the same event with similar expressions. If it has been continued to apply the same infringement standard of fictitious works to determine the infringement, it will limit the use of historical facts that are already available in the public domain. Thus, in order to keep the balance between the copyright owner and the public interests, a strict standard of determination of the infringement of works inspired by nonfictions shall be applied.

2.4. A plagiarism comparison table should be attached to the judgment

The main reason why many parties are not satisfied with the infringement determination by the court is there are only the amount and the proportion of the similar expression in the text of judgment. In practice, deep plagiarism is a frequent occurrence and the plagiarism parts are dispersed, from dozens to hundreds words (from the range of 20–2,000 words). Therefore, the courts should organize parties to cross-examine the evidence of the content regarded as plagiarism paragraph by paragraph (which is similar to the comparison in patent cases). Then the court can make the determination based on the comparison. Such a plagiarism comparison table should be attached to the judgment, so that the parties will understand the reason for the judgment.

In conclusion, the originality of the works inspired by nonfictions should be determined based on whether the authors explore their creative space with creative expression. Meanwhile, when determining the infringement, the courts should make the decision case by case based on analyzing the conditions including creative space, comparison of the works etc.

—**Comments by FENG Gang**

Case 10. Infringement of the Right of Adaptation

Beijing TCCM Media Co., Ltd. v. Beijing Juhai Media Co., Ltd.
Case of the Infringement of the Right of Adaptation Dispute
Case Index: *Beijing TCCM Media Co., Ltd. v. Beijing Juhai Media Co., Ltd.*; Chaoyang District People's Court of Beijing, Chao Min Chu Zi [2011] No. 24269, January 17, 2012; Beijing No. 2 Intermediate People's Court, Er Zhong Min Zhong Zi [2012] No. 04623, March 19, 2012.

Facts:

The Plaintiff, Beijing TCCM Media Co., Ltd. (hereinafter, "TCCM") alleged that: TCCM exclusively enjoy the right of adaptation to adapt the video drama *Old Boy* (hereinafter, "the involved drama") to a stage play. In April 2011, the Defendant Beijing Juhai Media Co., Ltd. (hereinafter, "Juhai") performed the stage play *Farewell Li Xiang* (hereinafter, "the involved play") to the public in 1919 Theater in Chaoyang District of Beijing. By comparison, the characters and their relationships, the main plots and drama conflicts, the characters' image design and the use of music in the involved play are same or similar to those of the involved drama. Such an act is an unauthorized use the content of the involved drama into the form of stage play, thus should be identified as the adaptation of the involved drama. Such an act of unauthorized adapting the involved drama by Juhai constitutes the infringement of the right of adaptation of the involved drama owned by TCCM, which has caused great economic losses to TCCM, and caused confusion to the public. Therefore, TCCM claimed that: Juhai should stop performing the involved play; make a public apology in the *Beijing Evening* to eliminate any negative influence; compensate the economic losses of RMB 460,000 and reasonable expense of RMB 30,400.

The Defendant Juhai argued that: the Plaintiff's claim in relation to the right of adaptation of the involved video drama to stage play shall be dismissed because of insufficient evidence. The involved play was created, directed and performed by Juhai without adapting the involved video drama. Despite that themes of the involved play and the video drama are similar, and there are huge differences between the two, including length, characters, plot, use of music. Since the Plaintiff also failed to prove the economic losses caused by Juhai, thus the claim of compensation cannot be established. To sum up, Juhai requests the Court to dismiss the claims by the Plaintiff.

The court found that: Xiao Yang and the production branch office of the China Film Group Corporation (hereinafter, "CFGC") signed an agreement titled "Agreement on producing the movie *Old Boy*." According to the agreement, as the producer of the movie, CFGC is responsible for demanding the production, giving opinion for modifications, checking the quality, and promoting. Xiao Yang is responsible for scriptwriting, filming, and post-editing, and guarantees the originality of the film script and music for copyright protection. CFGC, Youku Company and Xiao Yang are entitled to the copyright and related rights of the movie.

On October 28, 2010, the involved video drama was first shown on Youku Company's website. According to the movie information, the drama was co-produced

Chapter 3: Determination of Copyright Infringement

by CFGC and Youku Company, directed and scripted by Xiao Yang, and CFGC was the production manager.

On April 2, 2011, Xiao Yang and TCCM signed a license agreement, stipulating that Xiao Yang's right to adapt the video drama to stage play and the right to perform the stage play were exclusively licensed to TCCM. The term of license is thirty-six months. Meanwhile, Xiao Yang licensed TCCM to use the songs owned by Xiao Yang in the play and agreed to perform in first five *Old Boy* performances in the stage name of "Chopsticks Brothers" for free, as well as agreed to help TCCM to adapt the script and provide such materials as photos and attend the press conference arranged by TCCM. After obtaining the authorization from Xiao Yang, TCCM took full responsibility for the script adaptation, rehearsal and performing. At the time of the litigation, TCCM stated that they were adapting the involved video drama to play, but the play was in the process of preparation.

From April 7 to 24, 2011, Juhai performed the involved play in 1919 Theater in Chaoyang District of Beijing. According to the Juhai, the involved play was totally performed twelve times during the period. There were 250 seats in 1919 Theater. In the ticket of the involved play, it is stated that Juhai is the producer. Before the premiere of the involved play, the information of the play was reported by www.youth.cn, www.qq.com and www.xijucn.com. According to the reports, the involved play by Juhai was performed in 1919 Theater every Thursday, Friday, Saturday and Sunday from April 7 to 24, with twelve plays in the first round.

By comparison, the involved video drama and play are similar in the storyline, characters and the relationships of characters, and the main plots, despite that there were few differences in specific arrangement of some plots and characters.

Ruling and Reasoning:

In the second instance, Beijing No. 2 Intermediate People's Court affirmed the facts found by the first instance.

Beijing No. 2 Intermediate People's Court held that: Xiao Yang is entitled to the right of adaptation of the involved video drama to play, while TCCM exclusively obtained the right of adaptation of the involved video drama in accordance with the license agreement.

The involved video drama is identified as a cinematographic work under the copyright law. In the process of creating the cinematographic work, the relationships among characters are always interactive with the plots. They jointly form the expression to express the ideas and personal emotions of the creator. Thus the original content combined by characters and relationship and the specific plots should be protected by the copyright law. When determining whether the use of one work constitutes the infringement of the other work, the court shall compare not only the characters, the relationships of characters and the specific plots, but also the content intermingled by the three elements, to make a comprehensive comparison.

According to Article 10 of the *Copyright Law*, the right of adaptation is the right to change a work to create a new work of originality. In general, the adaptation should be the new creation that based on the original content of the original work. Thus, when determining whether a work is adapted from another work, one should consider not only the change of the types of work but also whether the new work revises the content of the original work. In this case, since there are some specific plots and characters in the involved play that are not expressed in the involved video drama, it can be concluded that there are original content within the involved play. However, the entire story and storyline of the two are substantially similar. Particularly, the arrangements, characters and relationships, major specific plots are substantially similar, even such details as the characters' names and dialogues are the same. Therefore, after comparing the entire content combined by the characters, character relationships and specific plots, it can be concluded that the two plays are substantially similar. Such similarity cannot be explained as coincidence. Meanwhile, the involved video drama was published before the involved play, which means that Juhai has access to the involved video drama.

Based on the above grounds, the Court held that: The involved play exploited the original content of the involved video drama by changing the involved video drama to create the new involved play. Such an act constitutes the adaptation of the involved video drama. In the absence of the authorization from the copyright owner, Juhai infringed the right of adaptation of TCCM, and caused confusion to the public regarding the relationship between the involved video drama and stage play.

Regarding the compensation, the Court comprehensively considered the reputation of both the involved video drama and play, the license fee of the right of adaption, the size of 1919 Theater, the duration of the performances, the ticket price and the degree of the infringement and subjective wrong of Juhai to determine the amount of compensation.

Commentary:

The key issue of the case is the standard of the infringement of the right of adaptation. Besides, whether a reasonable percentage of benefits should be left to the owner of the illegally adapted work when determining the amount of compensation and whether the new work can be protected by copyright are also two issues to be clarified.

1. The approach and standard of the infringement of the right of adaptation

According to Article 10 of the *Copyright Law*, the right of adaptation is the right to change a work to create a new work of originality, which means that the right of adaptation is a right to create new original work by changing the form or purpose of the original work. Adaptation is by nature one of the deducting behaviors, reserving the plot and content of original work to create a new one with originality by changing the form or purpose of the work. As one of the important economic rights of copyright, it can be exercised by the copyright owner to prohibit any unauthorized exploitation and also can be transferred to others. Thus, in the Chinese judicial practice, the approach to determine copyright infringement is a three-step-test: Step 1, examining the ownership of the right of adaptation; Step 2, judging whether the act in the case can be identified as adaptation; Step 3, ensuring whether there is any statutory exemption.

Chapter 3: Determination of Copyright Infringement

In this case, it can be identified that Xiao Yang is entitled the right of adaptation to adapt the involved video drama to play according to the "Agreement on producing the movie Old Boy" with CFGC. On April 2, 2011, Xiao Yang and TCCM signed a license agreement, exclusively licensing Xiao Yang's right of adaptation to TCCM for thirty-six months. Thus, TCCM obtained the right of adaptation of the involved work and has the capacity to sue for any infringement of the right of adaptation.

The key issue in this case is whether the alleged act by the Defendant can be determined as an act of adapting the Plaintiff's work. According to the copyright law, the core characteristic of the right of adaptation is whether the alleged act changes the original work and creates a new work of originality. Moreover, the adapted work and original work must be substantially similar in their expressions. An act of adaptation must be not only creating new work by changing the original work, but also keeping the basic expressions of that original work. Otherwise, it will be an independent act of creating a new work, instead of an act of adapting a prior work, since there is no connection between the two works. Therefore, in the copyright cases of the right of adaptation, it is of great importance to determine whether the two works are substantially similar. While comparing the similar parts of the two works, the ideas and non-original expressions should be excluded at first, and then the original expression parts should be compared for substantial similarity, that is, whether the new work uses the basic expression and core plot of the prior work to form the adapted work.

In this case, the entire story and storyline of the involved play is basically the same as the involved video drama. Moreover, the arrangements, characters and relationships, and major specific plots of the involved play are almost the same or substantially similar to that of the involved video drama, even including such details as the characters' names and their dialogues. Thus, comparing from the entire content combined by the characters, relationships and specific plots, the two works are substantially similar. Meanwhile, there are some specific plots and characters in the involved play that are not expressed in the involved video drama. For instance, the plots relating to the character "Xi Li" exist only in the involved play but not in the video drama and the relevant plots relating to the character "Campus Belle" are more developed in the involved play than that of the video drama. Thus, it can be determined that the involved play is adapted from the involved video drama.

It is clear that the involved play is adapted from the video drama without any authorization from the right owner TCCM. However, does such an act necessarily constitute the infringement of the right of adaptation? To answer this question, there is also a need to take the rule of fair use into consideration. According to Article 22 of the *Copyright Law*, in the case of free-of-charge live performance of a work that neither collecting fee from the public nor paying remuneration to the performers, the work may be exploited without permission from, and without payment of remuneration to, the copyright owner, provided that the name of the author and the title of the work shall be mentioned. Since the involved play adapted by Juhai was commercially performed in 1919 Theater in Chaoyang District of Beijing, and the name of author and the title of the original work were not mentioned, it cannot be considered as a fair use and exempted from the infringement liabilities.

2. Whether an illegally adapted new work shall be protected by copyright

According to the copyright law, the right of adaptation is to change a work into a new work of originality. Despite that the adapted works are not authorized, they are still new works of originality. According to Article 2 of the *Regulations for the Implementation of the Copyright Law*, the term "works" means intellectual creations with originality in the literary, artistic or scientific domain, insofar as they can be reproduced in a tangible form. Adaptation is a factual behavior, so the approval of the owner of the original work is not a prerequisite. Despite the absence of authorization, the act of adaptation is still intellectual endeavor and contains certain creativity. The adapted work is a new derivative work that is independent from the original work.

Whether an illegally adapted new work shall be protected by copyright is still under debate. The Copyright Law does not explicitly clarify this issue. However, given that, the copyright law protects intellectual creations with originality insofar as they can be reproduced in a tangible form; adapted works should be protected by copyright no matter whether it has been authorized by the owner of the original work. However, since the acquisition of rights is illegitimate, the protection of adapted works should be different. As a reference to China, the U.S. copyright protection only covers the part created by the adaptation, but not any part of the original works. According to the rules set by the 1990 *Abend* case, the parts created by the adaptation in deductive work are the property of the author of the deductive work, but the elements extracted from the prior work are still the property of the author of the prior works.[4] In another word, the protected parts of unauthorized adapted work should be the contents created by the adaptation, that is, the new expressions different from the original work. This means that any communication of the unauthorized adapted work may constitute copyright infringement, because the communication of an adapted work definitely involves the original work. As a result, in practice, the copyright of adapted works is only passive, that is, only when someone use the new expressions created in adaptation, the owner of the adapted work may claim for protection.

3. Whether a reasonable percentage of benefits should be left to the owner of the illegally adapted work when determining the amount of compensation

In copyright infringement cases, the amount of compensation should be first determined according to the actual losses of the right owner. However, usually it is difficult for right owners to provide evidence of the losses caused by the unauthorized adaptation. In this case, TCCM has not yet adapt the involved video drama and just made some preparations, but its potential benefit from the play market may be inevitably affected due to Juhai's infringement which is hard to calculate. When the actual losses are difficult to calculate, the compensation can also be determined

---

4. *Stewart v. Abend*, 495 U.S. 207 (1990).

according to the illegal income. In the case, the involved play was totally performed twelve times. The capacity of the 1919 Theater was approximately 250 seats and the ticket prices were RMB 120, 180 and 380. However since there was no evidence in relation to the attendance and the advertising revenue, the illegal income could not be calculated either. Therefore, the Court determined the amount of compensation based on the overall consideration of the influence and visibility of the involved video drama and play, as well as the degree of subjective wrong of Juhai.

However, there are different opinions regarding whether a reasonable percentage of benefits should be left to the owner of the illegally adapted work when determining the amount of compensation. According to the copyright law, when determining the amount of compensation, the nature of the infringing act of the infringement should be taken into consideration. Since the nature of the infringing act may be affected by many factors, there is an argument by some scholars that: Since the copyright of adapted works is only passive, thus the owner of the adapted works cannot obtain any benefit from communicating the work, therefore the court should not determine to leave any benefit to the infringer. On the other hand, some scholars raise the second opinion that: Despite that the involved play is an infringing work, but it is created by the intellectual endeavor, thus the infringer should be paid for corresponding proportion of benefits according to the rate of his creation from the whole work. Otherwise, it will be obviously unreasonable and against the legislative purpose of the copyright law for encouraging creation.

The second opinion seems fair and reasonable. However, the legislative purpose of the copyright law is not only encouraging creation, but also encouraging the communication of works. The legislative purpose is achieved by providing protection to copyright owners for their works. The protection should be vested on the legitimate works but not the works created by unauthorized creations. Since the works created by unauthorized creations are lack of right basis, the communication of such works will be definitely prohibited by the owner of the original work. Therefore, there will not be any legitimate benefit generated from the works created by unauthorized creations. Meanwhile, a work is considered as one. Despite that one may be able to distinguish the part of the original work from the adapted work, the benefit of the whole work cannot be equally calculated based on each of the parts. It is not only because the contribution for benefits cannot be calculated, but also because the adapted work itself cannot exist alone without the original work. Therefore, the Court did not determine to leave a percentage of benefits to the Defendant.

—**Comments by ZHANG Lingling**

Case 11. Protection of the Right of Authorship of Expressions of Folklore

Anshun Municipal Bureau of Culture & Sports of Guizhou Province. v. Zhang Yimou and Zhang Weiping
Case of the Copyright Infringement Dispute
Case Index: *Anshun Municipal Bureau of Culture & Sports of Guizhou Province. v. Zhang Yimou and Zhang Weiping*; Xicheng District People's Court of Beijing, Xi Min Chu Zi [2010] No. 2606, May 24, 2011; Beijing No. 1 Intermediate People's Court, Yi Zhong Min Zhong Zi [2011] No. 13010, September 14, 2011.

Facts:

The dispute in this case is relating to "Anshun Dixi," which is a type of traditional local drama in Anshun city of Guizhou Province. Since June 2006, Anshun Dixi has been identified by the State Council as a National Intangible Cultural Heritage. In 2005, the film titled *Riding Alone for Thousands of Miles* was released. In this film, the drama *Riding Alone for Thousands of Miles* of Anshun Dixi was played. However, it was named as "Yunnan Mask Drama" in the film.

In regard to the use of Anshun Dixi in the film *Riding Alone for Thousands of Miles*, Anshun Municipal Bureau of Culture & Sports argued that: Anshun Dixi, as a National Intangible Cultural Heritage, is classified as an expression of folklore stipulated in Article 6 of the *Copyright Law of China*. However, in the film involved in this case, Anshun Dixi was named as Yunnan Mask Drama, instead of Anshun Dixi. Such act violated the relevant provisions for protecting authorship right of expressions of folklore under the *Copyright Law*, therefore constituted the infringement of the authorship right of Anshun Dixi as an expression of folklore. Thereafter, Anshun Municipal Bureau of Culture & Sports sued Beijing New Screen Pictures Co., Ltd., which was the producer of the film *Riding Alone for Thousands of Miles*, Zhang Weiping, who was the product manager, and Zhang Yimou, who was the director. The Plaintiff claimed that the Defendants must clarify to the public that the drama in the film should be Anshun Dixi instead of Yunnan Mask Drama.

Ruling and Reasoning:

In the first instance trial, Xicheng District People's Court of Beijing held that as a National Intangible Cultural Heritage, Anshun Dixi should be protected and preserved by the state in accordance with related laws. Users including the producer, product manager, screenwriter and director should respect and protect it. However, the film *Riding Alone for Thousands of Miles* took Anshun DIxi that exists in the reality as a material for literary creation in the film *Riding Alone for Thousands of Miles*, and made the expression of Anshun Dixi to meet the need of film creation. In the film, the Defendants made some adjustments to the accompanying musical instrument and stage form of the drama show, and called it as Yunnan Mask Drama, which does not exist in reality. This deductive technique conforms to the laws of filmmaking, so the film *Riding Alone for Thousands of Miles* is different from documentaries that cannot be fictitious. The Defendants had no subjective intention or negligence to infringe the intangible cultural heritage. On the whole, they did not exert any negative influence including distortion, depreciation, or misleading confusion prohibited by laws on Anshun Dixi. Hence, according to Articles 3, 6, 9, 10, and 11 of the *Copyright Law* and Article 9 of the *Regulations for the Implementation of the Copyright Law*, Xicheng District People's Court of Beijing ruled that the claims of Anshun Municipal Bureau of Culture & Sports were dismissed.

Anshun Municipal Bureau of Culture & Sports filed an appeal. In the second instance, Beijing No. 1 Intermediate People's Court held that this case is on the protection of Anshun Dixi. Anshun Dixi has been communicated, inherited, and enriched by Anshun people from generation to generation, thus it does not belong to any specific civil subject. Therefore, if someone makes damages to it, it is difficult for a specific citizen, legal person, or other organization to make claims. As the governance and protecting organ of Anshun Dixi, the Plaintiff Anshun Municipal Bureau of Culture & Sports is qualified as the representative of Anshun to claim rights and bring a suit. Therefore, as a party of direct interest, Anshun Municipal Bureau of Culture & Sports was entitled to file an appeal of this case as the Plaintiff.

Regarding whether the Defendant, including Beijing New Screen Pictures Co., Ltd., Zhang Weiping, and Zhang Yimou, should bear civil liability for the infringement, the court held that: Under the *Copyright Law*, despite that there is no explicit provision on who shall bear civil liability for film-related disputes, it is explicitly provided that producers are copyright owners of cinematographic works. Based on the principle of "equal rights come with equal responsibility," the producer of a cinematographic work shall certainly bear relevant civil liability relating to the film. Hence in this case, the producer Beijing New Screen Pictures Co., Ltd. shall bear liability for any infringement. Neither Zhang Yimou nor Zhang Weiping was the producer of the film *Riding Alone for Thousands of Miles*, thus they shall not bear any liability.

The key issue of this case is whether use of Anshun Dixi in the film *Riding Alone for Thousands of Miles* constituted infringement of authorship right of Anshun Dixi. The court held that under the *Copyright Law*, Article 10 clarified that the right of authorship is the right to claim authorship and to have the author's name indicated in connection with the work. Thus it is explicated that authors are the owners of authorship right, the subject matter is the work, and the content of the right is to put the author's name on the work. If someone exercises the unauthorized act of signing names on the work, then he may infringe the authorship right. In this case, Anshun Dixi was not the subject matter of the authorship right. Despite Anshun Dixi was called Yunnan Mask Drama in the film *Riding Alone for Thousands of Miles*, this act of using could not be recognized as the act of signing name under the *Copyright Law*. Hence, according to the *Copyright Law*, the act did not constitute an infringement of the authorship right. Therefore, Beijing No. 1 Intermediate People's Court ruled that the claims were dismissed and the original judgment was affirmed in accordance with Article 153 of the *Civil Procedure Law of China*.

Commentary:

Since the dispute at issue was to seek copyright protection for an item of the National Intangible Cultural Heritage Anshun Dixi, this case drew great public attention. Despite that both the Court of First Instance and the court of second instance ruled the case by different approaches, they eventually dismissed the claims of the Plaintiff Anshun Municipal Bureau of Culture & Sports, and held that the use in the film *Riding Alone for Thousands of Miles* did not constitute infringement of authorship right under the *Copyright Law*. After the ruling had been made, there were some dissenting opinions. As the judge of this case in second instance, I would like to further explain the judgment, so that the readers may understand the inquisitions of this case.

1. Relationship between the *Intangible Cultural Heritage Law* and the *Copyright Law*

Since the issue involved in this case was the protection by copyright of National Intangible Cultural Heritage, it is necessary to clarify the relationship between the protection from the *Intangible Cultural Heritage Law* and that from the *Copyright Law* in the first place. The *Intangible Cultural Heritage Law* is designed mainly to provide administrative protection for those items of intangible cultural heritages, emphasizing on determination, protection and preservation of them. For civil protection on intangible cultural heritage, there is no provision in the *Intangible Cultural Heritage Law*. In addition, in the *Intangible Cultural Heritage Law*, Article 44 clarifies that when intellectual property issue occurs during the use of intangible cultural heritages, the intellectual property laws shall be applicable. Hence, the fact that Anshun Dixi is identified as a National Intangible Cultural Heritage only means it shall be protected by the *Intangible Cultural Heritage Law*. Whether Anshun Dixi is protectable under the *Copyright Law* shall be decided in accordance with the *Copyright Law*.

2. Legal basis for the protection of expressions of folklore

The Plaintiff argued that Anshun Dixi was not only a National Intangible Cultural Heritage but also an expression of folklore under the *Copyright Law*, thus the Plaintiff made the claims concerning the authorship right of Anshun Dixi.

Regarding the protection of expressions of folklore, there is no explicit provision in the *Copyright Law*, except that Article 6 stipulates that measures for the protection of expressions of folklore shall be formulated separately by the State Council. So far, the State Council has not provided any relevant measures for protecting the copyright of expressions of folklore. This however does not mean that it is impossible to provide copyright protection for expressions of folklore. Since the *Copyright Law* explicitly states that expressions of folklore shall be protected, all future measures for protecting expressions of folklore by the State Council must comply with the relevant provisions of the *Copyright Law*. Accordingly, in the absence of relevant protecting measures, the court shall rule the cases concerning expressions of folklore in accordance with the basic principles and provisions of the *Copyright Law*, including the protection on authorship right.

3. Interpretation of authorship right

Since the Plaintiff's claims were made based on the authorship right of Anshun Dixi as expression of folklore, the key issue was how to interpret the authorship right under the *Copyright Law*. In the *Copyright Law*, Article 10 clarifies that the right of authorship is the right to claim authorship in respect of, and to have the author's name mentioned in connection with, a work. As it can be read directly from this provision, the owner of the authorship right is the author; the subject matter of the authorship right is the specific concrete work; and the content of the right is to mark author's name on the work. The "authorship" in the authorship right refers to the name of the right owner (the author) rather than that of the subject matter (the work). In addition, the *Interpretations of the Copyright Law of the People's Republic of China* further explains that the owner of authorship right (the author) has the right to or not to display his identification in the work. In case others use the work without marking the author's name, such an act constitutes the infringement of authorship right. Whether the name of the work is marked is not in the scope of authorship right.[5]

On the basis of the above interpretation of authorship right, since the Plaintiff claimed for the authorship right of Anshun Dixi, therefore such claim may stand unless both of the following two conditions are met: first, Anshun Dixi can be classified as a work (the subject matter of authorship right); second, Anshun Dixi can be identified as the name of the author (the owner of authorship right). Otherwise, the Plaintiff is not entitled to prohibit others to indicate the name of Anshun Dixi.

Whether Anshun Dixi can be treated as a work shall be determined in accordance with the fundamental principles of copyright. According to the principle, only the specific expressions of ideas may be classified as copyrighted works. Similar to other traditional Chinese local dramas including Beijing opera and Ping opera, Anshun Dixi is a "type" of dramas. The term "Anshun Dixi" refers to all dramas with certain features in common. Since the type of dramas does not contain "concrete" expression of ideas or feelings, Anshun Dixi as such cannot be treated as a work, which is the subject matter of authorship right. Hence, there is no owner of the copyright of Anshun Dixi.

Even Anshun Dixi cannot be classified as work, it does not mean that any specific drama show of Anshun Dixi cannot be a work. Some specific drama shows (such as *Riding Alone for Thousands of Miles* used in the involved film) are works under the *Copyright Law*, since they are the concrete expressions of ideas and feelings. Hence, the authorship right of specific drama shows is enjoyed by the relevant civil subjects. However in this case, the Plaintiff explicitly claimed for the authorship right of Anshun Dixi, rather than that of the specific drama show such as *Riding Alone for Thousands of Miles*. Therefore, the court did not mention the issue in the decision.

---

5. The Plaintiff argued that the "authorship" in right of authorship shall cover the name of the author as well as the name of the work. This argument was incorrect.

Since only authors can own the right of authorship, and Anshun Dixi is obviously not a civil subject, hence it is impossible for Anshun Dixi to be an author and certainly cannot own the right of authorship. However, when considering the protection on expressions of folklore, the special characteristics of expressions of folklore are taken into consideration. The *Interpretations of the Copyright Law of the People's Republic of China* states that comparing with other types of works, individual authors of expressions of folklore are usually uncertain (i.e., difficult to determine who the author is) and not individual (i.e., the author is usually a social group such as a nation and a community).[6] Hence, when considering what and how an expression of folklore shall be signed, those special characteristics should be taken into consideration. Since the Plaintiff's claims were dismissed due to the subject matter reason but not the way of signing, it is not appropriate to analyze further in this book. However, it shall be emphasized that whether the way of signing in this case is within the scope of copyright cannot be decided by the reason that Anshun Dixi is not a civil subject.

4. Interpretation of the act of signing

To prove the Defendant's act constitutes the infringement of authorship right, the Plaintiff shall also prove that the alleged act of signing is within the scope of authorship right under the *Copyright Law*. If the Plaintiff failed to do so, even if the Plaintiff is entitled to claim, the Defendant's act still cannot be identified as an infringement of authorship right.

The alleged act was the act that Anshun Dixi was called Yunnan Mask Drama in the film. When deciding whether such an act was considered as an act of signing within the scope of authorship right, it has to be found whether the Defendant tried to indicate author's name in that alleged act. Therefore, if Yunnan Mask Drama is not the name of an author, the act of using Yunnan Mask Drama shall not be considered as an act of signing within the scope of authorship right. Based on the evidence, it is insufficient to prove the alleged act is an act of signing. Therefore, the use of Yunnan Mask drama in the film was for identifying the type of drama, but not a signing act under the *Copyright Law*.

5. Difference between the case of *Anshun Dixi* and the case of *Wusuli Boat Song*

In regard to the protection of expressions of folklore, just few precedent cases can be found from the judicial experience in China. The only famous case is the *Wusuli Boat Song* case tried by Beijing Higher People's Court.[7] In that case, the court had supported the claims of the Plaintiff. Therefore, In the case of *Anshun Dixi*, the Plaintiff was encouraged to take the *Wusuli Boat Song* case as a precedent and requested the court

---

6. In *The Protection of Traditional Cultural Expressions: Draft Articles* of World Intellectual Property Organization, Art. 1 clarifies that protection of traditional cultural expressions shall be extended to the local nation or community.
7. *See* Beijing Higher People's Court Gao Min Zhong Zi [2003] No. 246 civil judgment. The Plaintiff was Si Pai Hezhe Town Government in Raohe County, Heilongjiang Province, and the Defendant was Guo Song and China Central Television.

to support its claims. However, since the two cases are different in the following two aspects, the *Wusuli Boat Song* approach shall not be applied in this case.

First, the two Plaintiffs' claims are made upon different subject matters of copyright. In the *Wusuli Boat Song* case, the Plaintiff claimed the copyright of two "specific" Hezhe folk songs (*Miss My Lover* and *My Hunter Brother Returned*) rather than "general" Hezhe folk songs. The two specific folk songs certainly can be classified as copyrighted works, so they are protected by authorship right without any doubt. However in the *Anshun Dixi* case, the Plaintiff made its claims based on Anshun Dixi, which was a "type" of drama, instead of "specific" dramas. Since Anshun Dixi is not a work, it certainly cannot be protected by copyright as such.

Second, the alleged acts in the two cases are different. In the *Wusuli Boat Song* case, the alleged act was the Defendant (Guo Song)'s act of indicating his own name as the author in the adapted work *Wusuli Boat Song*. The act of signing is an act that marking the author's name in the work, so the Defendant's act obviously was within the scope of authorship right under the *Copyright Law*. However in the *Anshun Dixi* case, the alleged act was the act of calling Anshun Dixi as Yunnan Mask Drama. Given that the evidence was insufficient to prove the alleged act is an act of signing, such an act cannot be determined as an act of signing under the *Copyright Law*.

—**Comments by RUI Songyan**

Case 12. Scope of Protection of Architectural Works

National Stadium Co., Ltd. v. Panda Fireworks Group Corp., Ltd.; Liuyang Panda Fireworks Co., Ltd.; Beijing Panda Fireworks Co., Ltd
Cases of infringement of copyright disputes
Case Index: *National Stadium Co., Ltd. v. Panda Fireworks Group Corp., Ltd.; Liuyang Panda Fireworks Co., Ltd.; Beijing Panda Fireworks Co., Ltd.*; Beijing No. 1 Intermediate People's Court [2009] No. 4476, Zhong Min Chu Zi, June 20, 2011

Facts:

On November 13, 2003, National Stadium Co., Ltd. (hereinafter, "National Stadium Company") commissioned Herzog & de Meuron Architekten AG (H&deM), Ove Arup & Partner Hongkong Ltd., and the China National Architectural Design and Research Group to design the National Stadium. According to the agreement, National Stadium Company is entitled to the economic rights of the copyright of the National Stadium.

The National Stadium, also known as its popular name "Bird's Nest," was completed and accepted on June 27, 2008. The characteristics of the National Stadium (*see* Picture 1) are as follows: (1) Regarding the overall shape, the east-west part is narrow and high, the north-south part is wide and low, in the shape of a three-dimensional saddle. (2) The aspect ratio is 1:0.88. (3) Regarding the steel frame structure, the appearance of a seemingly casual steel trusses is interwoven around an internal football field. (4) Regarding the colors and lines, with the lights on, the steel racks of the National Stadium appear grayish blue, the back of the spectator stand is red and the gray-blue steel frame envelopes the red stands. (5) Regarding the torch, at the top of the northeastern side, a torch is set up to ignite the Olympic flame. (6) Regarding the lighting, the lighting fixtures of the National Stadium are installed on the elevation between the top and bottom chords to make the lights go to the track field. (7) Regarding the track and field, inside the National Stadium, there is a green football field and a red outer race track.

On January 14, 2009, the agent of the National Stadium Company purchased three "Flying Bird's Nest" fireworks at a price of RMB 140 (*see* Picture 2). The product exhibits the following characteristics: (1) Regarding the overall shape, it is in three-dimensional saddle, with two narrow sides high and two wide sides low. (2) Regarding the aspect ratio, the length is 40 cm, and the width is 33.5 cm, so the aspect ratio is 1:0.84. (3) Regarding the frame structure, The external drawing paper draws lines that are similar to the seemingly casual steel truss of the National Stadium. Its curved angle, curvature and frequency of interweaving are similar to those of the National Stadium. (4) Regarding the colors and lines, the external color is a mix of gray and blue lines covering the red body. (5) Regarding the torch, "Flying Bird's Nest" placed the ignition point of the firework on one side of the top. (6) Regarding the lighting, "Flying Bird's Nest" draws a light pattern on the elevation between the top and bottom chords. (7) Regarding the track and field, "Flying Bird's Nest" has set up a green football field and a red outer track pattern inside.

On the package of the "Flying Bird's Nest" firework, it is stated that: the product is manufactured by Liuyang Panda Fireworks Co., Ltd. (hereinafter, "Liuyang Panda"), supervised by Panda Group, and distributed by Beijing Panda Fireworks Co., Ltd. (hereinafter, "Beijing Panda").

National Stadium Company alleged that: National Stadium Company is the copyright owner of the architectural works of the National Stadium "Bird's Nest." Supervised by Panda Group, manufactured by Liuyang Panda and distributed by Beijing Panda, the "Flying Bird's Nest" firework product imitates the unique artistic characteristics of the "Bird's Nest," plagiarizing the Plaintiff's creativity. From the infringement of the Plaintiff's copyright, the Defendants obtained huge illegal benefits. Therefore, the Plaintiff claimed that the Defendants shall: (1) cease the infringement of the copyright immediately; (2) eliminate the negative impact by making apology on national newspapers; (3) compensate the Plaintiff RMB 4,000,000 for economic losses.

The Defendant Panda Group argued that: (1) Panda Group was neither the manufacturer of the involved infringing product nor the distributor of the product. As the supervisor of the involved infringing product, it is only responsible for quality control and technical support for the production of Liuyang Panda's fireworks. The Plaintiff has no factual or legal basis to request to bear the infringement liability. (2) The evidence provided by the Plaintiff can only prove that it enjoys the economic rights of the relevant work, not the moral rights of the works. Since the elimination of negative impact and apology only applicable to the infringement of moral rights, the Plaintiff's claim of elimination of negative impact and apology shall not be supported. In conclusion, Panda Group requests to dismiss all the claims by the Plaintiff.

The Defendant Liuyang Panda argued that: The "Flying Bird's Nest" firework product did not infringe the copyright of the National Stadium architectural work. First of all, Article 22 of the *Copyright Law* stipulates that "copying, painting, photographing, and recording of works of art that are set up or displayed in outdoor public places" is a fair use of the works. Even if the packaging pattern of the "Flying Bird's Nest" firework imitates the National Stadium, it is also a fair use of the architectural works and does not constitute any infringement. In conclusion, Liuyang Panda requests to dismiss all the claims by the Plaintiff.

The Defendant Beijing Panda argued that: Beijing Panda was only a distributor of the "Flying Bird's Nest" firework products. The product had a legitimate source, and Beijing Panda had already conducted a reasonable review of the infringement of the intellectual property rights due to the particularity of the purchased product, and fulfilled a reasonable duty of care. The sale did not constitute an infringement of the copyright of the Plaintiff. In conclusion, Beijing Panda requests to dismiss all the claims by the Plaintiff.

Ruling and Reasoning:

Beijing No. 1 Intermediate People's Court held that:

1. Whether the Plaintiff has the copyright in the National Stadium architectural works

The National Stadium can be identified as an architectural work in accordance with the *Regulations for the Implementation of the Copyright Law*. The steel trusses used are intertwined around the appearance of a bowl-shaped building. The space structure is scientific and concise. The architecture and structure are complete and unified. The design is novel and the structure is unique. The architecture is equipped with artistry which is independent of its utility, reflecting a considerable level of originality. Therefore, according to the *Regulations for the Implementation of the Copyright Law*, the National Stadium can be identified as an architectural works. The Plaintiff has obtained the economic rights of the architectural work of the National Stadium. The above rights enjoyed by the Plaintiff should be protected according to the copyright law.

2. Whether the manufacturing and distributing of the "Flying Bird's Nest" firework products constitute the infringement of the plaintiff's copyright in architectural works

The protection of the copyright of architectural works is mainly to protect the artistic aesthetic value of architectural works that can be separated from their utility. Therefore, in the absence of any legitimate basis of fair use or the authorization of the copyright owner of the architectural works, any act of plagiarism, reproduction, distribution, etc. to improperly exploit the artistic aesthetic value in architectural works, which prejudice the legitimate rights and interests of copyright owners, constitutes an infringement of the copyright of architectural works.

The "Flying Bird's Nest" firework product has an elliptical shape and a hollow in the middle. It adopts the original features same or similar to the appearance of the National Stadium in terms of its overall shape, aspect ratio, steel frame structure, colors and lines, and torch, etc. The highly imitation of the architectural works of the National Stadium is a reproduction of the original intellectual achievements of the National Stadium architectural works, and is essentially similar to the National Stadium. The manufacture and sale of the "Flying Bird's Nest" firework products constitute the reproduction and distribution of architectural works of the National Stadium.

As mentioned above, the protection of the copyright of architectural works is mainly the protection of the artistic aesthetic value that is reflected in architectural works that can be separated from their utility. As long as the authorization of the right owner is not granted, the exploitation of the artistic aesthetic value in the architectural works constitutes an infringement of the copyright of the architectural works, regardless of whether such exploitation is used in works in the sense of copyright law or in industrial products. That is not limited by the medium of fixation. Therefore, even the Defendant Liuyang Panda argued that the "Flying Bird's Nest" firework product is an industrial product, not a work in the sense of copyright law, thus there is no legal basis for the plagiarism or reproduction, such an argument cannot be established.

Despite that Article 22 of the *Copyright Law* stipulates that copying, painting, photographing, and recording of works of art set up or displayed in outdoor public places are fair uses of the works, the provision explicitly limits this fair use to the four modes of "copying, painting, photography, and video recording," and does not include any use other than these four methods. Since the Defendants in this case used the artistic aesthetic value of the National Stadium to manufacture and sell fireworks, such an act obviously is not within the scope of the above four methods. Second, the purpose of fair use rule is mainly to protect public interests. The Defendants exploited the Plaintiff's architectural works to firework products purely for commercial purposes. Such exploitation is against the legislative purpose of fair use rule. Third, when determining whether it constitutes fair use, it is necessary to consider whether the use will affect the value or potential market of the work, that is, whether it will affect the normal exploitation of the work by the copyright owner. The normal exploitation of works refers to the various ways in which people may reasonably expect to use their works, including the actual use of works that the author expects and the possible use of works in the future. The application of architectural design to other products is a foreseeable use. The Defendants' acts directly affect the Plaintiff's secondary commercialization of the works, and will unreasonably prejudice the Plaintiff's legitimate interests. Therefore, the Defendants' use of the National Stadium architectural works does not fall within the scope of fair use as stipulated in Article 22 of the *Copyright Law*. The Defendant Liuyang Panda's argument cannot be established.

In conclusion, in the absence of evidence to prove that the Defendants obtained the authorization from the Plaintiff, the manufacture and sale of the "Flying Bird's Nest" firework products infringed the Plaintiff's right of reproduction and the right of distribution of architectural work of the National Stadium.

3. Civil liabilities of each Defendant

Since the Defendants Liuyang Panda and Panda Group infringed the right of reproduction and the right distribution of the architectural work of the Plaintiff by plagiarism, reproduction and distribution, they shall jointly bear the civil liabilities of stopping the infringement and compensation for economic losses. Since the Defendant Beijing Panda is the distributor of the "Flying Bird's Nest" firework products, it shall only bear the liability of stopping the infringement. Apology and eliminating the negative impact are the remedies for damage of moral rights. Since the Plaintiff are not entitled to any moral right in the architectural works of the National Stadium, the Plaintiff's claim for the apology and the elimination of the negative impact are lack of factual and legal basis.

In conclusion, it is ruled that: The Defendants Panda Group and Liuyang Panda shall stop the manufacture and sale of the "Flying Bird's Nest" firework products, and jointly compensate the Plaintiff for economic losses of RMB 100,000, and the reasonable expenses of RMB 2,974. The Defendant Beijing Panda shall stop the sale of the "Flying Bird's Nest" firework products.

After the judgment of the first instance was made, no party appealed.

Commentary:

Architectural works are the newly added subject matter of copyright protection when China amended the *Copyright Law* in 2001. Article 4 of the *Regulations for the Implementation of the Copyright Law* stipulates: *"Architectural works are works with aesthetic effect which are expressed in form of buildings or structures."* Despite that the above provision gives a clear definition of architectural works, there is no specific scope of the protection of architectural works. Therefore, in the Chinese judicial practice, there are still controversial arguments in relation to the interpretation of the scope of protection. During the trial of this case, what the Court needed to answer were the following two questions: First, whether the protection of architectural works limited to the medium of building. Second, whether the application of architectural design to other industrial products constitutes a fair use of the architectural work.

1. Whether the protection of architectural works limited to the medium of building

From the definition of architectural works, it particularly emphasizes that architectural works should be represented in the form of buildings or structures. In the Chinese judicial practice, it has been a consensus that the unauthorized copy of one building from another building constitutes infringement. However in this case, the Defendants copied the building design of the Plaintiff's "Bird's Nest" to the firework products, but did not reflect the architectural design of the "Bird's Nest" in the form of buildings or structures. So, the question is whether the protection of architectural works only limited to the medium of building. To answer this question, the protection subject matter of architectural works must be clarified first.

What to be protected by copyright law are intangible works. The intangibility is the key characteristic for works to distinguish them from any material good. The medium is the intermediary to perceive the works. It is not the work itself, nor does it constitute part of the work. Despite that no work can be without its medium, the work itself is not the medium. Therefore, the medium is not the subject matter of copyright protection, and logically, it should not be a limitation of the protection of the work.

Since architectural works are one type of works, they also have the characteristic of intangibility. Although architectural works are represented by buildings or structures, the medium of a building or structure has meaning only when the architectural works are distinguished from other types of works, and cannot be a limitation when protecting architectural works. In this case, the Court emphasized that the protection of architectural works is mainly the protection of artistic aesthetic value that is reflected in architectural works separated from their utility, and the artistic aesthetic value can be separated from its medium.

Whether it is represented in buildings or structures is only for identifying the type of works, but not for determining whether it can be protected. Therefore, the protection of architectural works should not be limited to the medium of the building. In the case,

Chapter 3: Determination of Copyright Infringement

the Defendants' application of architectural design of the Plaintiff to the fireworks constitutes the infringement of the architectural works.

2. Whether the application of architectural design to other industrial products constitutes a fair use of the architectural work

According to the copyright law, the author enjoys copyright for his works. Others may not use without the author's authorization. However, the copyright law also imposes exemptions on the rights of copyright owners. Under certain circumstances, others are allowed to freely use the existing works without obtaining any permission from the copyright owner and or paying for the use. This is the fair use rule. The purpose of the fair use rule is to take care of public interests and prevent copyright owners from abusing their rights so as to better promote the development of science and technology as well as cultural prosperity. The main purpose of this rule is to ensure the free expression and exchange of ideas, particularly in the cases of nun-commercial use of works.

Article 22 of the *Copyright Law* stipulates twelve circumstances for fair use. One of the circumstances is "copying, painting, photography of works of art set up or displayed in outdoor public places." There are two conditions for this circumstance: First, from the perspective of object, it should be limited to the works in outdoor public places. Second, from the perspective of usage of architectural works, it should be limited to two-dimensional reproduction by copying, painting, photographing and video recording.

Besides utility, architectural works are also of artistic aesthetic value in the same time. Thus, architectural works is a kind of artistic works. The limitation concerning the object of outdoor public places should be applicable to "Bird's Nest." Therefore, the usage of architectural works is the key to determine whether the uses constitute fair use.

In this case, the three-dimensional shape of the "Flying Bird's Nest" firework manufactured and sold by the Defendants was completely imitated by the shape of the "Bird's Nest" architectural works. Meanwhile, it was decorated in a printed paper with a steel frame structure and a night view effect so that the audience could feel clearly that the fireworks took advantage of the "Bird's Nest" architectural works. Therefore, the "Flying Bird's Nest" fireworks do not use the "Bird's Nest" architectural works in a two-dimensional reproduction such as copying, painting, photographing, and video recording, thus do not constitute fair use according to Article 22 of the *Copyright Law*.

Despite that the *Copyright Law* enumerates certain specific circumstances of fair use, it cannot be determined whether it is fair use in judicial practice simply by whether or not it is included in the mentioned specific circumstances. When determining whether a defendant's act is fair use, the following factors should be taken into consideration, include the purpose and nature of the use, the nature of the work, the amount and substantive part of the work used as a whole, and the effect on the potential market value of copyrighted works. Therefore, the ruling of this case also discussed from the aspects of the purpose of fair use and whether the use by the Defendant will affect the value of the Plaintiff's work or the potential market, and then made the conclusion that the Defendants' exploitation does not constitute fair use.

—**Comments by JIANG Ying**

Chapter 3: Determination of Copyright Infringement

Case 13. Infringement Relating to Internet TV

Beijing Union Voole Technology Co., Ltd. v. TCL Group Corp., Ltd.; Shenzhen Xunlei Network Technology Co., Ltd.; and etc.
Case of the Infringement of Right of Dissemination via Information Networks Dispute
Case Index: *Beijing Union Voole Technology Co., Ltd v. TCL group Limited by Share Ltd, Shenzhen Xunlei Network Technology Co., Ltd.;* *Beijing No. 2 Intermediate People's Court, Er Zhong Min Chu Zi [2010] No. 17910, September 27, 2010; Beijing Higher People's Court, Gao Min Zhong Zi [2010] No. 2581, April 20, 2011.*

Facts:

Beijing Union Voole Co., Ltd (hereinafter, "Union Voole Co.") alleged that: it has the exclusive right of dissemination via information networks about the film "Lavender," the Defendant TCL Group Limited by Share Ltd (hereinafter, "TCL Co.") produces "MiTV Internet TV" which has a built-in automatic search function module to download film involved in the case, the search, download and other fixed operations involved in the case point to the Defendant Shenzhen Xunlei Network Technology co., LTD. (hereinafter Xunlei) video search platform and video resources portal, search and download technology is also provided by the Defendant, Xunlei Co. Hence, without the Plaintiff's authorization, the two Defendants jointly infringed the rights of information network transmission enjoyed by the Plaintiff. The Defendant, Gome Electrical Appliances co., LTD. (hereinafter, "Gome") knew that the function of "MiTV Internet TV" was to download and broadcast film and TV work before, Gome still highlighted it as a unique selling point to seek illegal interests. Hence, Gome shall bear corresponding responsibility in accordance with the law. Hence, the Plaintiff requested the Court to order that:

> 1. The Defendant shall cease the production of "MiTV Internet TV" immediately. Meanwhile, the Defendant shall dismantle the Internet function module of TV without selling out. The Defendants, TCL Co. and Xunlei Co. stopped disseminating the involved work Lavender through the information network. The Defendant shall immediately stop selling the infringing products. 2. Defendants, TCL Co. and Xunlei Co. shall respectively publish a statement of apology to the Plaintiff in the most prominent position on the homepages of their official websites in the same manner as other official texts. The statement should be approved by the Court in advance and be retained for one month. 3. The three Defendants shall compensate the Plaintiff RMB 200,000 for economic losses and the reasonable expenses for preventing act of infringement RMB 12,000 and bear the costs of litigation.

> The Defendant, TCL Co., argued that: (1) the Plaintiff did not have the right to disseminate information on the Internet and had no right to file a lawsuit in this case. The movie Lavender involved did not obtain the "License for Public Projection of Films" and could not be released. The Plaintiff did not submit the legal CD of Lavender. Moreover, the certification of the right to issue had flaws, which could not prove that the original right holder of the film involved was Jia He Film (China) Co., Ltd. It could not prove that the Plaintiff obtained the right to disseminate the information on the film work involved in the case. (2) There was no legal basis for the Defendant to require TCL Co. to stop the production of TV

involved in the case or to dismantle its Internet function modules. The "MiTV Internet TV" produced by TCL Co. had added an Internet search and download function module to traditional TV, through which consumers could search and download relevant content to be broadcasted by the television, which had substantial noninfringing use. Even if the Plaintiff's Right of Dissemination via Information Networks was infringed, the company should only bear the legal responsibility of stopping the dissemination of the works involved in the Internet. 3. TCL Co. was a network equipment provider. When a user used an Internet TV, TCL Co. could not select, edit, and copy the videos downloaded by users, but passively received them. Hence, TCL was not a provider of Internet content, but the provider of terminal equipment. 4. TCL had no fault subjectively. As an emerging industry, the development mode of Internet TV is still in the process of exploration, and cooperation between TCL Co. and the other organizations did not violate the relevant regulations and was subjectively fault-free. The Plaintiff failed to perform the corresponding notice service. After the suit, the Defendant, Xunlei Co., deleted the works involved in the case and the Internet TV could no longer search for the involved works. Therefore, TCL Co. asked to dismiss the Plaintiff's claim.

The Defendant, Xunlei Co., argued that: 1.It was not clear whether the Plaintiff was the right holder of the film work involved. Xunlei Co. had obtained the authorization of Hong Kong Power Film Co., Ltd. through Guangzhou Port Laohui Co., Ltd., which included the film Lavender. 2. Xunlei Co. only provided technical services to TCL, which was the basic index database for Gougou search engines. It did not involve video content and should not bear the legal liability. Xunlei Co. provided real-time search and nondirectional download services under the entire Internet environment, when the TV users searched and downloaded, this process was also searched on the entire Internet network, and ultimately provided third-party source addresses to the users. Xunlei Co. had not implemented direct Infringement. There were a large number of free legitimate videos available on the Internet. Xunlei Co. could not judge whether the video files in the search results were authorized, nor could it simply presumed that all the TV dramas searched from the Internet were infringing works. Moreover, the search results page of the television set in question should be controlled by TCL Co. and Xunlei Co. did not and could not make any sort of editing and sorting of search results, and did not have subjective guidance or objective assistance to assist infringement. 3. Xunlei Co. provided search engine services. The Plaintiff did not send rights notice in any form. Xunlei Co. should not assume any responsibility. After being sued, Xunlei Co. promptly carried out simple keywords screening on the three websites it controlled, and fulfilled its copyright protection responsibility. Therefore, Xunlei Co. asked to dismiss the Plaintiff's claim.

The Defendant, Gome Company, argued that The MiTV Internet TV involved in the case had legal sources of purchase. Gome had no infringement and infringement facts and should not be jointly and severally liable with other Defendants. Therefore, the Court was asked to dismiss the Plaintiff's claim against Gome.

Ruling and Reasoning:

The Beijing No. 2 Intermediate People's Court held that: The dispute between the parties involved in the case was whether the Plaintiff Union Voole Co. had the right to disseminate information on the Internet in the movie Lavender; and whether the Defendants Shenzhen Xunlei Network Technology Co., Ltd, TCL Group Limited by

Chapter 3: Determination of Copyright Infringement

Share Ltd, or Gome's involvement in the case infringed the information network transmission right enjoyed by the Plaintiff Union Voole Co. and whether it shall assume the corresponding legal responsibility.

First, on the issue of whether the Plaintiff Union Voole Co. had the right to disseminate information on the Internet in the film Lavender.

In accordance with the provisions of the Copyright Law of China, if there is no contrary proof, the citizen, legal person or other organization whose name appears on a work shall be the author. The production unit involved in the film Lavender was Golden Harvest Company Ltd. (China). Therefore, Golden Harvest Company Ltd. (China) should be the copyright owner of this cinematographic work involved in the case. The Certificate of Distribution Rights and other relevant evidence presented by the Hong Kong Motion Picture Industry Association Ltd (MPIA) and submitted by the Plaintiff Union Voole Co. indicated that Golden Harvest Company Ltd. (China) awarded the exclusive information network transmission right of the film Lavender to Golden Harvest Company Ltd. (China). Golden Harvest Company Ltd. (China) also awarded the exclusive information network transmission right to Union Voole Co. Therefore, the Plaintiff enjoyed exclusive rights to the dissemination of information on the movie Lavender in this case.

The Defendant, Shenzhen Xunlei Network Technology Co., Ltd., claimed that it had obtained the authorization for the film involved in this case from Guangzhou Gang Laohui Culture Communication Co., Ltd. and submitted the Video Copyright Assignment to prove that the copyright owner of the film, the Dynamic Film Co. Ltd., permanently transferred the television copyright of the film to Guangzhou Gang Laohui Culture Communication Co., Ltd. However, it did not prove that the Dynamic Film Co., Ltd. was the copyright holder of the film, and the signature of Dynamic Film Co., Ltd. did not appear in the movie Lavender. Therefore, although the Defendant TCL Group Limited by Share Ltd, and Shenzhen Xunlei Network Technology Co., Ltd. objected to the Plaintiff Union Voole Co. regarding the rights to dissemination of information on the film Lavender, and considered that the relevant evidence submitted by the Plaintiff was defective, it did not challenge the evidence presented by the Plaintiff. As a result, this Court would not accept the above defense.

Second, there were problems about whether the Defendants, Shenzhen Xunlei Network Technology Co., Ltd. and TCL Group Limited by Share Ltd's involvement in the case, infringed the information network transmission right enjoyed by the Plaintiff Union Voole Co. and whether it shall assume the corresponding legal responsibility.

Third, according to the facts ascertained in this case, the Defendant Shenzhen Xunlei Network Technology Co., Ltd. authorized the Defendant TCL Group Limited by Share Ltd, to integrate CE version downloadable software of Shenzhen Xunlei Network Technology Co., Ltd. in its internet television in accordance with its cooperation agreement with Shenzhen TCL Group Limited by Share Ltd, and to provide the TCL Group Limited by Share Ltd, with the information of Movie Information Database, including audio and video names, columns, keywords, categories, languages, director information, starring information, release time, length, content, location, origin and evaluation. The Defendant, Shenzhen Xunlei Network Technology Co., Ltd., recognized that its permission to module installed by TCL Group Limited by Share Ltd, in the internet television involved in this case was the same as the search function on the internet website Gougou. After being inspected by the Court, the search results for related videos using "Gougou Search" were BT, eDonkey, mobile video, HD and other types.

Notarially, when searching for the related movie Lavender in MiTV Internet TV, the page of search results included information about the movie, "Download Technology Powered by Xunlei" and it was accompanied by Xunlei Co.'s icon and showed only two Seed file links. Although the Defendants, TCL company and Xunlei Company, objected to the authenticity of the notarial deed for the purchase of the Internet television set and for the purpose of Internet forensics, it was verified by the Court that the Internet TV set involved did not appear to be out of control of the staff of the notary office. Therefore, this Court did not accept the above defense. The two seed files on the above search results page indicated that the search results belong to the BT type. According to the existing evidence in this case, the right holder of the film works involved in the film, although the Union Voole Co. had authorized a third party to disseminate the film work involved through the Internet. However, the Plaintiff and the relevant licensee did not make the movie work as a seed file and published it through the Internet. According to this, it was determined that the video file provided by the source address of the seed file appearing in the search results should be an infringing work without permission. Although the Defendant, Xunlei Company, argued that the relevant websites currently provided P2P services in the industry that purchased the copyright of the film and television works and then made the seed files to be published on the Internet. Hence, they could not determine whether the seed files in the search results were unauthorized sources of infringement. It did not provide sufficient evidence to prove this, so this Court did not accept its defenses.

The Defendant, Xunlei Co., as a search service provider involved in the case, provided TV users with a P2P search service for the film works involved by the internet television set produced by the Defendant, TCL Company. According to the corresponding content of the above-mentioned notarized search results page, the Defendants could be deemed to have edited and arranged related search results, and they should be known that the linked works are infringing works, but still helped the chained persons to implement the infringement of the Plaintiff. This behavior was subjective fault, and the Defendants, Xunlei Company and TCL Company shall assume joint tort liability in this regard. The Defendant, as a network equipment provider, did not select or edit the users' choice. Hence, TCL did not have subjective fault, and should not assume the infringement liability defense claim. The Defendant, Xunlei Company, proposed to provide search technology service only. It was impossible to judge whether the video files in the search results were authorized and should not bear the legal defense claims. Because of the lack of evidence, the Court would not accept them. Although the Defendants, TCL Company and Xunlei Company, both claimed that the search results page were made by the other side. Xunlei Company also considered that the company, as one of the shareholders, Guangzhou Huaneng Technology Co., Ltd, actually controlled the search results page according to the technical monitoring results in the notary process. None of them submitted sufficient evidence to prove it, so the Court did not accept its defense.

Chapter 3: Determination of Copyright Infringement

Although the technical monitoring conducted during the notary process showed that the seed resource of the movie Lavender involved in the movie was from the Defendant's website, it could not prove that the film work was directly from the Xunlei Company's network server. Hence, the Plaintiff, Union Voole Co. claimed that the Defendant, Xunlei Company, transmitted the film work involved in the internet and should bear the corresponding legal liability for direct infringement. The lack of evidence was not supported by this Court.

Third, whether the Defendant's sale of the Internet TV set involved in the case infringed the right of the Plaintiff to enjoy the right to disseminate information on the Internet, and whether it should bear corresponding legal responsibilities.

According to the relevant provisions of the Copyright Law, the Defendant, Gome's Internet TV involved in the sale of the case had a legitimate source and should not bear legal liability. In view of the fact that Gome's Internet TV sets involved Xunlei's provision of an internet function module for the movie "Lavender" downloading and viewing services, GOME shall bear the responsibility of stopping the sale of the Internet TVs involved in the case. The Plaintiff, Union Voole Co., advocated that the Defendant, Gome Company, used the infringement function of the Internet TV as a selling point to promote and achieve illegal profits, and demanded that Gome Company should bear the joint legal liability with the other two Defendants, TCL Corporation and Xunlei Corporation. Based on the deficiency, the Court would not stand by.

In summary, the Plaintiff as the right-of-information disseminator of the film work, Lavender, accused the Defendants, TCL Corporation and Xunlei Company, of infringing its right to disseminate information networks, and asked them to jointly stop the infringement and to compensate the economic losses and reasonable expenses for litigation expenses. This was justified and the Court supported them. With regard to the specific ways of stopping the infringement, the Court would determine according to the specific circumstances of the case. With regard to the compensation for economic losses and the amount of reasonable expenses due to litigation expenses in this case, the Court would consider the Defendant TCL Company and Xunlei Company's infringement methods, scope, subjective faults, and the duration of the infringement and profitability and other factors. In view of the Plaintiff's claim that the right to disseminate information on the Internet belonged to property rights and did not have the attribute of personal rights. The Plaintiff requested the Defendants, TCL Company and Xunlei Company, to publish the apology statements on the official website. Based on the deficiency, the Court would not stand by.

In summary, according to the Copyright Law of the People's Republic of China amended on October 27, 2001, Article 10(1)(12), No. 2, No. 48, "Protection of the Right to Information on the Internet" In accordance with Article 23 of the Regulations, The Beijing No. 2 Intermediate People's Court ruled that: (1) TCL Group Limited by Share Ltd and Shenzhen Xunlei Network Technology Co., Ltd. ceased to provide downloading and viewing services for the movie Lavender through "MiTV Internet TV" of Shenzhen Xunlei Network Technology Co., Ltd. starting from the effective date of this judgment. (2) Gome Electric Co., Ltd. ceased to sell the "MiTV Internet TV" with the Internet function module of Shenzhen Xunlei Network Technology Co., Ltd. to watch the movie Lavender from the effective date of this judgment. (3) TCL Group Co., Ltd.

and Shenzhen Xunlei Network Technology Co., Ltd. jointly compensated Beijing Union Voole Co. for an economic loss of 10,000 yuan and reasonable expenses for the litigation expenses of the case for RMB 411,500 within ten days from the effective date of this judgment. (4) The other claims of the Plaintiff were dismissed.

After the verdict was handed down, TCL and Xunlei filed appeals separately. Beijing Higher People's Court made a second instance judgment and rejected the appeal and upheld the original verdict.

Commentary:

In China, the development of Internet TV and the copyright infringement issues have experienced different stages of development. The infringement of Internet TV copyrights involved in this case occurred early in the development of China's Internet TV caused by irresponsible related administrative supervision. The Internet TV industry at that stage was seen by the regulatory authorities as "infringing upon the legitimate rights and interests of the copyright owner which was not authorized by the competent authority of the industry, disrupting the order of transmission of audiovisual programs on the Internet, and was once suspended by the regulatory authorities." However, with the development of integration technology of three networks, the attitude of the regulatory authorities on Internet TV has changed from prohibition to regulation and guidance, and since then, as the content service providers, integrated service platforms, and hardware manufacturers operate under the respective license rights, the Internet TV industry has gradually become normalized, but it has produced new issues such as third-party applications breaking regulatory restrictions, it also brought about new copyright issues.

1. Subjects involved in the operation of Internet TV

In accordance with the policy of the line management and supervision department, at present, various parties involved in the copyright infringement case need to be differentiated and determined responsibilities respectively in the regulation of the production and operation of Internet TV. The first is the content service platform. At present, in the content service of Internet TV, the on-demand service of news programs is only operated by broadcasting and television broadcasting organizations. The on-demand services and graphic information services for television dramas can be carried out by the broadcasting and television broadcasting agencies in cooperation with institutions that have copyright resources, China has fourteen radio and television broadcasting agencies that are qualified to provide Internet TV content currently. The second is the copyright owner. Such entities can cooperate with the above-mentioned fourteen content service platforms to provide TV drama on-demand services and graphic and text information services. The third is integrated broadcast control platform. The integrated broadcast control platform integrates the content provided by the content service platform into data information and sends it to the terminal. At present, there are only seven integrated broadcast control platforms licensed by SARFT. Fourth, Content Delivery Network operators, commonly referred to as CDN operators, provide technical services for the smooth dissemination of audiovisual programs. Fifth, manufacturers of Internet TV equipment, include integrated Internet TV manufacturers and external set-top box manufacturers.

When the infringement took place in this case, all aspects of Internet TV operations have not yet been standardized, and the concepts and operational qualifications of the content service platform and integrated broadcast control platform have not yet emerged. In this case, TCL Company's production of Internet TVs involved in the case was mainly attributed to the manufacturers of Internet TV equipment; and Xunlei Company integrated the CE version of Xunlei Download Software in the Internet TV produced by the company, and was responsible for providing the company with information on the AV library. Internet TV provides users with P2P search services related to film works in this case. It is neither a content service platform under current normative operation nor does it belong to an integrated broadcast control platform. It can only be said that the Internet search service providers appearing on the Internet when the relevant administrative supervision department has not restricted the direct connection of Internet TV.

2. The content of copyright of Internet TV

Internet TV is one of the important applications of triple play. The interconnection of telecommunication networks, radio and television networks, and the Internet and the sharing of resources have made the dissemination of works more convenient, which has also brought about the boundary issue of related copyright rights. According to the current Copyright Law in china, the right to broadcast refers to the right to broadcast or disseminate works in a wireless manner, disseminate broadcast works to the public in a wired manner and disseminate broadcast works to the public through loudspeakers or other similar tools that can transmit signals, sounds and images. The right to disseminate information on the Internet is to provide works to the public in a wired or wireless manner so that the public have the right to obtain the works at their personally selected time and place. The dissemination of works in the triple play is carried out by means of cable, which brings about the following issues concerning the contents of copyright rights: First of all, when the subject that has the right to broadcast re-promotes the work, once it involves a wired method, the subject should have the right to disseminate information on the Internet. In the case of diversified forms of communication, some forms of communication will cause disputes among right subjects; Second, although the current relevant administrative regulations have limited the functions of the Internet TV integration platform to video on demand and graphic and text information services, the possibility of access to technical services for live broadcasting of radio and television programs has been ruled out.[8] However, in the field of copyright civil tort, there may still be cases of infringement of broadcasting rights through cable relay, and there is no clear restriction on the access of telecommunication networks to the live services on radio and television programs; Third, as the dissemination methods covered by the right to disseminate information on the

---

8. State Administration of Radio, Film and Television: Holding Operational Management Requirements for Internet TV License Organizations.

Internet are increasingly diversified, more and more copyright licenses will no longer be subject to the provisions of Article 10 of the Copyright Law, but will show a tendency of fine differentiation. In the related disputes, there will be more cases of concurrence between breach of contract and infringement of rights, and the content involved is often a specific content under the right of dissemination of information networks.

3. Analysis of infringement of providing links and search services in Internet TV

According to the current regulatory measures, the above-mentioned operators of the five types of Internet TV can only access specific platforms and cannot access the Internet. However, this prohibitive measure did not exist when the infringement took place, so there was a situation that Xunlei Company provided Internet search services. Even at present, there are some illegally listed Internet TV devices and third-party video software. Whether or not they violate administrative regulations belongs to the issue of administrative departments. However, when it involves civil torts, it also involves providing infringement analysis of links and search services.

1) Definition of the infringement: "server standard" or "user perception standard"

In the determination of "network communication behavior," there have been differences in practice regarding whether "server standards" or "user perception standards" should be applied. The "server standard" refers to whether or not the accused infringer has implemented the "Internet communication behavior" based on whether the work is uploaded to the server by the accused infringer. The "user perception standard" refers to the perception of the average user. If the user subjectively feels that the work is from the accused infringer, it is determined that the accused infringer has implemented the "network communication behavior." The application of these two standards will result in different legal characterizations of the link behavior of online communication behavior and even affect the verdict.

In this case, although the technical inspection conducted during the notary process revealed that the seed resource of the film work "Lavender" was from the defendant's website, it could not prove that the film work was directly related to the case originated from Xunlei's web server. Therefore, the Plaintiff, Union Voole Co., advocated that the defendant, Xunlei Company, distributed the related film work through the Internet, and demanded that it should bear the corresponding legal liability for direct infringement. It lacks basis and the Court will not support it. Obviously, the Court adopted the "server standard" instead of the "user perception standard."

After the judgment in this case, the Supreme People's Court issued the "Provisions on Several Issues Concerning the Application of Law in the Trial of Cases of Civil Dispute over Information on the Right of Dissemination of Information on the Internet." Instead of using the "server standard" to define information network communication behavior, the information network transmission behavior is broadly defined. The information network communication behavior is defined by direct provision of the rights holders' works rather than the server standard. The information network communication behavior can be divided into the provision of the work behavior and other information network communication behaviors, while other information network communication behaviors are the behaviors of the network intermediate services provided by its technology and facilities, namely, providing services rather than directly providing works. This is because, with the development of technology, without the storage or transfer of the server, the related works can be placed on the information network through technologies such as file sharing. It is not accurate enough to define the information network communication behavior with a simple "server standard." It is also difficult to cope with the rapid development of network technology. Therefore, the information network communication behavior should be divided into work offering behavior and network service provision behavior. It is of fundamental significance to build a responsibility system for copyright protection under the network environment. Based on this distinction, the distinction between direct and indirect infringement liability arises. Direct infringement liability corresponds to the work provision behavior while indirect infringement liability corresponds to the network service provision behavior.

2) Identification of Fault

The network service provider provides services such as automatic access, automatic output, information storage space, search, link, P2P (point-to-point) services for the service objects, and provides technical and facility support for the service objects to spread information on the network, and such acts do not constitute direct information network dissemination. In this case, the actions of the two defendants were not direct information network transmissions, and they were indirect information network infringements.

According to the Regulations on the Protection of the Right of Communication through Information Network, if network service provider provides search or link services for their clients and actually knows or should have known that the linked works, performance, and sound and video recordings are infringing, it shall bear joint-torts duty. The Guiding Opinions of Beijing Higher People's Court on Several Issues concerning Network Copyright Dispute Cases (I) (Trial Implementation) specifically explain this principle on the reverse side: Network service provider who automatically provides information storage space, search, link, and P2P (point-to-point) services for alleged infringing works, performance, sound and video recordings through the information network, and does not edit, modify or select the alleged infringing works, performance, sound and video recordings, unless the network service provider knows or has reasonable grounds for knowing that there are other cases of infringement, the network service provider should not be presumed to fault. Internet service provider who provides services such as search, link, and P2P (point to point) services according to their own will, and on the basis of collecting, sorting, and classifying, making corresponding classifications and lists of alleged infringing works, performance, and sound and video recordings can be deemed to be at fault if it knows or has reasons to know that the infringed works, performance, and sound and video recordings are infringed.

In this case, the defendant Shenzhen Xunlei Network Technology Co., Ltd recognized that its permission to module installed by TCL Group Limited by Share Ltd in the internet television involved in this case was the same as the search function on the internet website Gougou. After being inspected by the Court, the search results for related videos using "Gougou Search" were BT, eDonkey, mobile video, HD and other types. After comparison, the search results and interface of the website Gougou are different from that displayed on the internet television. The number of internet television search results is less than that of the website Gougou. The interface of the internet television also adds information such as the introduction of the movie which differs from the interface of the website Gougou. According to the corresponding content of the above-mentioned notarized search results, the defendants Shenzhen Xunlei Network Technology Co., Ltd and TCL Group Limited by Share Ltd can be deemed as subjective faults as they had edited and collated relevant search results, and they have a reasonable reason to know that the linked works are infringing works while they still help the linked persons to infringe the right of dissemination of the information network enjoyed by the Plaintiff Union Voole Co., LTD.

If the network service provider actually knows or should have known that the linked works, performances and sound and video recordings are infringing, it shall bear joint-torts duty. At this time, haven rules cannot be applied for exemption. After the judgment in this case, the Supreme People's Court issued the Provisions on Several Issues Concerning the Application of Law in the Trial of Cases of Civil Dispute over Infringement of Information on the Right of Information on the Internet, and gave a more detailed explanation of how the People's Court decided whether or not the network service provider constituted "should have known of the particular fact, matter, circumstance or other item."

4. Substantial noninfringement use and technology neutrality—analysis of infringement liability of Internet TV equipment manufacturers

In 1984, the case of *"Global Film Production Company v. Sony Corporation"* was ruled in the U.S. Supreme People's Court. The judgment result was that, in order to "change the viewing time" in the home by recording TV programs using video recorders constituting "fair use," it was considered that as long as the product could have a potential "Substantial noninfringing uses," manufacturers and distributors of the products did not assume "help tort liability." In the next twenty years, the "Household Recording Act," "Millennium Digital Copyright Act" passed by the U.S. Congress, and the technical standards for video recording equipment enacted by Federal Communications Commission had firmly limited the scope of "fair use" of video recorders to recording the free show.

In this case, the defendant TCL Corporation proposed that it was a network equipment provider and did not perform operations such as selecting and editing movies and television works that users downloaded to watch, so it did not have subjective errors and should not be held liable for infringement liability. The Court of second instance divided TCL's relevant actions in this case into two aspects: First, the act of creating Internet TV sets involved in the case. The second is the participation in the editing and managing of the content of the Internet TV sets involved in this case. When discussing the production and sales of Internet TV sets, the Court further determined that "Internet TV involved in this case was only a tool for searching, downloading, and playing," "Internet TV as a neutral player and not specifically used for infringement." If the Internet TVs involved did not have preexisting content of film works, and the Internet TVs involved were not specifically used for infringement, TCL did not infringe on copyrights by making Internet TVs involved in the case.

Although the company's technology for manufacturing Internet TVs was neutral in itself, based on the facts identified in this case, users were searching, linking and downloading infringing movies "Lavender" through the video and audio information database technology set up in TCL Internet TV sets. After entering the keywords, the system would automatically compare them with the data in the audio and video information database, and would display all the introductory data of the film and television works, which showed that both the defendant company and the defendant Xunlei company have participated in editing and managing the content of the infringing film and television works spread by Internet TV sets. These search and download contents were not automatically generated based on system technology. Therefore, the Court decided that TCL corporation constituted infringement, which was not based on its manufacturing of the Internet TV itself, but because it had implemented other acts to provide aid for the infringement.

—**Comments by CUI Ning**

Case 14. Liability of Service Providers of E-commerce Platform

China Youyi Press Co. v. Zhejiang Taobao Network Co., Ltd. and Yang Hailin
Case of the Right to Publish Infringement Dispute
Case Index: *China Youyi Press Co. v. Zhejiang Taobao Network Co., Ltd. and Yang Hailin*; Dongcheng District People's court of Beijing, [2009] No. 2461, June 19, 2009; Beijing No. 2 Intermediate People's Court, [2009] No. 15423, September 20, 2009

Facts:

The Plaintiff, China Youyi Press Co. (hereinafter, "Youyi") alleged that: The Plaintiff enjoys the exclusive right to publish the book *The Graver Robbers' Chronicles (4th Volume)* in China. The right to Publish was infringed by Yang Hailin, who sold the pirated *The Graver Robbers' Chronicles (4th Volume)* in his online shop on the website of www.Taobao.com. As the operator of the e-commerce platform, Zhejiang Taobao Network Co., Ltd. (hereinafter, "Taobao") did not fulfill the duty of examination and facilitated the sale of the involved pirated books. Therefore, Taobao constituted joint infringement with Yang Hailin, and shall be liable for the joint liabilities.

In the first instance, Dongcheng District People's Court of Beijing found that: After searching the keywords "complete works of The Graver Robbers' Chronicles" on the home page of Taobao, 121 results are displayed, with the prices from RMB 11 to RMB 25 (with or without postage). After searching the keywords "The Graver Robbers' Chronicles" on the home page of Taobao, over 4,000 results are displayed, with the prices less than RMB 10. After searching the keywords "*The Graver Robbers' Chronicles (4th Volume)*" on the home page of Taobao, filtered with "Seller's location: Beijing" and indexed the price from high to low, the seventh search result is "*The Graver Robbers' Chronicles (4th Volume)* by Nan Pai San Shu" with the price of RMB 8, and the seller is "Yangfan Bookstore." On December 18, 2008, Motie Company was entrusted by Youyi to issue a copyright infringement notice to Taobao, informing the Defendant Taobao of the copyright infringement for selling the involved books. In this notice, Motie Company requested: (1) Taobao shall delete all the links of the infringing books. (2) Taobao shall give warning to the operators of the involved online shops. (3) Taobao shall provide the real names, addresses and contact information of the operators of the involved online shops. On December 22, 2008, Taobao issued a letter to Motie Company, stating that Taobao had examined the infringement information and had deleted twenty-eight pieces in total, and provided the involved sellers' registration information to the Plaintiff. The Defendant Yang Hailin is the operator of the involved online shop "Yangfan Bookstore." By comparison, it has been found that the infringing books were marked as "Published by Youyi," but the edition number, printing quality and catalog style were different from the original books printed by the Plaintiff. Thus, Youyi declared that the involved books were not published by it.

Dongcheng District People's Court of Beijing ruled that: The Defendants Yang Hailin and Taobao shall jointly compensate the Plaintiff RMB 2,000 for economic losses. Taobao appealed.

Ruling and Reasoning:

Beijing No. 2 Intermediate People's Court held that: (1) Youyi enjoys the exclusive right to publish the involved book. Yang Hailin infringed the right of Youyi for selling the infringing books and shall bear the corresponding liabilities. Taobao is the service provider of a huge e-commerce platform for various types of goods. Except for the goods that are explicitly prohibited by laws and administrative regulations, all commodities can be circulated on this e-commerce platform. (2) The sellers on e-commerce platforms can be classified as individual sellers and enterprise sellers. Generally, there are huge amounts of individual sellers on the e-commerce platforms, who can be individual businesses and natural persons to sell their own goods. As the service provider of e-commerce platform, Taobao had examined the individual seller Yang Hailin's real name and ID number. Since there is no specific law or administrative regulation to stipulate that service providers have the duty to examine the business qualification of individual sellers, Taobao did not violate any relevant regulations for not requesting Yang Hailin to provide any certificate of business qualification. The price of the original books published by Youyi is RMB 32.8, which is much higher than that of the infringing books. However, given the huge number of commodities on e-commerce platforms, laws and administrative regulations only explicitly list the prohibited goods, but do not request e-commerce platform providers to review whether the price of goods is significantly lower than the market price. Thus, Taobao did not violate any regulations for not reviewing Yang Hailin's low price of the infringing books. After receiving the copyright notice, Taobao immediately deleted the information of infringing books, which had fulfilled its obligation.

Since Taobao has fulfilled its obligation in examination and remediation and did not violate laws and administrative regulations, it was not a copyright infringement to offer facility to Yang Hailin who infringed the exclusive right to publish of Youyi. Therefore, Taobao does not constitute joint infringement. The Court revoked the first-instance judgment, and ruled that Yang Hailin should compensate RMB 2,000 for the Plaintiff's economic losses.

Commentary:

With the rapid development of the Internet technology and application, Internet-related disputes are becoming much more sophisticated. The determination of the Infringement liabilities of service providers of e-commerce Platform is one of the complicated issues of the Internet-related disputes.

1. Legal status of e-commerce service providers

E-commerce platform service providers are the operators to provide network services for trading information and trading transactions. From a certain perspective, it seems that one can conservatively consider that an e-commerce platform is a virtual conventional shopping mall on the Internet, whose legal status is the same as or similar to the legal status of a conventional shopping mall in the real world.

Despite that e-commerce platform and conventional shopping mall is similar in their functions, there are huge differences between the two. First, they are different in their categories of goods. Except for goods that are explicitly prohibited by laws and administrative regulations, all commodities can be circulated on e-commerce platforms. By contrast, conventional shopping malls generally sell some certain kinds of commodities that has been reviewed and approved by the industrial and commercial administrations.

Second, the sellers are different. The sellers on e-commerce platforms can be classified as individual sellers and enterprise sellers. Generally, there are huge amounts of individual sellers on the e-commerce platforms, who can be individual businesses and natural persons to sell their own goods. By contrast, the sellers in conventional shopping malls are limited in quantity as they must be the registered and approved by the industrial and commercial administrations in accordance with relevant laws and regulations.

Third, the obligations of examination are different. Regarding the enterprise sellers, e-commerce platform service providers shall examine the license of the business corporation. Regarding the individual sellers, since there is no a specific law or administrative regulation to stipulate that service providers have the duty to examine the business qualification of individual sellers, e-commerce platform service providers just examine the real names and ID numbers of the individual sellers in practice. By contrast, the operators of conventional shopping malls are obliged to examine the license of the business corporation, license of individually owned business etc.

Based on the above grounds, it can be deduced that if the same obligations of examination of the conventional shopping malls are applied on the e-commerce platforms, it would be impossible for the e-commerce platforms to survive. The provision needs to be redefined if a law would cause a serious imbalance for different subjects, rather than just simply apply the same method to regulate different subjects. To keep the balance of interests is the nature of laws.[9]

2. The identification of e-commerce platform service providers

E-commerce platform service providers can be identified as self-operated service providers and intermediary service providers. Regarding the identification of e-commerce platform service providers, the experience concerning the identification of Internet content providers (hereinafter, "ICP") and Internet service providers (hereinafter, "ISP") can be referred. On the one hand, whether ICP or ISP is not a fixed identity, since many operators both manage their own information and provide information from the users others uploaded. Thus, it is the act of providing whether content or service to decide whether the operator is an ICP or ISP. Therefore, it makes sense to clarify the identities of ICP or ISP only in the particular case. On the other hand, if a platform service provider (which is one type of ISP) asserts that an infringement is

---

9. Edgar Bodenheimer (Translated by Deng Zhenglai), *Jurisprudence*, CUPL Press, 2004, p. 415.

committed by a third-party party, it should bear the burden of proof to identify itself as a mere ISP. If it fails to prove so, then it will be presumed as an ICP, and should bear the liabilities for direct the infringement of the right of communication of information on networks. Such experience of ICP and ISP can be a good reference to identify whether an e-commerce platform service provider is a self-operated service provider or an intermediary service provider. In particular cases, the involved e-commerce platform service provider should be required to bear the burden of proof to prove that the involved information or corresponding transaction is operated by other online sellers who take advantage of the e-commerce service from the provider.

3. The liabilities of e-commerce platform service providers

3.1. The liabilities of self-operated service providers

Regarding the issue of liabilities of self-operated service providers, a consensus has been made that self-operated service providers should be determined as the distributors and bear direct liabilities when they provide infringing transaction information to public or make their own infringing transactions. However, in the case that the copyright owners fail to prove their actual damages, the self-operated service providers who only provide infringing transaction information to public do not need to bear the liability of compensation, but shall bear the liability of cease the infringement. This situation is similar to the liabilities concerning "offer for sale" infringement cases under the patent law.

3.2. The liabilities of intermediary service providers

The indirect infringement by intermediary service providers can be further identified as infringement of the intermediary service providers by aiding and infringement of the intermediary service providers by abetting. In both cases, the indirect infringers have subject wrong for the infringement.

3.2.1. Infringement of the intermediary service providers by aiding

Article 36 of the *Tort Liability Law* stipulates the legal basis for the determination of liabilities for intermediary service providers. According to jurisprudence, intermediary service providers shall bear indirect liabilities for infringing others' intellectual property based on the establishment of direct infringement. Therefore, the intermediary service providers shall be considered as indirect infringers when they fail to take any necessary measures in time, knowing that online sellers infringe others' intellectual property by their Internet service. Intermediary service providers and online sellers shall bear joint liabilities for the losses after knowing the infringement. The liabilities of intermediary service providers are based on the infringing transactions by online sellers with the aid of the service providers. How to determine "knowledge" is of great difficulty in judicial practice. The determination can be only made on a case-by-case basis to deduce the subjective intention of the intermediary service providers from particular details. The details to be taken into consideration are: (1) Whether the alleged infringing transaction information is located in obvious position of the homepage or other important webpage. (2) Whether the alleged infringing transaction information has been edited, selected and recommended. (3) Whether the notification of copyright owners can make the service providers know the alleged infringing transaction information has been spread by the service or make service providers believe there is a higher possibility of infringement. (4) Whether there is a clear indication in the transaction information that the online seller is not authorized by the copyright owner, which is enough to convince service providers that there exists greater possibility of infringement. (5) Other circumstances on intermediary service providers' knowledge of alleged infringing transaction information or corresponding transaction.

As previously mentioned, "knowledge" means such individual actually knows or should have known of the particular fact, matter, circumstance or other item. That means the service providers actually knows the particular fact of online seller infringing copyright or should have known the fact of infringement according to the principle of "balance of interests" and the principle of "reasonable prevention." Thus, the determination of "should have known" is within the scope of legal judgment, which depends on the duty of care of the intermediary service provider. The duty of care should be reasonably determined based on the provider's nature of the service, the method of the service, the capability of examining the information. If the intermediary service provider obtains economic benefits directly from the transactions of online sellers, then it shall bear higher duty of care for the infringement. It must be emphasized that "should have known" is a presumed situation that "an artificial reasonable person" will know the relevant fact under the reasonable duty of care. In this situation, it can be presumed that the service provider "knows" the infringement, but still aid such direct infringement.

3.2.2. Infringement of the intermediary service providers by abetting

Article 9 of the *Tort Liability Law* stipulates that one who abets or assists another person in committing an infringement shall be liable jointly and severally with the infringer. Therefore, if the intermediary platform service provider induces or encourages online sellers' infringement by promoting technical support, reward points, etc., it can be determined that the provider is abetting the infringement. Regarding such infringement by abetting, the intermediary service providers and the online sellers shall bear joint liabilities.

—Comments by ZHOU Duo

Chapter 3: Determination of Copyright Infringement

Case 15. Contributory Infringement by the Act of Inducement

LeTV Information Technology (Beijing) Corp., Ltd. v. Hangzhou Beinfo Co., Ltd. and China Unicom Corp., Ltd.
Case of Copyright Infringement Dispute
Case Index: LeTV Information Technology (Beijing) Corp., Ltd. v. Hangzhou Beinfo Co., Ltd. and China Unicom Corp., Ltd.; Xicheng District People's Court of Beijing, Xi Min Chu Zi [2011] No. 20126, September 23, 2011; Beijing No. 1 Intermediate People's Court, Yi Zhong Min Chu Zi [2011] No. 18027, December 2, 2011

Facts:

The plaintiff LeTV net information technology (Beijing) co., Ltd., (abbreviation LeTV net) is the right person of communication through information network of the film involved in the case. The defendant Hangzhou Zaixin Technology Co., Ltd., (abbreviation Hangzhou Zaixin Co.,) operates website to provide information storage space service. Users uploaded the films involved to the site without the plaintiff's permission for other web users downloading or viewing online. The plaintiff argues that the defendant's act of providing information storage space service for network users' behavior of uploading constitutes a joint infringement and shall bear the corresponding civil liability.

In this case more attention should be paid to the following facts: The defendant's website contains a film section in which the film is stored. The website also includes categories such as "Latest Love Movies," "Latest Comedy Movies," "Latest Action Movies," and corresponding lists. Furthermore, the website pages also contain words such as "massive movies, games, software's, etc. free to download ... ." Also, there are words like "Files exceed 20M, recommending you to download for watching" and "This file sizes over 5M, recommending using client to download" appeared in the download pages of relevant films.

In view of the plaintiff's grounds for prosecution, the court analyzed the case from the angles of aiding infringement and abetting (luring) infringement and pointed out that the focus of this case was how to determine the information storage space provider's duty of care for the contents of "film" section, and whether the act of establishing the "film" section on the website without taking any restrictive measures constitutes an infringement. On this basis, the court finally determined that the alleged infringement constituted both aiding and abetting (luring) infringement, and ordered the defendant to stop the infringement and compensate for the loss of RMB 30,000.

Ruling and Reasoning:

Xicheng District People's Court of Beijing held that: In accordance with the copyright Law, LeTV net Company enjoys the exclusive right of communication through information network of the works involved. Hangzhou Zaixin Company is the operator of the website and should bear legal liability for the infringement concerned with the website.

As a network service provider providing information storage space, Hangzhou Zaixin Company set up "romance," "comedy" and "action film" under the title of "Resource Center" and "Movie" on the website, and also set up "the latest Love Story," "the latest comedy," "the latest action" and other lists containing the names of specific cinematographic and television works. Although it is the Internet users who upload the cinematographic and television works in the "Resource Center," the actions of presetting the above-mentioned movie columns and lists on the website involved not only play a role in guiding network users to upload orderly and also sorting out the shared files of the uploaded cinematographic and television works. Under this circumstance, Hangzhou Zaixin Company has a higher duty of care to the existence of infringing works on the website, and it cannot be exempted from liability for publishing disclaimers on the website. As a website operator providing video file sharing, Hangzhou Zaixin Company ought to know that the right owners of cinematographic works will not authorize Internet users to upload the related films to its websites for disseminating freely. In this case, it still provides by category the storage space which can be shared for the cinematographic and television works suspected of infringement, and its subjective attitude toward the network users' direct infringement is "ought to know," thus whose operation behavior is at fault. Hangzhou Zaixin Company has not been authorized by the copyright owner to the above-mentioned network communication behavior, nor has it fulfilled reasonable duty of care to the copyright, thus infringing upon the right of communication through information network enjoyed by LeTV net and shall bear joint civil liabilities for the infringement committed by network users, ceasing the infringement and paying compensation for damages. LeTV net company accepts that there is no television drama involved on the website related to the case, and the act of infringement has been stopped, so the court no longer requires it to cease the infringement. Since the plaintiff's actual losses or the defendant's unlawful gains cannot be determined based on the existing evidence, the court, in light of the circumstances comprehensively of the popularity and market value of the involved works, the infringement, the reasonable expenses of the lawsuit, decides on compensation. Xicheng District People's Court of Beijing judged that, in accordance with Article 130 of the *General principles of Civil Law*, Article 10, paragraph 1 (12), Article 15, Article 48 (1), Article 49, paragraph 2 of the copyright Law, Article 148 of the Supreme People's Court's Opinions on Several Issues Concerning the Implementation of the General Principles of the Civil Law of the People's Republic of China (Trial), Hangzhou Zaixin company shall pay compensation for economic losses and reasonable expenses of LeTV net company totaling RMB 30,000.

Hangzhou Zaixin company did not accept it and appealed to the Beijing No. 1 Intermediate People's Court.

Beijing No. 1 Intermediate People's Court held that: Since Hangzhou Zaixin company set up a "film "section mainly for the purpose of attracting Internet users to upload the whole cinematographic and television works that are still under protection and the "film" section set up on the website without taking any corresponding restrictive measures directly led network users to upload cinematographic and

Chapter 3: Determination of Copyright Infringement

television works that infringe upon other's copyrights, the act of Hangzhou Zaixin company constitutes abetting infringement.

whether the act committed by Hangzhou Zaixin constitutes aiding infringement, the court held that, seeing that the act of uploading the films involved by Internet users directly infringes upon the right of communication through information network enjoyed by LeTV net, however, LeTV has no evidence to prove that Hangzhou Zaixin clearly knew that the involved films uploaded by Internet users on its website infringed on its right to communication through information network and that the subjective attitude of Hangzhou Zaixin was "knowingly." Therefore, the key to judge whether the act of Hangzhou Zaixin constitutes aiding infringement is whether it is subjectively "known" that uploading behavior by users constitutes infringement. In this case, due to the high investment in cinematographic and television works, it is nearly impossible for the right owners to authorize network users freely to upload them on video sharing website based on considerations of economic interests, which is supposed to know by Hangzhou Zaixin. Under such circumstance, Hangzhou Zaixin has set up a "movie" section on its website without taking any measures to prevent Internet users from uploading cinematographic and television works that infringe upon the copyright, inevitably resulting in a high risk of infringement of the content of this section, which is also supposed to know obviously by Hangzhou Zaixin. Under this circumstance, Hangzhou Zaixin Company should have a higher duty of care to the contents of the section than to other contents. This duty of care demands that all contents of such section should be checked timely and the infringing contents should be removed promptly. If Hangzhou Zaixin had fulfilled the above duties, it should have noticed that there are contents uploaded without permission involved on its website and ought to know subjectively that network users have infringed on the rights directly. In summary, the alleged act of infringement carried out by the Hangzhou Zaixin Company also constitutes aiding infringement.

Accordingly, the Beijing No. 1 Intermediate People's Court, in accordance with the provisions of Article 153, paragraph 1 (a) of the Civil Procedure Law of the People's Republic of China, decided to reject the appeal and uphold the original judgment.

Commentary:

The typical feature of this case is that the court commented on the tort liability of providing information storage space service from the perspectives of aiding infringement and abetting (luring) infringement. Thus, this case becomes the first case in our country to identify the infringing nature of information storage space website from the angle of abetting (luring) infringement.

Joint tort in civil law includes two forms: aiding tort and abetting tort. The above two forms of infringement are clearly stipulated in the existing laws of our country. Article 148 of the Supreme People's Court's Opinions on Several Issues Concerning the Implementation of the General Principles of the Civil Law of the People's Republic of China (Trial) stipulates that those who abet and assist others to commit infringements are joint tortfeasors and shall bear joint civil liabilities. In this case, because the plaintiff has not made it clear that which type of joint infringement the alleged tort belongs to, it is necessary for the court to identify the alleged tort from the angles of two types of tort at the same time.

1. The establishment of "film" section and determination of aiding infringement.

In the sense of civil law, the act of aiding tort usually refers to the act of giving help to the direct tort of others under the condition of subjective knowing or ought to know. There is a causal relationship between the helping behavior and the damage suffered by the victim, and the helping behavior contributes to the ultimate damage.[10]

By applying the above basic theory of civil law to the service of information storage space, the following elements should be considered to judge whether the service of information storage space constitutes an act of aiding infringement: first, The act of uploading the film involved by the network user has not been authorized by the right owners, and the uploading action is a direct infringement; second, the defendant "knows" or "ought to know" the users' upload behavior is an infringement act, but still provides the storage space service for the users.

As for this case, cause the behavior of the Internet users uploading the works involved in the case was not permitted by the plaintiff, the key to the determination of the case was whether the defendant had "ought to know," the key of this case determination is whether the defendant should be aware of the infringement subjectively of the user's uploading behavior. The court points out that the identification of "should know" should usually be considered as the following elements: First, only if the defendant knows that the involved website contains the content of the case, it may have knowledge of whether the user uploading behavior constitutes infringement. Therefore, the defendant objectively knows that the Internet users have uploaded the movies to the relevant website is a prerequisite for subjective knowledge. Second, with knowledge of the fact, the defendant should recognize that user-uploaded content is not licensed by the right holder based on the cognitive ability and the duty of care that the defendant should have.

By the specific analysis of the case based on the above two elements, it can be seen that the facts of this case are sufficient to prove that the defendant's subjectively knowing that the uploading behavior of internet users constitutes infringement. As it is widely known, cinematographic and television works usually have a high economic investment, which makes it nearly impossible for the right owners to authorize network users freely to upload them on video sharing website based on considerations of economic interests, which is supposed to know by the defendant. Under such circumstance, the defendant has set up a "movie" section on its website without taking any measures to prevent Internet users from uploading cinematographic and television works that infringe upon the copyright, inevitably resulting in a high risk of infringement of the content of this section. Under this circumstance, the defendant should have a higher duty of care to the contents of the section than to other contents. This duty of care demands that all contents of such section should be checked timely and the infringing contents should be removed promptly. If the defendant had fulfilled the

---

10. Wang Liming, *Research on Tort Liability Law*, China Renmin University Press, 2010, p. 539.

above duties, it should have noticed that there are contents uploaded without permission involved on its website and ought to know subjectively that network users have infringed on the rights directly. Thus, the defendant's behavior completely compliance with the requirements for the identification of the aiding infringement, and its behavior constitutes the aiding infringement.

2. The establishment of "film" section and determination of abetting (luring) infringement.

Abetting (luring) infringing action usually refers to the act intentionally subjective of abetting a person to commit a certain tort by means of words or acts. Although the abettor's abetting act is not the sufficient condition for the infringement, it constitutes the necessary condition for the damage, and they have quite a causal relationship. [11]

Regarding the determination between information storage space "film" column and abetting (luring) infringement, second instance court made the first attempt in this case, putting forward the principle that "if the defendant commits the act of abetting a network user to upload a film and television work which is copyrighted by another person, and the act of abetting directly leads to the uploading behavior of the network user to a certain extent, then determining that the act committed by the defendant constitutes an act of abetting (luring) infringing," under the circumstances of the following specific analysis of the principle in the light of the facts of the case, the court ultimately found that the act described above constituted an act of abetting (luring):

> 2.1 The purpose of the defendant setting up "film" section without taking the corresponding restrictive measures is to abet net users to upload cinematographic and television works copyrighted by others.
> First, the defendant set up a "film" section mainly for the purpose of attracting Internet users to upload the whole cinematographic and television works that are still under protection.
> In this case, the defendant argued that the purpose of setting up the "Movies" column was to attract users to "legitimately" upload movies and television works. Theoretically speaking, the contents of the "Movies" column can be regarded as "legitimately" uploading under the following conditions: first, the video files made by the network users; second, movies and television works uploaded by network users with the permission of the right owners; the third is the film flower, the trailers, the introduction comments of the film and television works which are still in the period of protection, and the fourth is the movie and television works which have passed the copyright protection period. Therefore, if the defendant can prove that the facts of the case meet the above requirements, the defendant's claim will stand. However, the court did not endorse the defendant's claim in the light of the case-by-case analysis of the four facts.
> For the first case (i.e., video files produced by the Internet users themselves), the court pointed out that although there is a large number of self-produced video content in the existing network environment, however, this kind of content does not meet the general public's definition of "film and television drama," and the content made by the Internet users is generally classified as

---

11. *Ibid.*, p. 534.

"original" content by websites and Internet users rather than "film and television drama." Web users do not usually upload such video files to the "movie" category, so it is obvious that the defendant should be aware of the fact that such content is rarely found in the "film" category in practice.

For the second case (i.e., film and television works uploaded by network users authorized by the right owners), the court held that which are also rarely found in practice. The reason is that movies and TV dramas are usually heavily invested, to recover their investment to the maximum extent and gaining benefits, although the right owners of film and television works currently will also adopt the method of network dissemination, they usually only have a limited amount of "compensated" authorization rather than allowing "web users" to upload their work "freely" to information storage space. Therefore, the "film" section of the website involved in the case is basically difficult to appear film and television works through the obligee's authorization and the defendant is certainly aware of this.

With regard to the third case (i.e., the floral, trailers, introductory comments, etc. of the film and television works that are still under protection), the court pointed out that there are indeed cases in which users upload such content in practice, and such content is also likely to be uploaded by the right owners themselves or by other Internet users authorized by themselves. However, it can be seen from the facts of the case that the defendant set up the "Movies" section is not intended to attract Internet users to upload the above content. As known, the length and file size of the whole film and television productions are significantly different from the length and size of their floral, trailers, introduction comments, etc. The latter usually has a very short playing time, and the file size is much smaller than that of the whole film and television dramas. The current technical means can completely distinguish the two from each other to avoid the Internet users uploading the whole films and TV dramas. The website involved appears some hints when network users download the whole films and TV dramas that "Files exceed 20M, recommending you to download for watching" "This file sizes over 5M, recommending using client to download," which also indicate that the defendant's technical level can do this. However, instead of taking any technical measures to distinguish the two types of content, the defendant suggests users to download them for watching in order to give the network users a better user experience when the relevant files are larger than a certain value. The fact shows that it not only knows, but also wants Internet users to upload the whole films.

As for the fourth case (i.e., film and television works that have passed the copyright protection period), the court pointed out that online users can surely upload them to the information storage space legally and freely for others to share. However, this fact alone does not prove that the purpose of the defendant setting up this column is to attract users to legally upload such film and television works. The reasons are as follows: first, since the implementation of the Copyright Law, the proportion of film and television works which have passed the protection period of 50 years is minimal in all film and television works, and their absolute number is also relatively limited. Under this circumstance, if the defendant wants to allow network users to legally upload such content, it should take corresponding restrictive measures. However, the defendant not only did not take any restrictive measures, but instead advertised on its website that its website contained "massive films and televisions … ." This fact can explain to a great extent that most of the contents uploaded by Internet users to the "Movies" section are works that are still in the protection period. The defendant is not only aware of this fact, but also hopes it occurs. Second, the website involved not only set up movie columns, but also set up columns such as "the Latest Love Movies" and attached lists. The defendants clearly knew that the film and television works that these columns are pointing to are still in the protection period. Therefore, this practice also indicates to a considerable extent that the defendant wants Internet users to upload such works, which are still under protection, or even during the period of hot release, rather than films and television works that have passed the protection period.

In summary, the defendant's main purpose of setting up the "film" section without taking any restrictive measures is not to attract Internet users to upload content that conforms to the above four situations, but to attract network users to upload the whole film and television works that are still under protection.

In addition, there is a close connection between the setting of the "Movie" section and the profitability of the website involved in the case, which also supports the defendant's motivation to set up this section from another perspective. In practice, while information storage space sites typically do not charge network users who share its website content, the benefit of the website directly or indirectly derives from the number of users. The defendant also admitted that the purpose of the "movie" column setting is to attract more users. Because what really attracts network users is usually the whole films and TV dramas, not the movies and television dramas that have passed the protection period, and the floral, etc. of the film and television works that are still under protection. In order to attract more users, the defendant apparently wants Internet users to upload the whole film and TV series that are still under protection so that the sites involved will eventually be able to make a better profit.

2.2 Web users are also often "aware" that the site's "movie" program is designed to attract Internet users to upload the whole movies and TV plays.

Although the defendant has the subjective intention of inducing the network users to upload the whole films, if the network users do not understand the intention of the defendant, the defendant's behavior cannot constitute an act of abetting (luring) infringement. In this case, although the content involved in the film column may objectively include four legal situations, given the online user's usual understanding of column names such as the "latest love movies," "latest action movies," as well as the usual needs of network users for the content of movies and TV dramas, in the absence of the defendant's associated restrictions and prompts, Web users will think that the content of the program is mainly whole films, not anything else.

2.3 The act of setting up the "film" section on the website involved without taking any corresponding restrictive measures results in directly to a considerable extent an infringement act of uploading cinematographic and television works infringing upon others' copyright committed by network users.

Although the establishment of the act of abetting (luring) should be based on the premise that there is a causal relationship between abetment and direct infringement, the recognition of the inducement of the act of infringement belongs to the category of the subjective state of the perpetrator. The nature of the subjective state makes it generally only inferred on the basis of existing facts, and it is objectively difficult to make a definite and sole determination. Therefore, this requirement of direct causality does not mean that the act of instigation should be the only inducement of the direct infringement, as long as it leads to the occurrence of the direct tort to a "considerable extent," the existence of this causality can be determined. Otherwise, it will make it difficult for the abetting (luring) to exist objectively.

Since the court has determined that the "film" section of the website involved set without any restrictions "is enough to make the Internet users aware that" they can upload the whole films and television series to the site. However, the existing evidence cannot prove that the related upload behavior of network users has other inducements. Combining with the network users' perception of the tort nature of the uploading behavior of film and television works, the court cannot determine that the defendant's abetting act is the only inducement of the direct infringement of network users although, it can be reasonably believed that the above behavior directly led to the occurrence of the network user uploading behavior to a certain extent.

In conclusion, the court finally held that the alleged infringement has constituted an act of abetting (luring) joint infringement. However, the court also pointed out that this finding does not mean that any act of setting up a "movie" section in the information storage space constitutes, of course, an act of abetting (luring) infringement. In this case, the setting up of the "movie" column is only one of the factors considered for the reason why the defendant's act constitutes an act of abetting (luring) infringement. The more important consideration factor is that when the defendant has the ability to take appropriate measures to prevent network users from uploading movies and TV works that infringe the copyright of others without permission, they do not take corresponding restrictive measures to avoid the occurrence of infringement.

—**Comments by RUI Songyan**

Chapter 3: Determination of Copyright Infringement

Case 16. Infringement of the Right of Communication by Apple's App Store

Encyclopedia of China Publishing House Co., Ltd. v. Apple Electronic Products Trading (Beijing) Co., Ltd. and Apple Inc.
Case of Copyright Infringement Dispute
Case Index: *Encyclopedia of China Publishing House Co., Ltd. v. Apple Electronic Products Trading (Beijing) Co., Ltd. and Apple Inc.*; Beijing No. 2 Intermediate People's Court, Er Zhong Min Chu Zi [2011] No. 10500, September 27, 2012

Facts:

The Plaintiff, Encyclopedia of China Publishing House Co., (hereinafter, "Encyclopedia Company") is entitled to the copyright of the *Chinese History* of the *Encyclopedia of China (First edition)*. In October 2010, the Plaintiff found that: After downloading and installing the iTunes software via the website operated by the Defendant Apple Electronic Products Trading (Beijing) Co., Ltd. (hereinafter, "Apple Trading"), people can enter the "App Store" that is managed by the Defendant Apple Inc. to purchase and download a large number of applications containing the content of the *Encyclopedia of China* for reading on iPhone and iPad. The application "China Encyclopedia (simplified and traditional Chinese version)" is priced for USD 20.99, which includes all content in the third volume of the *Chinese History* of the *Encyclopedia of China (First edition)*. The Plaintiff alleged that the behavior of the two Defendants caused it huge economic losses. Hence, the Plaintiff claimed that: (1) The Defendants shall cease the copyright infringement of the Plaintiff's works immediately. (2) The Defendants shall jointly compensate the Plaintiff RMB 500,000 for economic losses, and RMB 39,467 for the reasonable expenses.

The Defendant, Apple Trading argued that: It is just a retailer of Apple hardware products. Since the involved iTunes and App Store business are not operated by it, Apple Trading is irrelevant to any infringements relating to iTunes and App Store. The Defendant, Apple Inc. argued that: Despite that the involved iTunes and App Store were developed by it, iTunes and App Store are not operated by it but by iTunes S.A.R.L, which is a wholly owned subsidiary registered and established in Luxembourg. Since the alleged infringement was not committed by it, even if there is an infringement, it will be iTunes S.A.R.L. but not Apple Inc. to bear the liabilities.

Ruling and Reasoning:

Beijing No. 2 Intermediate People's Court held that: The Plaintiff is entitled to the copyright of the *Chinese History* of the *Encyclopedia of China (First edition)* that shall be protected by the copyright law. "App Store," which is operated by Apple Inc., provides downloading services for the alleged infringing application "China Encyclopedia (simplified and traditional Chinese version)" for the price of USD 20.99. Since the whole contents within the involved application are the same as partial contents within the *Encyclopedia of China* in the absence of any authorization by the Plaintiff, it can be determined as an infringing application that infringes the Plaintiff's right of communication of information on networks. Since Apple Inc. failed to prove that the involved infringing application was developed by a third-party developer, it shall be presumed that the application was developed by Apple Inc. Since Apple Inc. independently developed and provided the commercial download service of the involved application in the App Store without any authorization of copyrights owner, Apple Inc. infringed the Plaintiff's right of communication of information on networks, and shall bear the liabilities of stopping the infringement and compensating the economic losses. Even if the application was developed by a third-party developer in accordance with the signature in the application, Apple Inc. still indirectly infringed the Plaintiff's right of communication of information on networks and shall bear the liabilities. Since Apple Inc. participated in the developing process of the application, selected and decided independently to distribute it in the App Store, and gained fixed proportion of profit from the sales, Apple Inc. in fact constituted a joint infringement with the third-party developer for providing the infringing application to the network users for commercial purpose. Since the Plaintiff failed to prove that Apple Trading was involved in the infringement, the Plaintiff's claims against Apple Trading are not established.

In summary, the Court ruled that: Apple Inc. shall cease the infringement, and make compensation to the Plaintiff for the economic losses of RMB 500,000 and reasonable expenses of RMB 20,000.

Commentary:

App Store is an open platform operated by Apple Inc. The so-called Internet open platform refers to an open platform that exposes its application programming interfaces or functions so that external programs can increase the function of the software system or use the resources of the software system. Given that the open platform business model can bring an all-win situation to application developers, network users and platform operators, well-known Internet enterprises are willing to build up such platforms. App Store operated by Apple Inc. is one of the typical open platforms. In order to determine the infringement of App Store, it is necessary to analyze the business model in the first place.

1. The business model of App Store

App Store is different from the general online stores, since it is not an e-commerce website, but rather an open platform based on iTunes software. Therefore, the identity of the operator cannot simply be determined in accordance with the normal procedures for general website operators, that is, by checking the ICP license, the registration number, and the information of domain name and server, but should be analyzed and determined by the relevant contact details and copyright notice from the website of the open platform.

Specifically, when registering an account, network users are able to choose whether accept or reject the terms and conditions of App Store, such as "The use of App Store and the purchase by App Store are to be tied by the agreement between you and

Chapter 3: Determination of Copyright Infringement

iTunes S.A.R.L;" "iTunes is a provider of the relevant stores;" "iTunes is operated from its office in Luxembourg." In addition, according to the *iOS Developer Program License Agreement*, if a third-party developer chooses to sell his application in China via App Store, he must authorize iTunes S.A.R.L. of storing the software, providing downloading service to end users, issuing invoice of the sale, paying the service fee for the service etc. Judging by the above information, it seems that the App Store is operated by iTunes S.A.R.L. However, the relevant information of the App Store can be found that the *Apple Developer Program License Agreement* is provided by Apple Inc., and Apple Inc. is the contract party. The name of Apple Inc. may be found not only in the invoice to the users, but also in the users' interface of App Store. By contrast, the name of iTunes S.A.R.L. cannot be found either during the purchase of applications or the users' interface of App Store. Based on the above grounds, Apple Inc. can be identified as the operator of App Store.

During the operation of App Store, there are three parties to be involved in:

(1) Apple Inc. as the operator: It is the core and hub of the whole operation, and plays multiple roles in the process of operation. First of all, Apple Inc. is responsible for the development, technical support and management of trading platform. Second, Apple Inc. also develops applications and sells them in App Store. Third, Apple Inc. licenses third-party developers to use Apple's coding and testing software to develop applications running in iOS, providing developers with related OS, documentation, software (source code and object code), application, demonstration code, simulator, tools, storage of applications, API, data services etc. Fourth, Apple Inc. makes decision of whether to accept the third-party developers' applications to be sold in App Store. Fifthly, Apple Inc. takes the full license fee from the network users, then share with relevant developers in proportion. Regarding iTunes S.A.R.L. mentioned by Apple Inc., it is a wholly owned subsidiary registered and established in Luxembourg with a registered capital of just EUR 12,500, which is obviously incapable of operating the App Store.

(2) Third-party developers: They are mainly the providers of applications. After providing its detailed information to Apple for registration, they can pay license fee to use Apple software platform to develop applications and submit them to Apple Inc. With Apple Inc.'s approval, the applications may be downloaded for free or purchased by users in App Store. Then the third-party developer can share the purchase money with Apple Inc. or its designated affiliates.

(3) Network users: They are the consumers of the applications. First, they need to become a registered user by downloading the iTunes software including App Store from a website operated by Apple Inc. Then the registered users can download free applications or purchase applications online by credit card in App Store.

2. The determination of App Store's act

Based on the business model of App Store, it can be identified that there are two sources of applications that can be downloaded for free or purchased by users in App Store, which are the applications developed by Apple Inc. itself and the applications developed by third-party developers. When the applications from App Store constitute copyright infringement, the liabilities of Apple Inc. are also different due to the different sources of the applications.

In the case where the infringing application is developed by Apple Inc. itself, since Apple Inc. develops and communicates the infringing application in App Store so that network users may access the work at a time and place selected by them, such an act constituted the infringement of the right of communication of information on networks of the copyright owner. According to the copyright law, Apple Inc. shall bear the direct infringement liabilities.

In this case, Apple Inc. was identified as the developer of the infringing application. As the direct infringer, Apple Inc. shall bear the corresponding liabilities. It should be pointed out that Apple Inc. did not agree that the involved application was developed by itself, but argued that "Zhou Lianchun," who signed his name in the application, should be the developer. However, despite that Apple Inc. held the information of its partner third-party developers from the *iOS Developer Program License Agreement* etc., Apple Inc. did not provide any evidence concerning this "Zhou Lianchun," even after the Court suggested it to do so. Therefore, in the absence of the evidence to prove the infringing application was from a third-party developer, the Court determined that Apple Inc. is the developer.

If it can be confirmed that the infringing application is developed by a third-party developer, then what kind of liabilities should Apple Inc. bear? There are two controversial answers for this question.

The first opinion is that Apple Inc. is the joint direct infringer, and shall bear the liabilities for the direct infringement. As is mentioned above, Apple Inc. licenses third-party developers to use Apple's coding and testing software to develop applications running in iOS, providing developers with related OS, documentation, software (source code and object code), application, demonstration code, simulator, tools, storage of applications, API, data services etc. In addition, Apple Inc. makes decision of whether to accept the third-party developers' applications to be sold in App Store. Finally, Apple Inc. takes the full license fee from the network users, then share with relevant developers in proportion. Thus, together with the third-party developer, Apple Inc. in fact jointly commits the act of communication of information on networks. Therefore, Apple Inc. is a joint direct infringer, and shall bear the liabilities for the direct infringement.

The second opinion is that Apple Inc. only provides technology platforms and service support for third-party developers to develop application, which is not necessarily involved to the infringement of application content. The developer of the application shall bear the liabilities of infringement. For applications developed by third-party developers, Apple Inc.'s App Store only provides information storage service, thus should be identified as an "information storage service provider."

Chapter 3: Determination of Copyright Infringement

According to Article 22 of the *Regulations on the Protection of the Right of Communication of Information on Network*, "A network service provider which provides an information storage space to a service recipient, thus enabling the service recipient to make available to the public through information network a work, performance, or sound or video recording, and which meets the following conditions, bears no liabilities for compensation: (1) it clearly indicates that such information storage space is provided for the service recipient, and it makes known to the public its name, the person to be contacted and network address of the network service provider; (2) it does not make any modification to the work, performance, or sound or video recording made available by the service recipient; (3) it does not know or has no reasonable grounds to know that the work, performance, or sound or video recording made available by the service recipient is an infringement; (4) it does not gain any direct financial benefit from the service recipient making available the work, performance, or sound or video recording; and (5) upon receiving a written notification of the right owner, it removes, in accordance with the provisions of these Regulations, the work, performance, or sound or video recording which the right owner believes to be an infringement." Although Apple Inc. does not need to bear the direct infringement liabilities, it actively chooses applications, sells applications under its own name, collects fees and shares interests with third-party developers when providing the information storage space services, which obviously surpass the scope of "Safe harbor" rule which is an exemption of liabilities for neutral technological service providers. Therefore, Apple Inc. is an indirect infringer, and shall bear the liabilities for the indirect infringement.

I agree with the first opinion. Apple Inc. licenses third-party developers to develop applications that can only by the devices manufactured by Apple Inc. Besides, Apple Inc. makes decision of whether to accept the third-party developers' applications. This means that Apple Inc. takes part in the development of the applications. Apple Inc. requests developers to agree Apple Inc.'s sale method, which means that the communication of works by App Store is solely determined by Apple Inc. Meanwhile, Apple Inc. takes the full license fee from the network users, then share with relevant developers in proportion. Based on the above facts, it can be determined that Apple Inc. is not merely a provider of information storage space during the sales process of applications developed by third-party developers, it is also a co-developer, upload decision maker, application seller, and joint beneficiaries of the related software. Its act is not simply to help the infringement, but a direct infringement jointly with third-party developers by providing applications and sharing profits.

In this case, the judgment also indicates that even if the application was found to be developed by the third-party developer "Zhou Lianchun," Apple Inc. and the involved third-party developer still constituted a joint infringement of the copyrights owner's right of communication of information on networks, thus should also bear the corresponding liabilities.

—**Comments by ZHOU Duo**

Case 17. Internet Service Providers' Infringement of the Right of Communication Relating to Cloud Video Technology

Shanghai Jidong Network Corp., Ltd. v. Wuhan Radio & Television Bureau and Wuhan IPTV Corp., Ltd.

Case Index: *Shanghai Jidong Network Co., Ltd. v. Wuhan Radio & Television Bureau, Wuhan IPTV Co., Ltd.*; Wuhan Intermediate People's Court of Hubei Province, E Wuhan Zhong (Zhi) Chu Zi [2012] No. 3, June 18, 2012; Hubei Province Higher People's Court, E Min San Zhong Zi [2012] No. 184, September 4, 2012.

Facts:

The Plaintiff, Shanghai Jidong network Co., Ltd. (hereinafter, "JIDONG") alleged that: The Plaintiff spent a total of RMB 1.6 million to purchase the exclusive information network dissemination right of the forty-two episode drama "Boss Happiness." The drama was premiered on CCTV during the "Two Sessions" on March 4, 2010, was causing concern from all walks of life and setting a new high for audience ratings of CCTV in 2010. The "Huanghe TV" website (www.whtv.com.cn), which was filed by the Defendant Wuhan Radio and Television Bureau and was actually operated by the Defendant Wuhan IPTV, provided the online broadcast service for the show without permission by the Plaintiff. On September 23, 2011, the Plaintiff performed evidence preservation on the Defendant's infringement. The Defendant Wuhan Radio and Television Bureau (hereinafter, "WRTB") as the industry competent department, the Defendant Wuhan IPTV as a professional online media, arbitrarily uploaded the television drama "Boss Happiness" to the alleged infringing website and stored and broadcasted it. The subjective fault was obvious, which seriously impacted the TV drama's ratings in the Internet field and the Plaintiff's distribution of copyright, and affected the credibility of the Plaintiff's cooperation with business partners and the economic benefits of the Plaintiff. Hence, the Plaintiff requested the court to order that: First, the two Defendants shall stop the infringement, and remove the television drama "Boss Happiness" from the website involved, and eliminate the negative impact by publishing a statement concerning the infringement; Second, the Defendant shall compensate for the loss by infringement RMB 50,000, and the lawyer's agency fee paid for the purpose of stopping the infringement is RMB 5,000, total of RMB 55,000; Third, the Defendant shall bear the litigation fee.

The Defendant WRTB argued: The alleged infringing website was specifically operated by the Defendant Wuhan IPTV, and the bureau shall not bear the civil liability. The Defendant Wuhan IPTV argued that Beijing Sina Company which provided the works to the alleged infringing website "Huanghe TV" with "Cloud Video" technology have the license of the involved TV drama, and the alleged infringing website did not upload or store the works, thus it did not infringe the rights of Plaintiff.

Chapter 3: Determination of Copyright Infringement

Ruling and Reasoning:

In the first instance trial, Wuhan Intermediate People's Court of Hubei Province identified: In 2009, the plaintiff SJN was authorized by the copyright holder to obtain the exclusive right to information network dissemination on the television drama "Boss Happiness." The authorization term was five years from the date when the program was first broadcast on CCTV. On March 4, 2010, the drama was premiered on CCTV 1. On March 18, 2010, SJN (Party B) and Beijing Sina Company (Party A) signed the "Contract on Authorized Use of Film and TV Works" on the copyright authorization of the TV series "Boss Happiness." Section 3.1 of the contract stipulates: Under the precondition that Party A fully pays the cooperative amount, Party B provides Party A with its legally owned programs in a way for Party A to operate on its self-operating or operation platform (including but not limited to www.sina.com.cn website and its subpages), Party B grants Party A nonexclusive right of information network dissemination on the Internet. Section 4.1 of the contract stipulates: Party A shall only use it on its own broadband application platform, and shall not use on other application platforms or other approaches or transfer the contents of this agreement to third parties. Otherwise, Party A shall bear all legal liabilities and the liabilities for breach of contract. Article 4.2 of the contract stipulates: Party A shall be responsible for incorporating the video program resources provided by Party B into Party A's network system for consumption of network users. The contract stipulates: the term for Party A to use the authorized works is two years from March 18, 2010 to March 17, 2012.

On January 14, 2011, Beijing Sina Company issued the "Sina Video Play Power of Attorney," authorizing Beijing Ruobo Kesi Company to promote and serve the "Sina Cloud Video" project. The authorization term was from December 1, 2010 to January 31, 2012. Li Yanling, an employee of Beijing Ruobo Kesi Company, has been responsible for promoting the "Sina Cloud Video" project to the media since 2011, and has also cooperated with the WRTB as a media partner. During the promotion of the project, Li Yanling had sent Qian Ying, employee of WRTB, via QQ to send electronic files such as "Sina Video Player Power of Attorney," "Sina Cloud Video Project Cooperation" PPT, and "Sina Cloud Video Code Summary and Code Placement Method."

According to the "Sina Cloud Video Project Cooperation" PPT, "Sina Cloud video code summary and code placement methods" and other projects' promotion documents, the involved "Sina Cloud Video" technology has the following characteristics: (1) "Sina Cloud Video" relies on video on-demand and Streaming Media technology which is a massive copyrights video simulcasting platform that enables video content and audiences to access and allocate multiple points in the cloud; (2) "Sina Cloud Video" cooperation is based on the playing page (player code embedded in the partner's final page), according to the video headlines, video charts and the whole channel and other forms of modules for cloud video content output, cooperative media access module code can be placed on the home page, channel page, or the creation of a new second-level domain name, in the form of an entire channel to establish a new video channel; (3) No Sina outside chain, thus do not split the flow of cooperative media; (4) The cooperation site does not need to install the player, neither bandwidth and technology, also can customize their own page style; (5) "Sina cloud video" can be implemented by embedding video headlines and video lists in the cooperative media homepage or other pages, embedding full-motion video channel content into second-level domain of cooperative media, embedding playing page in the terminal of cooperative media; (6) Cooperative media is required to use "Cloud Video" code and its placement methods to achieve "Sina Cloud Video" function.

On September 23, 2011, under the supervision of a notary, the entrusted agent of the plaintiff SJN preserved the relevant cyber evidence at the notary office: Enter www.whbc.com.cn in the address bar to access the homepage of the website; Click on the "Huanghe TV Wuhan IPTV" logo at the top of the page to display the website homepage of www.whtv.com.cn, the bottom of the page displays information such as "E. ICP 05022490;" "I want to see" area on the left side of the page shows "Cloud Video" movie stills list, category and search box; enter the title "Boss Happiness" in the search box and click Search to display the search results; click on the title to display the "Boss Happiness" text profile and each episode list; click the episodes 1, 16 and 41 show embedded online playing pages. The IE browser icon and the "Cloud Video—Windows Internet Explorer" text are displayed at the top of the page where the work involved is located, and the first half of the address displayed in the address bar closely below is http://www.whtv.com.cn/whtv2011_yuntv/. In the upper left corner of the player page of the works involved, there are texts and an icon in the Chinese "Xin Lang Shi Pin" and the English "Sina." Above the player page, there are still remained icons of websites or column such as "Huanghe TV Wuhan IPTV" and "Wuhan Meeting Room."

Wuhan Intermediate People's Court of Hubei Province held that: When "Huanhe TV" broadcast the involved works, there was no redirect in the homepage address of the website, the original column names and layout design of "Huanghe TV Wuhan IPTV" and "Wuhan Meeting Room" set on the page did not change. Based on this, it can be concluded that the alleged infringing website used the "Sina Cloud Video" technology to broadcast the involved works. The "Cloud Video" code and its placement method were obviously a technical measure to adjust and control in a way to attain relevant works through the "Sina Cloud Video" technology. The dependence of alleged infringing website on the "Cloud Video" code and its placement method also confirms the fact that the alleged infringing websites must be subject to Beijing Sina Company when broadcasting the works involved, which further excludes the possibility of the alleged infringing websites uploading their own or storing the involved works in their web server. Therefore, the defendant's website did not store the involved work on its own server. Instead, it formed a new type of link with the website of the Beijing Sina Company to achieve the purpose of broadcasting the works involved in the case.

After Beijing Sina Company obtained the right of information network dissemination of the works involved from the SJN, it provided the "Sina Cloud Video" service to the defendant's website, which was essentially an act of uploading works to its own server, this behavior was not sublicense that the Beijing Sina Company granted the nonexclusive right of information network dissemination to the alleged infringing website. Therefore, Beijing Sina Company used certain technical method to make the works stored on its own server while played on the alleged infringing which did not violate the contractual agreement with SJN. The alleged infringing website used "Sina Cloud Video" technology and related code to obtain and play the works that had been uploaded to the Internet by Beijing Sina Company, it was an act of voluntarily accepting the "Sina Cloud Video" service which also did not infringe right of information network dissemination of SJN on the works involved in the case. Accordingly, Wuhan Intermediate People's Court of Hubei Province dismissed the plaintiff SJN's petition.

The plaintiff SJN refused to accept the first-instance judgment, filed an appeal within the statutory deadline, requested the revocation of the first-instance ruling and continued to claim its first-instance litigation request. During the second instance, the plaintiff SJN applied to revoke its appeal and the Hubei Province High People's Court granted.

Commentary:

American scholar Paul Goldstein said: "Copyright was the child of technology from the very beginning."[12] In a sense, copyright law is the product of communication technology and it continues to develop with innovations in printing, radio, television, and the Internet. In particular, the rapid development of Internet technology has made technical issues and legal issues intertwined, which has spawned many new topics for the protection of network copyrights. This case is a typical case that has been raised by the development of new technologies on the Internet.

1. Legal Issues of New Type Network Copyrights Caused by Cloud Video Technology Services

Cloud Video is an application mode of Cloud Computing. Regarding the concept of Cloud Computing, the U.S. National Institute of Standards and Technology defines it as: "Cloud Computing is a kind of ubiquitous, convenient and on-demand way to access configurable computing resources (including networks, servers, storage, applications and services) through the Internet, these resources can be quickly deployed and require only minimal administrative costs or intervention of service providers."[13] The core of the concept of Cloud Computing is to migrate the client's computing work to the cloud server. However, the cloud server is a service network cluster that is completely transparent to the user. The cloud server carries the user's specific application computing tasks, thus making the user face the terminals greatly simplified from the device to the software, the final form will be a free-maintenance software terminal, which greatly simplifies the user's hardware devices, and put complicated and

---

12. Paul Goldstein (Translated by Jin Haijun), *The Road to Copyright: From Gutenberg to Digital Jogger*, Peking University Press, 2008, p. 22.
13. *See* Peter Mell & Timothy Grance. The NIST Definition of Cloud Computing[EB/OL]. http://csrc.nist.gov/pub-lications/nistpubs/800-145/SP800-145.pdf.(2011-9). [2012-09-10]. Quoted from Bao Zhengye, Analysis of the Copyright of Cloud Computing—Taking the SaaS Model as an Example, *Jinan Journal*, 2 (2013).

changing hardware and software into the cloud, and is maintained by professional persons. Combined with the concept of development, the "Zhu Cloud" analysts team believe, Cloud Video refers to video network platform services based on cloud computing business model applications.[14] Cloud Video technology aims to free users from complicated terminal tools, hardware maintenance, and difficult-to-manage software, and puts the above work into the hands of professionals and professional servers in the cloud. In short, Cloud Video makes end-users feel as easy as turning on a TV when they are enjoying video services.

According to the traditional classification standards, service providers in the network environment can be divided into two types: network service providers (ISP) and network content providers (ICP). ISP is a network service provider which provides physical infrastructure services like network connections, access or links to a wide range of network users. ICP is a content provider that provides network information services and value-added services to a wide range of users. Usually, People's courts determine the legal status of defendants according to the classification standards of ISPs and ICPs in cases of infringement of network copyrights and whether they shall bear the tort liability. As the act of network services and network content are relatively independent activities, the classification standard of definition of responsibilities between ISP and ICP are relatively clear, the act of providing network content without the authorization of the copyright owner would directly infringes the rights of information network dissemination of copyright owners, and provides network services, however, constitute an accessory infringement if without fulfilling reasonable diligence. However, the basic characteristics of Cloud Computing are: "As software or behavior of service provider, it is a web browser to perform certain application functions through the software in a remote server, and its application results can be stored in a remote server, or download to the user's local computer."[15] In a word, Cloud Computing provides network services by the software, and transforms the traditional Software-as-a-Service application framework into a Platform-as-a-Service network environment. As a result of the network environment of service, "Cloud Computing as a technology of works transmission makes the distinction between the technology (equipment) and the service emphasized by the principle of technology-neutral blurred."[16] Under the Cloud Computing, the distinction between ISP and ICP is no longer as obvious as it used to be. This poses a challenge to the People's courts in determining infringement.

The originality of Cloud Video technology has created a brand-new network culture business model, moved the computational tasks undertaken by the complex hardware and software originally owned by the client to the cloud server in the cloud. In this case, for example, Sina Cloud Video technology has the following new features: First, Beijing Sina Corporation is responsible for providing Internet "Cloud Video" technical services to the cooperative website, and works can be freely played on the

---

14. *See* http://baike.baidu.com/view/4678792.html?fr = aladdin, the last visit: 2014-09-16.
15. *See* Liang Zhiwen, Cloud Computing, Technology Neutrality and Copyright Liability, *The Science of Law*, 3 (2011).
16. *Ibid.*

Chapter 3: Determination of Copyright Infringement

cooperative media website by means of content output, the copyright of the works belongs to Beijing Sina Company; Second, "Sina Cloud Video" is based on playing pages (play code embedded in the partner's final page), and the cloud video content is output in the form of video headlines, video charts, and entire channels, etc. To realize the Sina Cloud Video function: the cooperative websites use "Cloud Video" code and its placement methods. After acquiring the module code, a new video channel may be established in the form of an entire channel. Third, when playing video works, the interface of the player displays Sina Cloud Video logo icons such as Chinese "Xin Lang Shi Pin" and English "Sina," but the website address of the playing page of the work is still cooperative website's, the original column names, layout design, border settings and commercial advertisements of the cooperative website are all remained. Fourth, the cooperative website cannot control the play service of Sina Video, if the Beijing Sina Company's web server for storing video works fails or stops the online access and playing output of all Sina Cloud Video content, the cooperative website will not be able to continue to acquire and play video works.

The above technical features of the Sina Cloud Video service show: Beijing Sina Company provides a storage server which is open to public for video works, when a cooperative website plays a video works, the works is directly retrieved from the server, therefore, for a cooperative website, neither it uploads video works to its own server nor obtains through searching method to play works online, instead it transmits the video works provided by Beijing Sina Company by way of linking. In the past, the two most common linking methods in judicial practice, one is "Direct Linking," also known as "Home Linking," which refers to clicking on the hypertext links symbol on the current web page to make the browser's content redirect from one web page to another or part of another web page;[17] The other one is "Deep-Link," it can be summarized in judicial practice: hyperlinks that link directly to a text, a picture, etc., which not as usual to link to the main web page, or after clicking on the link, download or open files online from linked website without disconnecting the website itself.[18] In Deep Links, visitors generally do not see the link icons, and do not feel the change of information such as URL changes caused by the link. For the link technology involved in Cloud Video technology, the judgment of the first instance held that the alleged infringing website "using a new link with the Beijing Sina Company's website to achieve the purpose of broadcasting the works involved." Some judges summarized the characteristics of this new type of link as: "Beijing Sina Company authorized the alleged infringing website to access Beijing Sina website without any changes to its original page border and website address by using this technique in a way to achieve technical effects that embedding the film and television works of the Beijing Sina Company server into the alleged infringing websites."[19] This new type of link is

---

17. *See* Zhu Xiu, *Several Issues on the Deep Link and Information Network Communication Right*, in The Trial Practice of New Type of Difficult Copyright Cases, Jiang Zhipei (ed.), Law Press, 2007, p. 72.
18. *See* Chen Jinchuan, *Interpretation and Practice Guidance of Copyright Judgment Principles*, Law Press, 2014, p. 201.
19. Li Peimin, The Judicial Review of the Infringement of Cloud Video Works, *People's Justice-Case*, 14 (2013).

actually a linking technique similar to "Framing-link," that is, accessing content of other websites without changing the borders and URL of the website so that the contents of other websites appear on its own website, and the information on the column settings and commercials displayed on the borders of own website are not affected. The novelty of the Cloud Video business service model has brought new challenges to the People's courts in the trial of cases involving violations of the right of information network dissemination.

2. Judgment on Whether Cloud Video Dissemination Behavior Infringes the Right of Information Network Transmission

Article 10, paragraph 1 (12), of the Copyright Law of the People's Republic of China stipulates: "The right of information network dissemination, that is, the right to provide the public with works by wired or wireless means, so as to make the public able to respectively obtain the works at the individually selected time and place." Article 26 of the "Regulation on the Protection of the Right to Communicate Works to the Public over Information Networks" stipulates in paragraph 1: "The right of information network dissemination, means to provide works, performances, or audio and video recordings to the public in a wired or wireless manner so that the public have the right to obtain works, performances or audio and video products at the selected time and place." Article 2 of the "Provisions of the Supreme People's Court on Several Issues concerning the Application of Law in Hearing Civil Dispute Cases Involving Infringement of the Right of Dissemination on Information Networks." It is defined as: "For the purposes of these Provisions, 'information networks' means the Internet, radio and television broadcasting networks, fixed communication networks and mobile communication networks, with computers, TV sets, fixed telephones, mobile phones and other electronic devices as receiving terminals, as well as local area networks open to the public." Above all provisions of the law and judicial interpretation show, that the power structure of the right of information network dissemination includes three parts: the first is the interactive dissemination method; the second is the openness of the dissemination behavior; the third is the information network dissemination behavior.[20] The dissemination method of video works of Cloud Video services openly disseminate video works to network users in the computer network environment of the Internet, the behavior of the video works provided by the website and the behavior of users accepting video works also have the characteristics of interactive transmission, user can obtain the work at a selected time or in a selected place. Therefore, the transmission method of Cloud Video conforms to the characteristics of the information network dissemination, and the copyright case caused by the Cloud Video technology service belongs to dispute in infringement on right of information network dissemination.

Infringement forms that infringe on the right of information network dissemination can be further divided into "Direct Infringement" and "Indirect Infringement." According to the above provisions of the "Copyright Law of the People's Republic of

---

20. *See* Liang Zhiwen, *Digital Copyright—Centered on the Protection of Information Network Communication Rights*, Intellectual Property Publishing House, 2007, p. 14.

China," Direct Violation of the right of information network dissemination should be an act of "providing works to the public," the definition of "providing" can be understood as: "as long as the work is 'uploaded' to or placed on the Internet where for the public network users to download or browse, it constitutes a 'providing' of the works, regardless of whether anyone has actually downloaded or browsed."[21] In this case, although the alleged infringing website broadcasted the video works involved online, the website did not upload the video work to its own server, either placed the video work on its server, but through the "Framed Link," in this way, under the premise of not changing the border settings of this website, the address of webpages and the content of advertisements, instead playing works involved provided by Sina Cloud Company's cloud server with the dissemination technology embedded in the "Sina Cloud Video" player module. Therefore, the alleged infringing websites obviously did not constitute "Direct Infringement" of the right of information network dissemination.

Whether the alleged infringing website constitutes "Indirect Infringement," it should first examine whether the Sina Website providing video works constitutes "Direct Infringement." Article 8 of the "Tort Law of the People's Republic of China" stipulates: "Where two or more persons jointly commit a tort, causing harm to another person, they shall be liable jointly and severally." The first paragraph of Article 9 of the Act stipulates: "One who abets or assists another person in committing a tort shall be liable jointly and severally with the tortfeasor." The above legal provisions show that the precondition for the establishment of "Indirect Infringement" is the existence of "Direct Infringement," and the subject of infringement liability, including both the direct tortfeasor of the infringing act and tortfeasor who abets or assists another person in committing a tort. The above provisions, as general legal provisions on civil torts, of course apply to the specific situation of infringement of intellectual property rights. As the Italian scholar Musso pointed out, "even though the responsibility for assisting or indirectly participating in (copyright) infringement is not regulated by Copyright Law, however the general principles of Tort Law can be applied to it."[22] Therefore, in the determination of infringement of intellectual property rights cases: "The 'Indirect Infringement' is premised on the existence or impending implementation of 'Direct Infringement'."[23] In this case, the alleged infringing websites apparently did not have "Abetting Infringement" or "Induced Infringement," whether or not the alleged infringing website constitutes "Assisting Infringement," the key is to see whether the Sina Website which it collaborated with the cloud video business constitutes "Direct Infringement." The right of information network dissemination is a property-based economic right, according to the provisions of Article 10, paragraphs 2 and 3 of the "Copyright Law of the People's Republic of China," the copyright owner may license another person to exercise it, or may transfer it in whole or in part, and may receive

---

21. See Wang Qiang, *Internet Copyright Law*, China Renmin University Press, 2008, p. 68.
22. See Alberto Musso & Mario Fabiani, ITA International copyright law and Practice Scope11[1][a][ii], Matthew Bender & Company, Inc.(2002). Quoted from Wang Qian & Wang Linghong, *Indirect Infringement of Intellectual Property Rights*, China Renmin University Press, 2008, p. 8.
23. See Wang Qian & Wang Linghong, *supra* p. 5.

remuneration as agreed upon in the contract or in accordance with the relevant provisions in this Law. Judging from the facts ascertained by the court, SJN and Beijing Sina Company signed the "Contract for Authorized Use of Film and TV Works," and in the contract licensed Beijing Sina Company's nonexclusive right of information network dissemination for the involved television drama "Boss Happiness." It can be seen from this that Beijing Sina Company obtained the right to disseminate information on the television drama through the right holder's permission. The company's exercise of its rights within the contractual authorized period does not constitute "Direct Infringement." Based on this, it can be concluded that in the case that Beijing Sina Company does not constitute "Direct Infringement," the cooperative website that cooperated with the "Sina Cloud Video" business does not constitute "Indirect Infringement" either.

Question on whether the alleged infringing website constitutes "Licensed Infringement." In the intellectual property legislation and related precedents of Anglo-American legal system countries, there is a common type of "Indirect Infringement" called "Licensing Infringement." For example, Article 16 of the Copyright Act of the United Kingdom expressly states: "Without the consent of the copyright owner, any person who authorizes another person to perform a copyrighted proprietary right constitutes infringement."[24] There are similar provisions in the Copyright Act of Canada and the Copyright Act of Australia.[25] With regard to the use of copyright licenses, Article 26 of the Copyright Law of the People's Republic of China clearly stipulates that: "Without the consent of the copyright owner, if the copyright holder has not expressly permitted or transferred the rights in the contract for licensing and transferring, the other party shall not exercise such rights." According to this provision, in the litigation of copyright infringement, "if defendant claims it has been authorized by the copyright owner, he is obliged to prove that his actions do not exceed the copyright holder's permission."[26]

In this case, the "Contract for Authorized Use of Film and TV Works" signed between SJN and Beijing Sina Company stipulates that SJN will provide Beijing Sina Company with its own legally owned programs for Beijing Sina Company to operate on its self-operating or operation platform(including but not limited on the www.sina.com.cn website and its subpages), it granted Beijing Sina Company an nonexclusive right to disseminate information network on the Internet, and Beijing Sina Company shall only use it on its own broadband application platform, and shall not use on other application platforms or otherwise methods or license the contents of this agreement to the third parties. The key to interpret the above contractual agreement lies in the definition of "self-operating or operation platform (including but not limited to www.sina.com.cn and its subpages)." In the Cloud Video technology service model, the behavior of Beijing Sina Company provided the "Sina Cloud Video" service to the

---

24. *See* Wang Qian & Wang Linghong, *Research on Indirect Intellectual Property Infringement*, China Renmin University Press, 2008, p. 11.
25. *See* 17 USC 106; (Canada) Copyright Act, s. 3 (1); (Australia) Copyright Act 1968, s. 13 (2).
26. *See* He Huaiwen, *Study on Rules for Determination of Copyright Infringement* (2012 Edition), Intellectual Property Publishing House, 2012, p. 129.

alleged infringing website, video works was virtually "Uploaded" by Beijing Sina Company in its own cloud server; Beijing Sina Company provided video works through cloud video dissemination from "Cloud" to "Client," still belonged to Beijing Sina Company's self-operating or operation platform which is not limited to www.sina.com.cn and its subpages with regard to the using of the video work, the act did not license its "nonexclusive" information network dissemination right to the alleged infringing website. Therefore, the Beijing Sina Company provided the video works stored on its cloud server to the online broadcast of the alleged infringing website through the cloud video technology and it did not infringe the contract between Beijing Sina Company and SJN. The third-party website that accepted the "Sina Cloud Video" service, namely the alleged infringing website's dissemination of the video work involved in the case, which also did not infringe the right of information network dissemination of SJN who enjoyed in the video works involved.

3. Balance of Interests in Network Copyright Protection Considerations

The balance of interests is an important principle of the intellectual property system. As some scholars said: "The intellectual property law is a law based on the balance of interests, and the balance of interests constitutes the cornerstone of intellectual property law."[27] Under the Internet environment, the protection of network copyrights is more complicated. It involves not only inspiring the copyright owners to innovate and safeguarding the use of the public, but also relates to the development of emerging Internet cultural industries and new Internet business models. It can be said that "traditional copyright protection mainly involves the balance of interests between copyright owners and the public, while network copyright protection involves the balance between the interests of copyright owners, network service providers and the public, and network service providers became the important part of measurement of the balance of interests."[28]

From the point of view of western developed countries' network copyright protection, they attach great importance to the interest balance mechanism of network copyright protection and reasonably determine the tort liability of network service providers. For example, judging from the judicial practice in the U.S., in 1984 the U.S. Supreme Court established the "Technology Neutrality" principle in the Sony case, and according to this principle, U.S. Supreme Court affirmed that Betamax video recorders have "substantial noninfringing function" produced by Sony noncommercially which could change the user's time to watch television programs for personal purposes,[29] as a result, technical service providers have cleared up legal obstacles in developing high-tech products and technologies, and have achieved a balance between copyright protection and high-tech development. In the *Netcom* case in 1995, the court overturned the "Frena" judgment ruled in 1993 that network service provider should bear

---

27. *See* Feng Xiaoqing, *The Theory of Balancing Intellectual Property Interests*, China University of Political Science and Law Press, 2006, p. 23.
28. *See* Kong Xiangjun, *Basic Issues in the Application of Intellectual Property Law: Judicial Philosophy, Judicial Policy, and Judgment Methods*, China Legal Publishing House, 2013, p. 543.
29. *See Sony Corporation of American et al. v. Universal City Studio, Inc.*, et al. 464 U.S. 417, at 442.

direct infringement liability, and developed the theory of Indirect Infringement.[30] In this case, the court found that network service providers could not constitute direct infringement without intention when copying, distributing, displaying, etc., and could only constitute infringement if content of Direct Infringing was not deleted in time.[31] Since then, the development of the Internet has shown that the establishment of the "Indirect Infringement" principle in the *Netcom* case has played a crucial role in balancing the interests of all parties in the Internet environment. In the United States' Digital Millennium Copyright Act (DMCA) in 1998, the liabilities of network service providers were finally confirmed by law. The second part of the DMCA, "Limitation of Online Copyright Infringement Liability" added with the section 512 of the U.S. Copyright Act, it expressly stipulates exemptions for network service providers which could be divided to four categories: provide transmission channels, system caching, information storage, and information search services shall not bear the liability for Infringement.[32]

In turn, China's protection of network copyright also needs to balance the interests of copyright owners, network service providers and the public. Taking the Cloud Video technology service involved in this case as an example, the Cloud Video technology service move the client's computing work to the cloud, and the cloud server carries the user's computing tasks and is maintained by professional personnel, so that the terminal equipment and software that the user faces become greatly simplified. It should be said that the application of Cloud Video not only embodies the technical advantages of emerging network video services, but also satisfies the actual needs of the vast majority of network users, and greatly facilitates the dissemination of outstanding cultural achievements. The use of Cloud Video technology to disseminate video works may infringe upon copyright, but Cloud Video technology clearly has the legitimacy of "substantial noninfringement function," according to the principle of "Technology Neutrality," Cloud Video technology service itself should not be regarded as infringement. In addition, for the third-party websites that accept Cloud Video technology services, their online play of video works is controlled by Cloud Video technology service providers, and third-party websites themselves do not provide video works by uploading or storing. When the provider of the Cloud Video has obtained the authorization of the copyright owner, if it is determined that the third-party website constitutes infringement, it would inevitably affect the promotion of the Cloud Video service and the development of Cloud Video technology. Therefore, the judgment of this case well reflected the balance of interests in the protection of network copyright and enriched the judicial practice of the protection of network copyright.

—**Comments by TONG Haichao**

---

30. *See Religious Technology Center v. Netcom On-line Communication Services*, 907 F. Supp. 1361, at 1368–1370 (N.D.Ca.1995).
31. *See* Wang Qiang, *Research on Copyright Protection in Network Environment*, Law Press, 2011, p. 215.
32. *See* Wu Handong, On the Responsibility of Copyright Infringement of Internet Service Providers, *Chinese Law*, 2 (2011).

Chapter 3: Determination of Copyright Infringement

Case 18. The Nature of Real-Time Online Rebroadcast and Copyright Infringement

CCTV International Network Co., Ltd. v. Beijing Baidu Netcom Science Technology Co., Ltd. (Beijing Sohu Internet Information Service Co., Ltd. as 3rd Party)
Case of Copyright Infringement Dispute
Case Index: *CCTV International Network Co., Ltd. v. Beijing Baidu Netcom Technology Co., Ltd.*; Haidian District People's Court of Beijing, Hai Min Chu Zi [2012] No. 20573, December 12, 2012; Beijing No. 2 Intermediate People's Court, Yi Zhong Min Chu Zi [2013] No. 3142, May 2, 2013.

Facts:

This case was relating to a copyright infringement dispute. The work involved in this case was the "Spring Festival Gala Evening 2012" (hereinafter, "Chunwan"), and the copyright owner was China Central Television. The Plaintiff, CCTV International Network Co., Ltd. (hereinafter, "CCTV"), was entitled the exclusive right to use the work. During the live broadcast of the Chunwan, CCTV found that Internet users could directly watch the real-time rebroadcast of the Chunwan on the *Beijing Baidu Netcom Technology Co., Ltd.* (hereinafter, "Baidu") website (www.baidu.com). CCTV claimed that the act was a real-time rebroadcast of the Chunwan and constituted an infringement of copyright. CCTV required Baidu to compensate RMB 1 million for the economic losses. In the trial of the first instance, CCTV claimed that Baidu violated Article 10 (17) of the *Copyright Law of China* concerning the other rights enjoyed by copyright owners.

The Defendant denied the claims made by CCTV. The main defense was that Baidu provided only the service of network linking. Although online users could watch the video on Baidu's website directly, the "Sohu Video" was included in the search results illustration. The sign of "the video from the Sohu Video" displayed on the video playback page could all be noticed that the video was from the Sohu Video. As for why users were able to watch the video on the Baidu page, Baidu explained that it was because of the use of the i-frame technology. The technology allowed users to display the videos of the linked websites on the search results page directly without entering the pages of the linked websites.

Ruling and Reasoning:

Haidian District People's Court of Beijing held that: Chunwan was a compiled work; as the compiler of the Chunwan, CCTV was the copyright owner. In regard to Baidu's acts, the court held that due to the display of "From Sohu Video" next to the video play icon, and "Sohu Video" was displayed at the top of the screen, and "Sohu Video Broadcasting" was displayed at the top right of the screen, so the video involved in this case was provided by the third-party Sohu Video. Baidu provided only the service of linking, thus did not infringe CCTV's broadcasting right. According to the provisions of Article 10 (11) of the *Copyright Law of China*, the court decided to dismiss all the claims made by CCTV.

CCTV refused to accept the first-instance judgment and made an appeal to the Beijing No. 1 Intermediate People's Court.

The Beijing No. 1 Intermediate People's Court held that according to the certificate of authorization issued by CCTV, it could be concluded that CCTV had not only broadcasting rights for Chunwan, but also the right of communication of Information on networks and other rights stipulated in the provision of Article 10 (17) of the *Copyright Law of China*. The existing evidence submitted by the Defendant Baidu was insufficient to prove that it only provided linking services. Therefore, it should be determined that the Defendant Baidu website directly provided the real-time rebroadcast of the Chunwan. In the lack of permission of the copyright owner, the Defendant's act of real-time online rebroadcast constituted the infringement of the broadcasting right of the Plaintiff. According to the provisions of Article 170 (2) of the *Civil Procedure Law*, the court abrogated the judgment of the first instance and ruled that Baidu should compensate CCTV for the economic loss of RMB 60,000.

Commentary:

The determination made in this case is of typical significance on two issues.

1. Nature of the real-time online rebroadcast

One of the key issues in this case is how to determine the legal nature of the real-time online rebroadcast. In the ruling of the second instance, a more detailed analysis of this issue was provided by the court. Based on the different initial transmission methods, the alleged acts could be separately recognized to be within the scope of broadcasting right of Article 10 (10) and other rights of Article 10 (17) of the *Copyright Law*. Such determination was made for the first time in the Chinese judicial practice.

This case is distinctive from other prior copyright cases. The controversial opinions regarding the legal nature of the real-time rebroadcast were raised from not only the parties but also the judges of different courts. In the second instance, even the Plaintiff CCTV itself raised the opinion which was different from the opinion in the first instance first instance. In the first instance trial, CCTV believed that this act should be within the scope of Article 10 (17). However in the second instance trial, CCTV still insisted that this act constitutes a copyright infringement but stated that it could not determine which right to be infringed. The court of the first instance held that the act should be within the scope of broadcasting rights of Article 10 (11).

Under this circumstance, in the second instance trial, the first question presented to the court was whether CCTV was allowed to adjust the application of different rights in the second instance trial. Eventually, taking into account the complexity of the nature of the alleged acts and the lack of prior cases, the court held that CCTV had reasonable grounds for changing the applicable copyright provisions in the second instance trial. Under this premise, in order to accurately define the nature of the real-time online rebroadcast, the court of the second instance made a comprehensive analysis of all the rights enumerated in Article 10 of the *Copyright Law* regarding the legal nature of the act from the following three rights: the broadcasting right of Article

Chapter 3: Determination of Copyright Infringement

10 (10), the right of communication of information on networks of Article 10 (12), and the other rights of Article 10 (17).

Regarding whether the real-time online rebroadcast shall be within the scope of the right of communication of information on networks, the ruling of the second instance pointed out that Article 10 (12) of the *Copyright Law* stated that the right of communication of information on networks means "the right to communicate to the public a work, by wire or wireless means in such a way that members of the public may access these works from a place and at a time individually chosen by them." The key characteristic of the right is to enable the public to access the works at the time and place chosen by them. The act to be regulated is the "act of interactive communication." Therefore, the act of communication that does not contain "interactive" characteristic obviously does not fall within the scope of the right of communication of information on networks. For the real-time online rebroadcast in this case, because network users cannot obtain the broadcast content at the time and place of their own choice, it does not have interactive features, thus such act is not within the scope of the right of communication of information on networks.

Regarding whether the real-time online rebroadcast shall be within the scope of broadcasting right, the ruling of the second instance pointed out that Article 10 (11) of the *Copyright Law* stipulated that broadcasting right means "the right to publicly broadcast or communicate to the public a work by wireless means, to communicate to the public a broadcast work by wire or relay means, and to communicate to the public a broadcast work by a loudspeaker or by any other analogous tool used to transmit symbols, sounds or pictures." According to this provision, there are three types of acts within the scope of broadcasting right: wireless broadcasting, cable rebroadcasting, and publicly broadcast received broadcasts.[33] Of these three acts, the "wireless broadcasting" is crucial. It is not only a separate broadcast, but also the initial step of the other two types of broadcast. The other two types of broadcast are broadcast after receiving wireless broadcasting. When judging whether a certain act is within the scope of the broadcasting right, the key decisive factor is whether initial propagation is wireless broadcasting. Among the existing methods of transmission, only broadcasting stations, television stations and satellite broadcasting organizations adopt wireless methods.[34] As a result, "wireless broadcasting" as "initial broadcasting" usually refers to the broadcasting activities by broadcasting stations, television stations, and satellite broadcasting organizations. Correspondingly, the "rebroadcasting" based on wireless broadcasting should also be the dissemination of broadcasts by radio stations, television stations and satellite broadcasting organizations.

Specific to the real-time online rebroadcast, usually the initial transmission may adopt both wireless methods (from radio stations, television stations or satellite broadcasting organizations), and wired methods (from other websites). Therefore,

---

33. *See* Wang Qian, *Intellectual Property Law Course*, China Renmin University Press (中国人民大学出版社), 2012, p. 141.
34. *See* Li Mingde & Xu Chao, *Copyright Law*, Law Press（法律出版社）, 2009, p. 84.

based on the previous analysis, whether the real-time online rebroadcast is within the scope of broadcasting right should be determined based on different situations. Only the initial transmission of the real-time online rebroadcast by the "wireless" method (from radio stations, television stations or satellite broadcasting organizations) is within the scope of broadcasting right. If the initial transmission adopts "wired" real-time online rebroadcast, then it can only be regulated by other solutions.

Since the initial transmission of the real-time online rebroadcast by the "wired" method does not meet any conditions for the application of any specific right in Article 10 of the *Copyright Law*, it is necessary to determine whether the miscellaneous provision of Article 10 (17) of the *Copyright Law* shall cover such activity. This is the key issue to be clarified in this case.

The Principle of Numerus Clausus is the fundamental principle for granting the exclusive rights of copyright. In regard to the application of the miscellaneous provision of Article 10 (17), a higher standard must be adopted in order to avoid setting up new rights beyond the statutory rights that may jeopardize the Principle of Numerus Clausus. However, if some activities are obviously against the Principle of Fairness, then the miscellaneous provision shall be taken into consideration. This approach shall be applicable in the case of initial transmission of the real-time online rebroadcast by the "wired" method. Compared with the initial transmission regulated by the broadcasting right, the use of "wireless" real-time online transmission, the difference between the two activities is only the adoption of different technical means (use of wired or wireless). Under this circumstance, if the initial real-time online transmission is a "wired" method rather than a "wireless" method prescribed in the broadcasting rights, it is deemed that the activity is not within the scope of copyright protection. It means that for the same two transmission activities, different infringement determinations are made simply because they use different technical means. Such a conclusion is not only obviously unfair but also violates the basic principles of setting and distinguishing specific rights of copyright. Under the circumstance, the distinction of different rights should be based on the characteristics of the activities, rather than the specific technical means adopted in the activities. In other words, only the distinction in technical means will not affect the identification of the nature of the activity. At present, this principle has been adopted in the setting of various rights in the *Copyright Law*. The use of technical means as a basis for distinguishing broadcasting right in the *Copyright Law* is caused by legislative defects rather than the general Principles of Application.[35] Based on the above grounds, in order to make up for the legislative defects of "broadcasting right" as much as possible, it is reasonable to apply Article 10 (17) of the *Copyright Law* to cover the real-time online broadcast of the "wired" method

---

35. The "right of broadcasting" provisions of the *Copyright Law* are derived from Art. 11 of the *Berne Convention for the Protection of Literary and Artistic Works*, and it was not common for the Cable Broadcasting Act of the *Berne Convention* to be last amended in 1971. This activity has not been included in the scope of broadcasting right. *See* WANG Qian, *Intellectual Property Law Course*, China Renmin University Press (中国人民大学出版社), 2012, p. 143.

Chapter 3: Determination of Copyright Infringement

for initial transmission. [36] The prior judicial practice also supports such approach. [37]

In summary, regarding the legal nature of real-time online rebroadcast, the second-instance ruling concluded that: according to the difference in the means of initial transmission, real-time online rebroadcast should be subject to different legal provisions. If the initial transmission was a "wireless" approach, then the broadcasting right of Article 10 (11) of the *Copyright Law* should be applied. If it adopted a "wired" approach, the miscellaneous provision of Article 10 (17) of the *Copyright Law* should be applied. In addition, it should be pointed out that real-time online rebroadcast is not within the scope of the adjustment of the right of communication of information on networks of Article 10 (12) of the *Copyright Law*.

In this case, the content of authorization acquired by CCTV included the rights of both Article 10 (11) and Article 10 (17) of the *Copyright Law*. Therefore, regardless of whether the initial transmission method involved in the case is a wireless broadcast or a cable broadcast, CCTV has the right to prohibit it. According to the existing evidence, it can be determined that the initial transmission method of the real-time online rebroadcast in the case is "wireless broadcasting," so the activity is within the scope of the broadcasting right. The real-time online rebroadcast implemented by Baidu without the permission of the copyright owner constitutes an infringement of the broadcasting right.

2. Evidentiary requirements regarding deep linking

Another typical issue presented in this case is that: in the ruling of the second instance, the evidentiary requirements regarding deep linking was raised by the court. The ruling of the second instance stated that the deep link provider should provide the "absolute network address" of the linked content on its webpage in principle, and ensure the network users click on this address to obtain the content. Only the relevant mark on the web page cannot be the evidence to prove that what it provides is link service.

In this case, Baidu argued that what it provided was just a search link service. According to the notarial certificate of the case, during the entire process of search and play of the Chunwan, network users do not have to enter the corresponding page of the Sohu website to view the video. Therefore, if Baidu actually provides a link service, the service should belong to the "deep link" in the link service. It can be seen that the key to proof of Baidu is how to prove that it is a deep linking.

At present, although the judicial interpretation[38] of the Supreme Court and the Guiding Opinion of the Beijing High Court[39] clearly define the burden of proof of link

---

36. *See* Hu Kangsheng, *China Copyright Law Interpretation*, Law Press (法律出版社), 2012, pp. 63-64 Hu Er Zhong Min Wu (Zhi) Chu Zi [2008] No. 187.
37. Beijing Dongcheng District People's Court, Dong Min Chu Zi [2008] No. 7905.
38. Article 4 of the *Provisions of the Supreme People's Court on Several Issues Concerning the Application of Law in the Trial of Civil Disputes over the Dissemination of Information on the Right of Information on the Internet* (promulgated in 2012) stipulates that network service providers can prove that they only provide web services such as automatic access, automatic transmission, information storage space, search, linking, and file sharing technologies, and claiming that they do not constitute joint infringements, should be supported by the people's courts. The plaintiff claims that the form of the service provided by the network service provider

services on Internet service providers, few judgments have addressed specific evidentiary requirements. Under this circumstance, the second instance ruling in this case took full account of the possibility of the two parties' proofs, and made the following attempts:

1) Only having the mark on the webpage is insufficient to prove the linking provided by Baidu Company

In this case, Baidu claimed that the basis for the search linking service was the annotations on the two related pages (the "search results page" for the Chunwan on the Baidu website and the "play interface" for the Chunwan). The corresponding parts of the above two pages were marked with "Sohu Video." In this regard, the second instance ruling pointed out that the above evidences obviously did not have the corresponding probative force. There are two reasons: First of all, the tagged person in the "search results page" is Baidu, not the third party. Taking into account that the right to make changes to this mark is clearly in Baidu. If only based on this mark, it is determined that the content originated from Sohu Video, it seems to give Baidu too low burden of proof and the possibility of evading the law. Second, the tag of "Sohu Video" in the "playing interface" can only prove that Chunwan played on Baidu website "originated" from the Sohu website, but it cannot rule out that Baidu directly intercepted the stream of Sohu website's Chunwan video and cannot exclude the possibility of "storing" the broadcast on its server. Based on the above facts, it is obviously difficult to prove that Baidu only provided link services.

2) The deep link service provider should display the absolute network address of the linked content that can be clicked on the page

Baidu believed that the Baidu website's search results page can directly display the video of the linked website and provide deep link service, which was based on the use of i-frame technology. However, in view of the fact that the technology has substantial noninfringing uses, based on the Principle of Technology Neutrality, the act should be deemed to be legitimate. The second instance ruling did not support Baidu's claim. The reason is that network technology has substantial noninfringing uses, but technology itself does not constitute infringement does not mean that there is no restriction on the

---

misleads the user into thinking that the network service provider spread works, performances, and audio and video products, but the network service provider can provide evidence that it only provides services such as automatic access, automatic transmission, information storage space, search links, and P2P (point-to-point) services should not be considered to constitute the act of communication of information on networks.

39. The *Beijing Higher People's Court's Guiding Opinions on Several Issues concerning Network Copyright Dispute Cases* was promulgated in 2010. Article 4 (2) stipulates that the plaintiff claims that the forms of services provided by network service providers mislead users into thinking that they are network services. Providers disseminate works, performances, audio and video products, but network service providers can provide evidence that they provide only automatic access, automatic transmission, information storage space, search, links, P2P (point-to-point) services, etc. should not be considered to constitute the act of communication of information on networks.

specific form of use of network technology. When a website uses a particular technology, it should not only consider the benefits that the technology brings to the website, but also take into account the possibility of proof in future disputes, that is, how to prove that the occurrence of a certain situation is caused by a particular technology. The standard of this proof can neither be set too high, otherwise it will very likely make the website unable to be applied objectively because of the inability of proof or excessive difficulty, nor can it be set too low, otherwise it may cause the right holder to assume the burden of proof that should not be assumed, or influence the possibility of the right holder to raise contrary evidence. It means that the setting of this standard of proof can only be different from case to case and try to find a balance between the two interests. Specific to the i-frame technology, the use of this technology will enable users to display the linked content without having to enter the linked website. However, the use of the technology only exists in the background of the website, while most Internet users do not know it. Therefore, in consideration of the possibility and pertinence of the copyright owners' rights, the ruling requires that the website should provide the "absolute network address" of the linked content (in this case, the real-time rebroadcast page of Chunwan on the Sohu website). At the same time, it should be ensured that Internet users click the address enough to obtain the content.

The reason why such standard should be set is that on the one hand, this method is the closest approach to be consistent with the characteristic of link service, and it is possible and affordable for the providers and will not increase unreasonable burden. On the other hand, for the copyright owner, since the link address is an absolute address, if it is considered that the link is not true, it is possible to check the address for inspection. Moreover, it will not increase the burden of proof on the copyright owners, and it also protects the possibility of the right owners to raise rebuttal evidence.

If such standard is applied in this case, the whole playback process of Chunwan was in the Baidu page. Baidu did not mark the "absolute network address," and only labeled "Sohu Video" on the search results and playback page. This external manifestation was obviously difficult to make CCTV determine that the video was from Sohu website. To take a step back, even the CCTV can recognize this possibility, however since Baidu website does not tag the "absolute network address" of the live broadcast content, even if CCTV had the incentive to verify the direct source of the video, it still could not objectively verify it. If only relying on the above-mentioned label to determine that Baidu provided search link service, it would improperly increase the burden of proof of CCTV, and would have unreasonable influence on the possibility of raising rebuttal evidence. In summary, the existing evidence of Baidu had not satisfied the evidentiary requirements concerning deep link. On this ground, the court held that Baidu had implemented the real-time online rebroadcast. In the absence of evidence that it had been authorized by the right owner, the act constituted the infringement of the "broadcasting right" of CCTV.

—Comments by RUI Songyan

Case 19. The Nature of Partial Communicating and the Nature of Full Reproducing Without Communicating

Wang Xin v. Beijing Guxiang Information Technology Co., Ltd. and Google, Inc. Case of Copyright Infringement Dispute
Case Index: *Wang Xin v. Beijing Guxiang Information Technology Co., Ltd and Google, Inc.*; Beijing No. 1 Intermediate People's Court, Yi Zhong Min Chu Zi [2011] No. 1321, December 20, 2012; Beijing Higher People's Court, Gao Min Zhong Zi [2013] No. 1221, December 19, 2013.

Facts:

This case is the only case of copyright infringement disputes in China regarding Google Digital Library. The Plaintiff, Wang Xin, whose pseudonym is Mianmian, is the author of the involved work *Hydrochloride lover*. The Defendant, Google Inc., who is the creator of the Google Digital Library, copied full text of the Plaintiff's work in the process of making the digital library. Since then, the Defendant Google has provided the work to its affiliate in China, Beijing Guxiang Information Technology Co., Ltd (hereinafter, "BG"), and the latter has segmentally communicated the work to network users on its Google China website. (i.e., providing service of displaying two or three segments of the content on the webpage. Each segment consists of two or three lines. The webpage does not display the whole content of the work.)

The Plaintiff Wang Xin claimed that the two Defendants reproduced full text of her work and communicated it on Google's Chinese website without permission, which constituted copyright infringement of her right of reproduction and right of communication of information on networks. Therefore, the Plaintiff claimed that the two Defendants should cease the infringement and compensate for the economic loss.

The Defendant Google argued that since it only implemented the act of reproducing the Plaintiff's work, which occurred in the U.S., thus the Chinese court did not have jurisdiction. BG argued that Google China website only provided search services for books but not directly provided the works, and the website only presented the "segment" of works. Therefore, as the operator of the website, the Defendant BG had no subjective fault, thus should not bear the liability of infringement of the right of communication of information on networks.

Ruling and Reasoning:

The Beijing No. 1 Intermediate People's Court held that: As long as the *locus delicti* of the civil dispute is in China, the Chinese court has jurisdiction over the whole case. Since the Google China website in this case is located in China. The Chinese courts have jurisdiction over this case of infringement of the right of communication of information on networks. On this ground, the Court held that: since the Defendant BG failed to provide any evidence to prove that it was implementing a search link, it could be deemed that it was implementing the act of communication of information on networks. Despite that the Defendant BG implemented this act without the Plaintiff's permission; it did not constitute the infringement of the Plaintiff's right of communication of information on networks since the act satisfied the substantial conditions of fair use thus constituted fair use. For the Defendant Google's act of reproducing full text, the Court held that the act of reproducing full text conflicted with the normal exploitation of the Plaintiff's work, and would unreasonably prejudice the legitimate interests of the author by creating a potential risk over the market interest of the Plaintiff's work. This act of reproducing full-text did not constitute fair use. In the absence of the Plaintiff's permission, the Defendant Google's act constituted an infringement of Plaintiff's right of reproduction.

In summary, taken the Plaintiff's reputation, the word counting of the work, the remuneration rate of the industry, the mode of Google's use, and subjective malicious factors into consideration, the Court ruled that the Defendant Google should cease the infringement, and compensate the Plaintiff RMB 5,000 for economic losses and reasonable expenses of RMB 1,000.

The Defendant Google refused to accept the first-instance judgment and made an appeal to the Beijing Higher People's Court. The Beijing Higher People's Court dismissed the appeal and sustained the judgment of the first instance.

Commentary:

This case involves both the protection of copyright on the networks and the understanding and the application of traditional copyright theories. The following issues are particularly worthy of attention:

I. Whether the Defendant BG implemented the act of communication of information on networks

The Plaintiff claimed that Defendant BG's act of communicating her work to the public on its Google China website constituted the act of communication of information on networks. However, the Defendant BG claimed that the act was only an act of providing search and link service. Since the two mentioned activities have different criteria of copyright infringement, the Court must first determine the nature of the Defendant's activities.

What is the "act of communication of information on networks?" The *Copyright Law of China* does not stipulate explicitly. However, according to Article 10 (12) of the *Copyright Law*, the "right of communication of information on networks" refers to the right to communicate to the public a work, by wire or wireless means in such a way that members of the public may access these works from a place and at a time individually chosen by them. Since the right covers the corresponding act, thus the act of communication of information on networks is the act to communicate to the public a work, by wire or wireless means in such a way that members of the public may access these works from a place and at a time individually chosen by them. According to the above regulations, the key elements of constituting the act of communication of information on networks are including: "by wire or wireless means," "the public," "individually choosing a place and at a time," "act of communicating" etc. In this case, the controversial arguments between the Plaintiff and the Defendants were caused by the different understanding of the "act of communicating."

Regarding what is "act of communicating," there have been controversial discussions between the theory of "server standard" and the theory of "user perception standard" in the judicial practice. However, since the study on the act of communication of information on networks to be more sophisticated, this disagreement is gradually disappearing. Article 2 of the *Guiding Opinions on Certain Issues Concerning Online Copyright Disputes (I)* (promulgated by the Beijing Higher People's Court in 2010) confirms the "server standard." According to Article 2, if the work involved in this case is not on the Defendant's server, even if the Defendant's website's external appearance would mislead the network users to thinking that the Defendant is communicating the work, it still cannot be deemed that the act is an act of communication of information on networks. Since the promulgation of this provision, the judicial system in Beijing has basically reached a consensus on this issue.

Therefore, the "server standard" is applicable to determine the "act of communicating." The next question to be answered is that how to prove that the work involved in this case is in the Defendant's server. The key to the answer is the issue concerning the burden of proof, that is, whether the Plaintiff or the Defendant shall bear the burden of proof on this fact.

In this regard, Article 8 of the *Guiding Opinions* of the Beijing Higher People's Court and Article 4 of the *Provisions of the Supreme People's Court on Several Issues Concerning the Application of Law in the Trial of Cases of Civil Dispute over Information on Internet Dissemination of Rights* implemented in 2013 clearly stipulate that: The above provisions mean that, if a network user can obtain relevant content on the page of the Defendant's website under normal circumstances, unless the Defendant submits a rebuttal evidence, it can be presumed that the content is stored on the server of the Defendant's website, thus the Defendant has implemented such "act of communicating."

The reason for this presumption is that the Defendant's website server is under the control of the Defendant, and the Plaintiff can usually only make the fixation of the content displayed on the webpage of the website, but it is difficult to objectively prove the evidence for the specific storage location of the content. If the relevant content is on the webpage of the Defendant's website, it still cannot be presumed that the Defendant's web server has the content, which means that the Plaintiff cannot objectively prove that the information was implemented by any website unless the Defendant acknowledges that. Such situation is obviously unfair and imposes too much burden of proof on the Plaintiffs. Base on this ground, it is reasonable to make the above presumption based on the content displayed on the webpage, taking into account the possibility of the original Defendant's proof. Of course, this presumption is able to be overturned, however this burden of proof should be borne by the Defendant, that is, if the Defendant disapproves of this, he shall submit the relevant rebuttal evidence.

In this case, it can be deduced from the notary certificate submitted by the Plaintiff that the whole process of communicating work was within its website. Neither would it jump to the page of another website nor has the website address been changed. Therefore, the above situation can be preliminarily presumed that the works involved in the case were stored in the Defendant BG's server. Although the Defendant BG claimed that it provided a search link service, the work involved in this case was not stored in its server, and it did not submit the evidence to support. Meanwhile, the Defendant BG claimed to provide book search service, but the whole process was constantly staying on its webpage. When explaining, the Defendant BG just stated that it was a new business mode for book search service, but failed to further explain why the whole process was constantly on its webpage, and argued that the fact was objectively difficult to prove and could not be proved. Such explanation was understandably inconvincible. Therefore, since the Defendant BG failed to submit any rebuttal evidence or provide any reasonable explanation, it took into account that the whole process in the case was in the Defendant BG's website. The Court reasonably found that the work involved in this case was stored in the Defendant BG's server, thus the Defendant implemented the act of communication of information on networks. The argument by the Defendant BG that it provided search and link service was not accepted by the Court.

2. Whether the Defendant BG's act of segmentally communicating works constitutes fair use

To determine whether an act constitutes copyright infringement, generally the following elements should be taken into consideration: whether the act is covered by the copyright owner; whether the act has been authorized by the copyright owner; and whether the act constitutes a fair use.

In this case, given that the Defendant BG's act constituted the act of communication of information on networks and obviously such act was not authorized by the copyright owner, the key element to determine the infringement is whether it constituted a fair use of the Plaintiff's work.

Article 22 of the *Copyright Law* provides the rules of fair use. It explicitly enumerates twelve conditions of fair use, and there is no general clause for conditions other than the twelve. This indicates that any act outside of the scope of the twelve enumerated conditions should not constitute fair use. Since the act of segmentally communicating works is not in the twelve conditions, if the rule of copyright law is interpreted strictly, the act does not constitute fair use obviously.

However, in the judicial practice, some Chinese courts have expandedly interpreted the rule of fair use, so that some acts other than the mentioned twelve have been determined as fair use. For example, in the *Qin Shaoyin* case, the court found that the Defendant's use of the Plaintiff's works in the auction preview atlas constituted fair use. In the *Wu Rui* case, the court held that the use of segment of the Plaintiff's works in the book search website constituted fair use. The precedent cases indicated that the current regulations of fair use can be interpreted expandedly. In certain cases, if the activities are not determined as fair use, the public interest may be jeopardized. In this case, the key issue is that the alleged act of communication of information on networks was consistent with the "substantial condition" of fair use.

Considering the purpose of the rule of fair use, Article 22 of the *Copyright Law*, and Article 21 of the *Regulations for the Implementation of the Copyright Law*, even if an act is within the scope of copyright granted to copyright owners, in case that such act does not conflict with a normal exploitation of the work and does not "unreasonably" prejudice the legitimate interests of the copyright owner, then such act is consistent with the "substantial conditions" of fair use. Of course, there is no universal standard for "unreasonably" prejudice the legitimate interests of the copyright owner, thus the determination it should be made upon a case-by-case basis.

In this case, the Court had a positive attitude toward the expanded interpretation of fair use, taking into account the following factors:

(1) The alleged act of communication of information on networks did not constitute a substantive use of the Plaintiff's work. It was not significant to cause a substantial impact on the market value of the Plaintiff's work, or any marketing loss of the Plaintiff's work.

   In this case, the Plaintiff's work was a written work. The Plaintiff's fundamental purpose of creation was to convey her ideas and feelings to the readers via the literary expression. Therefore, if the use was not able for readers to perceive the author's ideas and feelings completely, then such use should not be considered as a substantial use. In this case, the Defendant BG's use of the Plaintiff's works was segmental. The content to be communicated to the network users was neither a "continuous" chapter of the work nor a "whole" paragraph of the work, but only a segment of the work. Each segment was generally two or three lines, and such segments were not consecutive. This use made it difficult for network users to fully understand the ideas and feelings expressed by the author. Based on this ground, the Court held that the alleged act did not constitute a substantial use of the Plaintiff's works. Meanwhile, the basic demands of the network users would not been satisfied by reading the segments of the works. If a network user intends to read the work, he will usually purchase a copy of the work according to the title of the work, the name of the author, and other relevant publication information provided by the webpage. Based on this ground, the Court held that the Defendant BG's act was not significant to cause a substantial impact on the market value of the Plaintiff's work, or any marketing loss of the Plaintiff's work.

(2) The alleged act of communication of information on networks was an act of segmentally communicating works. Since the function and purpose of segmentally communicating works were to provide a convenient and quick library information search service for the network users, such act was a transformative use of the Plaintiff's work. Hence, such act would not unreasonably damage the legitimate rights and interests of Plaintiff.

   In this case, the alleged act of communication of information on networks was an act of segmentally communicating works. The purpose of segmentally communicating works was not intended to simply reproduce the literary and artistic value of the original work or to achieve its internal ideographic function, but rather to provide network users with a more comprehensive and convenient book search services, so as to meet the demands of network users for more book information. Since the two fundamental principles of copyright law are protecting the interests of copyright owners and promoting the communication of works, the scope and degree of copyright protection for copyright owners should not affect the public's reasonable demand for works and information. Since the segmental use of works did not substantially reproduce the ideographic function of the Plaintiff's work and, to a large extent, it also provided a book information index function, thus such act constituted transformative use of the Plaintiff's work, which did not conflict with a normal exploitation of the work and does not unreasonably prejudice the legitimate interests of the author.

In summary, despite that the Defendant BG's alleged act of communication of information on networks was not permitted by the Plaintiff, since it did not conflict with the normal exploitation of the Plaintiff's work and did not unreasonably prejudice the legitimate interests of the Plaintiff, thus such act constituted fair use of the Plaintiff's, and did not constitute an infringement of Plaintiff's right of communication of information on networks.

3. Whether Google's full-text reproducing constitutes fair use

In this case, to determine whether Google's full-text scanning constituted the infringement of the Plaintiff's reproduction right, the key element was whether the act constituted fair use, which was similar to the early mentioned reasons regarding the act of communication of information on networks.

Based on the substantial conditions early mentioned for determining fair use, the Court found that the full-text reproducing did not constitute fair use, given the following factors:

3.1. In terms of the way of act, this "full-text reproducing" has been in conflict with the normal exploitation of the Plaintiff's work.

The normal exploitation of works of copyright owners should be limited to the specific exploitation methods specified in Article 11 of the *Copyright Law*. The most fundamental and important exploitation is reproduction. According to the copyright law, those who intend to reproduce a copyrighted work are obliged to pay the copyright owner a "license fee," which is the economic benefit brought to the copyright owner, and to issue a license is also a normal exploitation of works. Of course, not "any degree" of reproducing will be conflict with the normal exploitation of copyrighted works. Otherwise, there will be no fair use of reproducing. However in any case, whether the "full-text reproducing" with the highest degree is within the category is quite obvious.

If the full-text reproducing is not regarded as conflicting with the copyright owner's normal exploitation, it will inevitably make the copyright owner's control of the act of reproducing insignificant, and also make the provisions concerning reproduction right useless. Therefore, the Court held that the Defendant Google's full-text reproducing, which inevitably prejudiced the Plaintiff's interests of license fees, had conflicted with the Plaintiff's normal exploitation of the work.

3.2. In terms of the consequences of the act, this full-text reproducing caused potential risks to the market interest of the Plaintiff's work and unreasonably prejudiced the legitimate interests of the Plaintiff.

In this case, despite that the Plaintiff did not submit any evidence concerning whether the Defendant Google also implemented the follow-up act of communication after the full-text reproducing, the full-text reproducing would cause potential risks to the Plaintiff's market interest in the following two aspects:

- First, this full-text reproducing will largely facilitate Google's follow-up unauthorized exploitation of the works. In this case, it had been found from the facts that Google's purpose for full-text reproducing was not just reproducing itself, but rather communicating the corresponding works to the users, that is, the purpose of its reproducing was for "follow-up exploitation." Despite that the Defendant Google argued that the follow-up exploitation would be based on the cooperation with the copyright owner, it was obvious that the Plaintiff had no control over whether Google would obtain a license before using the work, considering that with full-text reproducing, Google's follow-up use of the Plaintiff's works would be convenient. The Court reasonably believed that the Defendant Google's full-text reproducing would cause great potential risks to the Plaintiff's interests.
- Second, this full-text reproducing will also largely facilitate the unauthorized exploitation of the works by "others." Despite that the Defendant Google argued that the copy of the Plaintiff's work was stored in the Google's servers, and it is not unmanageable for others to break through the technological measures or other methods to obtain the Plaintiff's work that stored in Google's servers. Therefore, Google's full-text reproducing will not only facilitate its own subsequent use of the Plaintiff's works, but also facilitate others to unauthorized exploit the Plaintiff's works.

Based on the above considerations, the Court held that the Defendant Google's reproducing of the Plaintiff's work was in conflict with the normal exploitation of the Plaintiff's work and would unreasonably prejudice the legitimate interests of the copyright owner. Such reproducing did constitute an infringement of Plaintiff's copyright, rather than a fair use.

4. Other relevant issues

In this case, in addition to determining the act of the reproduction and the act of communication of information on networks, the Court also reached a conclusion of the following issues:

4.1. Even the act of communication of information on networks by the Defendant BG constitutes fair use, it does not mean that Google's full-text reproducing also constitutes fair use.

Some scholars argued that the Defendant BG's act of communication of information on networks was based on the reproduction, thus if it was determined that act of communication of information on networks constituted fair use, then the Defendant Google's "full-text reproducing" also constituted fair use.

In this regard, the Court pointed out that despite that the Court has found the Defendant BG's act of communication of information on networks constituted fair use of the Plaintiff's work, and such act was based on the reproduction of the Plaintiff's work, however such an act of communication of information on networks was partial communicating, as the purpose was to enable Internet users to understand the Plaintiff's work at certain degree. For this purpose, only a part of the Plaintiff's work was to be reproduced, but not the full-text. There was no evidence to show that the Plaintiff's full work had been copied. Therefore, the act of communication of information constitutes fair use only means that the "partial" reproducing constitutes fair use, however it cannot be concluded that "full-text" reproducing by the Defendant Google constitutes fair use.

In addition, it must be emphasized that despite that the various types of fair use as stipulated in Article 22 of the *Copyright Law* are based on the premise of reproduction, this does not mean that any degree of reproduction is fair for the purpose of fair use. In principle, the full-text reproducing is difficult to be regarded as fair use.

For example, according to Article 22 of the Copyright Law, the "use of another person's published work for purpose of the user's own personal study, research or appreciation" constitutes fair use. Such use may include reproducing of other's works. However in the case of full-text copy, even if it is for personal learning purposes, it may still not be determined as fair use. This is because that the fair use rules stipulated in Article 22 of the *Copyright Law* must simultaneously comply with the three-step test stipulated in Article 21 of the *Regulations for the Implementation of the Copyright Law*. According to the three-step test, one of the prerequisites for fair use is that the use of work must not unreasonably prejudice the legitimate interests of the copyright owner. In case of full-text reproducing of a work, even if it is for personal learning, such a full-text copy will likely result in marketing damage, thus it is hard to assume that it did not cause any unreasonable damage to the interests of the copyright owner. Of course, not every act of full-text reproducing will definitely constitute copyright infringement.

However whether an act of full-text reproducing constitutes fair use must be determined carefully.

4.2. In principle, whether there exists follow-up use or communication of the copy does not affect the determination of whether the act of reproduction itself constitutes infringement.

Since the current evidence in this case can only prove that the Defendant Google had performed full-text reproducing, whether there was any "follow-up" use or communication of the Plaintiff's work was unknown, some scholars argued that the Defendant Google's "mere" reproducing does not cause any damage to the copyright owner, therefore should not be determined as infringement.

In this regard, the Court held that in accordance with the *Copyright Law*, anyone who "merely" reproduces others' work should obtain permission from the copyright owner and pay the license fee. Therefore in principle, even if there is no follow-up use or communication, the mere reproduction without copyright owner's permission still constitutes infringement, rather than inevitably constitutes fair use, unless it meets the relevant provisions and the essential conditions for fair use of the *Copyright Law*.

The reason why copyright law states that "mere" reproducing still constitutes infringement in principle is that in most cases reproducing is the prerequisite for the use of the work. It is reasonable to believe that to prohibit unauthorized reproducing will effectively prevent others to unauthorized use the work. This is true but not the fundamental reason. If reproducing is merely a prerequisite for follow-up infringement, then why the act of reproduction without any follow-up use can still constitute copyright infringement?

In this case, the Court pointed out that the reason that an act of mere reproducing still constituted infringement was that such mere reproducing would also prejudice the economic interests of the copyright owner. Such damages are mainly in the following two aspects:

- First, an act of mere reproducing may cause "actual" damage to the copyright owner's economic interests. This "actual" damage is usually derived from the act of reproducing the work for the purpose of "use." Although such type of reproducing will not make the copy available to the public, still the reproducer may use the work without purchasing a legitimate copy. This act of reproducing will inevitably affect the marketing of legitimate copies. Therefore, the act will cause actual damage to the copyright owner.

  For example, if a teacher makes ten unauthorized copies of a book and gives them to his students for free, such act does not constitute the act of distribution according to the *Copyright Law*. Therefore, in the whole process, only the act of reproducing is within the scope of copyright. However, such an act of mere reproducing is enough to enable the students to use this book without buying, resulting in the copyright owner loses the sale of ten copies, thus causes actual damage to the interests.

- Second, an act of mere reproducing may impose a "potential" risk to the copyright owner's economic interests. This "potential" risk usually comes from the act of reproducing followed by the act of "communicating works" (such as distribution, broadcasting, and communication of information on networks). In such cases, although the actual communication has not yet occurred, the act of reproducing for the purpose of communicating still causes obvious potential risk to the copyright owner's economic interests. If such act is not stopped immediately, it will inevitably cause actual damage. Therefore, this potential risk must be avoided by the *Copyright Law*.

Based on the above considerations, most counties clarify that the act of mere reproducing is within the scope of copyright, including China. This means that, even if there is no follow-up use or communication, the act of mere reproducing itself does not constitute fair use.

—Comments by RUI Songyan

Case 20. Infringement Relating to Making Available of Web Snapshot

Cong Wenhui v. Beijing Sogou Information Service Co., Ltd.
Case of Copyright Infringement Dispute
Case Index: *CONG Wenhui v. Beijing Sogou Information Service Co., Ltd.*; Haidian District People's Court of Beijing, Hai Min Chu Min Chu Zi [2013] No. 11368, June 24, 2013; Beijing No. 1 Intermediate People's Court, Yi Zhong Min Zhong Zi [2013] No. 12533, December 10, 2013.

Facts:

This case is about the determination of copyright infringement relating to making available of web snapshot. The work involved in the case is a sports commentary by Cong Wenhui entitled *Shameful gloat*. The word count of the work is approximately one thousand words. This work was originally published in the Tianya BBS. However, five months after Tianya BBS deleted the work, Cong Wenhui searched via the search engine website (www.sogou.com) operated by Beijing Sogou Information Service Co., Ltd. (hereinafter, "Sogou") and could still get the web snapshot of the work.

Cong Wenhui believed that Sogou's act of making available of web snapshot constituted an act of communication of information on networks that infringed his copyright of the works. Sogou did not agree with this and identified the act as an act of providing searching and linking service. Sogou also pointed out that due to the fact that Cong Wenhui did not send a notice for removing or blocking the web snapshot before filing the case, also Sogou had automatically deleted the linking of the work before filing the case, thus there was no subjective wrong for infringement, therefore Sogou should not bear any infringement liability.

Ruling and Reasoning:

Haidian District People's Court of Beijing held that the act of making available of web snapshot by Sogou was an act of system caching. Since the act did not comply with the safe harbor rule provided by Article 21 of the *Regulations on Protecting the Right of Communication of Information on Networks*, Sogou's act constituted copyright infringement. Given that Sogou had removed the web snapshot involved in this case, the Court no longer ordered Sogou to cease infringement, but Sogou should compensate Cong Wenhui for an economic loss of RMB 2,269.

Sogou appealed to Beijing No. 1 Intermediate People's Court against the judgment of first instance.

Beijing No. 1 Intermediate People's Court held that the alleged act of making available of web snapshot was neither an act of system caching defined by Article 21 of the *Regulations on Protecting the Right of Communication of Information on Networks* nor an act of providing searching and linking service defined by Article 23 of the *Regulations*. Such an act was an act of communication of information on networks defined by Article 10 (12) of the *Copyright Law*. Since this alleged act did not cause any substantial damage to Cong Wenhui's rights and the determination of the infringement would unreasonably prejudice the public interest, such an act was consistent with the substantial requirement for fair use, thus constituted fair use. Accordingly, although Sogou's act of making available of web snapshot was unauthorized, it did not constitute copyright infringement. In summary, Beijing No. 1 Intermediate People's Court ruled that the first instance judgment was revoked, and rejected all claims by Cong Wenhui.

Commentary:

The key issue of this case is how to determine the nature of the act of making available of web snapshot. Since judges and scholars have controversial opinions on this issue, despite that a similar case once was tried by a court in Beijing,[40] the determination in this case is still worth discussing. As one of the judges for the second instance, I would like to make the following analysis.

1. The nature of the act of making available of web snapshot

In this case, the Plaintiff, the Defendant, and the Court of First Instance had completely different views on the nature of the alleged act of making available of web snapshot. The Plaintiff Cong Wenhui believed that the act was an act of communication of information on networks. The Defendant Sogou claimed that the act was an act of providing searching and linking service. The Court of First Instance determined it as an act of system caching. Therefore, the first key issue for the court of second instance was how to determine the nature of the alleged act.

The court of second instance considered that the determination of the nature of the act should be based on its objective characteristics. Although making available of web snapshot was a kind of incidental service provided by a service provider when providing searching and linking service, it was not equivalent to the searching and linking service itself. A web snapshot was a copy of each web page made by a search engine spider program when searching web pages on the Internet, and was stored in the server of the search engine. If a web user clicked the "snapshot" option in the search results, the search engine will retrieve the web snapshot from its server to the web user. In this process, the search engine provided works to the web user. Such an act of making available enabled web users to access the work from a place and at a time individually chosen by them. Therefore, this act should be regulated by Article 10 (12) of the *Copyright Law*. Accordingly, it cannot necessarily be identified as the act of system caching of Article 21 of the *Regulations on Protecting the Right of Communication of Information on Networks* or the act of searching and linking defined of Article 23 of the *Regulations*.

---

40. *See Wang Lu v. Yahoo*, Beijing Higher People's Court, Gao Min Zhong Zi [2007] No. 1729.

2. Whether the act of making available of web snapshot may constitute fair use

Since the Court determined that the alleged act of making available of web snapshot was identified as an act of communication of information on networks, while Sogou's act was not authorized by the copyright owner Cong Wenhui, thus the key issue to the infringement determination was whether the act constituted fair use.

The rule of fair use is provided by Article 22 of the *Copyright Law*, which lists twelve situations of fair use. Since there is no general clause relating to fair use, any situation other than the enumerated twelve situations should not be fair use. Given that the Defendant's act was not within the scope of twelve situations, this act should not constitute fair use, if the *Copyright Law* is strictly interpreted.

However, in judicial practice, some courts have extendedly interpreted the rule of fair use, so that some situations that were not enumerated by Article 22 still constituted fair use. For instance, in *Qin Shaoyin* case, the court held that the defendant's use of the plaintiff's work in the auction brochure constituted fair use.[41] In *Wu Rui* case, the court held that the defendant's partial use of the plaintiff's work in the book search website constituted fair use.[42]

The precedent cases indicate that the rule of fair use may be extendedly interpreted. In certain cases, if the alleged acts cannot constitute fair use, the result may cause great damage to the public interest. Thus, the court of second instance in this case needs to determine whether the alleged act of making available of web snapshot meets the "substantial conditions" of fair use.

2.1 Substantial conditions of fair use

In consideration of the purpose of the rule of fair use, Article 22 of the *Copyright Law*, and Article 21 of the *Regulations for the Implementation of the Copyright Law*, the Court of second instance ruled that if an act was in the scope of copyright, but not cause "unreasonable" damage to the copyright owner's interests, and at the same time it was beneficial to the public interest, such an act could satisfy the "substantial condition" of fair use.

Meanwhile, the Court also pointed out that there was no unified standard for judging whether an act would cause "unreasonable" damage to the interests of the copyright owner, thus it should be determined case by case. For the act of communication of information on networks, since copyright owners have the right of authorize websites to communicate the works, which is a normal exploitation of the right of communication of information on networks, thus the unauthorized act of communication of information on networks will cause a "substantial substitution effect" to those authorized websites. As a result, web users may not visit the authorized websites and directly obtain the works via those unauthorized websites. In such cases, it should be determined that this act conflicts with the normal exploitation of the copyright owner's

---

41. *See* Beijing No. 1 Intermediate People's Court, Yi Zhong Min Chu Zi [2003] No. 12064.
42. *See* Haidian District People's Court of Beijing, Hai Min Chu Zi [2007] No. 8079.

Chapter 3: Determination of Copyright Infringement

work, thus it will "unreasonably" prejudice the legitimate interests of the copyright owner, or vice versa.

2.2 Whether the act of making available of web snapshot meets the substantial conditions of fair use

In this case, the court of second instance separately analyzed the nature of the alleged act from the perspectives of the copyright owner, web user, web cache provider and the public, then determined that the act meets the substantial conditions of fair use, because it would not "unreasonably" prejudice the interests of the copyright owner.

2.2.1 For web users, the web snapshot will not "substantively replace" the original web page.

One of the important factors in judging whether making available of web snapshot will "unreasonably" prejudice the copyright owner's interests is whether the act will substantially replace the normal exploitation of copyright owners. On the Internet, the most common exploitation of works by copyright owners is to communicate or authorize others to communicate their works. Therefore, if web users obtain relevant works by "web snapshots" instead of by "original web pages," it can be assumed that making available of web snapshot will substantially replace the normal exploitation of copyright owners.

In consideration of the following characteristics of web snapshots, the court of second instance held that the alleged act of making available of web snapshot was insufficient to change web users' way of web surfing. Therefore, it did not yet have a "substantive substitution effect" on the original web page:

- First, the web snapshot is only a copy of the "text" content. Despite that web snapshot is a copy of the original web page, the reproduced content is limited to text but not include files such as audio or video clips from the original web page. Since the text alone obviously cannot satisfy web users, web users prefer to visit the original web page to access the content, rather than the web snapshot.
- Second, the web snapshot is not updated "in real time." Limited by the current technology, the web snapshot cannot be updated in real time. Due to different algorithms of search engines or the level of activity of the original web pages, some web snapshots may have not been updated for several months or even years. Since web users will prefer to get "in-real-time" content rather than the "out-of-date" content, usually they will not choose web snapshot.
- Third, the web snapshot is only a copy of one "single" web page. Usually the source website will display one work, such as a book, in several web pages, so that the web users will need to click to get more content in the next page. However in the case of web snapshots, since it is only a copy of one "single" web page, web users cannot obtain the content from of original next page, but have to search again for the snapshot of the original next page. In general, web

users will prefer simple and convenient ways to access the search content. Therefore, usually web users will not choose web snapshot.
- Fourth, usually the logos of web snapshot are not obvious on the screen. Thus, web users usually do not intend to choose web snapshot to access the content. In addition, judging from the location of icons of web snapshot, it may be indicated that the snapshot providers still subjectively encourage web users to click on the search results, rather than the snapshot.

2.2.2 As the web snapshot providers, Sogou did not make available of web snapshot for any direct profit, and in fact there was no direct profit made from the act of make available of web snapshot.

In this case, Sogou only placed the "snapshot" logo in a corner of the web page, while placed the search results of the linked website in the most obvious position. This means that Sogou prefers web users to access the linked website instead of the web snapshot. Correspondingly, it also indicated that Sogou used the web snapshot as an alternative backup of the original web pages. It did not present a clear commercial purpose.

In addition, one of the factors for determining "unreasonable" damages of interests of the copyright owner is that whether the web snapshot provider obtains direct profit from the act of making available of web snapshot. However, the difference between the web snapshot and the original web page was that there was an extra frame outside the snapshot showing the information of the original page source, without any advertisement or commercial content. This indicated that the web snapshot involved in this case did not bring direct profit to Sogou.

2.2.3 As the copyright owner, Cong Wenhui never sent Sogou any notice to take down the web snapshot.

In determining whether "unreasonable" damages are caused by the act of making web snapshot available, not only the above-mentioned two factors are taken into consideration but the subjective intent of the copyright owner is taken into consideration. If the copyright owner has explicitly sent a notice to the snapshot provider requesting the removal of the web snapshot, the provider is obliged to delete it. Otherwise, it would be reasonable to conclude that the act has caused "unreasonable" damage to the copyright owner's interest, or vice versa.

The main reason for considering this factor is that the act of making available of web snapshot can be considered as an act of providing content service, which is independent from the act of providing search link service. Despite that such an act does not substantially replace the original web page, there is no doubt that it will, to some extent, prejudice the copyright owners more or less, especially in case that the original web page has been deleted whereas the web snapshot is still available to the public. Considering that the fundamental purpose of the *Copyright Law* is to protect copyright owners, and the standard of whether "damage" is "reasonable" can be interpreted flexibly. Therefore, the subjective intent of the copyright owner should also be taken into consideration to some extent. This consideration is also covered in Article 22 of the *Copyright Law*. Some articles of the *Copyright Law* stipulate that copyright owners can explicitly exclude others from their fair use. Under this circumstance, if the copyright owner explicitly requests the snapshot provider to delete the snapshot, it can reasonably be deduced that the copyright owner believes that the alleged act has caused unreasonable damage to his interests, thus the snapshot provider is obliged to delete it. However in this case, Cong Wenhui never sent Sogou any notice to take down the web snapshot before the lawsuit. By contrast, Sogou immediately deleted the web snapshot after it was sued by Cong Wenhui. Therefore, this factor should also be taken into consideration.

2.2.4 The act of making available of web snapshot has an "irreplaceable" substantial value to the general public

Whether an act does not have a substantial value to the general public is one of the key conditions for constituting fair use. In this case, the act of making available of web snapshot has an "irreplaceable" substantial value to the general public. This service has the following advantages for the original source web page, making it an irreplaceable substantial value:

- First, in some cases, the "source website" may be inaccessible due to hardware or network failure. In such cases, the web snapshot enables the web user to access the content of the "source website" during the failure. This function is of great significance to the source website.
- Second, in some cases, although the "source website" can be accessed normally by web users, the webpages in request in the website have been deleted, and the corresponding web snapshot is still stored in the search engine's server. In such cases, even the web users cannot get the content from source website, they can still get it from the web snapshot.
- Third, the web snapshot will highlight the keyword searched by the user. This highlight mode does not exist in the source web page. The user could accurately locate the specific location of the keyword in the snapshot without reading through the whole document, so as to effectively improve the efficiency of the search.

From the above analysis, the content of the web snapshot is from the source website, but the source website does not have the characteristics of the service. The above features are beneficial not only to the web users, but also to the source website (e.g., in the first mentioned case, the source website obviously hopes that web users can obtain content through the web snapshot). Thus, it may be concluded that the act of making available of web snapshot has an "irreplaceable" substantial value to the general public.

2.3 If it is determined that alleged act of making available of web snapshot does not constitute fair use, it will significantly prejudice the public interest.

To determine whether an act constitute fair use, the proof by contradiction can be applied. If the alleged act does not constitute fair use, then whether there will be a negative impact to the public interest should be taken into consideration.

In this case, if the alleged act does not constitute fair use, the corresponding legal consequence will be that if the source webpage has been deleted, regardless of whether the copyright owner sends a notice, the search engine provider should stop making available of the alleged web snapshot. Otherwise, this act will constitute an infringement of the right of communication of information on networks.

Such legal consequence obviously has a great negative impact to the public interest. The reason is that the existing technology cannot yet synchronize the web snapshot with the source web page. In other words, the search engine provider cannot yet delete the corresponding web snapshot timely when the source web page has been deleted. Even if the snapshot can be deleted, it is still impractical to do so due to the huge investment required. Regarding this status, if search engine providers want to minimize the legal risk, the most feasible approach is to totally stop providing any web snapshot service. Otherwise, a considerable proportion of acts of making available of web snapshot will unquestionably constitute a copyright infringement. However, given that the web snapshot has substantial "irreplaceable" value, it is undoubted that the total shutdown of the web snapshot will prejudice the public interest.

3. Other issues relating to act of making available of web snapshot

3.1 There is no positive causation between whether the source web page has been deleted and whether the act of making available of web snapshot constitutes fair use.

Since web snapshot and its source web page may not be updated synchronously, this may result in two situations in practice: first, the original web page of the web snapshot still exists; second, the original web page of the web snapshot has been deleted. In practice, copyright owners usually sue only in the latter situation. However, there is no positive causation between whether the source web page has been deleted and whether the act of making available of web snapshot constitutes fair use.

As mentioned earlier in this book, whether the act of making available of web snapshot constitutes fair use should be determined by whether it has a substantial value for web users and whether it will unreasonably prejudice the interests of copyright owners. In other words, web users get used to obtain the content by web snapshot rather than by visiting the original source web page, even if the source web page still exists, it should be determined that the act of making available of web snapshot has unfairly prejudiced the interests of the copyright owner, thus cannot constitute fair use. By contrast, if web users do not get used to obtain the content by web snapshot, even if the source web page has been deleted, the act may still constitute fair use, because it does not unreasonably prejudice the interests of the copyright owner. Therefore, it can be concluded that whether the source web page has been deleted does not substantially affect the determination of whether the act of making available of web snapshot constitutes fair use.

3.2 With the development of technology, the current situation that the act of making available of web snapshot constitutes fair use does not mean that it will always constitute fair use in the future.

The reason why the court of second instance found that the act of making available of web snapshot constitutes fair use is that the current technology determines that the web snapshot has some shortcomings (including copying documents only, updating asynchronously, and displaying only one page, etc.). Such shortcomings make web users usually do not choose the web snapshot service to obtain the content, so that the web snapshot does not substantially replace the source web page. However, such shortcomings of the web snapshot service may be overcome with the development of technology in the future. Then web users may prefer to obtain content by web snapshot service rather than by visiting the source web page. Under such circumstance, it cannot be assumed that the act of making available of web snapshot constitutes fair use. Whether it constitutes fair use should be determined in light of the technology of the day and the specific circumstances.

—**Comments by RUI Songyan**

Case 21. Infringement of the Right of Revision of Computer Software Works

Tencent Technology (Shenzhen) Co., Ltd. v. Shanghai Honglian Network Technology Co., Ltd. & Shanghai Woyao Network Development Co., Ltd.
Case of Computer Software Copyright Infringement and Unfair Competition Dispute
Case Index: *Tencent Technology (Shenzhen) Co., Ltd. v. Shanghai Honglian Network Technology Co., Ltd. & Shanghai Woyao Network Development Co., Ltd.*, Jiangan District People's Court of Wuhan City, Hubei Province [2009], An Zhi Min Chu Zi No. 4, July 5, 2011; Wuhan Intermediate People's Court of Hubei Province [2011], Wu Zhi Zhong Zi No. 00006, January 4, 2012.

Facts:

The Plaintiffs Tencent Technology (Shenzhen) Co., Ltd. (hereinafter, "Tencent Technology") and Shenzhen Tencent Computer System Co., Ltd. (hereinafter, "Tencent Computer") jointly alleged that: The Plaintiff Tencent Technology has developed the Tencent QQ Instant Communicating Software (hereinafter, "QQ Software") and is entitled to copyright and other rights and interests of the software. Tencent Technology authorized Tencent Computer to provide software downloads and other business activities on its own website *www.qq.com*. The Rainbow IP Exposure Software (hereinafter, "Rainbow Exposure Software"), produced and issued by the Defendant Shanghai Honglian Network Technology Co., Ltd. (hereinafter, "Honglian"), modified QQ Software during its operation, which infringed the Plaintiff's copyright of revision of the QQ Software. Honglian abetted web users to download and install the Rainbow Exposure Software, which was a plug-in program of QQ Software providing the functions of exposing the user's QQ friends' IP address and geographical location, and exposing online friends in invisible status. Some versions of the Rainbow Exposure Software were even bundled with commercial plug-ins and commercial promotion. Thus, Honglian's act constituted "free riding," which was unfair competition.

The Defendant, Woyao Network Development Co., Ltd. (hereinafter, "Woyao") provided technical support for Rainbow Exposure Software, and directly participated in the development of Rainbow Exposure Software. Meanwhile, Woyao also maintained the server of Honglian's website www.caihongqq.com and the downloading service of the Rainbow Exposure Software. The Defendant Woyao's act constituted a joint infringement that aided Honglian's infringement, so that Honglian and Woyao should bear the corresponding liability.

The Defendant Xu Zihua set up a download link of Rainbow Exposure Software at the website www.itmop.com, which aggravated the infringement damage of the Plaintiff. Thus, the Defendant Xu Zihua should cease the infringement.

Therefore, the two Plaintiffs sued for the following claims: (1) The Defendant Xu Zihua should immediately cease the infringement by taking down the Rainbow Exposure Software from www.itmop.com; (2) The Defendant Honglian and Woyao should immediately cease the copyright infringement of the Plaintiff's computer software and cease the unfair competition; (3) The Defendant Honglian and Woyao should make public apology to the two Plaintiffs at medias of national level; (4) The Defendant Honglian should compensate the Plaintiffs for the economic loss of RMB 500,000; (5) The Defendant Woyao should bear the joint liability for compensation; (6) The Defendant should be responsible for any expense of the litigation.

The Defendant Xu Zihua argued that he did provide the download service of Rainbow Express software at *www.itmop.com*, but it was free, and he stopped providing the software immediately after receiving the notice from the Plaintiffs.

The Defendant Honglian and Woyao argued that: (1) Regarding the copyright issue, Rainbow Exposure Software modified only the data loaded into the user's computer RAM when the QQ Software was running, but not the source code or object code of QQ Software, thus such act could not be identified as an act of alteration within the scope of copyright law. Accordingly, such act should not be determined as infringement of the right of revision of QQ Software. (2) Regarding the unfair competition issue, since QQ Software is an instant messaging software, while Rainbow Exposure Software is a software to provide functions of exposing QQ friends' IP address and invisible status, and Rainbow Exposure Software is for free, thus it is impossible for the Defendant to take QQ Software users away from the Plaintiffs. Since the two types of software do not have a competitive relationship, the unfair competition claims by the Plaintiff cannot be sustained.

Ruling and Reasoning:

In the first instance, Jiangan District People's Court of Wuhan City, Hubei Province, found that: the business scope of Tencent Technology and Tencent Computer are the development and sale of computer software and hardware, and computer technology and information services. Tencent Technology was the developer of QQ Software and authorized Tencent Computer to operate the service relating to all versions of QQ Software at www.QQ.com. Meanwhile, Tencent Technology authorized Tencent Computer to exclusively exploit the copyright of QQ Software, except Tencent Technology itself. In 2008, Honglian developed Rainbow Exposure Software for the use of QQ Software and provided free download of the software at its official website. Woyao participated in the development and operation of Rainbow Exposure Software, and maintained the official website of Honglian by providing the servers. Xu Zihua provided download service of Rainbow Exposure Software at his personal website. Rainbow Exposure Software is developed entirely for the use of QQ Software. Its main function is to destruct QQ Software's normal function of hiding QQ online friends' IP address, geographical location and invisible status. Appraisal report indicates that: (1) Rainbow Exposure Software cannot run independently without QQ Software, so it must be "attached" to QQ Software. Thus, Rainbow Exposure Software can run only based on QQ Software. (2) Rainbow Exposure Software places its file with the same name as msimg32.dll of Microsoft in the QQ Software's installation directory. When QQ Software is running, it needs to run msimg32.dll of Microsoft. Rainbow Exposure Software takes this advantage to get into the process course of QQ Software, then automatically run CaiHong.dll, which is the main file of Rainbow Exposure Software, so that it can be "imported" to QQ Software. During the operation, CaiHong.dll modifies nineteen object code instructions. (3) By modifying the object code instructions of QQ Software, Rainbow Exposure Software is able to expose QQ online friends' hidden IP address, geographical location and invisible status, so that the QQ Software's normal function of hiding IP address, geographical location and invisible status are destructed. (4) Rainbow Exposure Software attaches its user's interface into the user's interface of QQ Software. Web users may use Rainbow Exposure Software to remove the QQ Sidebar and other functions provided by QQ Software.

Jiangan District People's Court of Wuhan City, Hubei Province held that: Rainbow Exposure Software is affiliated to QQ Software. During the operation, Rainbow Exposure Software has modified the object code of QQ Software and destructs QQ Software's normal function of hiding IP address, geographical location and invisible status. The Defendant Honglian and Woyao wanted Woyao to maliciously develop and disseminate the software for commercial purpose. Such unauthorized modification of QQ Software infringed the right of revision of the Plaintiff Tencent Technology. The Defendants Honglian and Woyao operated the business relating to Rainbow Exposure Software as an affiliate of QQ Software to enjoy free access to the market resources obtained by the two Plaintiffs, destructed the normal functions of QQ Software, and made commercial profit by tying 360 Security Guards Software and pushing advertisements. Such acts seriously violated the principles of good faith and business ethics, and prejudiced the legitimate rights and interests of the two Plaintiffs, thus constituted unfair competition. The Defendant Xu Zihua provided download service of Rainbow Exposure Software at his personal website, which aided the communication of the infringing software, thus constituted joint copyright infringement of the Plaintiff.

Jiangan District People's Court of Wuhan City, Hubei Province ruled that: (1) The Defendant Xu Zihua must immediately cease the copyright infringement by stopping providing Rainbow Exposure Software relating to QQ Software. (2) The Defendants Honglian and Woyao must immediately cease the copyright infringement by stopping operating the business of Rainbow Exposure Software relating to QQ Software. (3) The Defendants Honglian and Woyao must make public apology to the Plaintiff Tencent Technology in national newspapers and magazines for the copyright infringement. (4) The Defendants Honglian and Woyao shall jointly compensate the Plaintiff Tencent Technology for the economic losses and the reasonable expenses in total of RMB 300,000 for the copyright infringement. (5) The Defendants Honglian and Woyao must immediately cease the unfair competition of using the Rainbow Exposure Software. (6) The Defendants Honglian and Woyao shall jointly compensate the Plaintiff Tencent Technology for the economic losses and the reasonable expenses in total of RMB 270,000.0,000 for the unfair competition. (7) Other petitions by the Plaintiffs Tencent Technology and Tencent Computer are dismissed.

Honglian and Woyao Co. refused to accept the judgment of the first instance and appealed to revoke of the judgment.

Chapter 3: Determination of Copyright Infringement

In the second instance, Wuhan Intermediate People's Court of Hubei Province found that: The facts found by the first instance are corroborated and the evidence is irrefutable.

Wuhan Intermediate People's Court of Hubei Province held that: Honglian and Woyao take advantage of QQ Software's operation mechanism that it needs to run msimg32.dll of Microsoft, thus leave their file of the same name in the installation directory of QQ Software, so that QQ will run their file when trying to run msimg32.dll of Microsoft. When their msimg32.dll (44k) get into the process course of QQ Software, it will run CaiHong.dll, which is the main file of Rainbow Exposure Software, so that it can be imported to QQ Software, then some of the original instructions of QQ Software in the process course will be replaced by the instructions of Rainbow Exposure Software. By doing so, the ordinary process, structure, order, organization, application of the original functions of the program etc. of QQ Software are modified, which causes nineteen object code instructions to be changed. The function of the computer software comes from the operation of the computer program. The change of the function is an external manifestation of the change of the computer program. It is due to the Rainbow Exposure Software's modification of the QQ Software object code that results in the dysfunction or change of the functions of QQ Software. In view of the above, Honglian and Woyao infringed the right of revision of the Plaintiffs' QQ Software. The purpose of the development of Rainbow Exposure Software and the function and operation mode of the software all indicate that the two Appellants took advantage of the parasitic software to misappropriate the potential market of QQ Software, separated QQ Software users, and got illegal profit from tying and pushing advertisement. Such act can be determined as free riding of the QQ Software. Relying on the above, the two Appellants violated the principle of good faith, thus constituted unfair competition.

Hence, the appeal by the Appellants Honglian and Woyao was dismissed and the first instance judgment was affirmed.

Commentary:

The famous U.S. Judge Boudin once asserted: "Applying copyright law to computer programs is like assembling a jigsaw puzzle whose pieces do not quite fit."[43] In the Internet era, disputes relating to unauthorized third-party software such as "plug-ins" and "patch" often arise, which are new challenges to copyright law. Rainbow Exposure Software is a third-party software developed for the popular QQ Software. Rainbow Exposure Software does not make static modifications to the source code or object code of QQ Software, but manipulates the dynamic data operated by QQ Software on the network to destruct QQ Software's normal function of hiding QQ online friends' IP address, geographical location and invisible status. The key issue of this case is whether such act constitutes the infringement of the right of revision of the copyright owner of QQ Software.

---

43. *See Lotus Development Corporation v. Borland International, Inc.*, 49 F3d 807, at 820 (1st Cir, 1995). Quoted from Wang Qian, *Intellectual Property Law Course*, Reming University Press, 2007, p. 95.

1. The provisions of the right of revision in China[44]

According to Article 3 of the *Copyright Law of China*, computer software is protected by the *Copyright Law*. Given that computer software is highly technological, Article 58 of the *Copyright Law* stipulates that the protection of computer software shall be separately prescribed by the State Council. Therefore, the copyright of computer software is protected by both the *Copyright Law* and the *Regulations on Protection of Computer Software* (hereinafter, "*Software Regulations*") promulgated by the State Council.

1) The right of revision under the *Copyright Law* is one of the moral rights

Article 10 of the *Copyright Law* enumerates four moral rights including the right of publication, the right of authorship, the right of revision and the right of integrity, as well as thirteen economic rights including the right of reproduction. According to Article 10 (3) of the Copyright Law, the right of revision is the right to alter or authorize others to alter one's work. According to this provision, the right of revision is a moral right enjoyed by copyright owners of all types of work. As for the scope of the right of revision, there are different academic opinions. The first opinion is that the right covers the partial modification of work or correction in words or expressions.[45] The second opinion is that the right covers the author's addition or deletion of the content of the work, correcting and supplementing the wrong or missing part. The right of revision has both positive and negative implications. From a positive perspective, the author is entitled to modify their own works; from a negative perspective, the author has the right to prohibit others from distorting or falsifying the work.[46] The third opinion is that the right is for author to modify his work after the work has been published. The function of the right is to protect the author's freedom of modifying the work without interruption. The act of interrupting the author from modifying his work is an infringement of the right.[47]

The differences among the above three opinions are on: (1) the degree of alteration, that is whether the modification can be only a partial change, or can be a major change due to the change of ideas; (2) the scope of the right, that is whether the right to prohibit others from modifying the work is within the scope of the right of revision.

Some scholars argued that according to the judicial practice, the right of revision also covers the right to prohibit others from modifying the work.[48] I agree with such

---

44. Current *Copyright Law* stipulates right of alteration, but *Draft Copyright Law* published by the Legislative Affairs Office of the State Council on Jun. 6, 2014 removed the right of alteration. The right of alteration is defined as: "The right to adapt the work into a new work of other genres and kinds, or to make works of audio, music, drama, etc. into audio-visual works, and to add, abridge, remove computer programs, change instructions and order of sentences or other modification."
45. Hu Kangsheng (Editor), *Interpretation of the Copyright Law of PRC*, Law Press, 2002, p. 43.
46. Wu Handong (Editor), *Intellectual Property Law* (Third Edition), Law Press, 2009, p. 72.
47. Li Mingde & Xu Chao, *Copyright Law* (Second Edition), Law Press, 2009, p. 65.
48. Li Chen, *Critique of Basic Theory of Copyright* (2013 Edition), Intellectual Property Publishing, 2013, p. 188.

opinion that this interpretation of the right of revision is in line with the legislative purpose of the *Copyright Law*. The wording of the *Copyright Law* clarifies that the right of revision covers both "the right to alter" and "the right to authorize others to alter" a work. Thus, the right of revision consists of two individual rights, which are a "right to self-use" for modifying his works and a "right to prohibit" for prohibiting any unauthorized modification of his work.

2) The right of revision under the *Software Regulations* is an economic right

Article 8 (3) of the *Software Regulations* stipulates the right of revision, that is, the right to add, delete, or change the order of instructions or statements of software. Regarding the nature of the right of revision, some scholars pointed out that the right to amend under the *Software Regulations* is an economic right.[49] According to Article 10 of the *Copyright Law*, copyright owners may assign the economic rights such as the right of reproduction to others in whole or in part. This article explicitly excludes the right of revision, which is a moral right. However, Article 8 of the *Software Regulations* explicitly stipulates that copyright owners of software enjoy the right of revision and may authorize others to exercise the copyright, and may assign the copyright in whole or in part and get paid. This indicates that the right of revision under the *Software Regulations* is the same as the economic rights such as the right of reproduction, which is also an economic right. The copyright owner of software is entitled to authorize others to exercise the right of revision and obtain economic benefits by means of licensing or transfer.

Moreover, according to Article 24 of the *Software Regulations*, those who unauthorizedly modify software shall be liable for damages. In addition, according to the *Drafted Copyright Law of China* issued by the Legislative Affairs Office of the State Council on June 6, 2014, in the next version of *Copyright Law*, the right of adaptation is an economic right, which will replace the right of revision of the current *Copyright Law*. Regarding the software protection, the *Drafted Copyright Law* states that the right of adaptation will include the right to add, delete, or change the order of instructions or statements of computer program, or other modification. The term of the *Drafted Copyright Law* is similar to that of the *Software Regulations*, except that it changes the term "software" into "computer program," and adds "or other modification." The new development of the *Drafted Copyright Law* further indicates that the right of revision under the *Software Regulations* is an economic right.

Therefore, it can be concluded that despite that both the current *Copyright Law* and *Software Regulations* vest the right of revision to copyright owners, those two rights of alteration are different in nature. The right of revision under the *Copyright Law* is a moral right, while the right of revision under the *Software Regulations* is an economic right.

---

49. Wang Qian, The Right of Alteration of Software Works: From the Perspective of Recent Cases including the *Rainbow Exposure Soft* Case, *The Jurist*, 1 (2013).

2. Whether the operation of unauthorized third-party software constitute infringement of the right of revision

As mentioned earlier, the right of revision under the *Copyright Law* is a moral right, while the right of revision under the *Software Regulations* is an economic right. However, the acts of alteration of computer software regulated by the two are consistent, including "adding, deleting, or changing the order of instructions or statements." Correspondingly, whether the operation of unauthorized third-party software constitutes infringement of the right of revision may also be determined from the two aspects of both moral right and economic right.

1) Classification of third-party software

Digital works, especially computer software, are often provided with an "end user license agreement (EULA)." The copyright owner is the first party, and the user is the second party of the EULA. [50] Third-party software refers to software developed by any organization or individual other than the copyright owner, with or without the authorization by the copyright owner to change the function of the original software by direct modifying the program or intercepting or manipulating the data to be transmitted by the software. Third-party software is also known as "plug-in," "patch," and MOD in video game software.[51] Based on its status of authorization, third-party software can be classified as authorized third-party software, such as the software developed for supporting Linux and unauthorized third-party software, such as the Rainbow Exposure Software of this case.

Based on the operating mechanism, third-party software may be further classified as the third-party software by modification and the third-party software by interception.[52] The third-party software by modification alters the function of the main program by directly modifying the source code of the main program. Since such third-party software by modification changes the "coded instruction sequence" of the main program, while such "coded instruction sequence" is protected as computer program according to Article 3 (1) of the *Software Regulations*, it can be concluded that the unauthorized third-party software by modification will infringe the right of revision of the copyright owner.

The third-party software by interception may be further classified as the third-party software by interception of local data and the third-party software by interception of network data. Interception of local data means the third-party software intercepts the data transmitted between the operating system of the local computer and the intercepted software. Interception of network data means the third-party software intercepts the data transmitted between the intercepted software and the network

---

50. *See MYD Indus. LLC v. Blazzard Entm't, Inc.*, 629 F.3d 928, 935 (9th Cir. 2010). Quoted from Wan Yong & Liu Yongpei (Editor), *Berkeley Technology and Law Review: Annual Review of American Intellectual Property Classics of 2012*, Intellectual Property Publishing, 2013, p. 35.
51. Qi Aimin & Zhou Weimeng, Analysis of the Legal Issues of Third-Party Software: From the Tencent v. 360, *Law Science Magazine*, 11 (2011).
52. Zhou Weimeng & Zhou Qing, Research on Unauthorized Third-party Software Infringement, *Journal of Chongqing University of Posts and Telecommunications*, 3 (2011).

server. Thus, the third-party software by interception of network data is aiming at the software running in the network. [53]

In this case, QQ Software is the software running in the network. Since Rainbow Exposure Software intercepts and manipulates the data transmitted between QQ Software and the network server, obviously it is third-party software by interception of network data. Given that the third-party software by interception of local data and the third-party software by interception of network data do not directly modify the source code or object code of the intercepted software, but modify the dynamic data, whether it can be determined as an infringement of the right of revision is still one of the controversial copyright issues under discussion.

2) Whether third-party software infringes the right of revision as an economic right

In this case, whether the development and operation of unauthorized third-party software Rainbow Exposure Software constitute an infringement of the economic right of revision of QQ Software is still under intensive discussion.

The first opinion is that Rainbow Exposure Software infringed the right of revision of QQ Software. For example, some Judges argue that Rainbow Exposure Software is affiliated to QQ Software, and it replaces and modifies QQ Software so that the normal function of hiding IP and invisible status are destroyed. When QQ Software is in operation, Rainbow Exposure Software deletes and adds instructions, and changes the order and statement sequence of QQ Software. Thus, it infringes the right of revision of QQ Software.[54] Some judges also argue that modifying the local software directly, modifying the data in RAM and modifying the data transmitted in the network should all be determined as modification of software.[55] Some scholars further argue that the term of computer program under the *Software Regulations* shall be extendly interpreted to cover all the digital data relating to third-party software. Thus both interception of local data and interception of network data should be determined as infringement of the right of revision and shall bear the liability.[56]

The second opinion is that Rainbow Exposure Software did not infringe the right of revision of QQ Software. Some scholars argue that only coded instruction sequence itself can be protected as computer program, the data transmitted by the coded instruction is not within the scope of computer program. For improving software performance and functionality, users should be allowed to use modification tool to modify the results of the software's operation during its operation, thus such act does not constitute infringement.[57] Some scholars also argue that third-party software does

---

53. *Ibid.*
54. Xia Lu, Identification of Infringement of the Right of Alteration of Main Program Software By Third-party Software and Unfair Competition: A Comment of the *Rainbow Exposure Software*, *Technology and Law*, 4 (2012).
55. Chen Huizhen, Analysis of the Harmfulness of Private Server and Plug-in, *Rule of Law Forum*, 5 (2004).
56. Liu Linlin, Thought of Third Party Software Infringing the Copyright of Main Program Software, *Software Engineer*, 7 (2012).
57. Wang Qian, The Right of Alteration of Software Works: From the Perspective of Recent Cases Including the *Rainbow Exposure Soft* Case, *The Jurist*, 1 (2013).

not modify the static code of the program, but only changes the function of the software by intercepting the transmitted dynamic data, which cannot be determined as infringement of the right of revision.[58] Some scholars analyze the U.S. cases of *Midway v. Artic* in 1983, *Lewis Galoob v. Nintendo* in 1992, and *Micro Star v. FormGen* in 1998 and conclude that the modification by third-party software within RAM does not constitute the infringement of the right of revision, and the right of revision cannot regulate third-party software.[59]

In addition, some foreign cases further support that unauthorized third-party software does not constitute infringement of the right of revision. For example, in *MYD v. Blizzard* in 2010, which is considered as the most famous case relating to plug-ins, Blizzard who is the owner of the online game *World of Warcraft* declared in the EULA to prohibit its users to use any cheats, while MYD developed a program called "Glider" to help users of the *World of Warcraft* to play the game automatically without running the game, which can be considered as an unfair advantage.[60] In that case, the Ninth Circuit Court of Appeals of the United States made it clear that the use of "Gilder," an external program for *World of Warcraft*, will not infringe any of Blizzard's proprietary rights, because it does not "modify or copy *World of Warcraft*."[61]

The key to this disagreement lies in the different interpretations of the definition of "computer program" and "the right of revision." In a narrow interpretation of the *Copyright Law*, "computer program" refers to a "coded instruction sequence" that can be executed by a computer to perform a task, but "coded data" is something that used by a "coded instruction sequence." Such data does not have the function of "coded instruction sequence."[62] In this case, Rainbow Exposure Software did not change the static source code of QQ Software, but merely changed the dynamic data in the operation process called by the "coded instructions." What has been modified is not the source code of QQ Software but the function of QQ Software. Therefore, it may be concluded that Rainbow Exposure Software did not modify the "computer program" of QQ Software, thus did not constitute an infringement of the right of revision.

On the contrary, in a broad interpretation of the *Copyright Law*, "computer program" refers not only to a "coded instruction sequence" itself, but also any relevant data that stored statically in the hard disk, stored dynamically in the RAM, as well as the data dynamically transmitted in network.[63] Based on such broad interpretation, since Rainbow Exposure Software replaced the file of Microsoft in the QQ directory, it

---

58. Zhou Weimeng & Zhou Qing, Research on Unauthorized Third-party Software Infringement, *Journal of Chongqing University of Posts and Telecommunications*, 3 (2011).
59. Ruan Kaixin, The Application of Software Alteration Right to Third-party Software in US, *China Copyright*, 5 (2012).
60. See *MYD Indus. LLC v. Blazzard Entm't, Inc.*, 629 F.3d 928, 935 (9th Cir. 2010). Quoted from Wan Yong & Liu Yongpei (Editor), *Berkeley Technology and Law Review: Annual Review of American Intellectual Property Classics of 2012*, Intellectual Property Publishing, 2013, p. 32.
61. Wang Qian, The Right of Alteration of Software Works: From the Perspective of Recent Cases including the *Rainbow Exposure Soft* Case, *The Jurist*, 1 (2013).
62. Ibid.
63. Shou Bu & Chen Yuehua, *Research on Legal Policy of Online Games*, Shanghai Jiao Tong University Press, 2005, p. 67.

should be determined to modify the object code of QQ Software, thus constitutes an infringement of the right of revision.

In my opinion, when the operating result of the main software is changed, the operation of unauthorized third-party software constitutes infringement of the right of revision. The reasons are as follows: First, according to Article 2 of the *Software Regulations*, computer software consists of computer program and related documents. Article 3 of the *Software Regulations* further stipulates that a computer program refers to a coded instruction sequence which may be executed by devices with information processing capabilities such as computers, or a symbolic instruction sequence or symbolic statement sequence which may be automatically converted into a coded instruction sequence for the purpose of obtaining certain expected results; the source program and object program of a computer program shall be deemed as one and the same work. According to this definition, the forms of computer program to be protected by copyright law are the source code and the object code, while the two may be adapted to each other.

Indeed, under normal circumstances, there is a corresponding relationship between the source code and object code of the same software, thus they are the same work under copyright law. However in the network environment, the change of the main software by the third-party software is no longer limited to the static modification of the source code or object code. Instead, it can be coded in the process of network data transmission. The modification of the "coded data" of the instruction "invocation" dynamically changes the function of the computer software. Therefore, unauthorized third-party software can be determined to be a modified computer program as long as the correspondence between the source code and the object code of the main software is changed.

Second, the value of software comes from its result of operation. From the perspective of the legislative purpose of the right of revision of the *Software Regulations*, the purpose of the right of revision is to protect the function and effect of the software. As some scholars have pointed out, "The right of revision is established for protecting and achieving the function of the software."[64] Therefore, the "dynamic modification" of its function during the software operating process should be within the scope of the right of revision.

Finally, in accordance with the *Software Regulations*, any unauthorized "supplement and deletion of software section" or "change order, statement sequence" will be determined as infringement of the right of revision. In the Internet era, the programming process of third-party software is independent from the main software. The procedures and documents of third-party software cannot be the same as the main program software. Therefore, the judicial determination of infringement of the right of revision by third-party software should not be limited to conventional approach of comparing source code, object code or related documents themselves. If the third-party software changes the relevant instructions of the main software during the operation, it should also be deemed as an infringement of the right of revision.

---

64. Feng Xiaoqing, *Copyright Law*, Law Press, 2010, p. 278.

In addition, Article 16 (3) of the *Software Regulations* stipulates the exemption relating to modifying software, that is, the owner of the legitimate copy of the software has the right "to make necessary alterations to the software in order to implement it in an actual environment of computer application or to improve its functions or performance, provided that such owners do not, except otherwise agreed in the contract, offer any third party the altered software without permission from the software copyright owner." According to this article, the modification shall be for the purpose of application, not for commercial purposes; besides, the modified software shall not be provided to any third party. This exemption is legislated to allow the normal use of the software by the legitimate users. Obviously, this exemption does not applicable for Rainbow Exposure Software in this case.

3) Whether third-party software infringes the right of revision as a moral right

Regarding the nature of right, there is a significant difference between moral right and economic right. The moral right is an absolute right, which is nontransferable, and can only be enjoyed by the copyright owner himself. Even if the author dies, the author's heir cannot inherit but can only exercise and protect the copyright. Moral right cannot be licensed or transferred as economic right. The reason is that "Moral right is not a commodity and cannot enter the market."[65] On the other hand, economic right can achieve the economic value of the work by the use of the work, thus it can be transferred in accordance with laws.

In this case, it may be deduced from the claims by Tencent Technology and Tencent Computer that the claims are based upon the right of revision of both economic right and moral right. According to the facts of the case that Tencent Technology authorized Tencent Computer to operate the business activities, it may be concluded that Tencent Technology is the developer of QQ Software and entitled to the moral right and economic right. As the licensee, Tencent Computer is only entitled to the economic right, but not the moral right of the work.

As the two Plaintiffs jointly claimed that the right of revision was infringed and requested the court to order the Defendants Honglian and Woyao to make public apology, while the right of revision is moral right according to the *Copyright Law*, Tencent Technology is entitled to the moral right, but Tencent Computer is not. Accordingly, the modification made by the Defendants Honglian and Woyao infringed Tencent Technology's moral right, but did not infringe Tencent Computer's moral right. Since making public apology is one of the remedies for the infringement of moral right, the Defendants Honglian and Woyao should make such apology to Tencent Technology for the infringement of the right of revision of QQ Software.

—Comments by TONG Haichao

---

65. *Ibid.*

Chapter 3: Determination of Copyright Infringement

Case 22. Infringement of Layout Designs of Integrated Circuits

Hi-trend Technology (Shanghai) Corp., Ltd. v. Renergy Co. and Achmarch Co.
Case of Copyright Infringement Dispute
Case Index: *Hi-trend Technology (Shanghai) Corp., Ltd. v. Renergy Co. and Achmarch Co.*; Shanghai No. 1 Intermediate People's Court, Hu Yi Zhong Min Wu (Zhi) Chu Zi [2008] No. 51, December 24, 2013; Shanghai Higher People's Court, Hu Gao Min San (Zhi) Zhong Zi [2014] No. 12, September 23, 2014

Facts:

The Plaintiff Hi-trend Technology (Shanghai) Corp., Ltd. (hereinafter, "Hi-trend") claimed that the Plaintiff had completed the integrated circuit layout design entitled "ATT7021AU" and obtained the layout design registration certificate. The Plaintiff found that without his permission, the Defendant Renergy Company copied the layout design, and sold the integrated circuit (RN8209CG chip and the RN8209 chip containing the layout design with the Defendant Achmarch Corporation for commercial purposes. The Plaintiff believed that the two Defendants' behavior infringed their exclusive right of integrated circuit layout design and appealed to the Court to request that the Defendants be ordered to: (1) Immediately stop the infringement of exclusive right of integrated circuit layout design; (2) Immediately destroy infringing products and promotional materials involving the product; (3) Publicly apologize to the Plaintiff in the prominent position of "Global Meter" or "International Electronic Business Conditions," and ensure that the Defendant no longer infringes upon the Plaintiff's exclusive circuit layout design in the future; (4) Compensate the Plaintiff for economic losses of RMB 15 million, including the Plaintiff's reasonable expenses for stopping the infringement.

The Defendant, Shenzhen Renergy Co. (hereinafter, "Renergy") argued that the layout design of the chip involved in the case was independently developed by Renergy and obtained the registration certificate, and also obtained the utility model patent right. The layout design of the chip is different from Hi-trend's layout design. Renergy has realized the improvement of chip functions through its originality; Hi-trend's layout design does not have originality and is a conventional design. In summary, Renergy does not constitute infringement and requests to dismiss Hi-trend's claim.

The Defendant Shanghai Achmarch Co. (hereinafter, "Achmarch") agreed with Renergy's reply.

Ruling and Reasoning:

The Shanghai First Intermediate People's Court found that on March 1, 2008, Hi-trend Company completed the layout design creation entitled "AT7021AU" and registered the layout design in the same year. There are sixteen layers of patterns registered in the integrated circuit layout design, and the "A brief description of the structure, technology, and functions of the ATT7021AU integrated circuit layout design" in the registration document is as follows: (1) Achieving the layout design of the same chip (single-phase energy metering) function/performance optimization area; (2) Digital-analog hybrid anti-interference/high static protection chip layout design; (3) Using circuit design technology and layout techniques such as metal layer, diffusion layer, and signal flow rational layout to achieve sensitive signal noise shielding and size signal interference isolation.

During the first trial, the Patent Reexamination Board of the State Intellectual Property Office did not find that Hi-trend's exclusive rights in the layout design involved in the case had defects that could be withdrawn under the "integrated circuit layout design protection regulations." Therefore, the Patent Reexamination Committee terminated the withdrawal procedure proposed by Renergy.

The Beijing Zitu Intellectual Property Judicial Identification Center (hereinafter, "Zitu Identification Center") was accepted by the Court of first instance for judicial expertise. Zitu Identification Center commissioned Beijing Xinyuanjing Software Technology Co., Ltd. to analyze the RN8209CG chip and the RN8209 chip respectively. After the comparison, the two chips have the same analysis report. Hi-trend Corporation claims that there are ten original parts in the ATT7021AU integrated circuit layout design. The appraisal opinions issued by Zitu Identification Center are as follows: (1) The RN8209 and RN8209G are the same as the original point 5 proposed by the Plaintiff (the layout of the digital ground track and the analog ground track); (2) The RN8209, RN8209G are the same as the layout of the two-zone independent booster circuit in the original spot 7 proposed by the Plaintiff (the layout of the analog-digital conversion circuit); (3) Based on the existing evidence, it should be determined that the above-mentioned 1 and 2 points are original and not conventional designs.

Renergy's website shows that in September 2010, RN8209 sales exceeded 10 million. Some VAT invoices seized from Renergy showed that the sales of the RN8209CG chip totaled 1,120 pieces. The unit price was mostly between RMB 5.50 and RMB 4.80. The unit price of invoices was about RMB 2. The sales volume of the RN 8209 chip was 6,610 pieces. The unit price was between RMB 4.80 and RMB 4.20.

On March 21, 2003, Zhuhai Juli Integrated Circuit Design Co., Ltd.(hereinafter, "Juli Company") signed a labor contract with Yang Jianming. Yang Jianming's job is an engineer in the R&D and Design Department of Juli Company. On March 31, 2007, the labor contract relationship between the two parties was terminated. Later, Yang Jianming went to the Defendant Renergy as a technical consultant. In May 2006, the Plaintiff signed a technology transfer contract and a supplementary agreement with Juli Company, which provided that Juli Company would transfer the proprietary technology of the energy metering chip to the Plaintiff. The total contract price is RMB 12 million. After receiving the proprietary technology, the Plaintiff carried out subsequent research and development, and applied layout design to the State Intellectual Property Office for registration, that is, the ATT7021AU layout design involved in the case. In 2006, the Plaintiffs signed labor contracts with Chen Qiang and Zhao Wei. The Plaintiff hired Chen Qiang as the sales manager and Zhao Lan was employed to work on IC design in the R&D department. The contract period was from 2006 to 2009. The Plaintiff also signed confidentiality contracts with Chen Qiang and Zhao Zheng, agreeing that they have the obligation to keep the Plaintiff's relevant technical and business information confidential. Later, Chen Qiang went to Renergy as the general manager and Zhao Hao also worked for Renergy.

Shanghai No. 1 Intermediate People's Court made a civil judgment on December 24, 2013:

> 1. The Defendant Renergy immediately ceased to infringe the exclusive right of the Plaintiff Hi-trend's ATT7021AU (registration number BS.08500145.7) integrated circuit layout design; 2. Within ten days after the judgment came into effect, the Defendant Renergy paid compensation for the Plaintiff's Hi-trend company's economic losses and reasonable expenses paid for stopping the infringement amounting to RMB 3.2 million; 3. Dismissed the Plaintiff Hi-trend's other lawsuit requests.

After the judgment of the first instance was announced, Hi-trend and JuRenergy appealed. Shanghai Higher People's Court issued a judgment on September 23, 2014, dismissed the appeal and upheld the original verdict.

The effective referee stated:

1. Is the layout design of the RN8209 and RN8209G chips involved in the case similar to the layout of digital ground rails and analog ground rails and the layout of independent booster circuits in Hi-trend's ATT7021AU integrated circuit layout design?

The Court held that due to the limited space for innovation in integrated circuit layout design, stricter standards were adopted in the determination of layout design infringement for the same or substantially similar determination of two layout designs. However, the layout design of Renergy's RN8209 and RN8209CG chips is still substantially similar to the "layout of digital ground rails and analog ground rails" and "independent booster circuit layout" of Hi-trend's ATT7021AU integrated circuit layout design. (1) Regarding the "layout of digital ground rails and analog ground rails," Hi-trend's claim that the "digital ground rails and analog ground rail connection layouts" for protection is mainly composed of "digital ground rails and analog ground rail links at the chip," "The east side is near the center," "Coupling place (i.e., four diodes) is in the shape of a field," "The two ground rails run north-south and pass through two 45-degree turns to the east, respectively, in the middle of the position of the horizontal and vertical two-corner layouts," "two ground rails are not touching, not connected" and other features. The layout design of Renergy's RN8209RN8209G chip is characterized in that the junction between the digital ground track and the analog ground track is located near the center of the chip on the east side, and four diodes are arranged in a field-like arrangement at the connection point. A ground track passes through two 45 degrees from the north to the south and then turns to the east. It passes through the top two diodes arranged in a square. Another track from south to north passes through two 45-degree angles and then turns eastward, crossing horizontally through the bottom two diodes arranged in a square. The two ground rails do not touch each other in parallel. It can be seen that the above features of the RN8209 and RN8209G chips' "layout of digital ground rails and analog ground rails" are the same as those of Hi-trend's "layout of digital ground rails and analog ground rails." Regarding Renergy's claim that the M2 layer layout is different, the Court held that although the interconnection circuit is one of the reference factors for integrated circuit layout, the layout design focuses on the three-dimensional structure of active components and components and interconnection lines. That is to say, in addition to considering the three-dimensional configuration of the interconnection lines, the combination of the elements connected by the interconnection lines in the three-dimensional space is more important when determining whether the layout designs are the same or substantially similar. In this case, although the direction of one of the wirings in the layout design of both sides is different after considering the M2 layer, the three-dimensional configuration of the combination of the wiring and interconnection elements does not substantially change. As for Renergy's claim that the position of the connection, the width of the rail, the layout of the specific layout, size, shape, etc., are all subtle, minor differences, but also did not substantially change the three-dimensional combination of wiring and interconnection components. Therefore, the opinions of the appraisal experts that the corresponding layout designs of the RN8209 and RN8209G chips involved are substantially similar to Hi-trend's "layout of digital ground-rail and analog ground-track connection" were approved by the Court. (2) Regarding "independent booster circuit layout." The "independent booster circuit layout" advocated by Hi-trend Company is mainly composed of "symmetry," "a unilateral labyrinthine circuit, two square plates, and two vertical dumbbells", "the labyrinth-like circuit is divided into four compartments and each cell has a small circuit," and "there is a feature such as a ridge-shaped layout between square and dumbbells and a short line perpendicular to the threshold." The layout design of Renergy's RN8209 and RN8209C chips is characterized as follows: bilateral symmetry; two grid-like layouts (corresponding to "dumb-bells") on the north; two horizontal lines on the south side of two grid-like layouts; two tubes The subdirection is perpendicular to the line (corresponding to the threshold pattern and a short line perpendicular to the threshold); there are three sets of tubes (1, 6, and 4) in the south, there are three pipes up and down in the middle and the middle is separated by a horizontal line (corresponding to "a labyrinthine circuit"); there are two rectangular capacitors (corresponding to "square pieces") between north and south. It can be seen that the above characteristics of the "independent booster circuit layout" of the RN8209 and RN8209G chips involved in the case are the same as those of the Hi-trend company's "independent booster circuit layout." As for the sizes of M1, M2, M3 and PL layer MOS tubes claimed by Renergy, they are subtle or minor differences. The difference in the ST layer is due to the use of different processes. Therefore, the above differences proposed by Renergy are not enough to affect the judgment that the corresponding layout design of the RN8209 and RN8209G chips is the same or substantially similar to Hi-trend's "independent booster circuit layout."

2. Whether the "convergence of digital ground rail and analog ground rail layout" and "independent booster circuit layout" in the Hi-trend's ATT7021AU integrated circuit layout design is original?

The Court held that according to the provisions of Article 4 of the "Regulations on the Protection of Integrated Circuit Layout Design" (hereinafter, "Regulations"), the originality of layout design means that the layout design is the result of the author's own intellectual work, and the layout design is not a conventional design among the layout-design creators and the integrated circuit makers at the time of creation. In addition, Hi-trend should bear the burden of proof on the originality of the integrated circuit layout design. However, Hi-trend company does not necessarily and cannot exhaust all related conventional layout designs to prove that its claimed layout design is an unconventional design. As long as the evidence and instructions provided by Hi-trend can prove that the claimed layout design does not belong to the conventional design, it should be considered that Hi-trend has completed preliminary burden of proof. In this case, Renergy claims that the related layout design is a conventional design, and provides an identical or substantially similar conventional layout design, which is enough to overturn Hi-trend's proposal on unconventional design.

First, in this case, Hi-trend claims that the "layout of digital ground rails and analog ground rails" and the "independent booster circuit layout" in AT7021AU integrated circuit layout design have originality and completed the initial burden of proof. First of all, Hi-trend's ATT7021AU integrated circuit layout design obtained the "Integrated Circuit Layout Design Registration Certificate." In the process of cancelling the layout design, the Patent Reexamination Board did not find that Hi-trend's exclusive right of layout design involved in the case could be revoked after examination. Second, the "ATT7021AU integrated circuit layout design brief description" in the "Integrated Circuit Layout Design Registration Certificate" states: "1. Achieved the layout design appeal of the industry's same chip (single-phase energy metering) performance optimization area; 2. Digital-analog mixed high anti-interference, high electrostatic protection chip layout design; 3. Adopt circuit design technology and metal layer, diffusion layer Layout techniques such as reasonable layout of signal flow enable sensitive signal noise shielding and large and small signal interference isolation." However, in the ATT7021AU integrated circuit layout design, the "layout of digital ground rails and analog ground rails" is used to remove noise and prevent static electricity and play a role in protecting the chips. The "independent booster circuit layout" is used to raise the voltage and is a necessary module for the amplifier circuit. Hi-trend company elaborated on the original creation point of the two-part layout design. And then, the "Identification Opinion" issued by the Zitu Identification Center also found that the "layout of digital ground rails and analog ground rails" and the "independent booster circuit layout" in AT7021AU integrated circuit layout design are original.

Second, Hi-trend has completed its preliminary burden of proof. The evidence submitted by Renergy in this case is not sufficient to deny the conclusion that "layout of digital ground and analog ground rails" and "independent booster circuit layout" in Hi-trend's ATT7021AU integrated circuit layout design are original. First of all, Hi-trend's claim that the "digital ground rails and analog ground rail connection layouts" for protection is mainly composed of "digital ground rails and analog ground rail links at the chip," "The east side is near the center," "Coupling place (that is, four diodes) is in the shape of a field," "The two ground rails run north-south and pass through two 45-degree turns to the east, respectively, in the middle of the position of the horizontal and vertical two-corner layouts," "two ground rails are not touching, not connected" and other features. The evidence submitted by Renergy is not enough to prove that the aforementioned "layout of digital ground and analog ground rails" is a conventional design. The reasons are: (1) In the first instance, evidence materials such as "ESD Circuits and Devices" provided by Renergy recorded the principle and diagram of ESD circuits rather than the layout design of ESD network electrical schematic diagrams in integrated circuit layout design. The diode layout shown in the layout design of BL6503 is a rectangular layout, with no field layout. The "rail-to-rail device connection" visible on the east side is not the same as Hi-trend's "layout of digital floor-to-rail simulations." The manufacturing process of the diode is reflected in the "CY6H process design rule of Shanghai Hua Hong NEC Corporation," not the integrated circuit layout design. The figure in the article "THEART OF ANALOG LAYOUT" written by Lin Zheng-Song shows that the diodes are arranged in a rectangular (ten diodes) or square (nine diodes) arrangement. (2) In the second instance, Renergy mentioned the layout of LTC3442 in the agency opinion. Because Renergy did not submit it as evidence, the Court could not verify the origin of the layout, that is, the origin and authenticity of the paper "PM Chip Reverse Design." (3) Prof. Wang Jiaji stated in Court that it is common practice to use bidirectional diodes in digital and analog ground rail circuits, and the most area-saving method for even-numbered devices is to arrange them into square or field shapes. The four elements in the integrated circuit layout design use a field-shaped layout as a general design. In the field of electronic meters, he did not find diode-shaped layouts. At present, he is unable to provide other layout designs that are the same or similar to the "layout of digital ground and analog ground rails" and the "independent booster circuit layout." The experts at the Zitu Identification Center stated that it does not matter how many diodes are used. Functionally, two and four diodes perform the same function. The number of diodes is determined based on the test results. In this case, the layout design of four diodes placed in a field shape was not a conventional design, and no similar layout design was found in similar chips. The BL6503 layout design provided by Renergy shows that the diodes in this layout design use a rectangular layout. Considering the existing evidence in the case, the Court held that saving area is one of factors that need to be considered when creating integrated circuit layout design, but it is not the unique factor. Other factors need to be considered, including achieving chip performance or optimizing performance through the layout design, for example, high anti-interference, high static protection, noise shielding and other properties. Even though the four-element layout is a conventional design in an integrated circuit layout design, the determination of the number of diodes needs to be selected experimentally. And when Hi-trend applied for the exclusive right of ATT7021AU integrated circuit layout design, no diode field layout design was found in the field of electronic meters. Therefore, when Hi-trend created the "layout of digital ground rails and analog ground rails," it was intellectual work to choose to arrange four diodes as field shapes. It should not simply deny the originality of the layout. Moreover, according to the provisions of Article 4 of the Regulations, the overall layout design which consists of conventional designs can be protected by law if it meets the originality requirements. To take a step back, even if Renergy's proposal for a conventional design was established, Renergy also failed to submit evidence to prove that Hi-trend's "layout of digital and analog ground rails" is a conventional design. Second, Hi-trend's "independent booster circuit layout" is characterized by "left-right symmetry," "a labyrinth of unilateral circuits, two square plates, and two vertical dumbbells," "the labyrinth-like circuit is divided into four compartments and each compartment has a small circuit," "there is a wedge-shaped pattern between square and dumbbell and there is a short line perpendicular to the threshold" and so on. In this case, the evidence submitted by Renergy is not enough to prove that the aforementioned "independent booster circuit layout" is a conventional design. The reasons are: (1) The "booster circuit layout" in BL6503 layout design does not have the feature of "left-right symmetry," and is different from Hi-trend's "independent booster circuit layout;" (2) ADE7755 layout design Although the "booster circuit layout" is symmetrical, the unilateral lower circuit is not divided into four compartments. There are two small and one large rectangles in the middle and seven "dumbbells" at the top. There are no "gate-like patterns" and "short lines perpendicular to the threshold." It is not the same as Hi-trend's "independent booster circuit layout."

3. Whether Renergy's production and sale behavior of RN8209 and RN8209G chips involved in the case infringe Hi-trend's exclusive right of ATT7021AU integrated circuit layout design

The Court held that Renergy's production and sale behavior of RN8209 and RN8209C chips involved in the case infringed Hi-trend's exclusive right of ATT7021AU integrated circuit layout design for the following reasons: First, according to Article 30 of the Regulations, unless otherwise specified, an actor must immediately stop the infringement without any permission from the owner of the layout-design right, and bear the liability for compensation: (1) copying all or part of the protected layout design; (2) providing a protected layout design, Integrated circuit with the layout design and products with the integrated circuits for commercial purposes, through import, sales, or other means. In this case, Renergy admitted that they had contacted Hi-trend's ATT7021AU integrated circuit layout design. Renergy produced and sold RN8209 and RN8209G chips without the permission of Hi-trend. The chips contained the original "layout of digital ground rails and analog ground rails" and "independent booster circuit layout" in Hi-trend's ATT7021AU integrated circuit layout design. Renergy's actions have infringed Hi-trend's proprietary right of ATT7021AU integrated circuit layout design and Renergy should assume corresponding civil liabilities. Second, Renergy proposed that their chip function is better than Hi-trend Company. The Court held that the originality of layout design is not directly related to the function of the chip. It is entirely possible that a layout design consisting of conventional designs can implement new chip functions, and it is also possible to realize the same function as other chips by independently designing a layout of an unconventional design. Therefore, the superiority of the layout design of the RN8209 and RN8209G chips cannot be a defense of Renergy. Third, Renergy also proposed that the infringement judgment standard of integrated circuit layout design should have the similarity concept (i.e., the ratio of similar parts to the total area of the chip). The Court held that according to Article 30 of the "Regulation," copying all or the original parts of the protected layout design constitutes infringement. It can be seen that any original part of the protected layout design is protected by law, regardless of size or role in the overall layout design. If the original partial layout design cannot be protected because the proportion of the overall layout design is low or not a core part, the copying of these parts will be uncontrollable. At the same time, it is impossible to encourage innovation in the noncore parts of layout design. The purpose of the Regulations to encourage innovation will also become empty talks. Ultimately, it will not be possible to promote design innovation in the entire IC industry through effective competition. Therefore, the layout design that accounts for a small proportion of the total integrated circuit layout design and noncore parts should also be protected by law. Judging whether part or whole of a layout design is the same or substantially similar is two different criteria. Only when it is determined whether the alleged infringing act belongs to the copy of all layout designs, it is necessary to judge the same or substantially similarity of the layout design of the whole chip, and it may involve the problem of overall similarity of two integrated circuit layout designs claimed by Renergy. The "layout of digital ground rails and analog ground rails" and the "independent booster circuit layout" involved in this case have conventional layout designs. Renergy can use these conventional designs or create different original layout designs through own research and development. However, Renergy did not take those approaches, but directly copied the "digital floor rail and analog ground rail connection layout" and "independent booster circuit layout" of Hi-trend's ATT7021AU integrated circuit layout design to manufacture and sell RN8209 and RN8209G chip. The behavior has constituted infringement. The proportion and role of the two layout designs in the entire chip are only factors considered in the case of infringement and do not affect the determination of infringement. Fourth, regarding whether Renergy's actions are subject to the provisions of Article 23 of the Regulations, the Court held that Article 23 of the Regulations stipulates "the following acts may not be subject to the permission of the layout-design right holder and shall not be paid to them: (1) copy protected layout designs for personal purposes or simply for evaluation, analysis, research, teaching, etc.; (2) on the basis of the evaluation and analysis of the protected layout designs according to the previous paragraph, create original layout design; (3) copy or put into commercial use of the same layout design as others created by him independently." Chips that implement the same or similar function must have similarities in the circuit principle, and the circuit principle does not belong to the portion of the Regulation that can be granted exclusive rights. Therefore, the law does not prohibit the reverse engineering of the layout design of other people's chips. Companies may imitate the chips of other people and do not constitute infringement. One possibility may be to obtain the permission of the layout-design right holders, and the other may be to redesign original layout designs based on reverse engineering. In the analysis and design process, companies must invest more time and cost. In the fast-growing IC industry, competitors' investment of this time and cost can ensure that the imitated company can retain competitive advantage within a period of time. This is also the reason why the law allows reverse engineering. However, the law does not allow the direct reproduction of other layout designs on the basis of reverse engineering, because this behavior will significantly reduce the investment of competitors in time and cost, thereby greatly weakening the competitive advantage of the imitated enterprise. Ultimately, it will reduce the enthusiasm of innovation in the entire IC industry. In this case, Renergy made a partial copy of Hi-trend's ATT7021AU integrated circuit layout design, which was neither for personal purposes nor for pure evaluation, research, teaching, etc., but for the development of new integrated circuits for commercial use. Renergy admitted to contact Hi-trend's ATT7021AU integrated circuit layout design, rather than through reverse engineering. Renergy directly copied the original "digital floor and analog ground rail connection layout" and "independent booster circuit layout" in Hi-trend's ATT7021AU integrated circuit layout design without permission to manufacture and sell the RN8209 and RN8209CG chips. Therefore, regardless of whether or not Renergy's RN8209 and RN8209G chip layout designs involved in the case are original, its behavior does not apply to Article 23 (2) of the Regulations. In summary, the ruling filed by Renergy about noninfringement cannot be established.

4. Determination of compensation amount

Renergy refused to provide relevant financial information, and should bear the unfavorable consequence of the inability to produce evidence. The quantity of 10 million pieces sold on Renergy's website, which Hi-trend claims, should be used as the calculation basis for the amount of compensation in this case. According to the existing evidence in the case, both parties did not submit evidence to prove the sales profit, and the appraisal report clearly stated that except for the infringement of the two parts of the layout design, the other parts were not the same or substantially similar. Taking into account the noncore role and small area of the two-part layout design of infringement in the chip, and the cost and time saved by Renergy by directly copying Hi-trend's corresponding layout, The Court of first instance adjudicated Renergy compensate Hi-trend's economic loss of RMB 3.2 million including reasonable expenses. The decision is reasonable.

Commentary:

Because of the general rules of "integrated circuit layout protection" and few relevant judicial practices, meanwhile integrated circuit layout design is also very professional, the determination standard of the infringement of integrated circuit layout design has been difficult to grasp in the jurisdiction. The difficulty of the determination of infringement of integrated circuit layout design is that: how to understand the word "any" in Articles 7 and 30 of the Regulations, how to determine the distribution of burden of proof and proof standard of the "originality" and how to ascertain the identification criteria of the "substantive similarity" of layout design. The trial of this case is based on the understanding of the legal provisions, respecting industrial practices, interpreting the principled legal provisions, in order to promote the innovation and development of the integrated circuit industry, as an infringement judgment standard that can be used in judicial practice. This case is a very typical case of integrated circuit layout design infringement disputes. The general idea of the Court in the trial is to strictly observe the protection scope of "all or any original part" stipulated in the Integrated Circuit Layout Design Regulations, to grasp whether there is infringement of illegal copy of layout design through strict and prudent "originality" and "substantial similarity" standards, to deal with specific integrated circuit layout design infringement cases through the construction of trial ideas. The Court took this case as an opportunity to explore the three aspects mentioned above, and tried to summarize the basic trial ideas and trial points in the determination of the infringement of the exclusive rights of integrated circuit layout design. The Court hopes this trial has a certain reference to solve cases of the infringement dispute of the exclusive rights of integrated circuit layout design.

I. The nonproportional standard

The nonproportional standard means that the protection span of integrated circuit layout design covers all units, regardless of how small the unit's volume accounts for the entire layout. Therefore, in the determination of infringement, the proportion of the layout design that is illegally copied does not take into account the proportion of the integrated circuit layout design, and it is not considered whether the layout design of this part is the core part of the overall layout design. Considering that the scope of protection of integrated circuit layout design will determine the threshold of the determination of infringement of integrated circuit layout design, it will affect the balance of interests of various groups in relevant industries and guide the domestic industry to judge the infringement or not. Therefore, when answering the question that "for the scope of protection of integrated circuit layout design, we should consider all copying constitutes infringement or partial copying also constitutes infringement? If copying a part constitutes an infringement, whether there is a proportional limit or an importance limit?" The Court has analyzed the legal regulations and judicial practices at home and abroad one by one and obtained the standard based on this.

(I) The most important reference case for the core protecting standards identified in the U.S. case *Brooktree* is the *"Browntree Corp v. AMD Inc."* that was the only case involved integrated circuit layout design after the issuance of the Semiconductor Chip Protection Act.[66] The Supreme Court established judgment standard under the SC.PA Act that in the U.S., it also constitutes a substantial similarity and thus infringes the exclusive rights of integrated circuit layout design as long as copying the core part of the protected layout design. The Court quoted the House of Representatives' legislative view in the judgment, "Percentage is not a criterion for judging whether or not the

---

66. Semiconductor Chip Protection Act, hereinafter, "SCPA."

infringement is based on the criteria for judging infringement on a case-by-case basis. Even a single unit layout design can be misappropriated, and sometimes the substantive part included in the masked work No. 2 contains is a unit of layout design, which contains creativity and commercial usage value." At the same time it also demonstrated its own view, "Although there are no hard and fast standards or percentages to determine what is substantively similar, even the copied percentage is quite small from the whole chip, substantial similarity may still exist because of the high importance of this copy in the mask work." From the existing U.S. jurisprudence, it can be clearly seen that it is the core part which has originality belonging to the U.S. protecting scope of integrated circuit layout design. It of the protection that. It would be protected by the SCPA method as long as it is the core part, regardless of the percentage of the part that occupies the volume of the entire integrated circuit chip.

Therefore, judging from foreign jurisprudence, for an integrated circuit layout design, regardless of the proportion of the part of the layout design illegally copied to the entire integrated circuit chip, this proportional relationship does not have a decisive influence on substantive similarity of the infringement.

(II) The nonproportional standard used in the case of *Jurui*

1. The nonproportional standard is based on the interpretation of "any" in the Regulations.

Based on the first paragraph of Article 7 and the first paragraph of Article 30 of the Regulations of China, it is stipulated that the object protected by the exclusive right of circuit layout design is "all or any original part of the protected layout design." According to the literal interpretation of this provision, as long as it is an original part of the layout design, regardless of the proportion of the whole layout design, or whether the part belongs to the core part of the entire layout design, it should be integrated circuit layout design protection. This is also the nonproportional standard described in this article. Because there is neither a requirement of proportionality nor an importance requirement such as that of the U.S. for a copy-designed layout unit that may constitute an infringement, it is larger, for perspective of protection scope, than the existing core protecting standards established by American jurisprudence.

2. Reflections on the application of nonproportional principles in domestic cases

There are extremely few cases in which the relevant judgments in China have come into force. In the case of *Xiwei Science Technology Service Co. v. Yuanzhifeng Co.*, since the parties directly copied and copied the entire chip, the fact of the illegal copying of the layout design was obvious, and there was no need to discuss the proportion. In the hearing of *Shanghai Jurui* case, the two parties' ICs, appraised by third part, have only two substantial similarities, whose proportion in the overall layout is less than 1%. The Defendant also argued that the two sides should layout. The design similarity is extremely low and there is no infringement. In this regard, the Court, on the basis of interpreting the Regulations that "copying all or any of the original parts of a protected layout design constitutes infringement," considers specific protection scope of circuit layout design in terms of technical characteristics and legislative objectives.

(1) From the aspect of technical characteristics, the nonproportional standard reflects that the existence of each unit of the layout design is required by the performance and all have market value.

Each part of the layout design unit embodies the designer's intellectual achievements and is of certain value. Since each layout design of the integrated circuit is set to have a certain execution function or performance at the time of development, the determination of each function or performance parameter needs to be corrected by many experimental data. Therefore, the layout design of each part is an integral part of the integrated circuit. Once the layout design of the part is changed, the previously set performance parameters of the layout design will also change accordingly. The layout parameters of other layout designs that are connected to the design will also be affected. Therefore, each part of the layout unit is carefully laid out and tested by the designer. As long as the parameters are not changed, a certain layout unit can be applied to different layout designs. The core unit may become an important core unit in other chips.

The layout design of a core part of an integrated circuit can only achieve the performance required for its design, with the aid of the noncore layout design matched with its performance. Because of the characteristics of electronic components and the limitations of design cost materials, any layout design in an integrated circuit as described above runs a specific design function. If a certain layout pattern is forcibly removed, the core design function of the circuit cannot be realized or necessary. The lack of auxiliary functions will eventually weaken the market competitiveness of integrated circuit products. This is what is said in the case of *Jurui*. The "digital ground track and analog ground track convergence layout" involving infringement reflects the chip's high anti-interference/high static protection characteristics, and the "independent booster circuit layout" part is the voltage counting the necessary parts of the circuit amplifies the monitored tiny voltage so that it can reach a countable value. If this part is missing, it may cause the energy count to be incorrect. If there is no two-part layout design that involves infringement, the circuit product is very likely to lose its commercial utility value.

Therefore, whether or not the layout unit core or the proportion is not the reason for whether it is protected by law, but the intellectual value of the designers contained in it is the basis for legal judgment of infringement.

(2) Starting from the purpose of legislation, the Regulations are formulated to stimulate the innovation and development of the integrated circuit layout industry. Regulations provide that any original part of the layout design which has originality deserves legal protection regardless of its size or role in the overall layout design. Moreover, the layout design of each part of the integrated circuit layout design has the feature of having independent functions but having influence on other parts, considering that if the original layout design is only because of its low proportion of the entire layout design Or if it is not the core part that cannot be protected, then the duplication of these parts will be arbitrary and will not encourage innovation in the noncore parts of layout design. Regulations aims to encourage the original intention of integrated

Chapter 3: Determination of Copyright Infringement

circuit technology innovation will also become empty talk, ineffective legal protection will lead to disorderly industrial competition, and ultimately cannot achieve the legislative objective of promoting the design and innovation of the entire integrated circuit industry through legal regulations and effective competition. Therefore, every part in ICs needs to encourage people to innovate. From the legislative purpose of the Regulations itself, the original layout design, which occupies a very small proportion of the entire integrated circuit layout design, is also unique and should be protected by law.

Therefore, the Court used a nonproportional standard that is more stringent than the U.S. core protection standard for the infringer in the case of *Jurui*, and considered that the noncore "digital ground track and analog ground track" occupying a small proportion of the entire integrated circuit layout design The originality of the layout design of the circuit and the "independent booster circuit" should also be protected by law, which is also based on actual needs and meets the standards prescribed by law.

II. The identification standard of "originality"

According to the nonproportional standard embodied in the aforementioned "Regulations," it indicates that integrated circuit layout design has been comprehensively protected by law in China. The examination of whether infringers infringe on the exclusive right of exclusive circuit layout design is even stricter than in the U.S. However, this does not mean that the scope of protection for integrated circuit layout design is infinitely extended, but this can fully reflect the legislative purpose of China to protect layout design innovation and IC industry development. However, according to industrial characteristics and industry practices, the IC innovation space is limited and there is a certain degree of mutual learning. Excessive protection of rights holders may cause other later designers to be afraid of the last generation to innovate and improve on the basis of the previous owners. It will also restrain the enthusiasm of industrial innovation to some extent. Furthermore, the law stipulates that only original layout design can be protected by the exclusive right of exclusive circuit layout design. Therefore, in order to balance the interests between the public interest and the interests of the parties, within the scope of delineated protection of layout design, the above-mentioned interests shall be balanced through the threshold of examination for the protection of layout-design protection with the statutory precondition of "originality." This is one of the important explorations made by the Court in the case of *Jurui*.

It is a factual issue to determine whether the layout design has "originality." It requires the parties to provide relevant evidence for their own original claims in the process of litigation. In this confrontation process, the Court has been trying to grasp the strict degree of determination of "originality" by distributing burden of proof and the scale of proof standard. The Court mentioned above had the balance of interests on the issue of "originality" identification. Therefore, the Court took this kind of consideration to form a preliminary rule on the distribution of the burden of proof and the standard of proof for the "originality" problem in the case of *Jurui*. Summarizing, in the course of litigation against the fact of originality, the Court measures the probative power of the evidence of the parties, provided that the Plaintiff provided evidence to prove the originality of its layout design and the Defendant denied the evidence provided by the Plaintiff's claim. That is, the "high degree of probabilistic" criterion is used to determine which side has more evidence, so as to support which side claims the facts to make a referee. If the evidence on both sides cannot enable the Court to reach a "highly probative" internal confirmation standard, it means that The Plaintiff of the original factual issue needs to bear the risk of unfavorable referees.

(1) The certification responsibility of "originality"

According to the principle of "who advocates and who gives proof" in the civil procedure proof rules, in the case of layout-design infringement, the Plaintiff should bear the burden of proof in its original circuit layout design, which means that once the Plaintiff even creates originality. The initial burden of proof cannot be fulfilled, and subsequent adversarial litigation activities do not need to be unfolded. Therefore, there is no judgment on the strength of evidence provided by the Court and the Plaintiff shall bear the corresponding burden of proof directly.

When the evidence provided by the Plaintiff reaches the level of initial proof burden, that is, when it meets the requirement of proof standard for initial proof originality, if the Defendant holds a negative opinion on the originality of the Plaintiff's layout design, the burden of proof is transferred to the Defendant at this time. The Defendant needs to provide evidence that the layout design does not have originality. When both parties of the original Defendant submit their claims on original facts and provide relevant evidence, the Court shall judge the probative power of the evidence on the basis of the proof standard of high degree of probative nature. If the evidential power of Plaintiff's evidence is obviously greater than that of the Defendant, then the fact that the layout design supported by the Plaintiff's evidence is original is highly probative, and the Court should make a judgment based on this fact; if the Defendant's evidence proves evident Greater than the Plaintiff, the fact that the layout design of the Defendant is not based on the high probability criterion is also supported. If both sides of the evidence cannot obtain an advantage in the evidentiary power of the evidence, the judge could not form an inner conviction on the fact judgment. According to the original facts, according to the "who advocates who claims evidence" rules of action, the Plaintiff shall bear the burden of proof that the evidence is insufficient to prove that his layout design is original.

In summary, on the issue of originality, when the facts of the case have been clarified after both parties have performed their subjective burden of proof, the judge will form a heart of conviction and make a judgment; but when the truth is not known, the rule of evidence is based on "who claims that who claims." The Plaintiff who claims that his layout design has originality bears the burden of objective proof, and the Court thus decides on the basis of this burden of proof. In terms of justifying the distribution of responsibilities, in the case of originality review, the Court's balance of interests is designed to take into consideration the legal interests of designing imitators in industry practice.

(2) The standard of proof in the proof process of "originality"

In the process of litigation confrontation, it has been clarified both sides' burden of proof on the originality of layout design, then the party who bears the burden of proof should prove to what level or extent the facts of his claim should be reached

Chapter 3: Determination of Copyright Infringement

before the judge can judge the transfer of burden of proof or It is a standard that one party's evidence is reached or both sides cannot achieve "probable advantage."

In the judicial practice of nonpersonal relationship civil cases, the "high probability" generally adopts a high probative proof requirement, that is, the party proves that claiming "facts" by the judge should be believed to be highly probable. This justification rule is only a general proof requirement for a general civil case, but it is due to the fact that different cases involve different legal facts and the need to protect different legal interests, the proof standard will change to different scales in different cases for different facts in different litigation stages. For the case of infringement of the exclusive right of circuit layout design, the fact that the layout design has originality, the "preliminary originality" evidence required by the Plaintiff and the two sides should be able to make the judge It is necessary to gradually find out the threshold of the above-mentioned certification standards in accordance with the relevant legal provisions, legal principles, industry practices, and relevant technical details of the case to form proof standards for all parties to obtain proofs of their inner convictions.

1. Initial evidence of start-up of the investigation on originality

In addition to the Plaintiff at the time of filing the case, as the exclusive right holder of the integrated circuit layout design to initiate litigation, in the process of hearing, the Plaintiff Hi-trend also had to bear initial responsibility for the fact that the integrated circuit layout design claimed by the Plaintiff was original. The burden of proof, for this responsibility, will be based on legal requirements, industry practice and case details.

Article 4 of the Regulations stipulates that for originality, the Plaintiff needs to prove two points. First, the layout design is the result of the creator's own intellectual labor; the second is the layout design creator and IC manufacturing. Among those who are not recognized as regular designs.

For the first point, the Plaintiff must prove that it is easier for him to create his own intellectual labor. Provided he provides corresponding unprovoked rights certificates, he can prove that the layout design of the Plaintiff is a result of his own intellectual work. In the case of *Jurui*, the Plaintiff provided a layout design registration certificate and a design creation contract signed by the layout design. During the litigation process, the Patent Reexamination Board maintained the exclusive right of the layout design during the cancellation process. Effectiveness can also reflect that the layout design has certain originality. It can be seen that the Plaintiff in this case proved that the layout design involved in the case was the result of his intellectual work.

As for the second point, the Plaintiff wants to initially prove that the creative result is an unconventional design. There are roughly two ways. One is the direct method, which is to require the Plaintiff to exhaust all relevant conventional layout designs for comparison, but this method is extremely costly. High and practically impossible to implement, so it is neither necessary nor possible. The second is the indirect approach, which can be used to prove that the layout design has certain originality. For example, in the case of *Jurui*, the Plaintiff proved this through two aspects of evidence. On the one hand, it is combined with the "integrated" maintained by the Patent Reexamination Board's cancellation process. The "circuit layout design registration certificate" records detailed descriptions of the original creation points of the disputed parts layout; on the other hand, the third-party verification organization has made original conclusions on the layout design of the disputed part. That is, the indirect evidence for the preliminary proof of the unconventional design is the characterization of the registration and the conclusion of the third-party verification. Moreover, the layout design of the Plaintiff in the *Jurui* case was authorized by the administrative agency. Although it was not subject to substantive examination, it was announced after a period of time before the Plaintiff obtained the right. If the party concerned is infringed, he should be able to discover it in time. Moreover, this case also went through the revocation procedure of the reexamination board, and it can also reflect to some extent that the layout design has certain originality.

With the above evidence, the Court held that the Plaintiff had provided basic evidence that preliminary proof of the originality of its layout design. Due to the limitations of the existing layout design registration management system, carpet search cannot be performed like a patent and corresponding search evaluation reports are provided. Therefore, from the perspective of cost efficiency and litigation effectiveness, the proof power of the Plaintiff's evidence in the *Jurui* case has reached To convince the Court that the part of its layout design that needs to be copied needs to be protected by the law, litigation resistance procedures can be initiated to further clarify the original facts.

2. The accused is accused of routine design anti-evidence

In the case of *Jurui*, the Court made it clear that as long as the Defendant can provide a conventional layout design that is the same or substantially similar to the original layout claimed by the Plaintiff, it is enough to overthrow the Plaintiff's claim on unconventional design, and it is also possible to achieve certification on whether the design of the figure has an original proof effect. That is, if the evidence provided by the Defendant can make the Court suspicious of the Plaintiff's original facts, the Court may support the Plaintiff's burden of proof whether the Defendant's power is dominant or the Court cannot form a conviction. The Defendant's conventional design claims.

In the case of *Jurui*, the evidence provided by the Defendant was merely related to the principle of the ESD circuit and the schematic or diode manufacturing process. They were all nonlayout designs, and the experts requested could not provide a similar conventional design layout. Therefore, in this case, the Court had reason to believe that the Plaintiff's two-part layout design was original.

Judging from the existing cases, the case of *Jurui* has already been discussed in more ingenious parts. The preliminary evidence of the Plaintiff and the counter-evidence of the Defendant overturning the claim of the Plaintiff all have a rough outline, which has blurred threshold of the proof degree. However, if there is more confrontational new evidence in the litigation, how to determine the original facts at this time still requires more practical cases to clarify whether the proof standard of high probability is reached.

In short, for the above-mentioned accused, the conventional design of counter-evidence, in terms of effect, not only alleviates the need for the Plaintiff's excessive burden of proof in the carpet search, but also provides the Defendant with an opportunity to easily prove his claim. In terms of implementation, both parties are designers of integrated circuit layouts. As professionals in this field, they should be able to know the existence of related layout designs. It is not difficult to find similar evidence.

II. Consistency of authorization standards and infringement standards in "originality"

There is a further problem in the determination of originality facts. If the Defendant provided the anti-evidence of the conventional design, how similar the comparative conventional design must be as the layout design of the Plaintiff in order to complete the routine design which could be falsification? The Court held that the judgment of the degree of similarity will determine whether the layout design of the Plaintiff is original and original, and whether or not it is originality is a precondition for granting the exclusive right of integrated circuit layout design. Therefore, the standard is the authorization standard. A similarity judgment will affect whether the Plaintiff layout design enjoys exclusive rights. The Court held that the similarity judgment should be consistent with the two layout designs in the infringement judgment, and adopt substantively similar judgment standards. Because in the judgment of infringement or not, the Court adopted a more stringent "substantive similarity" standard. If the two standards are inconsistent, such a situation will occur. The Court adopts strict standards in acknowledging one party's evidence, and in judging the same problem. At the same time, the adoption of the evidence of the other party is a loose standard, which will lead to unfairness in the litigation. Therefore, the two standards should be consistent.

III. The "substantive similarity" of the identification criteria

1. Take stricter "substantive similarity" criteria

In the case of *Jurui*, when the Court compared whether the two integrated circuit layout designs were substantially similar, they used relatively strict criteria to determine that only the entire or part of the alleged infringing integrated circuits and protected integrated circuits had originality. In the case of "extremely similar" nature of the layout design, it was determined to constitute "substantial similarity." The reason why the Court adopts a more stringent "substantially similar" criterion is to comprehensively consider the technical characteristics of the integrated circuit layout design and balance the legal norms and industry conventions.

First, from a technical point of view, the space for innovation in integrated circuit layout design is limited. This is because the integrated circuit needs to have the electronic function while designing, also have the physical property of the fixed object, and the design is in the ideal situation, the layout design is to make the ideal integrated circuit into a physical entity that exists in reality, so It is bound to be limited by objective conditions, so this has led to the limitation of many external factors. These limitations include layout designs that need to meet the constraints of integrated circuit parameters, are limited by the level of production technology and are limited by certain physical laws and material types. Therefore, the use of stricter "substantive similarity" criteria is subject to objective conditions.

Second, from the balance point of view, the Regulations are designed to stimulate the enthusiasm of innovation of integrated circuit layout designers and promote the development of the integrated circuit industry. In practice, both reverse laws and industry practices allow the existence of reverse engineering. Because reverse engineering can be used to design integrated circuits that are compatible with other people's integrated circuits on the basis of knowing other people's layout designs, it is possible to eliminate unnecessary duplicate studies and save social resources, and you can add your own Original research results promote faster technological progress. Therefore, there is a need to have a balance of interests between law and practice when trying such cases, both to protect the rights of right holders and to allow proper industry practices such as reverse engineering. On the other hand, as mentioned in the foregoing, according to the Regulations, the scope of protection for integrated circuit layout design should adopt the "nonproportional standard," which is a more favorable standard for right holders. Therefore, from the perspective of balance of interests, the courts should also pay attention to keep the balance of interests of all parties when applying the "substantive similarity" standard. Therefore, the adoption of a more stringent "substantive similarity" standard by the Court is in line with the needs of the interests of all parties in the industry.

2. Strictly "substantially similar" in technical operations

In the process of judging substantive similarity, because of the need for professional knowledge and technical experience, it often requires the participation of third-party appraisal agencies. However, the lack of relevant judicial practices in China leads to the lack of legal appraisal principles so that it is quite difficult for appraisal organizations to grasp substantive similarities. It can only be grasped from the relevant experience of professional technology. In the *Jurui* case, the Court determined that the criterion of "substantive similarity" required for infringement of the exclusive rights of integrated circuit layout design was more stringent. Such a standard measure is also an important guiding principle for the accreditation body.

(1) No protection for ideas, processes, methods of operation or mathematical concepts

In accordance with Article 5 of the Regulations, when comparing whether two layout designs constitute "substantial similarity," the factors of thinking, processing, operation methods or mathematical concepts should be removed, and the elements in the layout design should be considered purely as well as all or some of the three-dimensional configuration of the interconnection line. For integrated circuits, ideological factors are generally reflected at the conceptual level. At present, the conceptual level is specifically divided into five types of structures, eight types of technologies, and five types of functions (Table 1). These contents will not be taken into consideration within the scope of protection. For example, in the case of *Jurui*, the Defendant filed a defense: the size of the MOS transistors is not the same. In addition, one layout design uses N-MOS and the other is P-MOS, so the two layout designs are not substantially similar. According to the classification of the above conceptual levels, the types of MOS devices should be technical in nature, and they fall within the scope of Article 5 of the Regulations that is not protected by the rights of integrated circuit layout design. Therefore, the Court used the opinions of the accreditation body for the Defendant's defense in this case, and concluded that these differences did not affect the substantive similarity judgment.

Table 1   Classification of Layers of Concepts

Options	Content
Structure	Bipolar, MOS, Bi-MOS, Optical-IC, etc.
Technology	TTL, DTL, ECL, IIL, C-MOS, N-MOS, P-MOS, etc.
Function	Logics, Storage, Microcomputer, Linearity, etc.

In addition, when the case of *Jurui* was judged to be substantially similar, it also referred to the "process" issue. The process was the processing or processing of the material, and finally it became the method or process of the finished product, belonging to the treatment process of Article 5 of the Regulations. In the field of integrated circuits, designers draw integrated circuit layouts through computer-aided drafting (CAD) software, and these two-dimensional graphics form three-dimensional products through manufacturing processes. It can be seen that the process, as a processing process, actually displays the multi-layered two-dimensional graphics in the layout of the integrated circuit in a three-dimensional structure. For example, in the *Qi Rui* case, it was controversial whether the two sides had a substantial similarity judgment on the oral trap and the Tianzi trap, and the accreditation agency stated that the arrangement of the four capacitors in the shape of a square was a layout and was placed in several wells. Capacitors belong to the process rather than the layout. The Court took into account in the trial that N-type is a kind of process, and that CMOS devices prepared by this process, regardless of whether the use of square or square type, do not change the connection relationship between the four capacitive components in this case, and therefore do not constitute a substantial change in layout design.

(2) Considering the similarity of the layout design to the "priority criteria for component combinations"

In accordance with Article 2 paragraph 2 of the Regulations, the Court, in conjunction with the appraisal opinion, expressed its biased opinions on the order of factors to be considered when judging whether the two layout designs constitute substantive similarities. That is, in addition to considering the three-dimensional configuration of the interconnection lines, the configuration of the combination of elements connected by the interconnection lines in the three-dimensional space is more important when determining whether the layout designs are substantially similar.

First of all, from a technical perspective, the functions implemented by the chip actually depend on the configuration of the components. In the case of *Atera y. Clear*

Logic in the U.S., the District Court held that "the grouping and connection of duplicated transistors may constitute a violation of the SCPA. It also recognizes that the organization and layout of components are actually part of the masked work. The District Court allows the jury to confirm whether the similarity of these structures constitutes infringement, the masked work is different from an outline of an article or a chapter in the book and the configuration of these components actually determines which specific functions the chip will implement. The logical grouping of masked works is not An abstract concept, which is embodied in the chip products, affects the performance and efficiency of the chip, and it can be seen that when comparing the two parts of the integrated circuit layout design, the combination of the elements connected by the interconnection lines is the most direct configuration in the three-dimensional space. This affects the performance of the chip, so this configuration is most important when judging whether the layout design is substantially similar.

Second, after removing the aforementioned conceptual levels that do not fall under the scope of protection of integrated circuit layout design, from the concept level, the embodiment of originality is gradually strengthened, such as the comprehensive selection of various technologies at the conceptual level, the distribution of components, and the layout of components. Such as these, more originality can better reflect the designer's intellectual contribution, as shown in Figure 2, for the specific location of the components and the combination of components will reflect the originality of the integrated circuit layout designers to a very high degree. The exact location of the components will be subject to stricter legal protection.

Figure 2   Expression of Originality and Its Level of Protection

Layers to be protected	Content
Concepts	Five Structures, Eight technologies, Five functions
Choices	Component number, Integration level, Technical target, Material
Arrangement	Positions of the components
Interconnection	Connections within and among chips, signal relation
Parameter	Technical parameters for technical targets and functions

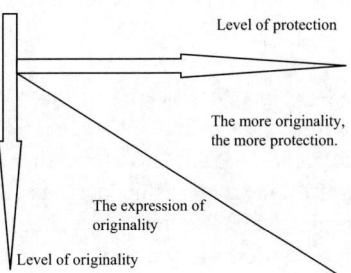

Finally, as mentioned above, the Court of Yan Rui believes that stricter "substantive similarity" criteria should be adopted, that is, only very similar layout designs are deemed to be substantially similar, thus constituting a copying act infringement. According to this standard, there is the possibility of evading the law and illegally copying other people's layout designs by making a slight change to the layout of the layout. This is because a slight change in the orientation of the interconnection lines in the three-dimensional configuration is not only technically and technologically difficult, but these slight changes in the interconnection lines do not affect the signal relationships or the technical parameters for implementing the functions. Therefore, it is necessary to distinguish the focus of judgment.

In the case of *Jurui*, the Defendant proposed that there is a difference in the routing direction of the "layout between a digital ground track and a simulated ground track" on the M2 floor, except that the wiring of the M2 floor is in another cloth in a layout. Change the adjacent layer in the figure. After combining the expert opinion of the Court, the Court analyzed that after considering the M2 layer, the combination and relative position of the components connected to the disputed wiring did not change, so the three-dimensional configuration presented by the combination of wiring and interconnected components was not changed. Without substantial changes, it is not sufficient to influence the juxtaposition of the layout design of the two parties. It can be seen that the Court has consistently adhered to more stringent substantive similarity criteria in the case of *Jurui*.

In summary, when the layout design is considered to be substantially similar, priority is given to the configuration of the components presented in the three-dimensional space, but it is not to say that the configuration of the interconnection lines in the three-dimensional space is not taken into account because there may be interconnection lines. Clearly different layout designs. At this point, it is necessary to consider whether the difference in the connection has an effect on the performance. If the impact is large, the three-dimensional dimension configuration is considered to be different and the layout design is not substantially similar.

Conclusion:

In summary, the scope of layout design protection follows nonproportional standards, and IC infringement cases are judged through originality and more stringent "substantive similarity" criteria. That is, regardless of whether the part of the layout design that was illegally duplicated occupies the entire integrated circuit layout design, or whether the layout design of this part is the core part of the whole layout design, the stricter "substantive similarity" criterion is adopted. To determine whether there is a substantial similar layout design, and then based on the evidence provided by the parties on the originality, with a "high degree of likeliness" as the standard of proof, to determine whether the existence of a substantial similar layout design needs to be protected by law. The process of constructing the infringement judgment standard of the integrated circuit layout design is the exploration process in which the Court balances the interests of all parties in the industry, protects the legitimate rights and interests, respects the industrial practice and fully and effectively encourages industrial innovation.

—**Comments by DING Wenlian**

CHAPTER 4
Other Issues concerning Copyright-Related Disputes

Case 23. The Principle of "Technological Neutrality" and Its Scope

Beijing Xingguangcanlan Technology Service Co., Ltd. v. BesTV Network Television Technology Development Co., Ltd.; Nanjing Sharp Electronics Co., Ltd.; and Beijing Dazhong Electrical Appliance Sales Co., Ltd.
Case of Related rights of Recorders Infringement Dispute
Case Index: ***Beijing Xingguangcanlan Technology Service Co., Ltd. v. BesTV Network Television Technology Development Co., Ltd.; Nanjing Sharp Electronics Co., Ltd.; and Beijing Dazhong Electrical Appliance Sales Co., Ltd.;*** Shijingshan District People's Court of Beijing, Shi Min Chu Zi [2012] No. 4913, December 6, 2013; Beijing No. 1 Intermediate People's Court, Yi Zhong Min Chu Zi [2014] No. 2641, May 20, 2014.

Facts:

Sony China Corporate (hereinafter, "Sony") is the producer of DVD albums *Looking Up*, *Missing Style* and *Fully Fire*. On December 15, 2010, Sony issued a power of attorney to authorize the Plaintiff Beijing Xingguangcanlan Technology Service Co., Ltd. (hereinafter, "Xingguangcanlan") to file lawsuits against any infringement of copyright and related rights of the sound and video recordings produced by Sony.

In March 2012, Xingguangcanlan notarized the purchase of a LCD-32LH440A TV produced by the Defendant Nanjing Sharp Electronics Co., Ltd. (hereinafter, "Sharp") from Beijing Dazhong Electrical Appliance Sales Co., Ltd. (hereinafter, "Dazhong").

In the first instance, the Court found that: After being connected to the server of BesTV Network TV Technology Development Co., Ltd. (hereinafter, "BesTV") via the

Internet, the involved Sharp TV is able to play the five music videos including *Looking Up*, *Defective Beauty*, *Re-understand Me*, *Missing Style* and *That Song*. They are identical to the five music videos claimed by Xingguangcanlan. In addition, another twenty-one music videos including *Fully Fire*, *Big City Little Love*, *Still in Love with You* were played by the involved TV. The sound content of the twenty-one works are basically the same in their basic melody, performer, orchestration, style, duration as the works contained in the sound and video recordings of Xingguangcanlan.

BesTV obtained the digital files of the involved music videos from Xingkonghuawen Company according to an agreement between the two companies. Then BesTV integrated the music videos in its digital broadcast platform, and make the music videos available to the users who purchase the involved Sharp TV to access to its digital platform by specific links via online method. Users of the involved Sharp TV can play the videos on-demand anytime, and do not need to pay separately for the play.

Ruling and Reasoning:

On December 6, 2013, Shijingshan District People's Court of Beijing ruled that: (1) BesTV shall immediately cease to make available to the public the music videos *Looking Up*, *Missing Style*, *Fully Fire* and other twenty-three videos. (2) Sharp and BesTV shall compensate Xingguangcanlan RMB 80,000 in total, which includes the economic losses of RMB 60,000 and the reasonable expenses of RMB 20,000. (3) The other claims by the Plaintiff are rejected.

Sharp and BesTV appealed to Beijing No. 1 Intermediate People's Court. Sharp appealed that: According to the principle of "technological neutrality," Sharp shall not be liable for the infringement. Therefore, the judgment of the first instance shall be revoked.

In the second instance, Beijing No. 1 Intermediate People's Court held that: Sharp connected the involved TV to BesTV's server by the specific links, which enabled the involved videos to be played online. Sine such an act and the act by BesTV constitute joint infringement of right of communication of information on networks enjoyed by the Xingguangcanlan, so Sharp and BesTV shall bear joint liability. Regarding the argument that the principle of "technological neutrality" shall be applicable, the TVs involved in this case are Internet TVs, which are different from ordinary TVs, because they have an extra special feature of connecting to the Internet. In terms of the Internet function, the involved TVs do not provide initial links, general links or links provided by search engines of the full Internet. Based on the commercial cooperation between Sharp and BesTV, the Sharp TVs only provide specific links to BesTV's server. Since Sharp selects BesTV as its exclusive content partner for the involved TV, it should take a higher duty of care for the content from BesTV. Base on the facts that what the involved TVs make available to the public are the specific links to specific database for commercial purpose, Sharp has obviously lost its position of technological neutrality and such principle should not be applicable. In summary, since the petitions by Sharp are lack of factual and legal basis, they are dismissed.

Chapter 4: Other Issues concerning Copyright-Related Disputes

Commentary:

Since technology is neutral, technology itself is not legal or illegal. Regarding the principle of "technological neutrality," one of the most important references for China is the 1984 *Sony* case in U.S. According to the *"Sony"* rule, also known as the "substantial noninfringement uses" rule, if a product has the function for both legal and illegal uses, the provider can be exempted from the infringement liabilities. However, from the U.S. legislative practice, such technologies are not always covered by the *"Sony"* rule. For example, according to the *1992 Audio Home Recording Act* (*AHRA*), digital recording equipment manufactured, sold, and imported into U.S. must have technological measures to control the copy, so that the copy cannot be reproduced; and manufacturers, sellers and importers of the digital music recording equipment must pay royalties in proportion of the sales price to compensate copyright owners. The *1998 Digital Millennium Copyright Act* (*DMCA*) clarifies not only the obligations relating to technological measures, but also the "safe harbor" rule for the liabilities of the Internet service providers, which is a response to the *"Sony"* rule regarding the responsibilities for third parties. This indicates that since the *Sony* case in 1984, legislators have banned or restricted products or business models that can provide substantial noninfringing uses on multiple occasions.[1] The principle of "technological neutrality" cannot be the excuse for manufacturers and service providers of dual-use technologies to ignore the potential harm to the copyright owners. To be more specific, manufacturers and service providers of use dual-use technologies should strive to take necessary measures to limit and minimize the potential damage caused by the illegal use.

In the Internet environment, the principle of "technological neutrality" is also known as "network neutrality." Network providers should not discriminate the content they transmit. The network is like a highway and its managers should take a neutral position. They should treated cars of different brands equally, and not distinguish or limit the brands of cars driving on the roads, and car manufactures and vendors. When the highway manager only allows specific cars to drive on, he certainly does not treat all cars equally, thus loses the neutral position. Logically, regarding the issue of copyright infringement, the principle of "technological neutrality" shall not be applicable to this kind of manufacturers and service providers.

The Internet TV involved in this case is a product that has become a "two-in-one" device, which can be used not only as a general TV, but also as an Internet terminal. While the function of Internet access has added new appeal to consumers, the involved TV also causes new Internet-related copyright issues. If the Internet TV manufacturers do not adjust their own thinking of the principle of "technological neutrality," and do not take necessary measures to restrict and minimize the risk of the infringement of the right of communication of information on networks, they may leave the scope of the principle of "technological neutrality." At present, Internet TVs usually have two modes of obtaining content, which are a specific database search and a full Internet

---

1. Liang Zhiwen, Cloud Computing, Technological Neutrality and Copyright Liabilities, *Law Science*, 3 (2011).

search. It is certain that the TVs of full Internet search are within the scope of the principle of "technological neutrality." Even considering the particularity of the TVs, the scope of the principle of "technological neutrality" can only be extended to the TVs of the search mode of all professional video websites all video databases. This approach is similar to that of the highway: in order to keep the normal function of highway, the managers can limit the minimum speed so that the slow cars are not allowed to travel on the road. To build in a function module in the Internet TV so that it can only be connected to specific database by specific links is similar to the case that the highway manager only allows the cars from specific company to travel on the road. Since this business model is not neutral to all the TV programs on the Internet, it is definitely not within the scope of the principle of "technological neutrality."

In this case, Sharp adopted a built-in function module in the Internet TV, which allowed the TV to be exclusively connected to BesTV's server for a specific database search. Sharp's decision of cooperating with BesTV as its only Internet content provider does not violate the law. However, while this business model has brought steady profits to Sharp, it also changed Sharp's position as a neutral manufacturer and pushed Sharp away from the scope of the principle of "technological neutrality." Based on the equivalent principle of rights and obligations, Sharp should also bear a higher duty of examination of the content played by the TVs for any copyright infringement. At the beginning of the cooperation with BesTV, Sharp should have examined the content within the database of BesTV in advance, and take necessary measures to review the content during the cooperation with BesTV. By doing this, Sharp can minimize its risk for copyright infringement. Meanwhile, Sharp can also help BesTV to pay more attention to protect the copyright on the Internet, making this commercial cooperation model of prosperity. However, in this case, Sharp ignored the new problems brought by the Internet TV, and did not examine the Internet content from BesTV. As a result, Sharp shall bear the joint infringement liability when BesTV directly infringed the right of communication of information on networks of the Plaintiff Xingguangcanlan.

—**Comments by QIANG Ganghua**

Case 24. Availability of Preliminary Injunction in the Cases of Infringement of Moral Rights

YANG Jikang v. Sungari International Auction Co., Ltd. and etc.
Case of application for Preliminary Injunction
Case Index: YANG Jikang v. Sungari International Auction Co., Ltd. and etc.; Beijing No. 2 Intermediate People's Court, Er Zhong Bao Zi [2013] No. 9727, June 3, 2013.

Facts:

Qian Zhongshu (deceased) was a famous Chinese writer and literary researcher. His wife Yang Jikang (pseudonym as Yang Jiang) is a famous Chinese writer and translator. The couple had a daughter Qian Yuan (deceased). The family used to communicate closely and frequently with Li Guoqiang, the editor-in-chief of the monthly magazine *Wide Angle* by letters. The personal manuscripts of the letter by the three should have been kept by the addressee Li Guoqiang. However, in May 2013, Sungari International Auction Co., Ltd. (Hereinafter, "Sungari") announced that it would hold a special auction event for Qian Zhongshu's correspondence manuscripts, and related preexhibitions and seminars at the 2013 Spring Auction. The number of the involved correspondence manuscripts written by Qian Zhongshu, Yang Jiang and Qian Yuan to Li Guoqiang is approximately one hundred. As soon as the announcement was made, a number of media reported on the matter and published some correspondences and research articles. The Applicant Yang Jikang expressed her disagreement with the publication of the copyrighted personal correspondence manuscripts for several times. In the absence of positive feedback, Yang Jikang filed an application to the court for a preliminary injunction to stop the copyright infringement, and provided a legitimate and effective guaranty.

The Respondent Sungari asserted: Sungari has made plans to hold special auction event for Qian Zhongshu's correspondence manuscripts, and related preexhibitions and seminars. The planned auctions include the letters written by Qian Zhongshu, Yang Jikang and Qian Yuan. Sungari did not review the status of copyright ownership of the involved letters in advance, and did not obtain authorization from the copyright owner.

Ruling and Reasoning:

Beijing No. 2 Intermediate People's Court held that: The copyright of the private correspondences involved as a written work protected by copyright law shall be enjoyed by the author, i.e., the sender. Any person, including the addressee and any other person lawfully obtaining the correspondence manuscripts, must not infringe upon the legitimate rights and interests of copyright owe in the disposition of the manuscripts. Given that the copyright owner explicitly disagree to make the involved works available to the public, Sungari's behavior of public preview and public auction constitutes the infringement of the right of publication of the copyright owner. If such behavior is not prevented promptly, it is likely to cause irreparable harm to the copyright owner. Therefore, in accordance with Article 10, Article 19, Article 21 and

Article 50 of the *Copyright Law*; Article 17 of the *Regulations for the Implementation of the Copyright Law*; Article 10 and Article 11 of the *Succession Law*; Article 100, Article 101 and Article 108 of the *Civil Procedure Law*; Article 30 of the *Interpretation of the Supreme People's Court on Issues Concerning the Application of Law in the Trial of Cases of Civil Dispute of Copyright*, Beijing No. 2 Intermediate People's Court ruled: Sungari shall not infringe the copyright of correspondence manuscripts written by Qian Zhongshu, Yang Jiang, Qian Yuan to Li Guoqiang by the way of publication, exhibition, reproduction, distribution, communication of information on networks in the activities of auction, preview and promotion. The ruling shall be executed immediately after delivery. If Sungari does not accept the ruling, it may apply to the Court for reconsideration within ten days from the date of delivery of the ruling. During the reconsideration period, the execution of the ruling will not be suspended.

After the injunction was issued, the Respondent Sungari immediately issued a statement to voluntarily stop the auction involved in the case.

Commentary:

The system of temporary injunction was officially introduced into China to enhance the protection of intellectual property after China became a member of the WTO. The rules relating to temporary injunction are further clarified in the *Copyright Law, Trademark Law, Patent Law* and judicial interpretations. Since 2000, the temporary injunction system has been well developed and widely applied in China. Temporary injunction plays an important role in protecting intellectual property, especially in the case of imminent infringements. This case is the first temporary injunction issued by the Chinese court concerning the infringement of moral rights, and it is also the first injunction against infringement of copyright after the implementation of the newly revised *Civil Procedure Law*.

Temporary injunction is a compulsory order that the court prohibits or restricts the perpetrator from engaging in certain behaviors in order to promptly stop the ongoing or pending infringement of the intellectual property rights according to the application of the party, the purpose in which is to protect the right owner' intellectual property rights from continuing infringement, preventing the irreparable damage as well.

The examination of the application of the preliminary temporary injunction, that is, under what circumstances the application of the applicant shall be approved, which may be expressed slightly differently in different countries, but their meanings are generally consistent. In the Chinese judicial practice, the factors that are commonly considered include that: The right on which the applicant makes the application is true and reliable; The alleged infringement is being or is about to be committed; The specific measures taken in the ruling beforehand can prevent applicants from being irreparably damaged; The measures taken in the ruling beforehand will not cause damage to the other legitimate rights and interests of the respondent, nor jeopardize the public interests. In the application of the preliminary temporary injunction, there are no uniform standards and detailed rules in practice in our country, and the application of rules still need further study and improvement. As for this case, how to timely and effectively protect the moral rights and relevant interests of copyright owners with correspondence manuscripts and how to balance the conflicts of interests between the Applicant and the Respondent are two major issues in the study.

1. The infringed moral rights can be protected by a preliminary injunction.

What kinds of damage can be decided to be irreparable? The court's judgment standards for "irreparable damage" are constantly evolving and changing over time. The U.S. Federal Court of Appeal has accumulated experience by judging, that to judge whether it constitutes irreparable damage or not, the following points should be considered comprehensively: (1)Timeliness of application by applicant; (2) Whether the damage can be remedied by the means of pecuniary compensation; (3) Whether the infringing act is ongoing. "Irreparable" damage emphasizes that it cannot be measured with money, and if the loss of the applicant can be measured and compensated for only by money, it is not the damage considered in the preliminary injunction. In a sense, the damage of nonproperty interests, such as goodwill and the declining of potential share of intellectual property and competitive position in the market, etc., whether the applicant delays the application intentionally, and whether the respondent constitutes a continuous injury, which are all considered in the preliminary injunction to confirm "irreparable damage." In the patent infringement case of *Amazon.com, Inc. v. Barnesandnoble.com, Inc. and Barnesandnoble.com, LIc*, the U.S. Federal Court of Appeal made a general interpretation of "irreparable damage" that the damage can be regarded as irreparable if the applicant's patent right is really valid and patent infringement was clearly evident. On the measurement of irreparable damage, the U.S. court held that the requirement for proof of the possibility of recovering could be reduced when there is clear evidence that irreparable damage exists. Because the existence of irreparable damage has largely proved the existence of respondent's infringement act; on the contrary, if it is possible to prove the possibility of recovering, then the burden of proof on the irreparable loss can be mitigated. This view has been accepted and widely used in American judicial practice, however, the degree of applying to which varies with different cases. In complex and difficult cases, it is not easy to prove the possibility of recovering, and then the weight of proof of applicant that serious irreparable damage would be brought about for the applicant's failure to take action should be increased. On the contrary, in cases where it is relatively easy to determine infringement or not, if there is a great possibility to prove the possibility of recovering, then the requirement upon applicant for proof of irreparable damage will be relatively weakened. Compared with the U.S. courts focusing on whether the respondent is infringing, British courts pay more attention to whether the respondent is capable of paying pecuniary compensation. In the 1970s, the *Polaroid Corporation v. Eastman Kodak. Co.* case in Britain summed up the following criteria. If applicants can make up for all losses in the form of monetary compensation in future litigation, the possibility of applying an injunction is very slim. By analogy, when the applicant has received sufficient monetary compensation before the review of the preliminary injunction is completed, and then the respondent should no longer be subject to an injunction.

In summary, in terms of intellectual property litigation, to determine the irreparable losses, the following factors may be considered generally that: (1) Plaintiff's personality interests are damaged. The good evaluation obtained by intellectual property right owners over a long period of time, such as goodwill, social status and so on, cannot be measured by the property interests once they have been infringed, and this kind of damage will bring great suffering to the spirit of the intellectual property right owners. It is also difficult to make up for the bad effects in a short period of time. (2) The plaintiff's loss is difficult to estimate, such as the change in market share, the loss of competitive position, the listing of new products and the immeasurable socio-economic value that the new products bring to the applicant. In *Hybritec Inc. v. Abbott Labs.*, the judge took into account the factors that the applicant's share in the market, how well the sales of respondent is in the market after infringement, how difficult it is for other competitors to enter the market and the development speed of the industry, etc. to decide whether to apply the preliminary injunction. For example, when a plaintiff encounters an overseas enterprise promoting a new product which infringes upon the plaintiff's existing intellectual property right in its own country or region. The plaintiff would apply for a preliminary injunction to prohibit the defendant from continuing to sell. In such cases, the plaintiff's original market share is damaged and could not be measured in terms of money.

The copyright law of our country stipulates four kinds of copyright-related personal rights, that is, the right of publication, the right of authorship, the right of revision and the right of integrity. Among them, the right of publication is also called the right of disclosure. The exercise of the right of publication is the premise for the copyright owners to obtain property interests and other spiritual interests, which plays a very important role for copyright owners. Under the copyright system of civil law countries, due to the principle of automatic acquisition of copyright, the creation of a work means the creation of copyright, which has nothing to do with the publication of the work, but it does not affect the significance of the right of publication. Italian copyright scholar Dessenktis once said that just as publishing right is the most important thing among the economic rights of literary works, copyright owners have the right of publication in the first place for the moral rights over all works. If they do not exercise his right of publication after the completion of the creation of the work, no other moral or economic rights can be exercised. Mr. Wei Zhi[2] also agrees that publication is the most important way to realize copyright, because only by publishing the work can the author realize the benefits he enjoys. I consider that the right of publication includes not only the author's right to decide whether to make a work available to the public and when, where and by which means to make it available to the public(i.e., the right of determination),but also the right to prohibit others from publishing their unpublished work and the contents of the work without authorization (i.e., the right of prohibition).The protection of intangible property rights is different from that of tangible property rights. Epistolary works involve the protection of intangible property rights such as copyright. Once they are auctioned and made public,

---

2. Wei Zhi, a professor of law at Huazhong University of Science and Technology, graduated from Ludwig Maximilian University in Munich, Germany, with a doctorate in Law.

the loss will inevitably be irreparable. In view of this situation, Copyright law expressly provides that "Where a copyright owner or an owner of a right related to the copyright who can present evidence to prove that another person is committing, or is about to commit, an infringement upon his right, which, unless prevented promptly, is likely to cause irreparable harm to his legitimate rights and interests, he may, before taking legal proceedings, apply to a People's Court for measures to order discontinuation of the infringement and to preserve property. The court may, at the request of the plaintiff, order the defendant to stop infringement. "In this case, the correspondence manuscripts in question are tangible in a view of several sheets of paper and could be kept by the defendant since they are addressed to him. But they also carry the work, and from the perspective of the work, the copyright attached to them has not been transferred, including the right of publication. The addressee shall not publish others' letters freely without their consent; otherwise it will result in infringement. Once the right of publication is infringed, then irreparable losses will be caused, because the right of publication can only be exercised once actively, and once exercised, the right is exhausted. The right of publication can be negatively exercised many times although only once be exercised actively. According to the above, it can be seen that making the work available to the public against the author's will does not constitute publication. The author's right of publication is still in place and the author can sue the infringer based on his right of publication. After that, if another person makes the work available to the public against the author's will, the author can still ask the law to punish the act in order to defend his own publishing interests.

2. Public interest and the balance of interests.

The public interest is not a necessary factor in the application of a preliminary injunction, but a very important reason for its applicability. There are multiple levels of understanding to the "public interest," not only the tangible benefits of most strangers that most people can recognize, but also social costs, freedom of speech, and many other aspects. When excessive protection limits free competition, it will discourage the development of innovation. From the perspective of economics, when the cost of applying a preliminary injunction to protect an intellectual property right is greater than the wealth created by the intellectual property right for society, the court should not decide to apply the preliminary injunction. The fact that the court issues an injunction before the verdict on the substantive issue of the lawsuit to require the defendant to act or not or even decides to not issue the injunction, would have an impact on the public interest. In most cases, therefore, courts have taken into account nonparty interest damages, regardless of whether they participate in the proceedings. Because the number of nonparty is very extensive, nonparty damage must be limited in the determination, that is to say, the third party must have the factual damage and be sufficient to obtain relief through the litigation. Of course, not every preliminary injunction concerns public interest, and sometimes the public interest may not be taken into account because of its transience, but if the subject matter of case itself is public interest, then the public interest is a very important consideration.

In addition, in order to stop infringement, court should consider both justice and efficiency and pay attention to the balance of interests when reviewing the preliminary injunction. Fairness and Justice are the fate or fundamental pursuit of law and justice. The concept of Justice for the prelitigation evidence preservation system, which is that not only to guarantee the realization of the legitimate rights of the right owners, but also to prevent the loss that may be caused to the respondent by wrong preservation. For the prelitigation evidence preservation system, due to the vague understanding to the purpose and boundary of the system and the practical difficulties caused by the nonspecific rules in practice, it is even more important to emphasize the principle of balance of interests in the exercise of judicial power.

Under the circumstances that people from all walks of life are paying close attention to the forthcoming large-scale exposure of Qian Zhongshu's manuscripts, the court took full account of the possible impact of the case on social public interests and accurately issued a judicial injunction, which not only effectively protected the rights of copyright owner, but also avoided the impact on auction company and related publics. It will contribute to the promotion of the protection of copyright and privacy of the sender by society, especially by the addressee.

—**Comments by LI Dan**

Case 25. Enforceability of a Contract of Transferring Copyright of an Unfinished Work

Shanghai Xuanting Entertainment & Information Technology Co., Ltd. v. WANG Zhong Case of Commissioned Works and Copyright Transfer Contract Dispute
Case Index: *Shanghai Xuanting Entertainment & Information Technology Co., Ltd. v. WANG Zhong;* Pudong District People's Court of Shanghai, Pu Min San (Zhi) Chu Zi [2010] No. 424, May 4, 2011; Shanghai No. 1 Intermediate People's Court, Hu Yi Zhong Min Wu (Zhi) Zhong Zi [2011] No. 136, May 4, 2012

Facts:

Shanghai Xuanting Entertainment & Information Technology Co., Ltd. (hereinafter, "Xuanting") was the operator of www.Qidian.com, a Chinese original literature portal. Since 2006, Wang Zhong (pseudonym as Mengrushenji) had published several works including *Buddha is Tao* and *Devil of the Black Mountain* on the website operated by Xuanting, and entered into several agreements with Xuanting whereby exclusively authorized or transferred his copyright, including the right of communication of information on networks, of the relevant works to Xuanting. In the meantime, Xuanting paid to Wang Zhong approximately RMB 2,000,000 in total for the remuneration.

On January 18, 2010, Xuanting (as Party A) and Wang Zhong (as Party B) signed the "Agreement on the Works of Platinum Writer." According to Article 3.2.1, Party B agrees and acknowledges to permanently transfer to Party A the right of communication of information on networks and the right to digitally compile, adapt, reproduce and publish all works created by him within four years from the effective date of the Agreement. (The "works of Agreement" include all versions in different languages, regardless whether the works have been completed, which means all finished and unfinished works.) Party B acknowledges and agrees that the above-mentioned assignment includes the exclusion of Party B from exercising on his own or transferring, authorizing to any third party to exercise or transfer the rights. According to Article 4.2.4, Party B represents and promises that it never digitally publishes, uses or develops, or authorizes any third party to digitally publishes, uses or develops, his works (including "works of Agreement") around the world. Where any of the above-mentioned situations occurs to Party B or any works of Agreement by Party B, Party B shall be deemed as breaching of the Agreement. In such case, Party B agrees to refund all relevant remunerations and expenses paid by Party A, and Party A is entitled to suspend, cancel and terminate the Agreement. Besides, Party B shall assume all legal liabilities thereby and indemnify Party A for any losses. In addition, according to Article 7.2.2, where Party B breaches Articles 3.2.5, 3.2.6, 3.2.8, 4.2.4, 4.2.5, it shall pay Party A the penalty of RMB 10,000 plus the sum for ten times of the total amount of fees obtained from Party A. Where the penalty is insufficient compensate for the losses of Party A, Party B shall indemnify Party A for the actual losses in addition to the penalty and Party A is entitled to suspend, cancel or terminate the Agreement immediately.

Moreover, on the same day, Xuanting (as Party A) and Wang Zhong (as Party B) signed the "Agreement on Creation of Commissioned Works." According to Article 3.2.1, both parties agrees that the ownership of copyright and relevant derivative rights in the works of Agreement created by Party B, who is the "exclusive author," on the commission of Party A (all the works commissioned by Party A, including but not limited to all types of works enumerated by Article 3 of the *Copyright Law*) are exclusively owned by Party A. (The exclusivity in this Agreement covers Party B. Party A exclusively enjoys the complete copyright of the works of Agreement which has been completed and delivered to Party A, or created under the organization of Party A, in regardless of whether Party B has finished the works of Agreement or has delivered all works to Party A.) The content of copyright of the works of Agreement owned by Party A includes, but not limited to all moral rights and economic rights enumerated by Article 10 of the *Copyright Law*. According to Article 1.1.7, without a written consent by Party A, Party B, as an "exclusive author," shall not transfer any type of works created by himself in his real name, pseudonym or any other name during the term of this Agreement (including works of Agreement) to any third party to publish, use or develop the works, or permit a third party to publish, use or develop the works, or create works for any third party. Such works include but not limited to all types of works enumerated by Article 3 of the *Copyright Law*. Party B is regarded as an "exclusive author" within the terms of the Agreement. Article 1.1.4 defines the "term of the Agreement" as the duration from the day this Agreement is executed to the day that all works of Agreement are completed and delivered to Party A by Party B. However, if Party B failed to finish any work for any reason, or any work finished by Party B does not meet with the outline of the works or does not fulfill with the commission purpose, the term of Agreement shall therefore expire on the date when all the works of Agreement recognized by Party A are finished. For the purpose of the Agreement, "the term of this Agreement" does not mean that this Agreement will lose its binding force and legal effect to both parties thereafter. Actually, it represents semantically a definition of time for both parties for implementing the Agreement. According to Article 3.2.2, Party B, as the "exclusive author" who is remunerated by Party A, warrants that it will create works for Party A exclusively, or it only creates the works of Agreement for Party A, which means the ownership of copyright and relevant derivative rights in the works created by party B during the term of the Agreement is exclusively owned by Party A (including the works commissioned by Party A, the works of Agreement and the works created for a third party, with or without Party A's written consent). The above-mentioned copyright includes, but not limited to moral rights and economic rights enumerated by Article 10 of the *Copyright Law*. Or else, Party B agrees to refund all associated amount from Party A and assume the liabilities for the breach of the Agreement. According to Article 4.1.6, when the copyright in any work other than the works of Agreement by Party B beyond the term of Agreement involves the use, assignment and authorization of use of such work, Party A shall precede over any third party to obtain the assignment or the authorization of use under the equal condition, and Party B shall provide Party A with necessary convenience to exercise such preemption. Unless Party A fails to exercise the preemption within thirty days after receiving a written notice from Party B, Party B shall not transfer any other

Chapter 4: Other Issues concerning Copyright-Related Disputes

work or permit any third party to exercise the copyright. Otherwise, Party B will be deemed as breach of the Agreement. According to the Article 4.2.1, Party B shall begin submit to Party A no later than January 25, 2011 and the minimum words of monthly submission shall be no less than 100,000. According to Article 5.1.1, the remuneration of Party B shall be calculated based on the word count of the works of Agreement at the rate of RMB 330 per 1,000 words before taxes. According to Article 5.2.1, Party A shall pay Party B RMB 100,000 as advance payment (from which the remuneration to Party B may be deducted) within thirty working days after the Agreement takes effect. According to 7.2.1, where Party B breaches Article 4.2, it shall pay Party A the penalty of RMB 400,000 plus the total amount of fees obtained from Party A. Where the penalty is insufficient compensate for the losses of Party A, Party B shall indemnify Party A for the actual losses in addition to the penalty, and Party A is entitled to suspend, cancel or terminate the Agreement immediately. According to Article 7.2.2, where Party B breaches Articles 3.2, 4.1.6, 7.2.3, or transfer or exercises (including transfers to any third party or authorizes any third party to exercise) any right (including the preemption owned by Party A) attributable to Party A in a manner of breaching the Agreement, it shall pay Party A the penalty of RMB 10,000 per 10,000 words of the work (including the works of Agreement), which Party B transfers or exercises any right without the written consent of Party A, in addition to the penalty provided in Article 7.2.1. Where the penalty is insufficient to compensate for the losses of Party A, Party B shall indemnify Party A for the actual losses in addition to the penalty, and Party A is entitled to suspend, cancel or terminate the Agreement immediately.

As agreed, on February 10, 2010, Xuanting paid Wang Zhong RMB 100,000 as the in-advance funds for creation.

On June 18, 2010, Beijing Huanxiangzongheng Network Technology Co., Ltd. (hereinafter, "Huanxiang") (as Party A) signed a "Contract of Labor" with Wang Zhong (as Party B). According to the Contract, Wang Zhong would act as the director of game design department of Huanxiang with a term of five years at the salary of RMB 5,000 per month. According to the Contract, the copyright in any work for hire created by Party B that are requested by Party A shall be owned by Party A, and it will be Party A's responsibility to settle all disputes relating to the works for hire. The job responsibilities of Party B include: Party B shall create works for hire that are requested by Huanxiang, and the words of monthly submission of the works for hire shall be no less than 100,000 but no more than 350,000. The total word count of each work for hire shall be over 2,000,000 words. Any work for hire with 300,000 words released on www.zongheng.com shall rank top ten of the most popular works on the website. Party B promises that all works for hire are original and do not infringe any others' intellectual property rights. Besides the basic salary, Huanxiang will offer party B bonuses depending on the performance by Party B. Meanwhile, the bonuses may be reduced in proportion if Party B breaches or fails to fulfill the above-mentioned job responsibilities. Meanwhile, the two parties signed an "Agreement on Intellectual Property Ownership and Confidentiality."

On July 18, 2010, Wang Zhong began to release his novel *The Eternal Life* on Zongheng (www.zongheng.com) with the pseudonym "Mengrushenji." By March 3, 2011, the work had 1,792,144 words released, which was still being uploaded.

In the first instance, Xuanting claimed that: (1) Wang Zhong shall continue to execute the "Agreement on the Works of Platinum Writer" and the "Agreement on Creation of Commissioned Works," and cease to release any work created by him on any other website (including but not limited to www.zongheng.com). (2) Wang Zhong shall pay the liquidated damages RMB 1,010,000. (3) The copyright of the work *The Eternal Life* created by Wang Zhong shall be owned by Xuanting. Wang Zhong filed a counterclaim, requesting that the "Agreement on the Works of Platinum Writer" shall be rescinded and the "Agreement on Creation of Commissioned Works" shall be terminated.

Ruling and Reasoning:

In the first instance, Pudong District People's court of Shanghai held that: The "Agreement on the Works of Platinum Writer" was signed between two equal parties, and represented their true intentions. It is reciprocal to both parties and satisfies the principle of "equality, free will and mutual benefit" of the contract law. Therefore, the "Agreement on the Works of Platinum Writer" does not satisfy the conditions for revocation according to the contract law. The "Agreement on Creation of Commissioned Works" is lawful and valid, thus it shall be allowed to continue. Since the novel *The Eternal Life* was created by Wang Zhong within the term agreed by both Xuanting and Wang Zhong, therefore Xuanting is the owner of the copyright of the involved work. Despite that there were two agreements between Xuanting and Wang Zhong, Wang Zhong still published the involved work on Zongheng (www.zongheng.com). Such behaviors had obvious intent to breach the agreements and should bear the liabilities. The Court ruled that: (1) Xuanting and Wang Zhong shall continue to execute the "Agreement on the Works of Platinum Writer" signed on January 18, 2010. (2) Xuanting and Wang Zhong shall continue to execute the "Agreement on Creation of Commissioned Works" signed on January 18, 2010. (3) Wang Zhong shall stop publishing of *The Eternal Life* on Zongheng (www.zongheng.com). (4) Wang Zhong shall pay RMB 200,000 to Xuanting as liquidated damages within ten days after the ruling takes effect. (5) Xuanting is the owner of the copyright of the work *The Eternal Life* created by Wang Zhong (except the rights that cannot be transferred under law). (6) Other claims of Xuanting are dismissed. (7) All claims of Wang Zhong are dismissed.

Wang Zhong and the third party Huanxiang in the first trial refused to accept, and appealed.

In the second instance, Shanghai No. 1 Intermediate People's Court held that: It is lawful that Xuanting shall be the owner of the copyright of the work *The Eternal Life*. However, if the agreements are performed continuously, such performance will lead to the consequence that Wang Zhong will be forced to create works. Due to the breach of agreements by Wang Zhong, the purpose of the agreements cannot be achieved. Thus, the agreements may be cancelled, but Wang Zhong should be liable for the breach of contract. Therefore, the Court ruled that: (1) Uphold the fifth item in the judgment of Pu Min San (Zhi) Chu Zi [2010] No. 424. (2) Reverse the first, second, third, forth, sixth, seventh items. (3) The "Agreement on the Works of Platinum Writer" and the "Agreement on Creation of Commissioned Works" shall be cancelled. (4) Wang Zhong shall pay RMB 600,000 to Xuanting as liquidated damages.

Commentary:

The case is relevant to the business model relating to the commission of creating works between Internet-based literature website and online writer. The validity and enforceability of the contract in which website operator bought out the unfinished works of online writer becomes a controversial issue, since there involves the behavior of writer's creation. The conclusion of the case successfully provided a solution to this issue, holding that when determining the legal nature of a copyright contract, the court should not regard the title of contract as the standard of determination, but to accord to the rights and obligations of both parties of the contract, as well as the purpose of the contract. Indeed, the agreement reached by parties concerning the transfer of the copyright of unfinished works has legal effect. However, neither party can claim to forcible execute the contractual obligation when it is relating to the behavior or freedom of writer's creation.

1. The nature of a contract and the rights and obligations

Wang Zhong and Xuanting signed two agreements on the same day, which were the "Agreement on the Works of Platinum Writer" and the "Agreement on Creation of Commissioned Works." There are similarities and differences in the two contracts, and the most significant difference is the way to dispose the copyright. Under the "Agreement on the Works of Platinum Writer," the relevant copyright shall be disposed by the way of assignment. By contrast, under the "Agreement on Creation of Commissioned Works," the relevant copyright shall be disposed by the way of commission for creation. In the trial, both parties confirmed that "Agreement on Creation of Commissioned Works" was signed later and it was the supplement and concretion of the "Agreement on the Works of Platinum Writer," modifying some terms. Thus, the rights and obligations of the parties should be identified in accordance with both contracts. If there is a conflict between the contracts, the later "Agreement on Creation of Commissioned Works" shall govern. When determining the nature of contract legal relation and the rights and obligations of parties, besides the title of contract, the terms concerning rights and obligations and the purpose of the contract pursued by the parties should be considered comprehensively. Although "Agreement on Creation of Commissioned Works" is under such name, the contract itself does not stipulate the content and form of creation in detail, but focuses on determining the ownership of the works of Agreement. Based on the "Agreement on the Works of Platinum Writer" signed on the same day, it can be inferred that the real purpose of both parties are "buying out" the copyright of all works created by Wang Zhong in some future period. The nature of contract is determined by its content. Thus, the contractual relationship in this case is the assignment of the economic rights of the works, instead of a contract for commission. After identifying the contractual nature between the parties, it is clear that both parties shall execute the contract accordingly: Wang Zhong shall transfer the copyright of the works created within the time specified by the contract to Xuanting, and Xuanting shall pay the agreed price.

2. The validity of the contract of transferring copyright of an unfinished work

The economic rights of copyright are prohibited to be transferred under the copyright law and contract law. In this case, the works in which the copyright to be transferred had not been finished when both parties signed the contract of transferring the copyright. Is this act of assignment valid? From the perspective of comparative law, some countries hold that such an act is valid, including UK, South Africa and India; while some other countries hold that such as act is conditional valid, including Germany, France and Brazil. In fact, there is no country in which such an act is explicitly void. According to Article 52 of the *Contract Law*, the contract is void only when it meets one of the five conditions stipulated by the article. Apparently, the other four conditions are not applicable to this case, except the condition concerning the protection of public interests. However, does this kind of contract need to be void for the protection of public interests?

From the perspective of public policies and the balance of interests, it is necessary to set up certain limitation for the validity of the contract of transferring copyright of an unfinished work. If a writer is poor and unknown in his early days, when a publisher is willing to make a contract for assignment of copyright with him, it is difficult for him to consider protecting the future interests. Even when the writer becomes famous, he could still be a writing machine of the publisher. The disparity between writers and publishers leaves the writers lack of equal capability to bargain with publishers. Under this circumstance, to impose certain limitations on transferring copyright of an unfinished work can help to protect the interests of writers to some degree. However, there are always two sides to everything. If contracts of transferring copyright of an unfinished work laws are recognized by laws, it would also have positive effect on promoting the creation and transmission of works. In copyright trade, commissioned creations are common. In most cases, there is no huge disparity between writers and transmitters. Besides the creation of writers, creations of works also rely on the support of capital. In such cases as the production of cinematographic works, capital investment plays a key role in the completion of works. It would be detrimental for literary and artistic creation to access funding if the rights of unfinished works are not allowed to dispose. Even to a writer who is at the beginning of his career, signing an unfinished works' copyrights assignment agreement with a publisher can help him have a stable income to finish the creation. In general, a contract of transferring copyright of an unfinished work has advantages and disadvantages. Its effect cannot be denied only on the basis of public interests. Such kind of activity of copyright trade is an essential business practice. According to the principle "absence of legal prohibition means freedom," in the term of respecting the autonomy of the parties, the validity of this agreement should be recognized under the situation that the laws are silent, the act of transfer should be approved and the breach of contract damages as stipulated in the contract should also be respected.

3. The enforceability of the obligation of creation

In this case, Xuanting petitioned that Wang Zhong should resume the performance of "Agreement on the Works of Platinum Writer" and the "Agreement on Creation of Commissioned Works" and stop publishing his works on other websites. Xuanting also petitioned to identify that Xuanting was the owner of the copyright of *The Eternal Life* created by Wang Zhong, and Wang Zhong was obliged to perform. The Court of the second instance held that: According to the "Agreement on Creation of Commissioned Works," as an "exclusive author," Wang Zhong's obligations were as follows: Creating "the works of agreement;" Prohibited to create works for others or ask any third party to publish his works; Offering Xuanting the preemption to the works created outside the term of agreement; Following Xuanting's deadline and length of the works. Since such obligations were relating to the behavior and freedom of Wang's creation, they were not applicable to compulsory performance in nature. Thus, Xuanting were not entitled to the right for forcing Wang Zhong to perform the agreement, when Wang Zhong breached the agreement. Instead, Xuanting was only entitled to the payment of liquidated damages and the actual losses. As for the assignment of copyright of finished works, it was not a matter of enforceability of the obligation, so it was legal for Xuanting to assert the copyright of *The Eternal Life*. Accordingly, the Court of the second instance reversed the original judgment.

The judgment of the Court of the second instance has legal basis and conforms to the legal requirements. From the perspective of both the trail and the enforcement of the judgment, it is difficult to request Wang Zhong to continue performing the obligation concerning creation of works. According to Article 110 of the *Contract Law*, the observant party cannot ask the default party to continue performing if the obligation is unable to be performed in law or the subject matter of the obligation is unfit for compulsory performance. As the general principle, the party who accuses the other of contractual breach cannot demand specific performance but can only accept monetary compensation. An order for specific performance is made only under the circumstance where need not the assistance of the accused.[3] The premise of a specific performance is that the contract is able to be performed. If the contract is impossible to be performed, neither in the terms of facts or laws, it cannot be enforced. The debts which are personal are not applicable to compulsory performance in nature, otherwise the liability for breach of contract would go back to the personal duty, which is against with the basic value of modern society to respect human dignity and protect freedom.[4] In German, Article 275 of *Civil code* also rules that the debt which is personal is impossible to perform.[5] In the assignment of copyright of an unfinished work, the creation is author's intellectual behavior and it is not applicable to compulsory performance. It is against the legislative purposes of copyright law to promoting creation and dissemination if limiting the creation freedom. Thus, to request the

---

3. P.S. Atlyah & Zhao Xudong (Translator), *Introduction to Law of Contract* (Fifth Edition), 2002, p. 451.
4. Han Shiyuan, *Law of Contract*, Law Press, 2004, pp. 704, 712.
5. Dirk Looschelders, Shen Xiaojun & Zhang Jinhai (Translator), *Law of Obligation: General Part* (Seventh Edition), Renmin University of China Press, 2014, p. 261.

compulsory performance of contracts which transfer unfinished works may lead to forced creation or limitation of creation freedom. It is unrealistic to enforce authors to create, and it is also a violation of the personal freedom of a citizen which is much more superior.

—**Comments by XU Zhuobin**

Postscript

It has been over thirty years since China started to launch the judicial protection of copyright in the 1980s. Particularly after China's entry into WTO, with the three amendments of the *Copyright Law*, the Chinese judicial protection of copyright has entered a new era. A complete judicial system and mechanism has been formed. Since the level of judicial protection has been improved, the leading role of judicial protection within the dual-track system has been further strengthened. After China's entry into WTO, it is of great significance to summarize the judicial experience and further strengthen the guidance of judicial protection.

With the careful planning and strong support of the Commercial Press, Prof. LUO Dongchuan, the member of the Judicial Committee and the Chief Judge of the Fourth Civil Tribunal of the Supreme People's Court of China, who is also the chief editor of the book *Selected Chinese Patent Cases*, organized the compilation of the book *Landmark Copyright Cases in China*. A number of intellectual property judges spent nearly two years to work hard and carefully on this book.

The judges involved in this book are (*order by surname name in Chinese*):

CUI Ning, Judge, Beijing No. 2 Intermediate People's Court
DING Wenlian, Vice Chief Judge, Intellectual Property Tribunal, Shanghai Higher People's Court
DING Wenyan, Research Fellow, China Institute of Applied Jurisprudence
FENG Gang, Judge, Beijing Intellectual Property Court
JIANG Ying, Chief Judge, First Tribunal, Beijing Intellectual Property Court
LI Dan, Judge, Beijing No. 2 Intermediate People's Court
LUO Dongchuan, Member of the Judicial Committee, Supreme People's Court of China; Chief Judge, Fourth Civil Tribunal, Supreme People's Court of China; First Degree Senior Judge; Professor
QIANG Ganghua, Vice Chief Judge, Fifth Civil Tribunal, Beijing No. 1 Intermediate People's Court
RUI Songyan, Judge, Beijing Intellectual Property Court
TONG Haichao, Judge, Intellectual Property Tribunal, Hubei Higher People's Court

XU Cui, Vice Chief Judge, Intellectual Property Tribunal, Hubei Higher People's Court

XU Zhuobin, Judge, Intellectual Property Tribunal, Shanghai Higher People's Court

ZHANG Lingling, Judge, Beijing Intellectual Property Court

ZHANG Xiaojin, Chief Judge, Second Tribunal, Beijing Intellectual Property Court

ZHOU Duo, Judge, Beijing No. 2 Intermediate People's Court